THE BASICS  W9-DJP-005
AMERICAN POLITICS

THE BASICS OF AMERICAN POLITICS

FOURTH EDITION

Gary Wasserman

Little, Brown and Company

Boston   Toronto

To Ann and Daniel

Library of Congress Cataloging in Publication Data

Wasserman, Gary, 1944–
    The basics of American politics.

    Includes bibliographies and index.
    1. United States — Politics and government.
I. Title
JK274.W249   1985   320.973   84–19376
ISBN 0–316–92436–9

Library of Congress Catalog Card No. 84–19376

ISBN 0-316-92436-9

9   8   7   6   5   4   3   2

HAL

Published simultaneously in Canada
by Little, Brown & Company (Canada) Limited

Printed in the United States of America

Drawings by David Omar White

Preface

The aims of this fourth edition remain what they were for the first three editions — to give students an introductory American government text that is basic, easy to read, current, and short.

The book has been shaped by teaching both at an inner city college and at an Ivy League university. Perhaps it was a surprise only to their teacher, but the needs of the two very different groups of students were basically the same. Both groups generally lacked a solid foundation in the structure and practice of American politics; both wished to acquire these basics quickly in order to spend time on issues they found more interesting. This text seeks to allow them to do that.

The fourth edition has been revised but, thanks to the advice of many teachers, only slightly expanded. The Presidency and Congress chapters now include discussions of the activities of the Reagan administration and the Ninety-eighth Congress. The Courts and Civil Liberties chapters are tied more closely together and updated by recent decisions on affirmative action and criminal rights. New topics in other chapters range from the President's media skills and the rise of public confidence in government, to the increasing strength of the national party organizations and the accelerating cost of political campaigns.

In *The Basics of American Politics*, politics is compared to a game in that it involves competing players more or less following certain rules and trying to win. But politics is no lighthearted sport; it is complex, important, and deadly serious. This book is intended to provide a start for both understanding and playing the political game.

A number of people helped on the text. Parts of the book still owe much to the contributions made by Ed Beard and Marsha Hurst. Richard Pious's contribution to the civil rights and liberties chapter was invaluable, as was that of

Ed Wasserman to the section on the media. Pat Walsh and Ann Stewart provided excellent research. The following people helped fashion the finished product: Charlie Clark, Ed Confino, Larry Flynt, Margaret Shapiro, Bruce Murphy, Herb Jacob, Harold Stanley, and Jeffrey M. Berry. Don Palm, Cynthia Chapin, and Judy Maas of Little, Brown improved the book with their customary courtesy and competence. Any errors remaining are mine. However, if this book does help someone learn about American politics, it is probably because of what my students taught me. In a sense the book is a way of thanking them.

G.W.

Contents

8 Interest Groups and the Media   221

9 Who Wins, Who Loses: Pluralism versus Elitism   253

Appendixes   267

Index   295

THE BASICS OF
AMERICAN POLITICS

What Is Politics? 1

THE FIRST DAY OF CLASS

"There are some very strange dudes teaching here this year. The first day of my American government class the prof comes in and asks us to sit in alphabetical order. Is this believable, I ask myself. Of course all the freshman sheep do it forthwith. But since I am sitting next to a most attractive lady I am very put out by this. So I ask him whether he might not want us to wear Mickey Mouse ears to his next class. A bit too cute perhaps, because he asks me if I think politics goes on in the classroom.

I reply, "No, we are alleged to study politics, but very few of us actually indulge."

"Incorrect," the dude responds, and would I mind removing myself from his class.

"Yes, I would very much mind," I say, "considering the costs of my first seven years at college."

"Will you *please* leave?" he says.

Seeing no gain from further dialogue, I start to exit. He then stops me and asks why I am departing. I remind the gentleman that while he may have missed it, he has just requested my absence. But he insists, inquiring why I'm doing what he asked. I am beginning to think I have missed something and I retort that he is numero uno here, the teach, while I am but a lowly student.

"In other words," he says, "my power or authority as the teacher of this class influenced you to do something you didn't want to do. In fact it influenced everyone's behavior by getting the class to sit in alphabetical order. So we just saw a process of influence in this classroom that affected a group of people. That's politics. Now you may sit down, and I'm sorry I put you through all that."

"Not at all," I graciously respond, "it was a pleasure to assist in instructing my fellow students."

This dialogue reveals a process of influence between the teacher and the students. This relationship is not only an educational one, but a political one as well. It is political in the sense of political scientist Harold Lasswell's definition of politics as *the process of who gets what, when, and how.* The teacher (who) gets the student to leave the class (what) immediately (when) by using his authority to persuade and threaten him (how). This indeed is politics.

Our definition of politics centers on interactions among a number of people involving influence. How do people get others to do what they wish? How does our society or any society (like that classroom) distribute its valued things, such as wealth, prestige, and security? Who gets these valued things, which political scientists call *values,* and how? The dialogue hints at an answer to these questions. That answer lies in the concepts of *power* and *authority.*

POLITICS AND POWER

Notice in the dialogue that the teacher influenced the student to do something the student didn't want to do (leave the class). The teacher demonstrated that he or she had power over the student. Power is simply *the ability to influence another's behavior.* Power is getting someone to do something he or she wouldn't otherwise do. Power may involved force (often called *coercion),* or persuasion, or rewards. But its essence is the ability to change another's actions in some way. The more power one has over another, the greater the change, or the easier the change is to accomplish. Having more power could also mean influencing more people to change.

Power always involves a relationship between people and groups. When someone says that a person has a lot of power, one should ask: power to influence whom to do what? What is the power relationship being discussed? Take the statement, "The United States is the most powerful nation in the world today." If this sentence means that because of its huge wealth, large army, and educated population, the United States can influence any other country however it wishes, the statement is wrong. These resources (wealth, army, and population) can give only a *capacity* for power. Whether this capacity is converted into effective influence will depend on the relationship in which it is applied. Certainly the United States had greater wealth, population, and troops than North Vietnam. Yet in attempting to halt a national movement with American troops in the Vietnam War, the United States had very limited power to change that small Asian country's behavior.

People generally do not seek power for its own sake alone. They usually want it for the other values it can get them — for the fame or wealth or even affection they think it will bring. Power, like money, is a means to other ends. Most people seek money for what it can buy, whether possessions, prestige, or security. Just as some people go after money more intently than others, so too some people seek power more than others. Of course power, just like money, does not come to everyone who seeks it.

Elites

Those who do gain power are often called a political *elite*. Elites are those who get most of the values society has available (such as wealth and respect). We could answer the "who" part of the question "who gets what, when, and how?" by saying the elite are those who get the most.

There may be different elites depending on what value is being considered. In a small town the owner of the largest business may be getting most of the wealth in the community, whereas the poor but honest mayor may have most of the respect. In most cases, however, the values overlap. The wealthy businessman will get plenty of respect, and the mayor will use people's respect for him or her to make income-producing contacts and investments.

To see the difference between an elite and the rest of us, we can look at one value (wealth) in one society (the United States). Clearly wealth is not distributed equally among the population — some (an elite) get more than others. The top

10 percent of the American population has an income thirty times that of the bottom 10 percent. The top 1 percent of the nation owns 33 percent of the wealth. Federal government figures show that more than 34 million Americans live below the official poverty line, the highest number since 1965. This 15 percent of the population includes 37 percent of blacks and 41 percent of families headed by women. These differences show the division between an elite and the bulk of the population in the way our society's value of wealth is distributed.

Authority: Legitimate Power

Often members of an elite reinforce their position by gaining authority. Authority is *legitimate power.* By *legitimate* we mean even more than "legal": the word implies a *rightness* or *correctness.* This rightness or legitimacy is connected in people's minds to both the position and the wishes of the authority. People may also think something is legitimate if it was chosen using an agreed-upon procedure, such as an election. People generally recognize certain others as having the right to influence their behavior in certain ways. Most people feel that a secretary of state *should* follow the wishes of the president; students *should* listen to their teacher; children *should* obey their parents. All these influences have a personal moral quality. Other reasons that people have for obeying authorities include habit, the authority figure's personal appeal, desire to be accepted by the group, and self-interest. But although they may not always follow it, people widely recognize authority as deserving obedience, and that is what gives it legitimacy.

Authority, then, is an efficient form of power. If people feel they *should* follow the wishes of an authority, then there is no need to force or even to persuade them to do so. The cost of influence is lowered for the authority. It takes little effort for police to get a group of teenagers to stay on the sidewalk — as long as they respect police authority. But in Liberty City, Miami's major black ghetto, on May 18, 1980, getting teenagers to obey required several thousand National Guardsmen. These teenagers, enraged at the freeing of white policemen accused of beating to death a black motorist, started a riot lasting two nights. Because the police had lost their legitimacy in the eyes of the teenagers, the cost to the police of influencing the teenagers' behavior went up. The police still could *force* agreement (and an element of force lies behind most authority); but anybody can clear a street with a gun. Only a recognized authority can do it with just a word.

Power and authority, then, are central to politics. They are also central to many other aspects of life — certainly almost all human interactions show people trying to influence others. In a political science course we could study the politics of a school or a hospital or a family — who influences, who is influenced, and what is the process of influence. But most of us are interested in a bigger question: How does the whole society decide who gets what, when, and how? To find out, we need to study the most important organization that decides who is to get the valued things of our society — government.

THE NEED FOR GOVERNMENT

Government is one of humanity's oldest and most universal institutions. History records very few societies that have existed with no government. *Anarchy* (a society without government) may be an interesting theory, but it seldom has been applied for long. Instead, people have lived under forms of government varying from the tribal council of an American Indian village to the complex government of the Soviet Union. Why is government so common?

One answer is that government is as common in society as is political conflict — disputes over distribution of a society's valued things. These values (such as wealth) are fairly limited, but people's demands for them are pretty unlimited. This imbalance means conflict. Whenever people have lived together, they have needed a way to regulate the conflicts among them. The question is not *whether* there will be conflict, but *how* the conflict will be handled. Who will decide on the rules that determine who wins and loses? And how does one get the loser to accept the decision? The usual way to channel political conflict and thus preserve society is to have some form of government.

Most governments in the world today claim to be democratic. A *democracy* is a form of government in which all people effectively participate. Because it is generally impractical for all the people to take part in their government directly, their participation is usually through representatives whom they choose in free elections. (What many countries call "free elections," however, without competing political parties and an independent press, would not impress Americans.) Hence the people rule themselves indirectly, through their representatives, and the government is often called a *representative democracy.*

Yet establishing governments, even democratic ones, to settle conflicts creates new problems. Government allows some people to have their way by coercing others even more effectively than they could if government didn't exist. And to control government is to have great power over many others. As the mass murders of Jews in Nazi Germany illustrated, having control of government may even mean having the power to kill millions of people.

In Chapter 2 we will see that the men who wrote the United States Constitution recognized this problem. They set up a number of checks and divisions of power to limit the future leaders of the United States government. Of course, these may not always work. In the early 1970s it was disclosed that for more than a year, in 1969–1970, the United States had engaged in a secret massive bombing of Cambodia. This act of war, overseen by President Nixon and his close advisers, was kept secret from the American public and from Congress.

What Is Government?

Government is a political association that does two things:

1. It makes rules determining who will get the valued things of a society.
2. It alone regulates the use of legitimate force in society.

The first part of the definition deals with how society distributes the values it has available — wealth, respect, safety, and so on. The second part deals with how these decisions are enforced. Government, then, has the final

word over who gets what and the ultimate say over how it will be done.

The government does not always *directly* determine who will get the valued things in a society. In theory, the United States government only protects and legitimizes private distribution of most of society's values. That is, our government is set up to allow people to get what they can without government interference. But this noninterference also can be viewed as a decision supporting the status quo or existing distribution of values in American society. The government not only refuses to interfere but also prevents others from interfering in the status quo. For example, it enforces laws such as those supporting repayment of debt and punishment of robbery. In practice these and other government functions, such as providing a sound currency, protecting from domestic unrest, and safeguarding private property, do mean government intervention. Most groups, whatever their political leanings, favor intervention if it is in their favor.

At the same time, the government sets limits on the private distribution of values. While allowing people to accumulate wealth, the government puts higher taxes on those with higher incomes (although tax loopholes used by the wealthy tend to undercut this adjustment). It also supports welfare programs to help the people who are getting the least of society's wealth. Both taxes and welfare illustrate the government's use of its legitimate power (authority) to place limits on the private distribution of this value of wealth.

Making and Supporting Decisions

The government may also intervene more directly in disputes among its citizens. Citizens of a town near a river may not be able to swim there because a paper mill dumps sewage into it. The citizens of the town or the owners of the mill may ask the government to settle the dispute. The appropriate part of the government may respond by passing a law, or by a ruling of an administrative agency such as the Environmental Protection Agency, or by a court decision on whether the town or the paper mill will get the use of the river (the "valued thing").

How the government supports its decision brings us to the second aspect of government — its exclusive regulation of legitimate force. In enforcing its decisions, the government may employ, allow, or prevent the use of force. Either the paper mill or the town's swimmers may be ordered not to use the river. If they try to, they may be fined or arrested. The government alone is allowed to regulate what kind of force is used, and how.

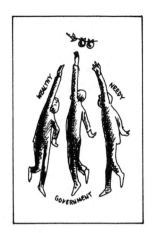

The government is not the only group in society that can legitimately use force. Parents may spank their children to keep them from swimming, or the paper mill may employ guards to keep people off their property. But only the government can set limits on this force. Most governments, although permitting parents to spank their kids, forbid cruel punishment of children. The paper mill's guards may be forbidden to use guns to keep swimmers out. Government does not *monopolize* the use of legitimate force, but it alone *regulates* its use.

THE STUDY OF POLITICS

What is the study of politics? One thing you will notice about political science is that it's a lot like other social sciences such as history, economics, sociology, and psychology. Each studies aspects of the interactions among people. In any large group of people many social relations are going on. Each of these disciplines may look at the same group and ask different questions about the relationships going on there. This division of labor is partly traditional and partly a way of separating complicated human relations into more easily understood parts. Political science fits in by studying one type of interaction between people — that involving power and authority. An example will make the approaches of the other disciplines clearer and distinguish them from political science.

Political Science and General Motors

What questions would an economist, a psychologist, and a historian ask about the operations of a "society" like the giant automobile maker, General Motors? An *economist* might ask questions about the production and distribution of the Chevys, Pontiacs, Cadillacs, and trucks that GM makes. How are the raw materials converted into a finished product? At what cost? How efficiently does the assembly line operate? How are the cars marketed? A *psychologist* would concentrate on the motives and interactions of people at GM. How do the workers or executives view their jobs and the company? Why? What is the psychological makeup of successful executives? of dissatisfied workers? A *historian* might look at the origins and development of General Motors. What factors within the company and in the country generally have accounted for GM's expansion? Why did it become the world's second-largest corporation (with assets of more than $41 billion) while competitors fell by the wayside?

Of course these fields overlap. Members of one discipline are often interested in the findings of another. The economist may find answers to his or her questions about the efficiency of the assembly line in the works of the psychologist. The historian might ask the economist about GM's marketing activities to determine why the corporation has expanded. Certainly the economist and psychologist would want to know about the history of the giant industry before studying their particular parts of it.

A political scientist, although interested in the other disciplines' findings, would be most likely to focus on our central question: *who is getting what, when, and how?* Who runs General Motors? How do they run it? How do the heads of GM reach decisions? How do unions or the government influence the decisions of GM? (Strikes? Taxes?) How do GM's leaders get their decisions carried out? How did these people get to the top and how do they stay there? Political science focuses on the study of power and authority — on the powerful, the ways in which they exercise their authority, and the effects they produce.

As Lasswell wrote, "The study of politics is the study of influence and the influential."[1] That is the core of what a political scientist would want to find out about General Motors.

Why Give a Damn about Politics?

After looking at what politics is and what government and political scientists do, you could still be asking one basic question: Who cares? Why give a damn about politics? Often students say: "Politics is just ego-tripping. I don't want to get involved in it." But you *are* involved. Apathy is as much a political position as is activism. Either position will influence who gets what in our society. Safe streets, good schools, clean food are political decisions influenced by who participates in them, who is prevented from participating, and who chooses not to participate.

Our lives are webs of politics. From the moment we wake up in the morning we are affected by someone's political choices. Think of what you've done today and how politics has influenced you. What you had (or didn't have) for breakfast was probably influenced by the price and availability of the food. The quality of the food you ate was regulated by a government agency that made sure those Grade A eggs were Grade A and that the milk was indeed pasteurized. The cost of that milk or those eggs was affected by the decisions of government to aid farmers, as well as the ability of farmers' groups to influence the government (through campaign contributions, for instance). The news you heard on the radio of what the government was doing for the economy was

[1] Harold Lasswell, *Politics: Who Gets What, When, How* (New York: World, 1936, 1958), p. 13.

conditioned by what officials felt they should tell the public, and what media editors felt was newsworthy. The lack of good public transportation to take you to school may have been a result of government decisions to put money into highways rather than buses or trains. The college you attend, the tuition you pay, the GI benefits or other aid you may or may not receive, are all the results of someone's choices in the political game.

Let's take a personal example to make the point clearer. Students of American government generally have agreed that federal regulatory commissions often do not effectively regulate the business they oversee. These commissions have tended to be closely tied to the powerful economic interests they supervise. The lesson was brought home some years ago.

In July 1972, the cargo door blew off an American Airlines DC-10 flying over Windsor, Canada, causing violent decompression. The pilot managed to land the empty jumbo jet safely. The independent National Transportation Safety Board investigated the near-disaster. Their recommendations went to the Federal Aviation Administration (FAA), the government regulatory commission in charge of airline safety. The Safety Board recommended that the FAA order that all cargo doors have modified locking devices and that McDonnell Douglas, the plane's builder, be required to strengthen the cabin floor.

The FAA, headed by a political appointee, was operating under a policy of "gentlemen's agreements" with the industries it was regulating. After discussions with the plane's manufacturers (who were large campaign contributors to President Nixon's reelection), they allowed McDonnell Douglas to modify the door on its own instead of under FAA supervision and simply to issue advisory service bulletins for the 130 or so DC-10s already in operation. McDonnell Douglas was allowed to reject as "impractical" the idea of strengthening the floor.

Somehow the changes were not made on the door of a DC-10 flown by Turkish Airlines. The plane, flying from

Paris to London in March 1974, crashed, killing all 346 people aboard. It was at the time the world's worst air disaster. The cargo door had blown off. This loss produced explosive decompression, collapse of the cabin floor, and loss of control. Passengers still strapped in their seats were sucked from the plane. A subcommittee of the House of Representatives, in a report on the crash, attacked the FAA for its "indifference to public safety" and for attempting to "balance dollars against lives."[2]

A teacher and friend of the author of this book, Professor Wayne Wilcox of Columbia University, was on the plane. With him were his wife and two children.

We have no choice over *whether* to be involved in the political game. But we can choose *how* to be involved. We can choose whether to be a *subject in* the political game or an *object of* that game. The question is not whether politics affects us. It does, and will. The question is whether we will affect politics. The first step in this decision is choosing how aware we wish to be of the game. This book may, with luck, be a start of your awareness and your willingness to be a *player* rather than merely *played upon*.

WHAT IS THIS BOOK ABOUT?

This book is, in a way, a scorecard covering the major players in the game of national politics. This first chapter introduces some of the terms and substance of politics — the means (power and authority) and goals (valued things) of the game. Chapters 2 and 6 cover the formal constitutional rules and the civil liberties and rights under which the competition proceeds. Chapters 3, 4, and 5 deal with the governmental players — the president and bureaucracy, Congress, and the federal courts — their history and structure, their strengths and weaknesses. Chapters 7 and 8 are

[2] The *Times* (London), December 29, 1974.

about several important nongovernmental players — voters, political parties, interest groups, and media. That they are not formal parts of the government does not mean they do not have great influence over the outcome of political conflicts. Finally, the last chapter goes into different theories of who wins and loses, who plays and doesn't play the game.

Let's be clear about this "game"; it is not Monday night football. It is vital, complex, ever changing, never ending, and played in deadly seriousness. Actually, many games are going on at the same time with overlapping players and objectives. They are games in which the participants seldom agree, even on the goals. For the goals (unlike the touchdown in football) vary with the objectives of the players. A business group may seek higher profits from its involvement in a political issue, a consumer organization may want a better-quality product, and a labor union may demand higher wages for its workers. They may all compete for their differing objectives over the same issue. They all seek to use power to obtain the values they consider important. We can analyze with fair objectivity how they play the game, but which side we root for depends on our own interests and ideals.

Another problem is that the players we've grouped together may not see themselves as being on the same team. Each participant, whether the bureaucracy, Congress, or the media, is hardly one player seeking a single goal. They are not only players but also *arenas* in which competition goes on. We may read of Congress opposing the president on an issue. But a closer look will find the president's congressional supporters and opponents fighting it out in the committees of Congress. Some of the media may oppose a certain interest group, while allowing or limiting the use of television and radio as an arena for publicizing the group's views.

Finally, in this brief introductory text all the political players are not discussed. State and local governments are certainly important in national politics. Ethnic groups and even foreign governments may have a role in the outcome of the competition. An even more fundamental omission, as one student remarked, are the people. What ever happened to the people in this game? Are they players or spectators?

For the most part, politics today is a spectator sport. The people are in the audience. To be sure, people do influence the players. The president and Congress are selected by election, labor unions depend on membership dues for support, and political parties need popular backing for their activities. But though it is played for the crowd and paid for by them, the game generally doesn't include them directly. Whether it will depends on the players, the rules and nature of the competition, and the people watching.

THOUGHT QUESTIONS

1. In the opening dialogue of this chapter, we discovered politics in a place that may seem unlikely — a classroom. Describe some other common situations in which politics goes on.
2. How do authorities gain legitimacy? How do they lose it? Can you think of recent examples of both?
3. Why do you think many people are apathetic about national politics? Is apathy encouraged? If so, how? By whom?
4. In what ways has your life been affected by governmental action? Did you have anything to say about those actions? If you didn't, do you know who did?

SUGGESTED READINGS

Golding, William G. *Lord of the Flies.* New York: Capricorn Books, 1959. Pb.
  A somewhat pessimistic novel on what happens to a group of British children on a deserted island without adults or government, but with lots of politics.

Korda, Michael. *Power.* New York: Ballantine Books, 1975. Pb.
  A witty bestselling manual about the role of power in our daily lives, with tips on how to "make it" in the power game.

Lasswell, Harold D. *Politics: Who Gets What, When, How.* New York: World, 1958.

A brief, well-known introduction to politics.

Orwell, George. *Animal Farm.* New York: Harcourt, Brace Jovanovich, 1946. Pb.

The famous barnyard tale in which the animals overthrow the farmer and set up a government in which pigs are more equal than others.

Schattschneider, E. E. *The Semisovereign People.* New York: Holt, Rinehart and Winston, 1961. Pb.

This landmark work presents a basic explanation of how and why some people get into the political game and some stay out.

The Constitution: Rules of the Game 2

So far we have discussed what the political game is about, what winning means, and why one plays. This chapter deals with the principles and procedures of the competition. The Constitution contains the official rules of the American political game; it also establishes three major players and their powers — the president, Congress, and the Supreme Court. Further, as we will see in Chapter 6 on civil liberties and rights, it places limits on how the game can be played and provides protection for the losers. And by establishing a central government sharing power with state governments, the Constitution marks out the arenas of play. What led to the adoption of these rules, what they mean, how they have changed, and how much influence they have today are the central questions of this chapter.

BACKGROUND TO THE CONSTITUTION

On July 4, 1776, the Declaration of Independence proclaimed the American colonies "Free and Independent States." This phrase symbolized the beginning not only of a bitter fight for independence from Great Britain, but also of a struggle to unify the separate and often conflicting interests, regions, and states of America. Only after a decade of trial and error was the Constitution written and accepted as the legal foundation for the new United States of America.

The men who gathered in Philadelphia in May 1787 to write the Constitution were not starting from scratch. They were able to draw on (1) an English legal heritage, (2) American models of colonial and state governments, and (3) their experience with the Articles of Confederation.

The English political heritage the framers were part of included the *Magna Charta*, which in 1215 had declared that the power of the king was not absolute. It also included the idea of natural rights, expressed by English philosophers, most notably John Locke, who wrote that people were "born free" and formed society to protect their rights. Many colonists felt that they were fighting a revolution to secure their traditional rights as Englishmen, which had been denied them by an abusive colonial government.

During their 150 years as colonies, the states had learned much about self-government that now went into the Constitution. Even the earliest settlers had been determined to live under written rules of law resting on the consent of the community: the *Mayflower Compact* was signed by the Pilgrims shortly before they landed at Plymouth in 1620. Similar documents had been written in other colonies, most of which had their own constitutions. Other aspects of colonial governments, such as two-house legislatures, also were later to appear in the Constitution. After the Revolution, in reaction to the authority of the royal governor, the colonists established the legislature as the most important branch in their state governments. Most of the colonies had a governor, a legislature, and a judiciary, a pattern that would evolve into the constitutional separation of powers. Most had regular elections, though generally only white, property-tied males could vote. There was even an uneasy basis for the federal system of local and national governments in the sharing of powers between the American colonies and a central government in England. Perhaps most important was the idea of limited government and individual rights written into the state constitutions after the Revolution.

But unity among the colonies was evolving slowly. Attempts to tighten their ties during the Revolution were a limited success. The First Continental Congress in September 1774 had established regular lines of communication among the colonies and gave a focus to anti-British sentiment. The Second Continental Congress, beginning in Philadelphia in May 1775 created the Declaration of Independence. At the same time a plan for confederation — a loose union among the states — was proposed. The Articles of Confederation were ratified by the states by March 1781, and went into effect even before the formal end of the American Revolution in February 1783.

The Articles of Confederation (1781–1789)

Pointing out the shortcomings of the Articles of Confederation is not difficult. No national government was really set up in the articles. Rather they established a "league of friendship" among the states, which didn't have much more authority than the United Nations does today. The center of the federation was a *unicameral* (one-house) legislature, the Continental Congress. Each state had one vote, regardless of its size. Most serious actions required approval by nine states, and amendments to the articles needed approval by all thirteen.

The confederation had no executive branch and no national system of courts. Perhaps most important, the Continental Congress had no ability to impose taxes; it could only *request* funds from the states. Each state retained its "sovereignty, freedom, and independence." Nor did the congress have any direct authority over citizens, who were subject only to the government of their states. In short, the congress had no ability to enforce its will on either states or citizens.

The confederation did have many strengths, however. Unlike the United Nations, it had the power to declare war, conduct foreign policy, coin money, manage a postal system, and oversee an army made up of the state militias. The articles were also startlingly democratic in requiring compulsory rotation in office. That is, no member of the congress could serve more than three years in any six. Finally, real accomplishments were made under the articles, such as the start of a national bureaucracy and the passing of the Northwest Ordinance, which established the procedure for admitting new states into the union.

But by 1787 the inadequacies of the articles were more apparent than the strengths. Too little power had been granted to the central authority. Fears about British, French, and Spanish threats to American territory were widespread. The confederation was in deep financial difficulty: Not enough funds were coming from the states, the currency was being devalued, and the states were locked in trade wars, putting up tariff barriers against each other. Shays' Rebellion in late 1786, an angry protest by Massachusetts farmers unable to pay their mortgages and taxes, reinforced the fears of many among the propertied elite that strong government was needed to avoid "mob rule" and economic disruption.

The Constitutional Convention

Against this background the convention met in Philadelphia from May 25 to September 17, 1787. The weather was hot and muggy, making tempers short. All the meetings were held in strict secrecy. One reason was that the congress had reluctantly called the convention together "for the sole purpose of revising the Articles of Confederation." Yet within five days of its organization the convention had adopted a Virginia delegate's resolution "that a national government ought to be established consisting of a *supreme* legislative, executive, and judiciary." In other words, the convention violated the authority under which it had been established and proceeded to write a completely new United States Constitution in a single summer.

The Constitution was a product of a series of compromises. The most important compromise, because it was the most divisive issue, was the question of how the states would be represented in the national legislature. The large states proposed a legislature with representation based either on the taxes paid by each state to the national government or on the number of people in each state. The small states wanted one vote for each state no matter what its size. After a long deadlock an agreement called the *Great*

Compromise established the present structure of Congress: representation based on population in the lower house (House of Representatives) and equal representation for all states in the upper one (Senate).

Other compromises came a bit more easily. Southern delegates feared the national government would impose an export tax on their agricultural goods and interfere with slavery. A compromise was reached that gave Congress the power to regulate commerce but not to put a tax on exports. In addition, the slave trade could not be banned before 1808. The slave issue was also central in the agreement that was perhaps the weirdest — the "Three-Fifths" Compromise. Here the debate was over whether slaves should be counted as people for purposes of representation and taxation. It was finally agreed that a slave should be counted as three-fifths of a person for both. (This provision was later removed by the Thirteenth and Fourteenth Amendments.) Another main issue, the right of a state to withdraw or *secede* from the union, was simply avoided. The questions of secession and slavery had to wait for a later generation to answer in a bloody civil war.

The Framers

Given the importance of the Constitution, it is a little surprising how quickly and painlessly it was drafted. No doubt the writing went so smoothly in part because of the wisdom of the men at Philadelphia. The universally respected General Washington chaired the meetings; the political brilliance of Alexander Hamilton and James Madison illuminated the debates: and Benjamin Franklin at eighty-two added the moderation of age. The delegates themselves possessed a blend of experience and learning. Of the fifty-five delegates, forty-two had served in the Continental Congress. More than half were college educated and had studied political philosophy. As a relatively young group, the average age being forty, they may have reflected a generation

gap of their own time. Having politically matured during
the Revolutionary period, they were less tied to state loyal-
ties than were older men whose outlook was formed before
the war. They were nationalists building a nation, not
merely defending the interests of their states.

But there was more to the consensus. The framers were
not exactly a representative sample of the population of
America at the time. They were wealthy planters, merchants, and lawyers. Fifteen of them were slaveholders,
fourteen were land speculators. The small farmers and
workers of the country, many of whom were suffering from
an economic downturn, were not represented at Philadelphia. Nor did leading liberals in the elite who might speak
for this poorer majority, such as Thomas Jefferson (who was
in Paris as ambassador) or Patrick Henry (who stayed away
because he "smelt a rat"), attend the convention. Only six
of the fifty-six men who signed the Declaration of Independence were at the convention. The delegates were a conservative, propertied elite, worried that continuing the weak
confederation would only encourage more and larger Shays'
Rebellions. Thus the debates at the convention were not
between the haves and the have-nots, but between the
haves and the haves over their regional interests.

Motives behind the Constitution

Much scholarly debate has gone on over the motives of
the framers since Charles Beard published his book, *An Economic Interpretation of the Constitution of the United
States*, in 1913. Beard argued that the convention was a
counterrevolution engineered by the delegates to protect
and improve their own property holdings by transferring
power from the states to an unrepresentative central government. Certainly the forty delegates who held nearly
worthless confederation securities stood to profit from a
new government committed to honoring these debts. Certainly their interests as creditors and property holders
would be better protected by a strong central government.

Nor did the delegates particularly favor democracy. Most thought that liberty had to be protected *from* democracy (which they thought of as "mob rule") and agreed with Madison's statement in *The Federalist Papers* (No. 10) that "Those who hold and those who are without property have ever formed distinct interests in society."

Critics of Beard's theory argue that the framers' motives were more varied. They reason that the delegates sought to build a new nation, to reduce the country's numerous political disputes, and to promote economic development that would benefit all. They point out that having a central government able to raise an army to protect the states from foreign attack appeared to be the most important reason that George Washington, among others, backed the Constitution.

But the arguments of the two sides don't necessarily cancel each other. The framers' *public* interest of building a strong nation and their *private* interest of protecting their property could work together. Like most people, they believed that what was good for themselves was good for society. That most of the population (workers, the poor, blacks, women) was not represented at Philadelphia was not surprising by the standards of the day. Nor should it be surprising that the delegates' ideas for a nation and a government not only did not work against their own economic interests but in many cases aided them.

Federalists versus Anti-Federalists

This is not to say that there were not divisions within this elite. Many of the debates during the writing and ratification of the Constitution divided the political elite into essentially conservative and liberal camps, the Federalists and the Anti-Federalists.

The Federalists (conservatives) generally favored a strong federal (national) government, with protection of private property rights and limits on popular participation in government. (Alexander Hamilton, a leader of the Federalists, described the people as "a great beast.") In the debates over the Constitution, the Federalists pushed for high property qualifications for voting, an indirectly elected Senate modeled after the English aristocratic House of Lords, a lofty indirectly elected president, and a strong nonelected judiciary. The Federalists, being more pessimistic about human nature (including the nature of the rulers), wanted these "cooling-off" devices in the government to filter down the popular will and create guardians of the people's real interests.

The Anti-Federalists (liberals) were more optimistic about human nature, though just as suspicious about the nature of those in power. Led by Thomas Jefferson, they favored strong state governments because they felt the states would be closer to the popular will than a strong central government would be. They wanted fewer limits on popular participation and pushed for the legislative branch to have more power than the executive and judicial branches. Believing that the majority was responsible, though agreeing that it might need cooling off, they wanted government to be answerable to elected officials.

The Constitution is a compromise between the conservative and liberal positions. It was designed to prevent tyranny both from the bottom (which the Federalists feared) and from the top (which the Anti-Federalists feared). Both sides generally believed that the government that governed best governed least.

Ratification and the Bill of Rights

The struggle for ratification of the Constitution focused the debate between the Federalists and Anti-Federalists. Conventions in nine states had to approve the Constitution before it could go into effect. Because a majority of the people were against the Constitution, the fight for ratification wasn't easy. The Anti-Federalists wanted a more rigid system of separation of powers and more effective checks and balances. Fearing that the president and Senate would act together as an aristocratic clique, they proposed compulsory rotation in office (as under the Articles of Confederation).

The Federalists criticized the Anti-Federalists for their lack of faith in the popular selection process and for ignoring the advantages of national union. They mounted a propaganda campaign using pamphlets and newspaper articles. The best known of these was a series of essays in a New York newspaper written by Madison, Hamilton, and John Jay, later republished as *The Federalist Papers.* The book stands today as the most famous commentary on the nature of the Constitution and what the framers thought of it.

The debate over including the Bill of Rights, the first ten amendments, in the Constitution became a key issue in the struggle over ratification. The Philadelphia convention, dominated by conservatives, had failed to include a bill of rights in the original document, not so much because of opposition to the ideals of the bill but from a feeling that such a statement was irrelevant. (A proposed bill of rights was voted down unanimously near the end of the convention partly because everyone was worn out and wanted to go home.) The Federalists, from their pessimistic viewpoint, believed that liberty was best protected by the *procedures,* such as federalism and checks and balances, established by their constitutional government. No matter what ideals were written down, such as freedoms of speech, press, and religion, the Federalists argued that support for them would depend on the "tolerance of the age" and the balance of forces established by the Constitution.

For the Anti-Federalists the Bill of Rights was a proclamation of fundamental truths, natural rights due to all people. No matter that another generation might ignore them, these rights were sacred. Any government resting on the consent of its people must honor them in its constitution. Although the Anti-Federalists had lost the battle in Philadelphia, they eventually won the war over the Bill of Rights. Massachusetts and Virginia agreed to accept the Constitution with the recommendation that such a proclamation be the first order of business of the new Congress. It was, and the Bill of Rights became the first ten amendments to the Constitution on December 15, 1791.

FOUR MAJOR CONSTITUTIONAL PRINCIPLES

In establishing a system of government, the United States Constitution did three things. First, it *established the structure* of government. In setting up three branches of government within a federal system, it gave the country a political framework that has existed down to the present. Second, the Constitution *distributed certain powers* to this government. Article I gave legislative powers, such as the power to raise and spend money, to Congress. Article II gave executive powers to the president, including command over the armed forces and wide authority over foreign policy. And Article III gave judicial power, the right to judge disputes arising under the Constitution, to the United States Supreme Court. Third, the Constitution *restrained the government* in exercising these powers. Government was limited, by the Bill of Rights for example, so that certain individual rights would be preserved.

The Constitution, then, both *grants* and *limits* governmental power. This point can be most clearly illustrated by looking closely at four major constitutional principles: *separation of powers and checks and balances, federalism, limited government*, and *judicial review.*

Separation of Powers and Checks and Balances

The first major constitutional principle is actually two: separation of powers, and checks and balances. But the two principles can't be understood apart from each other, and they operate together.

Separation of powers is the principle that the powers of government should be separated and put in the care of different parts of the government. Although never exactly stated in the Constitution, this principle had a long history in political philosophy and was in practice in the governments of the colonies. The writers of the Constitution divided the federal government into three branches to carry out what they saw as the three major functions of government. The *legislative function* — passing the laws — was given to Congress; the *executive function* — carrying out or executing the laws — was given to the president; and the *judicial function* — interpreting the laws — was given to the Supreme Court.

Though it is nice and neat, the principle is probably also unworkable. The purpose of the separation of powers was to allow ambition to counter ambition, to prevent any one authority from monopolizing power. Yet simply dividing the powers of government into these three branches would probably make the legislature supreme — as it did in the colonies. As the starter of the governmental process, the legislature could determine how, or even if, the other branches played their roles. Something else was needed to curb legislative power. That something was checks and balances.

Checks and balances create a mixture of powers that permits the three branches of government to limit one another. A *check* is a control one branch has over another's

---

MADISON ON GOVERNMENT

". . . If men were angels, no government would be necessary. If angels were to govern men, neither external or internal controls on government would be necessary. In framing a government, which is to be administered by men over men, the great difficulty lies in this: You must first enable the government to control the governed; and in the next place, oblige it to control itself." — James Madison, *The Federalist Papers* (No. 51)

functions, creating a *balance* of power. The principle gives the branches constitutional means for guarding their functions from interference by another branch. The principle of checks and balances mixed together the legislative, executive, and judicial powers, giving some legislative powers to the executive, some executive powers to the legislative branch, and so on, to keep any branch from dominating another.

There are a number of examples of checks and balances in the Constitution. The presidential veto gives the chief executive a primarily legislative power to prevent bills he dislikes from being passed into law by Congress. Congress can check this power by its right to override the veto by a two-thirds vote. The Senate is given an executive power in its role of confirming presidential nominations for major executive and judicial posts. Further, Congress can refuse to appropriate funds for any executive agency, thereby preventing the agency from carrying out the laws.

But the system of separation of powers and checks and balances is even more elaborate. The way each branch of government is set up and chosen also checks and balances its power. For example, Congress is divided into two houses, and both must approve legislation before it becomes law. Limited terms of office and varied methods of selection help keep any one person or branch from becoming too strong. The House of Representatives was to be popularly elected for two-year terms; Senators were elected for six years, originally by their state legislatures (changed by the Seventeenth Amendment to popular election); the president was elected for four years by an electoral college; and federal judges were to be appointed by the president and confirmed by the Senate, and to serve for life during good behavior. All these procedures were designed to give government officials different interests to defend, varied bases of support, and protection from too much interference by other officials.

The bodies that result from this separating and mixing of powers are separate institutions that in practice *share* the overall power of government. Each needs the others to make the government work, yet each has an interest in checking and balancing the powers of the others. This elaborate scheme of separation of powers and checks and balances was certainly not designed as the most efficient form of government. Rather, it was established "to control the abuses of government" — to oblige the government to control itself. It set up the structure that historian Richard Hofstadter has called "a harmonious system of mutual frustration."

Federalism

A second constitutional principle, *federalism,* calls for political authority to be distributed between a central government and the governments of the states. Both the federal and state governments may act directly on the people, and each has some exclusive powers. Federalism, like separation of powers, spreads out political authority to prevent power from being concentrated in any one group.

Actually, the men who wrote the Constitution had little choice. The loose confederation of states hadn't operated well, in their eyes, and centralizing all government powers would have been unacceptable to the major governments of the day — those of the states. Federalism, then, was more than just a reasonable principle for governing a large country divided by regional differences and slow communications. It was also the only politically realistic way to get the states to ratify the Constitution.

American federalism has always involved two somewhat contradictory ideas. The first, expressed in Article VI, is that the Constitution and the laws of the central government are supreme. This condition was necessary to establish an effective government, able to pass laws and rule directly over all the people. The second principle ensures the independence of the state governments: The Tenth Amendment *reserved* to the states or the people all powers not delegated to the central government. These substantial reserved powers include control of local and city governments, regulation of business within a state, supervision of education, and exercise of the general "police power" over the safety of the people (see Figure 2.1).

The conflict between the two principles — national supremacy and states' rights — came to a head in the Civil War, which established the predominance of the national government. That is not to say that the question was settled once and for all — even today, in issues such as school busing and abortion, state governments often clash with the federal government. But the conflict shouldn't be overstated. Even though the Constitution divided the powers of government by federalism, it also clearly set up the basis for national union. In the years since, the national government has grown far more important than state governments. As political issues — whether regulating the economy or protecting the environment — became national, so too did solutions come to center in the national government. But in practice today there are few purely national government domestic programs. Almost all require cooperation by the

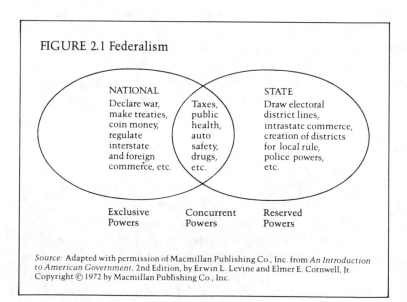

FIGURE 2.1 Federalism

NATIONAL
Declare war, make treaties, coin money, regulate interstate and foreign commerce, etc.

Taxes, public health, auto safety, drugs, etc.

STATE
Draw electoral district lines, intrastate commerce, creation of districts for local rule, police powers, etc.

Exclusive Powers

Concurrent Powers

Reserved Powers

Source: Adapted with permission of Macmillan Publishing Co., Inc. from *An Introduction to American Government,* 2nd Edition, by Erwin L. Levine and Elmer E. Cornwell, Jr. Copyright © 1972 by Macmillan Publishing Co., Inc.

states and often the cities. In the best cases this arrangement helps adjust the programs to local conditions; in the worst, it may delay needed changes. Either way, federalism now exists far less as separate boxes of powers than as a mix of overlapping relations between the states and the federal government, sometimes called a *marblecake*.

Limited Government

The principle of *limited government* means that the powers of government are limited by the rights and liberties of the governed. This principle is basic to the very idea of constitutional government: The people give the government listed powers and duties through a constitution, while reserving the rest to themselves. This *political compact* means that government actions must rest on the *rule of law*, approved, however indirectly, by the consent of the governed. Furthermore, the Constitution sets up procedures, such as separation of powers and federalism, to ensure that the government remains limited to its proper duties and powers. For example, the president may not exercise powers given by the Constitution exclusively to Congress.

Limited government guarantees citizens their *rights against* the government as well as *access* to the government. Civil liberties and rights guarantee the openness and competitiveness of the political process, which means not only the right to vote, but also the freedom to dissent, demonstrate, and organize to produce alternatives, in order to make the right to vote meaningful. Civil liberties also protect the citizen from arbitrary governmental power. Under these would fall a citizen's right to a fair and speedy trial, to have legal defense, and to be judged by an impartial jury of his or her peers. Further, government cannot take life, liberty, or property without due process of law, nor interfere with a citizen's right to practice religion, nor invade his or her privacy. In short, the people who make the law are also subject to it. (See Chapter 6 on civil liberties and rights.)

Judicial Review

An important means of keeping government limited and of maintaining civil rights and liberties is the power of judicial review vested in the Supreme Court. *Judicial Review*, the last constitutional principle, is the judicial branch's authority to decide on the constitutionality of the acts of the various parts of the government (state, local, and federal).

Although judicial review has become an accepted constitutional practice, it is not actually mentioned in the document. There was some debate in the first years of the Constitution over whether the Court had the power merely to give nonbinding opinions or whether it had supremacy over acts of the government. Most people at that time agreed that the Court did have the power to nullify unconstitutional acts of the state governments, but opinion was divided over whether this power extended to the acts of the federal government. In 1803, in the case of *Marbury* v. *Madison*, the Supreme Court declared that it did have the right to judge acts of Congress (see page 136). Since then, this power has become a firmly entrenched principle of the Constitution.

Judicial review has put the Court in the position of watchdog over the limits of the central government's actions, and made it the guardian of federalism. The latter function, reviewing the acts of state and local governments, has in fact been the Court's most important use of judicial review. Though relatively few federal laws have been struck down by the Court, hundreds of state and local laws have been held to violate the Constitution. As Justice Oliver Wendell Holmes said more than fifty years ago, "The United States would not come to an end if we lost our power to declare an act of Congress void. I do think the Union would be imperiled if we could not make that declaration as to the laws of the several states."

HOW IS THE CONSTITUTION CHANGED?

To say that the Constitution has lasted almost two hundred years does not mean it is the same document that was adopted in 1789. The Constitution has changed vastly; in practical ways, it bears little resemblance to the original. Most of the framers would scarcely recognize the political process that operates today under their Constitution. Changes in the Constitution have been made by four major methods: formal amendments, judicial interpretation, legislation, and custom.

Amendments

Although the amendment process is the first way we usually think of for changing the Constitution, it is actually the least common method. Only twenty-six amendments (including the first ten amendments, which can practically be considered part of the original document) have been adopted. (A twenty-seventh, the Equal Rights Amendment, and a twenty-eighth, the Washington, D.C. Voting Rights Amendment, were proposed by Congress but not ratified by the needed three-fourths of the state legislatures. They failed mostly because the process of adopting amendments is so difficult.) Though the Constitution's framers recognized the need for change in any such document, no matter how farsighted, they wanted to protect it from temporary popular pressure. Hence they required unusually large majorities for adopting amendments.

Article V of the Constitution provides a number of methods for adopting amendments (see Figure 2.2). Amendments may be *proposed* by a two-thirds vote of each house of Congress or (if requested by two-thirds of the state legislatures) by a national convention called by Congress. They must be

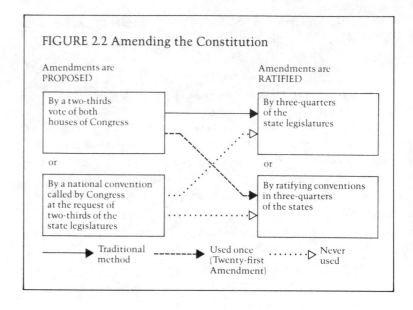

FIGURE 2.2 Amending the Constitution

ratified by conventions in three-fourths of the states, or by three-fourths of the state legislatures (the choice is up to Congress).

The national convention has never been used; all amendments have been proposed by Congress. (By 1984, however, thirty-two states had passed resolutions calling for a constitutional convention to draft a new amendment requiring a balanced budget.) Only the Twenty-first Amendment, repealing Prohibition, was ratified by state conventions. The idea behind this one use of state conventions was that the state legislatures were still full of the same representatives who had passed Prohibition in the first place, and conventions seemed likely to be the fastest way to change it. A major reason that the national convention method has never been used to propose amendments is Congress's jealousy toward another body trespassing on its powers. Another is worry over how many other amendments might be proposed by such a convention. After all, the Constitution was written by an earlier runaway convention set up only to amend the Articles of Confederation.

Judicial Interpretation

If the amendment process is the least-used method of changing the Constitution, interpretations by the Supreme Court are probably the most common. Practically every part of the Constitution has been before the Supreme Court at some time or another. The Court has shaped and reshaped the document. Recent Court decisions have allowed Congress great scope in regulating the economy, prohibited legal segregation of races, allowed local communities to determine the limits of obscenity, and established "one man, one vote" as a constitutional principle governing election to the House of Representatives (see page 89). The Court has also given practical meaning to general constitutional phrases such as "necessary and proper" (Article I, Section 8), "due process of law" (Amendments 5 and 14), and "unreasonable searches and seizures" (Amendment 4). No wonder the Supreme Court is sometimes called "a permanent constitutional convention."

Legislation

Although legislation is passed under the Constitution and does not change the basic document, Congress has been responsible for filling in most of the framework of government outlined by the Constitution. Congress has established all the federal courts below the Supreme Court. It has determined the size of the House of Representatives as well as of the Supreme Court. The cabinet and most of the boards and commissions in the executive branch have been created by congressional legislation. And most of the regulations and services we now take for granted, such as social security, have come from measures passed by Congress.

Custom

Custom is the most imprecise way in which the Constitution has changed, yet one of the most widespread. Many practices that have been accepted as constitutional are not actually mentioned in the document. The growth of political parties and the influence of party leadership in the government, the presidential nominating conventions, the breakdown of the electoral college, and the committee system in Congress are just a few customary practices not foreseen by the Constitution.

Custom has also changed some practices that, at least on the surface, seem to have been clearly intended by the framers. The Eighth Amendment, forbidding "excessive bail," has not prevented courts from setting bail for serious offenses that is too high for the accused to raise. Although Congress has the right to declare war (Article II, Section 8), presidents have entered conflicts that looked very much like wars (Korea, Vietnam) without such a declaration. Customs also have been broken and reestablished by law. The custom that a president serves only two terms was started by Washington and cemented by Jefferson. Broken with much debate by Franklin D. Roosevelt in 1940, the custom was made law in the Twenty-second Amendment, adopted in 1951.

WHY HAS THE CONSTITUTION SURVIVED?

All these ways in which the Constitution has been changed to meet different needs at different times do not completely explain its survival. Various explanations have been put forth for why the Constitution has endured to become the oldest written constitution of any country.

The major reason it has lasted probably lies not in the Constitution itself but in the stability of American society. Disturbances like the Civil War, the Indian campaigns and massacres, and foreign wars all have been handled within the same constitutional structure. The Constitution has been made more democratic so as to include potentially disruptive groups, such as immigrants, former slaves, women, and the poor, that were originally excluded from political participation. The Constitution's emphasis on procedures has served it well through the wars and depressions as well as the peace and prosperity of various ages.

Other explanations for the Constitution's durability focus on the document itself. One maintains that it is a work of genius. William Gladstone, the nineteenth-century British prime minister, described it as "the most wonderful work ever struck off at a given time by the brain and purpose of man." Incorporating centuries of English political traditions as well as the framers' own experience, the Constitution set out the principles and framework of government in concise, well-written phrases.

The *shortness* of the document (only some seven thousand words with all its amendments) is another major reason for its durability. Although it sets out the basic principles and structures of a government, the Constitution leaves much only generally stated or not mentioned at all. In a word, the Constitution is *ambiguous*. Many of the most enduring Constitutional phrases ("freedom of speech," "due process of law," "all laws which shall be necessary and proper," "privileges or immunities of citizens") have been applied differently at various times in our history. Other principles, such as majority rule and individual liberties, sometimes may seem contradictory. It is left to the political players of each age to resolve the conflicts among groups claiming constitutional support. This flexibility has been one of the Constitution's major strengths in adapting to new political pressures and allowing people to reach compromises under competing principles.

WRAP-UP

We have covered quite a bit in this chapter. In looking at the writing of the Constitution, we saw how the colonists drew from the tradition of English political thought, the models of colonial government, and experience with the Articles of Confederation in shaping the Constitution. But the framers were also influenced by who they were. As a wealthy elite they sought to establish a government that would further both the interests of the nation and their own economic concerns. They divided into conservative and liberal groups, known as the Federalists and Anti-Federalists, over how strong the government should be and how personal rights would be protected best. Ratification and the addition of the Bill of Rights forged an uneasy agreement between the two groups.

The Constitution as it has developed centers on four major principles: separation of powers and checks and balances, federalism, limited government, and judicial review. Although these principles remain fundamental to the document, the Constitution has been changed vastly by four main methods: formal amendment, judicial interpretation, legislation, and custom. The changes it has undergone have enabled the Constitution to endure. Perhaps more important to its survival, however, have been the stability of American society and the ambiguity of the document itself.

But does the flexibility and vagueness of the document mean that the Constitution as a body of rules governing the American political game is meaningless? That essentially it serves the interests of those in power and its interpretations change only as those interests alter? Perhaps. Certainly any document that has presided in olympian indifference over a political system that imported and enslaved most of its black residents, placed its citizens of Japanese descent in detention camps, allowed sweatshops and child labor, looked away from tremendous concentrations of wealth alongside severe poverty, has much to answer for. Is the Constitution an unworkable grab bag of obsolete principles used to rationalize domination by the few?

As we said in Chapter 1, politics is not primarily about words, it is about power and ideals. One cannot blame a body of principles and procedures for the power or lack of power, for the ideals or lack of ideals, of the players in the game. All great historical documents, from the Bible to the

Constitution, have been given vastly differing applications by different people at different times.

More than the rules of the game, then, the Constitution stands as a symbol of the ideals of a people. But this symbol does influence behavior. That a president violates the law does make a difference in whether he remains in power. That people have a constitutional right to demonstrate against a war can change the outcome of that war. That the press has the right to publish government documents (and the courts, not the administration, make the decision) does place limits on the bureaucracy. Even the hypocrisy of politicians in bowing to ideals they may wish to ignore shows the strength of the symbol.

Yet the substance of the principles in the Constitution must ultimately rest on the political relationships within each generation of players. The *right* to demonstrate is meaningless without the *will* to demonstrate. Freedom of speech means nothing if no one has anything critical to say. Freedom of the press, or judicial safeguards, or rights to privacy could be lost without anyone necessarily changing a word of the Constitution. Power without principle may be blind, but principle without power is impotent.

The rules of this game, then, are not fixed or unchanging. Though rooted in the traditions of the past, they are supported by the politics of the present. They are not only guidelines but goals as well. Therefore they remain unfinished, as must any constitution setting out to "secure the Blessings of Liberty to ourselves and our Posterity."

THOUGHT QUESTIONS

1. Do federalism and separation of powers and checks and balances support or restrict democracy?
2. What were some of the issues that the framers of the Constitution agreed on almost from the beginning? On which did they have to compromise, and what have been the historical effects of those compromises?

3. What makes the Constitution a flexible document? Do you agree that it is really that flexible?
4. How efficient are the political structures set up by the Constitution in dealing with contemporary problems? Do the goals of efficiency and democracy in the Constitution work against each other?

SUGGESTED READINGS

Beard, Charles A. *An Economic Interpretation of the Constitution of the United States.* New York: Macmillan, 1935. Pb.
The famous criticism of the framers' economic motivations in writing the Constitution.

Brown, Robert E. *Charles Beard and the Constitution.* New York: Norton, 1965. Pb.
Refutes Beard's analysis.

Hamilton, Alexander, James Madison, and John Jay. *The Federalist Papers.* New York: New American Library, 1961.
The classic work on what the framers thought about their Constitution.

McDonald, Forrest. *E Pluribus Unum.* Boston: Houghton Mifflin, 1965.
A lively account of the early days of the republic.

Vidal, Gore. *Burr.* New York: Bantam, 1974. Pb.
An accurate though fictional account of the nation's early years, well told from the viewpoint of Aaron Burr.

Wills, Garry. *Explaining America: The Federalist.* New York: Doubleday, 1980.
A well-written argument about what the Founding Fathers really meant by their Constitution.

The Executive Branch: The Presidency and the Bureaucracy

3

The superstar of the American political game is the president of the United States. Although at the head of just one of the three branches of the United States government, the president is the only official (along with the vice president) elected by the entire nation. As a result he often stands as the symbol not only of the federal government but of the country as well.

The Vietnam War and the Watergate scandal led many people to feel that the power of the president had grown so great as to be a threat to democracy. Underlying Richard Nixon's resignation in 1974 was the fear of the president's growing — and illegal — use of his authority. Later, complaints were heard about weakness and ineffectiveness in the White House. Jimmy Carter fell victim to this popular view that the president was too weak to resolve the country's major problems. When Ronald Reagan took office he faced the tricky problem of steering a course between too much and too little power as he attempted to use the presidency to limit the growth of the domestic programs of the federal government.

This chapter is about the executive branch of government and its chief executive, the president. We will trace the history of the growth of the presidency from the limited powers granted to the office in the Constitution. We will discuss different approaches to being president and the various roles of the office. The departments of the federal bureaucracy under the president, and the problems he has in controlling the bureaucracy, will take up another part of the chapter. Finally, we will look at three cases of the uses of presidential power and then draw some conclusions.

THE PRESIDENT AND THE CONSTITUTION

Article II of the Constitution lists the president's powers. It grants a president far less power and far fewer duties than it gives Congress in Article I. Yet the opening sentence of the article ("The executive Power shall be vested in a President of the United States of America") and other vague phrases ("he shall take Care that the Laws be faithfully executed") have been used by presidents to justify enlarging their powers. As we will see, presidential practice has vastly expanded the Constitution's ideas of executive powers.

In setting requirements for the office, the Constitution states that the president must be at least thirty-five years old, fourteen years a resident of the United States, and a native-born citizen. The president is immune from arrest while in office and can be removed only by impeachment. His term of office is fixed at four years. Under the Twenty-second Amendment, passed in 1951, presidents are limited to two terms. During the last months of his final term the president is often called a *lame duck:* Because he cannot be re-elected, his influence — and his accountability — are lessened. Jimmy Carter, between his defeat on November 4, 1980 and the inauguration of Ronald Reagan on January 21, 1981, was a lame duck president.

Presidents are not chosen by direct popular elections. All the votes across the United States are not added up on election day with the candidate receiving the most declared the winner. Rather, presidents are chosen through the *electoral college.* Each state is granted as many *electors,* members of the electoral college, as it has senators and representatives combined (the District of Columbia gets three votes). On election day the votes *within each state* are added up, and the candidate with the most votes receives *all* that state's votes in the electoral college. When the counting has been done in each state, the number of electoral-college votes for each candidate is added up. If any candidate has a majority (270 votes, which is 50 percent plus 1) he becomes presi-

dent. If no candidate wins a majority (because several candidates have split the votes), the Constitution then provides
that the election will be decided by a majority vote in the
House of Representatives with each state delegation casting
one vote.

The electoral college was created by the authors of the
Constitution as another way of filtering what they feared
might be the passions and prejudices of the mass of voters.
It was hoped that the members of the electoral college
would be cautious, sober people who would make a wise
choice. The development of political parties (see Chapter 7)
has undercut the purpose of the electoral college, for electors are now pledged to one party's candidate at the time
of the elections. Although there have often been calls for
replacing the "outmoded" electoral college with direct popular election (which would require a constitutional amendment), they have so far been unsuccessful.

The major official duty of the *vice president* is to preside
over the Senate. Although in recent years the vice president
has taken over more executive tasks, his main function is
to succeed the president if the office should become vacant.
(The Speaker of the House of Representatives and the president pro tem of the Senate are next in line.) The fact that
thirteen vice presidents have become president, and that
three of our last five presidents were vice presidents at some
time, has increased the political importance of the office.
Former Vice President Walter Mondale was termed "the
deputy president" by Jimmy Carter and given a unique
amount of influence as a close adviser. Vice President
George Bush recognized that his influence in the Reagan
administration depended on his relationship to President
Reagan. As Bush put it, "If I don't have his confidence, I'll
be going to funerals in Ecuador." Frequently, the vice president remains in a limited, frustrating position. As Harry
Truman, Franklin Roosevelt's vice president, remarked,
"Look at all the vice presidents in history. Where are they?
They were about as useful as a cow's fifth teat."

HISTORY OF THE PRESIDENCY

Forty men have been president of the United States, from George Washington, who took office in 1790, to Ronald Reagan, who began his second term in 1985 (see Table 3.1). Between Washington and Reagan, the influence and powers of the president have expanded considerably.

Most members of the Constitutional Convention in 1789 did not see a *political* role for the president. They pictured the president as a gentleman-aristocrat, who would stand above politics as a symbol of national unity. He would be selected by an electoral college chosen by the states, to ensure that he wasn't dependent on party or popular support. Congress, not the president, was to be supreme. Yet strong presidents confronting problems soon increased these powers, although at times weak presidents and popular sentiment have reduced executive power. In the twentieth century presidential power has expanded as a result of wars and domestic crises, such as economic depression.

George Washington sent troops to put down a rebellion among farmers in western Pennsylvania who were angered by a tax placed on whiskey. Washington's action in the Whiskey Rebellion was later claimed as the precedent for a president's *residual power* (also called inherent power) — powers not spelled out in the Constitution but necessary for the president to be able to carry out other responsibilities. The third president, Thomas Jefferson, had, as leader of the liberals, fought against establishing a strong executive in the Constitution. Yet as president he too expanded the powers of the office. By negotiating and signing the Louisiana Purchase, gaining the approval of Congress only after the fact (perhaps inevitable in an age of slow communication), Jefferson weakened the principle of checks and balances. Congress not only played a minor role in doubling the size of the country but also couldn't easily reverse the president's action once it had been taken.

Abraham Lincoln, the sixteenth president, disregarded a number of constitutional provisions when he led the North into the Civil War. Lincoln raised armies, spent money

Congress had not appropriated, blockaded the South, suspended certain civil rights, and generally did what he felt was necessary to help preserve the Union. He even sent money and troops to Virginia and helped create West Virginia, all without participation by Congress. Congress later approved these actions, but the initiative clearly lay with the president. This pattern of crisis leadership continued into the twentieth century with strong presidents like Theodore Roosevelt and Woodrow Wilson. They were followed, however, by a series of weak presidents in the 1920s (Harding, Coolidge, Hoover), who perhaps responded to a mood in the country that favored inactivity from the chief executive.

Franklin D. Roosevelt's coming into office in 1933 in the midst of a depression resulted in the president's taking virtually full responsibility for the continual shaping of both domestic and foreign policy. His programs (called the New Deal) in response to the depression, and his leadership of the United States into the international role it would play during and after World War II, firmly established the strong leadership patterns we find today in the presidency. Roosevelt thus is often called the first modern president. He probably influenced the shape of that office more than anyone else in this century.

TYPES OF PRESIDENTS

The seemingly inevitable growth of the presidency should not obscure the many types of people who have occupied the office. To simplify matters, we will talk about three general approaches that various presidents have adopted toward the office and see which chief executives fit into each category.

Buchanan Presidents

The first category has been called *Buchanan presidents,* after James Buchanan, who is known mainly for his refusal

Buchanan-Custodial

TABLE 3.1 Presidents and Vice Presidents of the United States

Year	President	Party	Year	President	Party
1789	George Washington		1892	Grover Cleveland	Democratic
1792	George Washington		1896	William McKinley	Republican
1796	John Adams	Federalist	1900	William McKinley	Republican
1800	Thomas Jefferson	Democratic-Republican	1901	Theodore Roosevelt[a]	Republican
1804	Thomas Jefferson	Democratic-Republican	1904	Theodore Roosevelt	Republican
1808	James Madison	Democratic-Republican	1908	William H. Taft	Republican
1812	James Madison	Democratic-Republican	1912	Woodrow Wilson	Democratic
1816	James Monroe	Democratic-Republican	1916	Woodrow Wilson	Democratic
1820	James Monroe	Democratic-Republican	1920	Warren G. Harding	Republican
1824	John Quincy Adams	Democratic-Republican	1923	Calvin Coolidge[a]	Republican
1828	Andrew Jackson	Democratic	1924	Calvin Coolidge	Republican
1832	Andrew Jackson	Democratic	1928	Herbert C. Hoover	Republican
1836	Martin Van Buren	Democratic	1932	Franklin D. Roosevelt	Democratic
1840	William H. Harrison	Whig	1936	Franklin D. Roosevelt	Democratic
1841	John Tyler[a]	Whig	1940	Franklin D. Roosevelt	Democratic
1844	James K. Polk	Democratic	1944	Franklin D. Roosevelt	Democratic
1848	Zachary Taylor	Whig	1945	Harry S Truman[a]	Democratic
1850	Millard Fillmore[a]	Whig	1948	Harry S Truman	Democratic
1852	Franklin Pierce	Democratic	1952	Dwight D. Eisenhower	Republican
1856	James Buchanan	Democratic	1956	Dwight D. Eisenhower	Republican
1860	Abraham Lincoln	Republican	1960	John F. Kennedy	Democratic
1864	Abraham Lincoln	Republican	1963	Lyndon B. Johnson[a]	Democratic
1865	Andrew Johnson[a]	Democratic (Union)	1964	Lyndon B. Johnson	Democratic
1868	Ulysses S. Grant	Republican	1968	Richard M. Nixon	Republican
1872	Ulysses S. Grant	Republican	1972	Richard M. Nixon	Republican
1876	Rutherford B. Hayes	Republican	1974	Gerald R. Ford[a]	Republican
1880	James A. Garfield	Republican	1976	James E. Carter	Democratic
1881	Chester A. Arthur[a]	Republican	1980	Ronald W. Reagan	Republican
1884	Grover Cleveland	Democratic	1984	Ronald W. Reagan	Republican
1888	Benjamin Harrison	Republican			

TABLE 3.1 Presidents and Vice Presidents of the United States (cont.)

Year	Vice President	Party	Year	Vice President	Party
1789	John Adams	Federalist	1892	Adlai E. Stevenson	Democratic
1792	John Adams	Federalist	1896	Garrett A. Hobart	Republican
1796	Thomas Jefferson	Democratic-Republican	1900	Theodore Roosevelt	Republican
1800	Aaron Burr	Democratic-Republican	1904	Charles W. Fairbanks	Republican
1804	George Clinton	Democratic-Republican	1908	James S. Sherman	Republican
1808	George Clinton	Democratic-Republican	1912	Thomas R. Marshall	Democratic
1812	Elbridge Gerry	Democratic-Republican	1916	Thomas R. Marshall	Democratic
1816	Daniel D. Tompkins	Democratic-Republican	1920	Calvin Coolidge	Republican
1820	Daniel D. Tompkins	Democratic-Republican	1924	Charles G. Dawes	Republican
1824	John C. Calhoun	Democratic-Republican	1928	Charles Curtis	Republican
1828	John C. Calhoun	Democratic	1932	John N. Garner	Democratic
1832	Martin Van Buren	Democratic	1936	John N. Garner	Democratic
1836	Richard M. Johnson	Democratic	1940	Henry A. Wallace	Democratic
1840	John Tyler	Whig	1944	Harry S Truman	Democratic
1844	George M. Dallas	Democratic	1948	Alben W. Barkley	Democratic
1848	Millard Fillmore	Whig	1952	Richard M. Nixon	Republican
1852	William R. King	Democratic	1956	Richard M. Nixon	Republican
1856	John C. Breckinridge	Democratic	1960	Lyndon B. Johnson	Democratic
1860	Hannibal Hamlin	Republican	1964	Hubert H. Humphrey	Democratic
1864	Andrew Johnson	Democratic (Union)	1968	Spiro T. Agnew	Republican
1868	Schuyler Colfax	Republican	1972	Spiro T. Agnew	Republican
1872	Henry Wilson	Republican	1973	Gerald R. Ford[b]	Republican
1876	William A. Wheeler	Republican	1974	Nelson A. Rockefeller[b]	Republican
1880	Chester A. Arthur	Republican	1976	Walter F. Mondale	Democratic
1884	Thomas A. Hendricks	Democratic	1980	George H. Bush	Republican
1888	Levi P. Morton	Republican	1984	George H. Bush	Republican

[a] Not elected to office, but succeeding to it through the death or resignation of predecessor.
[b] Nonelected vice presidents nominated by the president and confirmed by Congress.

to end southern secession by force in 1860. Presidents in this group view their office as purely administrative: The president should be aloof from politics and depend on leadership from Congress. Buchanan presidents adopt a *custodial* view of presidental powers: The president is limited to those powers expressly granted to him in the Constitution. Otherwise, they argue, there would be no limits on presidential power. Presidents who have followed this approach generally have been considered the less active chief executives. They include Warren Harding, Calvin Coolidge, and Herbert Hoover, Republican presidents in the 1920s and early 1930s.

Lincoln Presidents

Lincoln -Active

Second, there are the *Lincoln presidents.* In this approach, the president is an active politician, often rallying the country in a crisis. Abraham Lincoln did so in the Civil War; Theodore Roosevelt did it later when he moved against the large business monopolies called trusts. In this century the Lincoln president also originates much of the legislation Congress considers, he leads public opinion, and he is the major source of the country's political goals.

Lincoln presidents do not interpret the Constitution as narrowly as do Buchanan presidents. In their view the presidency is a *stewardship;* its only limits are those explicitly mentioned in the Constitution. The president's powers, then, are as large as his political talents. Following this approach have been activist presidents such as Andrew Jackson, Theodore Roosevelt, Franklin Roosevelt, Harry Truman, Lyndon Johnson, and Richard Nixon.

Eisenhower Presidents

These two approaches to the presidency were outlined by Theodore Roosevelt, who as the twenty-fifth president did much to expand the influence of the office. Another category has been added since then, a combination of the other two called the *Eisenhower president.* Like Buchanan presidents, the Eisenhower president seeks to avoid political leadership and to keep out of party conflicts. But the Eisenhower president is not merely a chief administrator. He sees himself as a *chief delegate,* representing and organizing a national consensus rather than the special interests he believes Congress reflects. Believing that the people are basically good and that government tends to corrupt, the Eisenhower president limits government on behalf of the people by intervening to veto ill-advised political measures passed by Congress.

Eisenhower - Chief Delegate

Modern Presidents

Of course presidents never fall into exact categories. (Recent studies of Eisenhower, for example, make him appear to be more of an active politician than he seemed at the time.) Modern presidents have all leaned toward the activist end of the scale. Lyndon Johnson combined an Eisenhower pose with the results of an activist president like Franklin Roosevelt. Johnson sought not only to represent a national consensus but to create and guide this coalition as well. President Johnson, a master politician, was well known for his midnight phone calls and political arm twisting to gain support for his proposals. Richard Nixon tried to create an image of the presidency being above politics while using his own powers as president for sometimes unconstitutional ends. Gerald Ford came to his brief presidency as the nation's first nonelected vice president. His calm tenure of low activity was marked by his issuing more vetoes of congressional legislation in a shorter time than had any other president in history.

President Jimmy Carter, though gaining high marks as a hard-working manager, was criticized for his lack of political leadership, especially in his deadlocks with Congress. Trained as an engineer, Carter thoroughly, and most often privately, surrounded himself with the details of the policy decisions he had to make. By the end of his term a widespread feeling that the country's problems — inflation and unemployment at home, Soviet advances abroad — were not being competently handled led to the president's defeat for reelection in November 1980.

Ronald Reagan came to the presidency with a career as an actor and two terms as Republican governor of California behind him. He excelled in the ability to communicate through the media while delegating wide powers to his subordinates. His relaxed, optimistic attitude toward the office, and his advanced age (seventy-three when he was reelected) led critics to accuse him of being a "nine-to-five" president. Yet his media and political skills helped get through Congress budgets calling for decreases in social programs, increases in defense spending, and large tax cuts. President Reagan's success lay in demonstrating that a president could get an effective program put into law; his shortcomings lay in the questioned fairness of those conservative policies.

A Psychological Approach

A well-known modern attempt to categorize presidents has concentrated on their psychological makeup. Political scientist James D. Barber uses this personality approach to focus on the style and character of various chief executives.[1] A president's *style* refers to his ability to act and to the habits of work and personal relations by which he adapts to his surroundings. A style is either *active* or *passive*. *Character* refers to the way a president feels about himself (his self-esteem). Character is either *positive* or *negative*. Putting style and character together, Barber comes up with four categories of personalities in which he places some of our recent presidents (Active-Positive, Active-Negative, Passive-Positive, Passive-Negative).

And so, for example, because of their activism in office, as well as their ability to gain satisfaction from their accomplishments, John Kennedy, Harry Truman, and Jimmy Car-

[1] James David Barber, *The Presidential Character: Predicting Performance in the White House* (Englewood Cliffs, N.J.: Prentice-Hall, 1977).

ter are labeled Active-Positive. Not so fortunate are Active-Negative types like Presidents Johnson and Nixon, who, though intensely active, suffered from a low opinion of themselves and gained little personal satisfaction from their efforts. Passive-Positive presidents (one of whom, Barber believes, is Ronald Reagan) are easily influenced men searching for affection as a reward for being agreeable rather than for being assertive. President Eisenhower fits into the final category, Passive-Negative, combining a tendency to withdraw from conflict with a sense of his own uselessness. Only his sense of duty leads the Passive-Negative type into the presidency.

This last category gives us a clue to some of the shortcomings of Barber's personality approach. Having been Supreme Commander of the Allied Expeditionary Force during World War II, and a five-star general, Eisenhower may have seemed Passive-Negative compared with other presidents but could hardly have achieved what he did if these charac-

---

FIRST LADY, FIRST TARGET

The First Lady, the president's wife, fills a difficult nonconstitutional role. She may represent the president in public and advise him in private. She is constantly on public view acting as the ideal wife and often criticized for everything from her hair style to her life-style. Ever since Dolly Madison was described as "fat, forty but not fair," presidents' wives have been faulted for various presumed flaws. Eleanor Roosevelt was considered "too public" while Bess Truman was "too private." Pat Nixon was "too plastic," Betty Ford was "too candid," and Rosalynn Carter was "too ambitious." Nancy Reagan was immediately labeled an "Iron Butterfly" and remarked, "I never got half a chance!" One can sympathize with President Johnson's wife, Lady Bird, who commented, "A politician should be born an orphan and remain a bachelor." — from Ellen Goodman, "First Ladies Can't Win," *The Washington Post*, January 17, 1981. — © 1981, The Boston Globe Newspaper Company/Washington Post Writers Group. Reprinted with permission.

teristics had dominated his entire career. It therefore seems
inadequate to explain any shortcomings of his presidency
solely in terms of his personality. The makeup of the executive bureaucracy, the strength of his party, the interests he
represented, and the political mood of the country are just
some of the factors needed to understand the direction of
Eisenhower's presidency. Studying a president's personality
will provide interesting insights into how and why he acts.
It does not, as Barber would agree, give us the full picture of
the staff, institutions, and political and economic interests
that shape the behavior of the office of the presidency.

PRESIDENTIAL ROLES

The reasons the presidency has expanded lie not only in
the history of the office and the personality of the occupant,
but also in the increased expectations focused on the president today. When a specific national problem arises,
whether it is military aid to a foreign ally, racial discrimination, or rising interest rates, the president is usually
called on to respond. The president is also required by law
to handle a number of important duties, such as drawing up
and presenting the federal government's annual budget. In
fulfilling these responsibilities the president plays six somewhat different roles that often overlap and blend into one
another.

Chief of State

The president is the symbolic head of *state* as well as the
head of *government*. (In England the two positions are separate: the queen is head of state, a visible symbol of the
nation, and the prime minister is head of government, exercising the real power.) As chief of state, the president has
many ceremonial functions, ranging from declaring National Codfish Week to visiting foreign powers, often in an

election year. Because of this role, many people see the president as a symbol of the nation, somehow more than human, a fact that also gives him a political advantage. The difficulty in separating his ceremonial from his political actions is evident when, after President Reagan makes television broadcasts, the Democrats ask for equal time. Is he speaking in his role as a nonpolitical chief of state, or as the head of the Republican party?

Chief Diplomat

One has only to remember the taking, holding, and negotiated release of the American hostages in Iran — with much of the resulting attention and blame focused on President Carter — to see the importance of the president's second role: chief diplomat. The president has the power to establish relations with foreign governments, to appoint United States ambassadors, and to sign treaties that take effect with the consent of two-thirds of the Senate. Over the years, the president has become the chief maker and executor of American foreign policy. Despite the Senate's power to approve treaties and Congress's power to appropriate money for foreign aid and to declare wars, the checks on the president's power over foreign affairs are fewer than those on his conduct in domestic matters. After World War II, in an age of cold war when the United States and the Soviet Union seemed to be competing in every sphere, this authority over foreign policy elevated the president's standing to ever greater heights. Often presidents went so far as to argue that the health of the economy, the effectiveness of the educational system, and even racial discrimination affected our standing abroad and thus involved the president in how they should be resolved.

The Watergate and CIA investigations in the early 1970s illustrated the dangers in this wide interpretation of the president's powers as chief diplomat. The Central Intelligence Agency, which is part of the executive branch, was created to protect American interests and security by gathering information in other countries. But instruments developed for influencing events abroad became threats to democracy at home. In the Watergate case, ex-CIA officials tapped the telephones of opponents of the Nixon administration. Similarly, investigations of the CIA revealed that the agency had violated its charter by spying on American citizens who opposed presidential policies.

The Senate's power to ratify or reject treaties also has been changed by practice. Since its refusal in 1920 to approve United States membership in the League of Nations, the Senate has seldom refused to ratify a treaty. A partial exception to this was the Strategic Arms Limitation Treaty (SALT II) with the Soviet Union, which in 1980 was withdrawn from consideration in the Senate because the Soviet invasion of Afghanistan had made it impossible to pass. However, most international agreements involving the United States never reach the Senate. Because *executive agreements* do not require the approval of the Senate, their use has increased to the point where a president may sign hundreds of them in a single year. Presidents argue that these agreements usually concern only minor matters, and that important issues, such as the Panama Canal Treaty in 1978, are still submitted to the Senate for ratification. Those who disagree have pointed to the many agreements kept secret from the public and Congress that involve matters of far-reaching importance. Both Wilson and FDR used executive agreements to aid the Allies in the two world wars and, by doing so, involved the country in those conflicts before war was formally declared. Attempts by Congress to limit the president's use of executive agreements have all failed, although Congress can refuse to appropriate funds to carry out the agreements.

Commander-in-Chief

Closely tied to his role as chief diplomat is the president's role as commander-in-chief of the armed forces. The idea

behind the president's acting as commander-in-chief is the
principle of *civilian supremacy* over the military: An
elected civilian official, the president, is in charge of the
armed forces. In practice, this authority is given to the
secretary of defense, who normally delegates his command
to members of the military. This role may be used to
limit other rights, as in Grenada, where newsmen were not
immediately allowed to cover the United States invasion
of that island. This role, too, is not limited to actions
abroad, as shown by President Kennedy's use of federal
troops in 1961 to enroll a black man, James Meredith, in
the University of Mississippi. Its political importance is
further reflected by the fact that national defense gets
almost $250 billion, some 30 percent of the government's
budget.

Although the Constitution gives Congress the power to
declare war, Congress has not done so since December,
1941, when the United States entered World War II. Presidents, in their role as commander-in-chief, initiated the
country's involvement in the Korean and Vietnam wars.
Congress supported both actions by appropriating money for
the armed forces. Criticism of the president's role in Vietnam led to the *War Powers Act* of 1973 to limit the president's war-making powers. The law, passed over President
Nixon's veto, limited the president's committing of troops
abroad to a period of sixty days, or ninety at most if needed
for a successful withdrawal. If Congress does not authorize
a longer period, the troops must be removed. The effectiveness of the War Powers Act remains uncertain. In signing a
law in October 1983, allowing American Marines to remain
in Beirut, Lebanon, President Reagan stated that the War
Powers Act did not apply because the troops were not involved in hostilities. The argument became hard to justify
after several hundred were killed, and the peacekeeping
force was withdrawn in early 1984. The act also does not
prevent chief executives from using supposedly secret force,
as President Reagan did aiding rebels fighting the Nicara-
guan government.

Chief Executive

The president is, at least in theory, in complete charge of the huge federal bureaucracy in the executive branch. His authority comes from Article II of the Constitution, which states: "The executive Power shall be vested in a President of the United States of America." Executive power here means the ability to carry out or execute the laws. By 1983 this had led to the president's heading a bureaucracy spending over $850 billion a year, employing 2.8 million civilians (60 percent of whom are men) on a payroll of around $68 billion. The federal government, with revenues larger than those of the top forty United States corporations combined, ranks as the largest administrative organization in the world. Criticism of the bureaucracy is widespread; President Reagan's promise in his 1980 campaign to get the government "off the backs of the American people" helped get him elected. He follows a long tradition of presidents who have made similar promises. We will take a closer look at the federal bureaucracy later in this chapter.

Chief Legislator

Although the Constitution gives the president the right to recommend measures to Congress, it was not until the twentieth century that presidents regularly and actively participated in the legislative process. The president delivers his "State of the Union" address to a joint session of Congress at the beginning of every year to present the administration's annual legislative program. He also gives an annual budget message, an economic message and report, and frequently sends special messages to Congress supporting specific legislation.

Most bills passed by Congress originate in the executive branch. Getting this legislation passed requires some presidential popularity in Congress and in the nation. The president often uses tactics like campaigning for a supporter's reelection or threatening to block a member of Congress's local public works project to get his legislative program enacted into law. There were widespread reports in the spring of 1981 that President Reagan's refusal to cut tobacco subsidies sprang from his need to gain the support of conservative southern senators for the rest of his budget cuts.

The president's main constitutional power as chief legislator is the *veto*. If a president disapproves of a bill passed by Congress, he may refuse to sign it and can return it to Congress with his objections. Congress may override the veto by a two-thirds vote of each house, though this has happened in only 3 percent of vetoes. Because the president does not have an *item veto* (despite President Reagan's attempt to gain this power), he cannot veto only the specific sections of the bill he dislikes. Rather he must approve or reject the whole bill that comes before him. The veto is most often used as a threat to influence the shape of a bill while it is still being considered by Congress.

Party Leader

A president is also head of his party. As party leader the president has a number of major duties: to choose a vice president after his own nomination; to distribute a few thousand offices and numerous favors to the party faithful; and to demonstrate that he is at least trying to fulfill the *party platform*, the party's program adopted at his nominating convention. The president is also the chief campaigner and fund-raiser for his party. He names the national chairperson and usually exerts a great deal of influence over the national party machinery.

The president's control over his party is limited, however, by the decentralized nature of American political parties. Local party organizations are usually stronger than the national organizations. Congressional members of the president's party often refuse to support his programs, and he has few sanctions to use against them. He has no power to refuse members of Congress the party's nomination, or to keep them from reaching positions of power in Congress through seniority. In a recent Congress, many Senate Republicans from farm states opposed President Reagan's efforts to drastically reduce the food-stamp program. Presidents also vary in how much they wish to be involved in their party's affairs. President Carter was often criticized for not strengthening the Democratic party, whereas President Johnson kept close control on the Democratic party organization.

THE PRESIDENT AND THE PUBLIC

A major result of the president's many powers and roles in his influence over mass opinion. His visibility, his standing as a symbol of the nation, and his position as a human being compared with a frequently impersonal government give the chief executive a great deal of influence in the political game.

Yet all this visibility may also work against him. After all, a president is chosen by election and has to keep the voters happy to keep himself and his party in office. Usually this duty means accomplishing his administration's goals as well as maintaining his own personal popularity. But these two aims are not always compatible. Two recent presidents, Lyndon Johnson and Richard Nixon, left office widely unpopular, Johnson because of the Vietnam War and Nixon because of Watergate. In both cases the public attention focused on them by the mass media probably hastened their decline. Jimmy Carter, who had fairly good relations with the press, lost his bid for reelection under the widespread perception that his was a "failed presidency." President Reagan has shown himself to be history's most skillful chief executive at using the media to directly reach people for support of controversial foreign and domestic policies. Although most recent presidents have lost popularity as their term progressed, with his publicized visits to China and Europe and an improved economy, Mr. Reagan won reelection by a landslide in November of 1984 (see Chapter 8).

While keeping up his standing with other branches of the government and the public at large, the president must still try to carry out the tasks of his office and the goals of his administration. In doing so, his most vital relationship is with the bureaucracy under him. What makes up this bureaucracy and how the president handles it are our focus in the rest of this chapter.

THE FEDERAL BUREAUCRACY

The federal bureaucracy carries out most of the work of governing. Despite the bad implications of the word, a *bureaucrat* is simply an administrator, a member of the large administrative organization — the bureaucracy — that carries out the policies of the elected officials of the government. The great growth of the national government and the tasks it has confronted during this century have produced an administrative system unequaled in size and complexity. Most of this bureaucracy is within, or close to, the executive branch. The structure of the bureaucracy can be broken down into the executive office of the president, the cabinet departments, the executive agencies, and the regulatory commissions (see Figure 3.1).

Executive Office of the President

The *executive office* was established in 1939 to advise the president and to assist him in managing the bureaucracy. It has grown steadily in size and influence until today it includes eight agencies and some 1,800 people (see Figure 3.2). Three of the most important agencies of the executive office are the White House office, the National Security Council, and the Office of Management and Budget.

The *White House office* is a direct extension of the president. Its members are not subject to Senate approval. In recent years centralization of executive power has increased

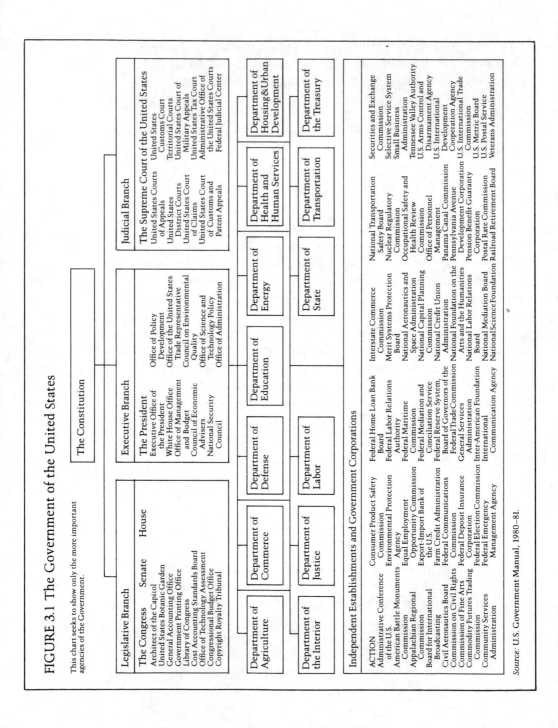

FIGURE 3.1 The Government of the United States

This chart seeks to show only the more important agencies of the Government.

Source: U.S. Government Manual, 1980–81.

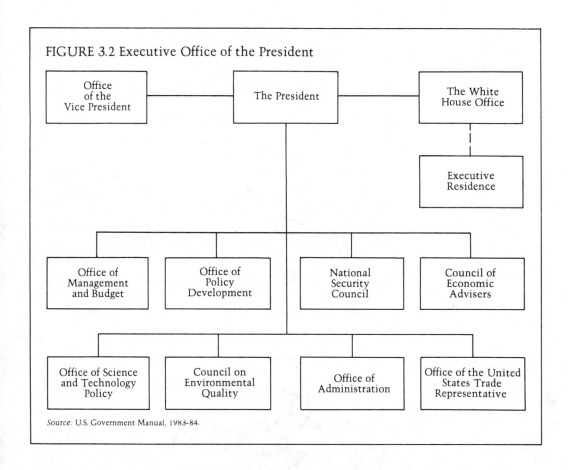

FIGURE 3.2 Executive Office of the President

Source: U.S. Government Manual, 1983-84.

the authority of the White House staff at the expense of the cabinet officers. Henry Kissinger, as Nixon's assistant for national security affairs, had such a leading role in foreign policy that his influence overshadowed that of the secretary of state. President Reagan depended so much on his White House staff that some conservative supporters charged that he was a captive of his more moderate staff. "Let Reagan Be Reagan" was the slogan they used in 1983 to illustrate this feeling. Though the president when first elected declared his belief in relying on the cabinet, the Reagan White House staff with its access to the president quickly established itself as the central player in the administration.

The *National Security Council* (NSC) was established early in the cold war (1947) to help the president coordinate American military and foreign policies. These policies mainly involve the departments of State and Defense, which are represented on the council. (The Central Intelligence Agency, though an executive agency, also falls under the authority of the NSC.) Presidents have varied in how much they wished to use the NSC. President Kennedy preferred more informal ways of getting advice on national security matters, but President Nixon restored the council to a dominant role in forming and executing policy.

The *Office of Management and Budget* (OMB) was created by President Nixon in 1970 to replace the Bureau of the Budget. Departments of the executive branch submit competing claims for shares in the federal budget to the OMB. Besides preparing the budget, OMB is an important general-management arm of the president. It helps the pres-

ident control the executive branch by overseeing all the agencies and their success in accomplishing their programs. Preparing and administering the annual budget (which is then submitted to Congress for approval) gives OMB tremendous power within the government. David Stockman, President Reagan's young director of OMB, illustrated this influence as architect of the administration's proposals for some $50 billion in spending cuts in its first budget.

The *Council of Economic Advisers* is another important unit of the executive office. It is a three-member council of economic experts, appointed with Senate approval, which helps the president form a national economic policy and gives him advice on economic developments.

The Cabinet Departments

The *cabinet departments* that are created by Congress are the major agencies of the federal government. Originally there were only three (the departments of State, War, and the Treasury); today there are thirteen. The expansion of the cabinet has been due largely to the growth of problems that people wanted the federal government to deal with. The raising to cabinet level of the Department of Energy in 1977 shows the recent interest in this area of both the public and the government. The former Department of Health, Education and Welfare was split into two new units, the Department of Education, and the Department of Health and Human Services, in May 1980. Although President Reagan promised in 1980 to abolish both the departments of Energy and Education, he had not done so by 1985.

Each cabinet department is headed by a secretary, who is appointed by the president with the consent of the Senate (which is usually given). Cabinet secretaries hold office as long as the president wishes. Because cabinet secretaries have large bureaucracies to manage, however, they have less loyalty to the president than do members of the executive office. Pressures from their staff and constant involvement with the problems of their agencies may cause secretaries to act more like lobbyists for their departments than representatives of the president.

How much the president uses the cabinet as a whole is strictly up to him, for the cabinet has no power as a body. Although many presidents, including Reagan and Carter, entered office promising to give the cabinet policymaking authority, things haven't worked out that way. More typical is a story about President Lincoln being opposed by his entire cabinet on an issue and remarking, "Seven nays, one aye; the ayes have it."

The amount of control each cabinet head has over his or her own department varies greatly. Often a department may be a loose structure containing strong, relatively independent groups. Although the attorney general has authority over the FBI, which is in the Justice Department, J. Edgar Hoover's lengthy rule as director of the FBI limited the cabinet secretary's influence. The Treasury Department under Donald Regan on the other hand, appeared to be much more tightly run by its secretary.

The Executive Agencies

Executive agencies are simply important agencies of the executive branch that are not in the cabinet. Their heads are appointed by the president with approval of the Senate, but they are not considered important enough to be part of the cabinet. Examples of these are the Veterans' Administration (VA), the National Aeronautics and Space Administration (NASA), and the Central Intelligence Agency (CIA).

Under executive agencies we might include *government corporations*, which were originally semi-independent but have come increasingly under presidential control. Government corporations, like private corporations, perform business activities such as operating a transportation system or developing and selling electricity. They are usually governed by a board of directors, have limited legislative control over them, and allow for flexible administration. The Tennessee Valley Authority (TVA) is a government corporation, set up in the 1930s to develop electricity for the Tennessee Valley. The United States Postal Service is another, established in 1970 when Congress abolished the Post Office as a cabinet department and set it up as a semi-independent government-owned corporation.

The Regulatory Commissions

Regulatory commissions are charged with regulating certain parts of the economy. Examples are the Interstate Commerce Commission (ICC), which regulates railroads, buses, and trucking, and the Federal Communications Commission (FCC), which oversees telephone, radio, and television operations. (The important Federal Reserve Board, under its chairman, Paul Volcker, is a special type of regulatory agency that determines general monetary policies, like interest rates, for Federal Reserve Banks.) Although the president appoints the members of the commissions and chooses the chairpersons, the commissions are relatively independent of all branches of the government. They are bipartisan (members come from both parties); the president has only a limited right to remove commissioners, who generally serve longer terms than the president; and there is no presidential veto over their actions. These commissions also have all three capacities of government: they can make rules that have the force of law (legislative), administer and enforce these regulations (executive), and conduct hearings and issue orders (judicial). Their decisions can be reviewed by federal courts, however, and their authority can be reduced by Congress.

The reason behind these agencies is the common view that private economic groups will not always act in the public interest unless they are forced to. The independence of these commissions from the rest of the government has meant, however, that the public has little control over their activities. The commissions often come under pressure from the groups they are regulating, and the lack of governmental controls has sometimes led them to negotiate with,

---

THE PRESIDENT AND THE MOUSE

The problems presidents have with their bureaucracy are not always limited to major policy matters. An example from the Carter presidency: "When a couple of mice scampered across the President's study one evening last spring, an alarm went out to the General Services Administration, housekeeper of Federal buildings. Some weeks later, another mouse climbed up inside a wall of the Oval Office and died. The President's office was bathed in the odor of dead mouse as Carter prepared to greet visiting Latin American dignitaries. An emergency call went out to GSA. But it refused to touch the matter. Officials insisted that they had exterminated all the "inside" mice in the White House and this errant mouse must have come from outside, and therefore was the responsibility of the Interior Department. Interior demurred, saying that the dead mouse was now inside the White House. President Carter summoned officials from both agencies to his desk and exploded: 'I can't even get a damn mouse out of my office.' Ultimately, it took an interagency task force to get rid of the mouse." — From Hedrick Smith, "Problems of a Problem Solver," *The New York Times Magazine,* January 8, 1978. Copyright © 1978 by The New York Times Company. Reprinted by permission.

---

rather than regulate, some important economic interests. They have often been charged with being captives of the wealthy economic groups they oversee. On the other hand, some commissions, like the Federal Trade Commission (FTC), were accused by Republicans in the 1980 election of overregulating the economy.

PROBLEMS OF BUREAUCRACY

The word *bureaucracy* is often used nowadays to imply incompetence and red tape; the faceless administrator unthinkingly following rules despite their impact on peoples' lives. The problems with bureaucracies seem to be related to their size rather than the nature of the public or private organizations they serve. Socialist bureaucracies don't appear to operate better than bureaucracies in capitalist countries. The size and complexity of a large bureaucracy makes it hard to tell who is responsible for a particular action, inhibiting public scrutiny and control. In the 1980 election public feelings against a bureaucracy with too much power under too little control helped propel Ronald Reagan into the presidency.

The fact that bureaucrats are experts in their own areas is a major source of their influence in government, but the limits of their vision also present problems. A member of Congress or a president wanting information or advice on tax policy, housing programs, or energy costs would probably go to the bureaucrat in charge of the subject. The problem is how to get these experts in the bureaucracy to see beyond their own narrow fields of expertise to the broader public interest. During the Vietnam War, bureaucrats often pursued their own departments' interests (the navy wanted more ships, the air force more planes, and the army more troops), rather than asking whether the war could ever be won.

Rise of the Civil Service

In the first century of the federal government, the usual method of choosing government bureaucrats was known as the *spoils system*. Taken from the phrase "To the victor belong the spoils," the spoils system meant that the victorious politicians filled government positions with their supporters. This system of widespread patronage got its start during the administration of President Andrew Jackson (1828–1836), when bureaucrats did not even need to be knowledgeable in their fields. But as the tasks expected of bureaucrats became more complex and corruption grew, pressure for reform also increased.

In 1881 President James Garfield was assassinated by a disappointed (and slightly crazy) office seeker. The new president, Chester Arthur, backed by public outrage over the murder, supported the Civil Service Reform Act (also known as the Pendleton Act), which was passed by Congress in 1883. The act set up a bipartisan Civil Service Commission under which government employees were chosen by merit through examinations. At first only about 10 percent of federal employees were covered by civil service, but the system has grown and now covers practically the entire bureaucracy. This influence has considerably diminished the spoils system and has added stability to government activity. The president today fills only about 5,000 patronage jobs, of which fewer than one-third are at a policy-making level. While weakening the spoils system, it has also weakened presidential control of the bureaucracy; the bureaucrats know they will have their jobs long after the current administration passes into history.

Controlling Bureaucracy

The size and growth of the federal bureaucracy has led some people to ask whether it has become the master of government, rather than its servant. Both liberals and conservatives have proposed ways of making bureaucracy more responsive to the government and public. Stronger executive control by the president has been the usual response, but many people fear the president is already too strong. Congress has been called on to watch the bureaucracy more closely. President Carter's Civil Service Reform Act of 1978 made it easier to fire incompetent employees and created a core of top civil servants (a senior executive service) who would exchange job security for large pay bonuses based on performance. Public involvement through consumer groups like Ralph Nader's "Raiders" has grown in popularity. Efforts to decentralize the bureaucracy and put parts of it under local control are another solution that has been just partly successful. This technique can work only where the community has adequate resources and awareness to both support and control the local bureaucracy. Political and bureaucratic interests have often halted all these attempts at reform.

President Reagan's efforts to control the bureaucracy have aimed at reducing its size and turning over some of its functions to the states. Soon after taking office the president imposed a job freeze, reducing federal employment in virtually all departments except Defense. He also severely limited the budget increases for many social programs and proposed to cut out some agencies entirely, like the Departments of Energy and Education. The president then proposed to combine many federal programs into four big *block grants* that would be given to state governments. Under the "New Federalism," each state would be given wide powers to decide how it wished to spend the money, with a minimum of federal oversight. Though reducing the role of the federal bureaucracy, the block grants would result in reduced spending for popular programs in areas like education assistance and health care. Although modified in the 1984 budget, the President's proposals got little support from Congress, the bureaucracy, or state governments. Like many attempts to reform the bureaucracy, the "New Federalism" seems to have been a nonstarter.

The President and the Bureaucracy

The bureaucracy at his disposal is an important support for the president. The federal bureaucracy gives the president access to more information than his opponents are likely to have and allows him to initiate policies to which others must react. Curiously, though, the bureaucracy also provides the major limit on a president's actions. To carry out his policies the president must rely on the information, advice, and actions of subordinates. Keeping control over the three million employees of the executive branch is a full-time job in itself. As political scientist Richard Neustadt commented, the president spends much of his time finding out what his subordinates are doing in his name.

Members of the bureaucracy may work to protect their own interests or may respond to pressures from economic concerns threatened by presidential policies. In doing so they may ignore the president's orders, and delay or even sabotage his programs. Often these departments have long rivalries with each other: Labor versus Agriculture on food prices, State versus Defense over foreign policy. The president must act as judge over these conflicts and yet maintain close ties with both sides. Even cabinet officials appointed by the president may represent their own departments' interests against those of the president. Does the secretary of defense represent the president to the Defense Department, or the department to the president? Clearly both, but conflict often results.

To operate in this fiercely contested bureaucratic puzzle the president must know how to bargain. Presidential power thus often boils down to the power to persuade. The president both influences and reflects the interests and powers in the government and country. His ability to gain acceptance for his policies, be they actions against budget deficits or for foreign military aid, depends on the interests he represents, his ability to bargain with the political elites, and his skill in controlling his own bureaucracy. Examples can be seen in the following cases of presidential confrontations with the steel industry.

Case Study: Three Examples of Presidential Power

Outlining the powers and duties of the executive branch will not necessarily tell us what a president can do in real situations. How successfully a president plays the roles of his office and uses the bureaucracy depends partly on what political situations he faces. And of course it also depends on his own experience and skill. These three cases, in which presidents Truman, Kennedy, and Carter faced similar conflicts with the steel industry, emphasize the difficulties, the advantages, and the uncertainties in using presidential power.

Truman and Steel (1952)

In 1952 the United States was involved in the Korean War, and both strikes and inflation were serious threats to the country. When union and management leaders in the steel industry deadlocked over union wage demands, President Truman faced a crisis. The Wage Stabilization Board (WSB), which had been set up to hold down wages and prices so as to reduce inflation, recommended a proposal that was accepted by the union but strongly opposed by management. It was also opposed by Charles Wilson, who headed the Office of Defense Mobilization, which oversaw the WSB. The president agreed with the WSB, and Wilson resigned.

Meanwhile, industry officials argued that a large price increase would be necessary to meet the union's wage demands. President Truman responded that if a price rise were needed "in the interest of national defense" it would be granted, but he refused to commit himself to any specific figure. The steel management then presented a wage offer lower than the WSB had recommended. The union turned it down and prepared for a strike.

Given the wartime situation, the president's problem was to avoid a strike without causing a large rise in the price of steel. He saw three alternatives: (1) He could use the Taft Hartley Law to seek an eighty-day cooling-off period in which no strike could occur (but he disliked this law, which he considered antilabor and which had been passed over his veto); (2) he could grant both the union's wage demands and the industry's increase (but he saw this as increasing inflation); or (3) he could seize the steel mills and put them under government management. Two hours before the strike was due to start, Truman ordered the mills seized.

Some of what followed was predictable. On April 8, 1952, the president went after public support. He bitterly attacked a "few greedy companies" for demanding "outrageous prices" that would wreck the entire price-control program. A spokesman for the steel industry responded in kind, accusing the president of having "transgressed his oath of office" and "abused" his power. Congress and the press were generally upset by what they felt was the president's overstepping the limits of his office in seizing the mills. The industry brought a suit against the seizure, and the case went quickly through the lower courts to the Supreme Court.

Things began to go badly for the president for a number of reasons. Truman's seizure of the mills was designed only as a tactic to give him time and an informal way to force an agreeable wage and price settlement. Essentially the seizure was designed to be so unattractive to both union and management that they would come to an agreement. But Truman's own secretary of commerce, who was ordered to administer the mills, opposed the seizure. Though he did not refuse to follow the president's orders, the secretary did drag his feet. By the time the plan was ready to take effect, it was too late. The Supreme Court ruled against the president's claim that as commander-in-chief he had the "inherent power" to seize the mills in the interest of national security. Such emergency powers rested only in Congress. Truman had lost.

Kennedy and Steel (1962)

Ten years later President Kennedy confronted the steel industry in a similar crisis. In this case, the Kennedy administration had persuaded the steel union to accept a moderate wage rise, under the impression that it would not mean a price increase. To the president's surprise, the leading steel company, United States Steel, then announced a sharp rise in price. This action was quickly followed by most of the other large steel corporations.

The next day, April 11, President Kennedy responded in a nationally televised press conference. He called the actions by the companies "a wholly unjustifiable and irresponsible defiance of the public interest." Referring to the "grave crises in Berlin and Southeast Asia," he stressed the need for "restraint and sacrifice" by every citizen. He charged that there was no economic reason for the increase because of the industry's already high rate of profit. He concluded that "a tiny handful of steel executives" had shown "utter contempt for the interests of 185 million Americans," adding, "Some time ago I asked each American to consider what he would do for his country. And I asked the steel companies. In the last twenty-four hours we had their answer."

But Kennedy did not merely use his position as chief of state to shame the steel executives with speeches. He backed up his statements with some pointed informal threats. The president warned the steel companies that the Department of Justice was exploring possible violations of antitrust laws in the way the companies set prices. The Department of Defense, a major steel buyer, might also decide to buy from those companies which had not raised their prices. Further, in his roles of chief legislator and party leader (the Democrats controlled Congress at the time), Kennedy hinted that Congress might change tax laws to the disadvantage of the steel industry.

After initial resistance, the steel corporations caved in. Two major companies announced they would not raise prices. The ones that already had raised them quickly canceled the increase. In concluding the conflict, President Kennedy remarked that his administration "harbors no ill will" against any industry in the American economy. It was easy for Kennedy to be graceful. He was a winner.

Carter and Steel (1977)

On May 6, 1977, two major steel companies raised the prices on their products by 8.8 percent. The price rise was widely expected. Steel workers had recently won an 11 percent increase in wages spread over three years, and five of the nine leading steel producers had lost money the previous year.

The Carter administration, though agreeing on the need for higher prices, thought that the increases were too large. Steel prices had already risen 12 percent in the last year, and these new increases for an essential product threatened the administration's program of voluntary wage and price restraints to fight inflation. The president, in a written statement, called the rise "unwarranted," and his Council on Wage and Price Stability (which had no formal authority to lower the prices) announced an immediate investigation of the increase.

At the same time the administration offered the steel companies an attractive incentive for moderating their prices. For years the steel industry had complained that foreign steel manufacturers had been illegally "dumping" their product in the American market. ("Dumping" consists of selling steel in the United States at a lower price than the price of steel in the home country of the producer.) More detached observers contended that the industry was inefficient and poorly managed and that limiting foreign imports would free the American producers from competition and would thereby raise prices. The Carter administration had been generally against restrictions on imports. Nonetheless, at a breakfast meeting with steel representatives, advisers to the president linked holding down prices by the companies to the administration restricting imports in the future.

The mutual back scratching seemed to have an effect. On May 10, United States Steel, which had not raised its prices, announced a 6 percent price rise. A rollback to 6 percent in the prices announced by the other companies quickly followed. High administration officials stated they were "very happy" with this figure. At the same time, leaks in the press announced that the administration was considering opening negotiations with foreign countries over their steel-pricing policies. A deal had been made. Each side had gotten something it wanted, which may be the nearest thing in politics to a draw.

What Made the Difference?

Why did Truman lose, Kennedy win, and Carter play to a draw? What do these cases tell us about presidential power? It is worth noticing that Truman used *formal power* in challenging the steel industry, whereas both Kennedy and Carter used the *informal influence* of their office. Employing his doubtful legal powers as commander-in-chief, Truman took direct action in seizing the steel mills. The companies responded by moving the playing field from the public arena to the courts. Here Truman, on weak legal ground, lost.

A major reason for Truman's taking such drastic action was his political weakness. He chose the formal action of seizure in order to increase his informal influence. But it didn't work. His own bureaucracy frustrated his efforts. Wilson resigned and the secretary of commerce defied him. The reasons he didn't fire the secretary probably lie outside the steel crisis. Truman in 1952 was an unpopular president, a lame duck nearing the end of his term. He had recently fired his attorney general and had dismissed the very popular General Douglas MacArthur for disobeying his orders. Truman felt he had to tolerate his secretary's delaying tactics.

Kennedy used both his symbolic position as a representative of the national interest and the informal influence of his office to put pressure on the steel companies. Like Truman, he "wrapped himself in the flag," pointing to threats from overseas and hurling thunderbolts of national indignation at the companies. But it is doubtful whether hard-headed steel executives would have cut into their profits out of patriotism alone. It was the threat to restrict government buying, to start antitrust suits, and to use tax laws against the companies that was probably more important in their switch.

Carter's low-key approach avoided a confrontation. Perhaps remembering that Kennedy's win had marked him as "antibusiness," Carter tried in a nonpublic, informal way to push the prices down. Although this tactic was at first successful, skirmishes continued. Soon the industry had an apparently unanswerable argument for government opposition to price increases — mill closings. In early fall, 1977, some 20,000 steelworkers were put out of work. Labor united with industry to lobby for restrictions on steel imports. By the end of the year the industry had raised their prices another 5.5 percent, and the administration announced a plan to limit low-priced foreign imports. Despite opposition from some of the bureaucracy to this plan (the independent Federal Trade Commission said in 1978 that it would cost consumers $1 billion a year), President Carter seemed to lose ground to an industry that could get its unemployed workers to symbolize its interests.

All three presidents had the same formal powers, yet their use of the powers differed. Kennedy combined the tools of presidential power with his political standing and smoothly used the media to bring his message to the public. Carter had more modest goals than either Kennedy or Truman, which may have led him to use more moderate methods. Carter's methods of influence involved less conflict than those of the other two Democrats, and though his achievement was more limited than Kennedy's, his losses were less visible than Truman's. Both Carter and Kennedy also had an advantage in coming after Truman — they could learn from the other's mistakes.

But we should hesitate in drawing too many conclusions from these cases. The use of presidential power is always surrounded by politics. Similar political conflicts are not the same as identical chemistry experiments. The ingredients and procedures of the chemistry laboratory can be repeated exactly to prove conclusions. Political events cannot. Too

much remains uncertain. Perhaps uncertainty over the results of the use of presidential power is the most useful
conclusion we can draw from these cases.

WRAP-UP

This chapter has introduced the executive players in the
political game — the president and the bureaucracy. We
have seen how the presidency has irregularly but vastly
grown in influence from a limited grant of constitutional
powers, and we have looked at three different presidential
styles as well as a psychological approach to a president's
personality. The six major roles a president fills — chief of
state, chief diplomat, commander-in-chief, chief executive,
chief legislator, and party leader — show how broad his
power has grown. In the last fifty years government power
has been centralized, in the federal government relative to
the states, and in the president relative to the Congress.

The bureaucracy within the executive branch generally
reinforces the president's power. Yet its size and the complexity of its structures, from the executive office to the
cabinet departments, executive agencies, and regulatory
commissions, limit the president's control over the bureaucracy. As the steel cases made clear, a president's power in
a real situation may be hindered as well as extended by the
rest of the executive branch.

The president as both an individual and an institution is
likely to continue to play a central role in the American
political game. The history of arbitrary actions by presidents abroad and at home has shown how powerful a president can be and how easily he can manipulate public
opinion. Yet, often, presidents have seemed weak and inef-
fective in managing the bureaucracy and getting their programs acted on by Congress. People have tended to focus
their dissatisfaction with government on individual presidents. Most of us still look for a presidential Moses to lead

us out of the wilderness of economic and foreign troubles. We often fail to realize that it was largely these public expectations that encouraged presidents' inflated powers and removed the presidency from the original limits of the office.

Presidents are people too. As political players they have performed neither better nor worse than most of the other players in the game. But the unrealistic expectations and powers given them have magnified their faults.

THOUGHT QUESTIONS

1. What are the major reasons for the growth in the power of the president? Do you think it has been inevitable?
2. How does the executive-branch bureaucracy both limit and support the power of the president?
3. Do you think the president and bureaucracy are too powerful or not powerful enough? Give some current examples to back up your argument.
4. What should a president do? Is it possible for any president to accomplish what people expect him to do?

SUGGESTED READINGS

Greenstein, Fred I. *The Hidden-hand Presidency: Eisenhower as Leader.* New York: Basic Books, 1982.
  Another look at General Eisenhower's presidency, with surprising conclusions about how effective this supposedly "nonpolitical" leader really was.

Hersh, Seymour. *The Price of Power.* New York: Summit Books, 1983. Pb.
  A bitter, impressive chronicle of the rise to power of Henry Kissinger, presidential assistant for national security and secretary of state under Nixon and Ford.

Kearns, Doris. *Lyndon Johnson and the American Dream.* New York: Harper & Row, 1976. Pb.
  Tantalizing behind-the-scenes looks at the character and career of Lyndon Johnson.

Lengle, James I., and Byron E. Shafer. *Presidential Politics*, 2nd ed. New York: St. Martin's, 1983.

A collection of articles examining how we elect a president, with topics ranging from campaign strategy to picking a president based on World Series results.

Neustadt, Richard E. *Presidential Power*. New York: John Wiley & Sons, 1976. Pb.

A classic work on the presidency with an added look at Johnson and Nixon.

Pious, Richard. *The American Presidency*. New York: Basic Books, 1979.

A comprehensive, balanced review of the powers and weaknesses of the modern presidency.

Safire, William. *Full Disclosure*. New York: Doubleday, 1977.

A former White House staffer's novel of a blind president struggling against an unkind media to hold on to his office.

The Legislative Branch: Congress 4

The framers of the American Constitution meant for the Congress to be the center of the American political game. Their experience with King George III of England and his often dictatorial or incompetent governors had left the colonists with a deep suspicion of strong executive authority. As a result, the Constitution gave many detailed powers and responsibilities to the Congress but far fewer to the president. And through its major function — lawmaking — Congress creates the rules that govern all the political players. Article I of the Constitution gives Congress the power to levy taxes, borrow money, raise armies, declare war, determine the nature of the federal judiciary, regulate commerce, coin money, and "make all Laws which shall be necessary and proper for carrying into Execution the foregoing powers, and all other Powers vested by this Constitution in the Government of the United States, or in any Department or Officer thereof."

Many of the powers given to the president are limited by the powers of Congress. The president was named the commander-in-chief of the armed services, but he could not declare war or raise armies. If he wanted an army, the Congress had to provide it. The president was to be the chief administrative officer of the government, but there would be no government to administer if the Congress did not create it. He could appoint executive officials and negotiate foreign treaties only if the Senate agreed. Although the president could veto a bill passed by Congress, the Congress had the power to override his veto and make the bill a law in spite of the president's wishes. Both the raising of money through taxes and the spending of it by the government required approval by Congress. Finally, Congress was given the power to impeach and remove the president, if in its judgment he was found guilty of "Treason, Bribery, or other high Crimes and Misdemeanors."

During the early years and through the nineteenth century, Congress often played the dominant role in shaping the nation's policies. Members of Congress such as Daniel Webster, Henry Clay, and John C. Calhoun molded the major issues of their times from within the legislature. As late as the end of the nineteenth century, Woodrow Wilson could proclaim, "Congress is the dominant, nay, the irresistible power of the federal system."

Wilson was later to change his mind, however, and most observers have gone along with him. During the twentieth century, and especially since the Great Depression and World War II, the executive branch of the government has greatly increased in influence compared with that of Congress. In recent years Congress has been often blamed by the public for many of the delays and failures of government to act on pressing national problems, from budget deficits to nuclear arms. Still, the Congress showed its muscle in the early 1970s with its successful opposition to President Nixon's sometimes illegal actions. Even with the president's central role in foreign affairs recent Congresses have shown new activism in shaping policies ranging from Central America to the nuclear freeze. With its control over the government's purse strings Congress remains a vital part of the political game. In this chapter we will examine the structure of Congress, how it was designed to operate, and how it actually carries out its functions today.

MAKEUP OF THE SENATE AND HOUSE

The Congress of the United States is *bicameral*, made up of two branches: the Senate and the House of Representatives. The Senate consists of two senators from each state regardless of the size of the state. House members are distributed according to population so that the larger the state's population, the more representatives it gets. The Constitution requires that each state have at least one representative, no matter how small it may be. These provisions are the result of a political compromise between the small states and the large states during the writing of the Constitution.

As the country has grown, so too has the size of Congress. The first Congress consisted of 26 senators and 65 representatives. With each new state added to the union, the Senate has grown by two, so that it now has 100 members. As the nation's population grew, the size of the House of Representatives grew also. In 1922 the Congress passed a law setting the maximum size of the House at 435 members, where it remains today (see Figure 4.2). In the first House each member represented around 50,000 citizens. The average representative now serves some 550,000 constituents.

THE NINETY-EIGHTH CONGRESS

The Ninety-eighth Congress was elected in the fall of 1982. Seventy-nine freshmen entered the House, and five entered the Senate. The new Congress has the lowest average age — 47 years — of any since World War II. Ten years ago, the average age was 52. Only seven of today's senators are 70 or over, compared with fifteen in 1971. Unlike the 97th Congress, which had twelve members 30 or younger, the new Congress has only one, Representative Jim Cooper, D-Tenn., 29. The youngest Senator is Don Nickles, 34, R-Oklahoma.

Catholics make up 26 percent of the Congress, whereas Jews compose about 7 percent. A record twenty-one representatives and two senators are women. Minority group representation includes twenty-one blacks, an increase of four from 1980, and eleven Hispanics, up six from the previous Congress. All except one of them are Democrats, and all sit in the House. Three Asians sit in the House, two in the Senate. Easily the most overrepresented group in Congress is astronauts, with two in the Senate — Harrison H. Schmitt (R-N.M.), and John Glenn (D-Ohio).

Role of the Legislator

There are many questions about what the role of a legislator should be, questions as old as the idea of representative assemblies. Should a representative do only what his or her constituents wish, or follow his or her own judgment about what is best? What should a representative do if the interests of his or her district seem to conflict with the needs of the nation as a whole? Should a legislator recognize a "greater good" beyond the boundaries of the district?

One reason for all these questions is that members of Congress are both *national* and *local* representatives. They are national representatives in that they make up one branch of the national government, are paid by that federal government, and are required to support and defend the interests of the entire nation. Yet they are elected by local districts or states. In running for election, legislators must satisfy local constituents that they are looking out not only for the national interest but for local interests as well. In controversial areas like cutting the budget, the legislator's view of the national interest may be very different from local popular opinion. Congressmen must both represent a small interest and compromise it to form a coalition large enough to pass bills. And they can't forget a warning heard often in Congress, "To be a good congressman, you first have to be a congressman."

Who Are the Legislators?

A member of the House of Representatives must be at least twenty-five years old, a citizen of the United States for seven years, and a resident of the state in which he or she is elected. A senator must be thirty years old, nine years a citizen, and a resident of the state that elects him or her. State residency is a fairly loose requirement, however. Robert Kennedy rented a New York City apartment and declared it his prime residence just before entering the New York Senate race in 1964.

Senators serve six-year terms and are elected by the entire state's population. Every two years, during the national elections, one third of the Senate seeks reelection. The other senators do not run because they are only one third or two thirds of the way through their terms.

The Constitution originally provided that members of the Senate would be elected by their respective state legislatures. The purpose was to remove the choice from the masses of citizens and try to ensure that more conservative elements would pick the senators. This procedure was changed by the Seventeenth Amendment, ratified in 1913. Senators are now elected by the voting public of each state, just like other elected officials.

Members of the House of Representatives (called "members of Congress," although Congress technically includes both the Senate and the House) serve two years. They are elected from congressional districts within the states. No congressional district ever crosses state borders (see Figure 4.1).

Congress is composed overwhelmingly of white males, and it tends to reflect the values of upper-middle-class America. Almost half the members of Congress are lawyers. Other common professions are business, banking, education, farming, and journalism. Women and blacks are underrepresented in Congress for many reasons, including (for blacks at least) the effects of malapportionment and gerrymandering, to be discussed in the following pages. Some other reasons are the selection of candidates by party organizations, lack of voter organization, and voter apathy. Recent elections, however, have brought more women and minority-group members into Congress, a trend that is likely to continue. (See Tables 4.1 and 4.2 for the characteristics of the Ninety-eighth Congress and the Ninety-third Congress.)

Another change in the makeup of Congress has been the trend toward *careerism* — the tendency for legislators to see service in Congress as a lifetime career. This tendency hasn't always held. Until the 1840s the average length of

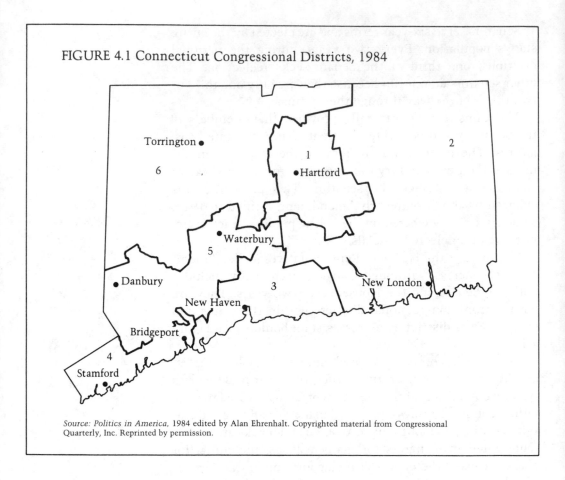

FIGURE 4.1 Connecticut Congressional Districts, 1984

Source: Politics in America, 1984 edited by Alan Ehrenhalt. Copyrighted material from Congressional
Quarterly, Inc. Reprinted by permission.

service in the House was less than two years, and in the
Senate less than four, meaning that many members were
resigning for better opportunities. By the 1960s the average
length of service was ten years in the House and twelve in
the Senate, with 60 percent of the Senate and nearly 90
percent of the House being reelected members. This proportion has lessened now because of the unusually large number of new members elected in recent Congress, so that well
over half of the House has been there less than ten years.
Nonetheless, the leadership positions in both the House and
Senate, because of custom and seniority, have tended to

TABLE 4.1 Characteristics of the Ninety-eighth Congress (beginning in January 1983)

	House (432 Members)*	Senate (100 Members)	Total
Party affiliation			
Democrat	267	46	313
Republican	165	54	219
Independent	0	0	0
Average age	45.5	52.5	47.0
Religious affiliation			
Roman Catholic	124	17	141
Jewish	29	8	37
Methodist	57	18	75
Episcopalian	42	20	62
Presbyterian	49	10	59
Baptist	38	10	48
Race			
Caucasian	397	98	395
Black	21	0	21
Hispanic	11	0	11
Oriental	2	2	4
Polynesian	1	0	1
Sex			
Male	411	98	509
Female	21	2	23
Occupation			
Agriculture	29	9	38
Business or banking	139	35	174
Education	42	12	54
Engineering	5	0	5
Journalism	21	7	28
Labor leader	2	0	2
Law	200	61	261
Law enforcement	5	0	5
Medicine	6	1	7
Public service or politics	49	2	51
Ministry	2	1	3
Science	3	2	5

Source: *Congressional Quarterly* Weekly Report, January 29, 1983, pp. 221–223. Reprinted by permission of Congressional Quarterly, Inc. Data on race from *U.S. News and World Report*, January 31, 1983. Copyright © 1983 by U.S. News and World Report, Inc. Reprinted by permission.

*3 vacancies

TABLE 4.2 Characteristics of the Ninety-third Congress (beginning in January 1973)

	House (432 Members)*	Senate (100 Members)	Total
Party			
Democrat	240	57	297
Republican	192	43	235
Average Age	51.1	55.3	52.0
Religion			
Roman Catholic	100	14	114
Jewish	12	2	14
Methodist	64	18	82
Episcopalian	48	17	65
Presbyterian	62	14	76
Baptist	45	8	53
Race			
Caucasian	417	99	516
Black	16	1	17
Sex			
Male	416	100	516
Female	16	0	16
Occupation			
Agriculture	38	11	49
Business or banking	155	22	177
Education	59	10	69
Journalism	23	5	28
Labor leader	3	0	3
Law	221	68	289
Law enforcement	2	0	2
Medicine	5	1	6
Public service or politics	353	97	450
Ministry	4	0	4
Science	2	0	2
Veteran	317	73	390

Source: Congressional Quarterly Weekly Report, January 1, 1973, and January 29, 1983. Reprinted by permission of Congressional Quarterly, Inc.

*3 vacancies

require long periods in office and an orderly climb up the ladder of lesser offices. Few legislators actually go on to higher offices in the executive or judicial branch. It seems ironic that although high-level administrators and judges may be appointed from outside fields, it's a lifetime career to become a leader in a representative assembly. The problem with careerism is that, although it may guarantee loyalty to their institution, it may also insulate members from a rapidly changing society.

Malapportionment and Reapportionment

The drawing of House districts is up to the various state governors and legislatures, who have often used these powers to boost their own party and penalize the party that is out of power. In the past, *malapportionment* (large differences in the populations of congressional districts) was common in many areas of the country. Districts would be drawn up so that minority-party districts included more voters than majority-party districts. In this way, each minority-party voter would count for less. In 1960, Michigan's sixteenth district had 802,994 people, whereas the twelfth had only 177,431.

In addition, the art of *gerrymandering* was practiced. The name comes from Massachusetts Governor Elbridge Gerry, who in 1812 helped to draw a long, misshapen district composed of a string of towns north of Boston. The story goes that one critic observed, "Why, that looks like a salamander!" and another retorted, "That's not a salamander, that's a gerrymander." The two most common forms of gerrymandering are "packing" and "cracking." *Packing* involves drawing up a district so that it has a large majority of your supporters, to ensure a "safe" seat. *Cracking* means splitting up your opponents' supporters into minorities in a number of districts to weaken their influence.

Such practices have long been attacked by reformers. In 1964 a Supreme Court decision held that legislative districts at both the state and national levels must be as close to equal in population as possible. Many of the worst abuses of malapportionment were ended by the Court's decision. The average House district now has about 550,000 people in it. But politics remains vital to the drawing of districts, as can be seen in the conflicts over the shifts caused by the 1980 census.

At the beginning of each decade the Census Bureau counts the nation's population, and the House of Representatives is reapportioned to reflect the change in each state's population. The population had not only grown since the last census in 1970 — up some 11 percent to 227 million — but had also shifted toward the South and West of the country. Because the number of seats in the House is limited by law to 435, seventeen seats switched to the so-called Sunbelt. New York was the big loser, with five of its seats being lost, and Florida the big winner, gaining four seats (see Figures 4.2 and 4.3). The state legislatures shaped the new districts, combining them in states losing population and splitting up districts in states gaining voters. Because the Democrats controlled most of the state legislatures, they drew districts in such a way as to help Democratic candidates.

Organization of the House of Representatives

The organization of both branches of Congress is based on political party lines. The *majority party* in each house is the one with the greatest number of members. Being the majority party is quite important because that party chooses the major officers of the branch of Congress, controls debate on the floor, selects all committee chairmen, and has a majority on all committees. For almost thirty years, the Democratic party was the majority party in both the House and the Senate; the Republicans were the minority party. In the 1980 elections the GOP ("Grand Old Party") won control of the Senate for the first time in twenty-eight years. Thus the Republicans became the majority party in the Senate, al-

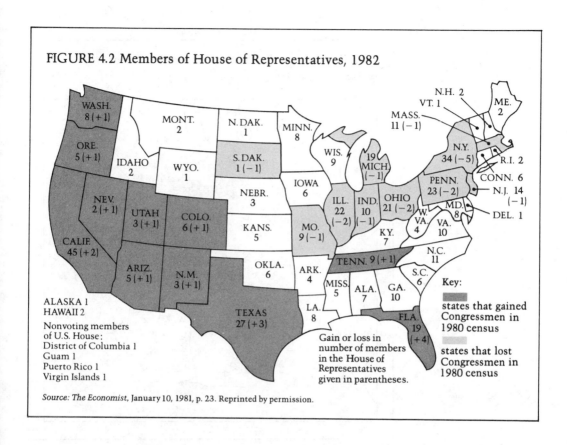

FIGURE 4.2 Members of House of Representatives, 1982

Source: The Economist, January 10, 1981, p. 23. Reprinted by permission.

though the Democrats remained the majority party in the House.

In the House of Representatives, the majority party chooses from among its members the *Speaker of the House.* He does not have to be the oldest or longest-serving member, but he will certainly be well respected and is quite likely to have served a long apprenticeship in other party posts. Until the twentieth century, the Speaker exercised almost dictatorial powers. The Speaker still retains considerable power, however. He presides over debate on the House floor, recognizes members who wish to speak, votes in case of a tie, and interprets procedural questions. He also influences the committee system, which we will look at

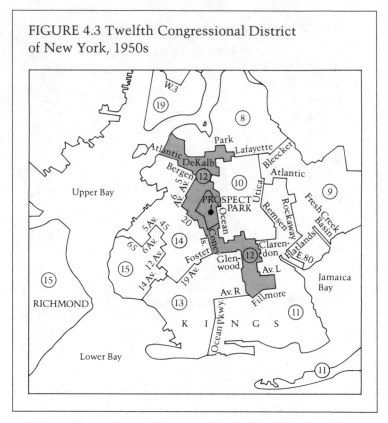

FIGURE 4.3 Twelfth Congressional District
of New York, 1950s

"There are very few Republicans in Brooklyn, and distributed in ordinarily shaped districts they would never make a majority anywhere. But
the Republican legislature strung G.O.P areas into a district winding
through the borough, and the result was Republican victories until this
year." — Anthony Lewis, *The New York Times*, November 27, 1960.

later in this chapter. The present Speaker is Thomas "Tip"
O'Neill, Democratic congressman from Massachusetts
since 1952, and Speaker since 1977. The selection of the
Speaker takes place every two years, at the beginning of
Congress, in the majority party caucus.

The *caucus* of each political party in the House or Senate

is simply a gathering of all the members of that party serving there. In recent Congresses the majority-party caucus has grown more assertive. The House Democratic caucus has shown a willingness to influence committee and floor action on legislation, to remove committee chairmen from their positions, and to attempt to unite Democrats around the leadership of the Speaker.

The majority-party caucus also chooses a *majority leader* who is second in command to the Speaker. The majority leader works closely with the Speaker and schedules legislation for debate on the House floor.

The Speaker and majority leader are assisted by *majority whips.* (The word *whip* comes from English fox hunting, where the "whipper-in" keeps the dogs from running away.) The whips help coordinate party positions on legislation, pass information and directions between the leadership and

---

ADVANTAGES OF INCUMBENCY

During elections to Congress, the advantages of *incumbency* (being currently in office) are considerable. The incumbent is well known, and by issuing "official" statements or making "official" trips to his district, he can get a lot of free publicity that his opponents would have to pay for. Members of the House have office and staff budgets of approximately $350,000 a year; senators are given at least that and often considerably more if their states are large. Both receive thirty-two government-paid round trips to their districts each year. Facilities for making television or radio tapes are available in Washington at a low cost. And there is the *frank,* the privilege of free official mailing enjoyed by Congress. Two hundred million pieces of mail, much of it quite partisan, are sent free under the frank every year. Despite the low public opinion of the effectiveness of Congress, congressmen often do well running for Congress by running against Congress. Coupled with the usually low voter turnout in congressional races, it is no wonder that most incumbents who seek reelection are returned to office.

other party members, make sure party members know when a particular vote is coming, try to persuade wavering representatives to vote with the leadership, and conduct informal surveys to check the likely outcome of votes. Being at the center of the congressional process, all these party leaders possess more information than other legislators, which adds to their power.

The minority party in the House, currently the Republicans, select in their caucus, known as a *conference*, a *minority leader* and *minority whips*. Like the majority party's leader and whips, their duties are to coordinate party positions. The minority leader is usually his or her party's candidate for Speaker should it become the majority party. (Gerald Ford was minority leader in the House before he was chosen vice president.)

The Democratic and Republican caucuses in the House run their affairs in slightly different ways. The Democratic party chooses a *Steering and Policy Committee* to function as an executive committee of the caucus. The Steering Committee helps chart party policy in the House. It assigns Democratic members to committees, with the advice of the committees' chairmen and senior members. It also nominates committee chairmen, although the nominations must be approved by the full caucus. The approval used to be a formality, but in 1975 the House Democratic caucus rejected three nominees for chairmen: the incumbent heads of the Armed Services, Banking, and Agriculture committees. The increasingly important role of the Steering Committee has also enlarged the power of the House Speaker, who, as leader of the congressional Democrats, is chairman of the committee. On the other hand, it has also weakened the ability of committee chairmen to act independently of the wishes of their party caucus.

SPEAKER OF THE HOUSE

Republican party committee assignments in the House are made by a *Committee on Committees*. This group contains a member from each state with Republican party representation in the House. These members have as many votes in the committee as their state's Republican delegation does in the House.

Organization of the Senate

The Senate has no Speaker. The *president of the Senate* is the vice president of the United States. He has the right to preside over the Senate chamber and to vote in case of a tie. This is a largely ceremonial function, one he fills only on rare occasions when an important vote is scheduled. Former Vice President Mondale presided over several sessions of the Ninety-fifth Congress, however, and made important procedural decisions, helping break a filibuster on the Senate floor. And in November 1983, Vice President Bush cast the deciding vote in favor of funding for nerve gas.

The honorary post of *president pro tem* (from *pro tempore,* meaning "for the time being") of the Senate is given to the senator from the majority party who has served longest in the Senate — currently Strom Thurmond (Republican, South Carolina). His only power is to preside in the absence of the vice president, but he hardly ever does so. Because the vast majority of Senate work takes place in committees, the job of presiding over a Senate chamber that may be dull and nearly vacant usually falls to a junior senator, who is asked to do so by the Senate majority leader.

The *majority leader of the Senate* is the nearest equivalent to the Speaker of the House. He schedules debate on the Senate floor, assigns bills to committees, coordinates party policy, and appoints members of special committees. The position is at present held by Howard Baker (Republican, Tennessee), who switched to majority leader from minority leader in 1981 when the Republicans became the majority party in the Senate. The Senate majority leader is assisted by a whip and assistant whips. The minority party in the Senate selects a *minority leader* and a *minority whip,* who likewise coordinate party positions and manage floor strategy.

In the Senate the Democrats have a *Steering Committee,* which makes committee assignments, and a *Policy Committee,* which charts legislative tactics. The Senate Democratic leader chairs the Democratic caucus (called the *Democratic Conference),* the Steering Committee, and the

Policy Committee. Senate Republicans are organized in much the same way. A *Committee on Committees* assigns members to committees; a *Policy Committee* coordinates strategy; and the *Republican Conference* consists of all Republicans in the Senate. One difference from the Democrats is that these groups are chaired by leading Republican senators, rather than by the Senate Republican leader.

HOW DOES CONGRESS OPERATE?

Most legislation may be introduced in either the House or the Senate, or it can be presented in both houses at the same time. The only exceptions to this rule are money-raising bills, which the Constitution states must originate in the House, and appropriations (spending) bills, which by custom also begin there. Approximately 20,000 bills are introduced in Congress each year (see Figure 4.4). These may be part of the president's program, they may be drafted by individual senators or representatives or by congressional committees, or they may be the result of alliances between Congress and the executive bureaucracy or private interests. Only 5 percent of these bills become law.

At present, after the large Republican electoral victories that gave them control of both the presidency and Senate, it is likely that the president will introduce the majority of all legislation passed by Congress. The Senate and House act separately, however, and may amend or revise bills as they see fit. For any bill to become law it must ultimately be passed by both branches of Congress in identical language and approved by the president or passed over his veto.

The Congress operates by division of labor. Most of the work of Congress goes on not on the House or Senate floor, but in committees. House committees may have anywhere from twenty to fifty representatives; Senate committees usually have ten to twenty senators. If they did not break down into committees, the Senate and House would move much more slowly and could deal with far fewer issues be-

FIGURE 4.4 How a Bill Becomes a Law

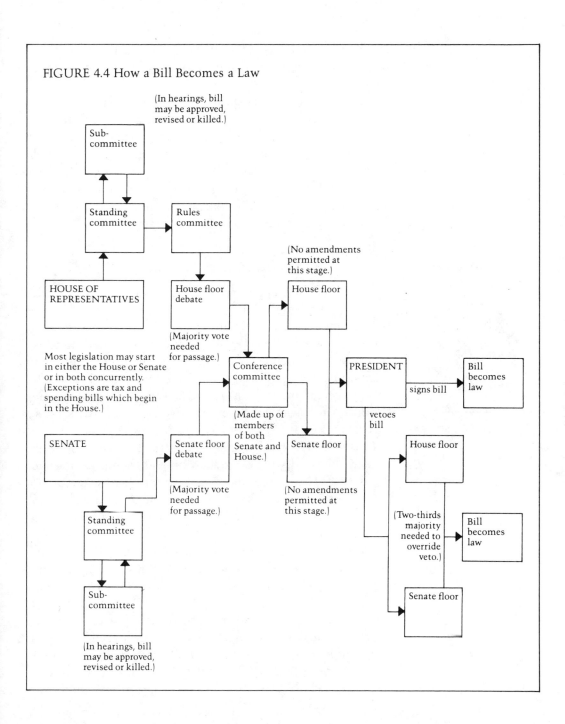

cause they could consider only one subject at a time. It is almost impossible to imagine Congress operating without the committee system.

When a piece of legislation is introduced in either the Senate or the House, it is assigned to a committee. The committee (or, often, one of its subcommittees) reviews the bill and decides whether to recommend it to the whole House or Senate. Between 80 and 90 percent of the bills introduced in Congress die in committee. Because the committee system is central to the operation of Congress, it will be discussed more fully later in this chapter.

Floor Debate in the House and Senate

Once a bill has been approved by committee (and in the House by the Rules Committee) it is sent to the House or Senate floor for debate. There it is placed on a calendar. *Calendars* are the business agendas or schedules in Congress. Certain calendars are for routine or minor legislation, others for more important bills, and one in the House, the "discharge calendar," can be used to try to force a bill out of committee against the committee's wishes. (It is rarely successful.)

In the House, floor debate is controlled by the Speaker. He schedules bills for consideration and then presides over the debate. House members are commonly restricted to a few minutes of talk each. The Senate, being smaller, is able to operate more informally. In general, power is more widely distributed in the Senate than in the House. Even junior (new) senators, for example, often chair subcommittees. The Senate majority leader schedules bills for debate, but his control during debate is much less than the House Speaker's.

When debate on a bill has ended, it is put to a vote. A simple majority of the legislators present is needed for passage. Whether a bill begins in the Senate or the House, it must sooner or later be submitted to the other branch, where the whole procedure of committee review and floor action will be repeated. Then, any differences between the House and Senate versions of a bill must be eliminated before it can be sent to the president for his signature or veto.

Both in committees and on the floor of either branch of Congress, members of the same political party do not always vote together. Indeed, one common division, which appeared in the fight over President Reagan's budget, has been between northern and western moderate to liberal Democrats joined by some liberal Republicans on one side, with southern Democrats and moderate to conservative Republicans on the other. The conservative side now seems to be in the majority in Congress, even though the most frequent division in Congress remains that between Republicans and Democrats.

Filibuster

In the Senate, except under very unusual circumstances, debate is unlimited. Senators may talk on a subject for as long as they wish and they will not be cut off. Never-ending talk by one or a number of senators designed to delay or block action in the Senate is called a *filibuster*. The original filibuster was a type of pirate ship. Its current meaning probably comes from the image of a lone individual defying society's rules. Senators engaged in a filibuster usually talk for several hours at a time (sometimes reading the Bible or the Washington phone directory) before giving up the floor to an ally. Senator Strom Thurmond of South Carolina set the individual filibuster record in 1957 by speaking against a civil rights act for twenty-four hours and eighteen minutes nonstop.

Rule 22 (of the Senate Rules — a set of regulations governing Senate behavior) protects the filibuster unless three fifths of the Senate votes for an end to debate. This is the only vote in Congress based on the total number of legislators. All other votes in both the Senate and House are based on the number of members who are present and voting. Voting to end debate is called *cloture*. Because many senators, whatever their political leanings, see advantages in having the option of a filibuster available, cloture is rarely successful.

Filibusters are most effective late in a session of the Senate when legislation has piled up. Senators are eager to adjourn, and they feel the pressures of any delaying tactic much more quickly. If the Senate is eager to move on, and if sixty senators cannot be found to invoke cloture, a compromise is likely: The offending legislation that provoked the filibuster is dropped for that session, the filibuster ends, and the Senate takes up other business. In general, however, the Senate feels that, as a smaller body, it can afford the luxury of unlimited debate. The House being larger and harder to manage, has decided it cannot, and so filibusters are not allowed in the House.

Presidential Veto

Even after it has been approved by both the House and Senate, a bill may still be killed by a presidential *veto*. The president may veto any legislation he wishes. He may not, despite President Reagan's attempt to gain this power, veto only a piece of a bill — referred to as an *item veto*. He must veto it all or accept it all. Still, the Congress has the last word: if Congress *overrides* a veto, the bill becomes law. To override a veto requires two-thirds approval of each house of Congress.

The president must act on a bill within ten working days. If he does not sign it within that period while Congress remains in session, the bill becomes law without his signature. If Congress adjourns before the ten days are up, and the president does not sign the bill, it does not become law; this is called a "pocket veto."

The ban on "item vetoes" gives Congress an advantage in any confrontation with the president by allowing Congress to use *riders*. A rider is a piece of legislation attached as an amendment to another bill, which may deal with a totally different issue. Commonly, the rider contains provisions that the president does not like, whereas the "parent" bill to which the rider is attached is strongly favored by the president. Because the president must veto all or none of the bill, he is faced with an unhappy alternative. Either he vetoes the rider he does not like and thus also the main bill that he desires, or he accepts the unwanted rider in order to get the rest of the bill.

Finally, passing a legislative proposal does not automatically make anything happen. If money is needed for the government's wishes (as expressed in a bill) to be carried out, the entire legislative process must be gone through *twice* — once to pass the bill authorizing the activity, and a second time to pass an appropriations bill granting the money to do it. The goals of the bill will not come into being if the appropriations process does not provide the funds.

THE COMMITTEE SYSTEM

As we have mentioned, much of the work of both branches of Congress takes place within committees rather than on the "floor" of the House or Senate. Often, although not always, floor debate is little more than a formality designed to make a public record. On an average day, a visitor to the Senate or House chamber might find a dozen or fewer members talking with each other while a colleague describes the superiority of Idaho potatoes or the reason Pennsylvania named the firefly its official state insect. At the same moment, many of the committee rooms would be filled with activity.

How Committees Work

The four types of committees in Congress are standing, conference, select, and joint.

Standing committees are the basic working units of Congress. They were started early in the nation's history because Congress found it could do more work faster if it broke down into smaller, specialized groups. There are twenty-two standing committees in the House and fifteen in the Senate, most focusing on one or two general subjects. Representatives serve on one or two standing committees, senators on three or four. Usually these committees break down into subcommittees for further division of labor. The House has two hundred subcommittees and the Senate ninety.

Before any bill can be sent to the floor for consideration by the entire Senate or House, it must be approved by a majority vote in the standing committee to which it is assigned. A committee's examination of a proposed bill may include holding public hearings in which interested parties, including the executive bureaucracies and lobbyists, are invited to testify. If the committee approves the bill, it will be sent to the floor of the Senate or House with a report describing the committee's findings and the reasons the committee thinks the bill should be passed. If the bill is considered unnecessary or undesirable by the committee, it will be killed. The bill's sponsors may resubmit it in a later Congress, but if the committee involved continues to reject it, it will fail again.

Often the actual work on a bill assigned to a standing committee goes on in one of its subcommittees. Subcommittees have become more powerful in recent Congresses. Because of the desire of the growing number of junior representatives and senators for a "piece of the action," more subcommittees have been created and given larger staffs and greater powers. Seniority has not been considered crucial in appointing subcommittee chairmen, especially in the Senate, where first-term Republicans will usually chair a subcommittee. This increased reliance on subcommittees was also a revolt against the power of committee chairmen who have lost much of their influence over the activities and membership of the subcommittees to the party caucus. This change, then, has spread out power away from committee chairmen to more junior members acting through the sub-committees and the party caucus.

A *conference committee* is a temporary body including both senators and representatives, created solely to iron out the differences between House and Senate versions of one bill. These differences come about because of amendments attached to the bill by one chamber but not the other or because the two houses have passed different bills dealing with the same subject. Before a bill can be sent to the president for his action, it must be passed in identical language by both houses.

House members of conference committees are appointed by the Speaker of the House, and Senate members by the Senate majority leader. They usually include senior members of the relevant committees. The conference committee engages in bargaining and trade-offs to reach a compromise; once this job is finished, it is disbanded.

When (and if) the conference committee reaches agreement, the new substitute bill is then sent back to the House and Senate floors for approval or disapproval. This bill cannot be amended; it must be accepted or rejected as is. If this rule were not in force, of course, the bill might be amended again in different ways in the House and Senate, thereby requiring another conference committee, and so on.

Select committees are set up to do specific, usually temporary, jobs, often to conduct an investigation. Recent examples include the Senate select committee charged with investigating the Central Intelligence Agency, and the House Assassinations Committee investigating the deaths of the two Kennedys and Martin Luther King.

Joint committees are permanent bodies including both senators and representatives. Usually these committees coordinate policy on routine matters, such as printing or the congressional library. The Joint Committee on Atomic Energy and the Joint Economic Committee, however, have important tasks. Reformers often favor much greater use of joint committees in Congress to save time, money, and confusion. The two branches are jealous of their separate pow-

LOBBYISTS

Many of the private individuals who help draft legislation and testify at committee hearings are *lobbyists.* The term *lobbying* originally came from the "lobby-agents" who waited in the lobbies of the legislature to catch legislators and pressure them for favorable treatment. A lobbyist is a representative of any private interest (a lobby) that tries to influence government policy. The common image of lobbyists is of people from private corporate interests looking for a tax break, and there are many of those. But groups such as the NAACP, the Moral Majority, or the Sierra Club also lobby Congress. Large labor unions maintain some of the most important lobbying organizations in Washington.

It is a fact of Washington life that special interests concentrate their efforts on committee members who are in a position to help them. This sometimes results in scandals such as *Abscam,* in which FBI agents claiming to represent wealthy Arabs successfully offered money to several congressmen. It is also true that constant contact between committee members and staff and interested private parties may lead to friendship and a sense of shared interests. This is what a super-lobbyist like Robert Gray does, making over $11 million a year for his company by doing it. And the goal of the lobbying is pretty direct, as one lobbyist put it: "The key is stopping and getting legislation." Whether this familiarity and its consequences are harmful to the public interest varies with the circumstances. (See pages 225–226.)

ers, however, and joint committees remain the exception rather than the rule.

Committee Chairmen and the Seniority System

Committee chairmen's considerable power has been lessened in recent Congresses. By the unwritten rule of *seniority,* the chairman of any committee is the majority-party member who has served longest (consecutively) on the committee. Some of the chairmen's power comes about naturally through the work of their committees, their understanding of congressional procedures, and their wide contacts within the government, results of long legislative service. They also generally influence the hiring and firing of majority-party staff, schedule committee meetings and agenda, and have something to say about the appointment of new members to their committees. The recent lessening of the chairmen's power has come about because of the increasing influence of the majority members of the committees, the subcommittee chairmen, the party caucus, and the budget committees.

The seniority system has been one of the most influential traditions in Congress, though it is not written down anywhere in the rules of the House or Senate. Still, for more than fifty years the custom was almost never broken. Then, in the fall of 1974, Wilbur Mills, chairman of the House Ways and Means Committee (which deals with taxation) was involved in several public incidents with a striptease dancer, Fanne Foxe. Mills even appeared on stage in a Boston burlesque house with Ms. Foxe. This behavior greatly embarrassed other House members, and finally Mills was forced to resign his chairmanship, which then went to the next most senior Democrat on the committee. Another sex scandal occurred two years later when Wayne Hays, chairman of the House administration Committee, was accused by Elizabeth Ray of keeping her on the committee payroll for services above and beyond the call of duty. In spite of his seniority, the Democratic party caucus quickly acted to force Hays's resignation.

Nonetheless, the seniority system (often called the "senility system") remains. Attacked as out of date and undemocratic, it has favored congressmen from one-party regions like the Deep South and the inner cities of the Northeast, where the same person is returned to Congress time after time. In spite of its rigidity and unresponsiveness, seniority ensures that an experienced, knowledgeable person will become chairman. More important, it has provided a predictable system of succession that has prevented constant fights over control of the chair. But clearly the newer members of Congress no longer feel the need to automatically follow a custom that limits their own influence. The hold of the seniority system is likely to continue to weaken, at least until the now junior members of Congress themselves gain seniority.

Specialization and Reciprocity

Two other informal rules, though recently weakened, support the power of committees in Congress. The first, *specialization,* is closely related to the second, *reciprocity. Specialization* means that once assigned to a committee or subcommittee, a member of Congress is expected to specialize in its work and become expert in that area. Particularly in the House, members are not expected to follow all legislation in Congress equally, or to speak out on widely varying issues. Rather, the accepted pattern is to work hard on committee business and leave unrelated issues to other committees designed to deal with them. The result of this system is that committees and their individual members develop close and extensive knowledge of their own work but may not know much about other areas.

This potential problem is resolved through the informal rule of *reciprocity.* Under this rule, members look for guidance in voting on legislation outside their committee's or subcommittee's field to members of committees that do specialize in it. Legislators tend to vote the way their party's representatives on the most closely concerned committee tell them to vote, because that committee knows most about the legislation and because the members want the same support and respect when their committee's business is involved. Specialization and reciprocity, then, are two sides of the same coin. You develop expertise in an area and other members follow your lead in that area. You in turn follow the lead of others more knowledgeable than you in areas outside your expertise.

This process has been slightly diluted in the Senate and

recently in the House. Because senators commonly serve on three or four committees, their areas of specialization are more varied and less intense. The rise in importance of the House majority-party caucus has meant that in some cases the caucus will help defeat committee recommendations on the floor. With so many subcommittees backed by recently increased congressional staffs pushing their own proposals, there is a lot more hustling for votes and a lot less automatic reciprocity. Still, the general pattern operates both in the Senate and the House. Indeed, were it not for specialization and reciprocity, the work of Congress would proceed much more slowly, with more confusion, and probably with much more conflict.

Members of Congress who do not abide by these informal rules are called *mavericks*. Mavericks may be popular with the media and in their home districts, but they are unlikely to be popular in Congress. They may receive unattractive committee assignments or generally be shunned by the majority of their colleagues. As Speaker Rayburn was fond of saying to the new members of Congress, "To get along you've got to go along." When former Representative Herman Badillo, an outspoken liberal, was first elected to Congress from a poor, urban district in New York, he was assigned to the Agriculture Committee, an area far from his and his constituents' interest (although one can argue that food prices ought to be of interest to city voters). After many protests, and after having been taught the penalties for being too outspoken, he was finally given a more attractive spot on the Education and Labor Committee.

Because of the importance of committee and subcommittee work and the existence of specialization and reciprocity, these assignments are vital to a legislator's power and effectiveness. These traditional patterns of influence tend to keep committees stable and discourage "hopping" from one to another. Once members of Congress have been assigned to a committee, they will not be removed against their wishes unless the party balance in Congress should shift so much as to change the total number of Democrats and Republicans on the committee. This imbalance came about in the 1980 elections when the Republicans gained thirty-three seats and the ratio of House Democrats to Republicans changed from three to two to about five to four. The relative proportion of Democrats and Republicans on committees had to shift in line with these changes. (The Democrats, however, refused to accept these changes on four key House committees, setting off Republican protest. Because the ratios are determined by the majority party, little could be done.) Of course, the result of representatives from rural areas preferring some committees while urban representatives prefer others is that some committees reflect a rural bias (Agriculture) and others an urban bias (Education and Labor).

The 1974 Budget Act and the Budget Committees

The "power of the purse" is one of Congress's basic Constitutional powers. Historically, the power to control government spending and taxes has not meant that Congress had the *ability* to control them coherently. The large number of committees and decentralized power bases in Congress has meant that overall spending (expenditures) was seldom related to taxes (revenues), and neither fit into a national economic policy. The responsibility for putting together a comprehensive government budget and national economic policy thus fell to the president.

In 1974, however, Congress passed the *Budget Act* (the Congressional Budget and Impoundment Control Act). The Budget Act enabled Congress to propose a coherent alternative to the president's budget based on an examination of all spending and tax measures and the overall needs of the economy. Rather than merely debating the merits of individual government programs, Congress could now examine formerly isolated parts of the budget and evaluate them for their influence on the economy and other spending priorities. The Budget Act did so in several ways.

First, the act set up House and Senate Budget committees. The House Budget Committee members were drawn mainly from the Ways and Means and Appropriations committees, with one member from each of the other standing committees. Members and the chairman were rotated periodically without regard to seniority. Members of the Senate Budget Committee are selected in the same way as members of other committees in the Senate. The committees guide the Congress in setting total spending, tax, and debt levels. Aiding the two Budget committees is a *Congressional Budget Office* (CBO) established by the act. The nonpartisan CBO provides experts to analyze the president's budget proposals and to match up Congress' numerous spending decisions with the established budget targets.

The budget works its way through Congress on a series of deadlines. The goal is to have a completed budget by the beginning of the government's fiscal year, October 1. Essentially the process starts when the president submits his budget to Congress in late January. All the committees in Congress then submit their estimates and views of the budget to the Budget committees, which gather them in a first resolution. Congress must vote on this resolution, which sets overall spending and tax levels, by May 15. The various parts of this first resolution then go back to the standing committees concerned with the particular subject or program. By mid-September the standing committees' recommendations have gone back to the Budget committees, which draw up a *second resolution* for Congress to vote on. This part of the process is called *reconciliation* because it attempts to balance the separate standing committees' decisions with the initial targets set by the first resolution. A more or less final budget is then passed by October 1.

This bare-bones outline of the congressional budget process ought to give an idea of its complexity and importance, which were demonstrated in 1981 when the Reagan administration used the budget process to cut more than $34 billion from government programs. Rather than merely setting targets, which could be ignored — and had been in the past — Reagan pushed through Congress a first budget resolution that *required* the standing committees to reduce spending in ninety-five programs ranging from food stamps to student loans. This demand appeared to be a drastic change in how Congress operated, shifting power from decentralized standing committees to the Budget committees and the administration.

By the time of the 1984 budget, however, Congress failed to act on schedule on any of the deficit-reduction measures required by its own budget resolution. The result was a deficit approaching $200 billion, and a divided Congress once again decentralized and seemingly unable to move. When a measure to reduce the deficit by some $60 billion over three years finally passed, it merely confirmed to many observers that Congress could not tackle difficult national issues without strong presidential leadership.

Major Committees in the House

Besides the Budget Committee, the most important standing committees in the House of Representatives are Rules, Appropriations, and Ways and Means. Almost all legislation approved by committees in the House must pass through the Rules Committee before reaching the House floor. (Exceptions are bills coming from Ways and Means or Appropriations.) The Rules Committee's name comes from its function: If the committee approves a bill for transmission to the House floor, it assigns a "rule" to that bill setting the terms of a debate. The Rules Committee can, for example, assign a "closed rule," which forbids any amendments and forces the House into a "take it or leave it" position. Or the committee may specify which portions of a bill may be amended and which may not, or even the exact wording of permissible amendments. Thus the Rules Committee acts as a "traffic cop." It has the power to delay or even kill legislation; it can amend bills or send them back to committee for revision. The Rules Committee commonly screens out legislation that might be embarrassing, foolish, or too costly.

Of course, the Rules Committee also has the power to stall or kill legislation supported by a House majority. In the past, it has often done so, particularly in civil rights and social welfare. A long history of such obstruction finally led to a revolt in the House in 1961, led by Speaker of the House Sam Rayburn and President John Kennedy. As a result, the Rules Committee was enlarged, with new members added to create a liberal majority. Early in 1975 the majority caucus gave the Speaker the power to nominate the Democratic members and the chairman of the Rules Committee. This change clearly brought the committee more under the control of the Speaker and the party.

The *Ways and Means Committee* deals with tax legislation, or the *raising* of revenue for the government. Because all money-raising bills begin in the House, any tax legislation goes first to the Ways and Means Committee. If approved by that committee and then by the Budget Committee to be sure it falls within the budget targets, it normally goes to the House floor under a "closed rule" (forbidding amendments). This rule keeps members of Congress from giving in to the temptation to attach amendments for special interests that haven't gone through the committee first. Ways and Means also deals with social security legislation, Medicare, unemployment insurance, and import tariffs.

In early 1975 an important change occurred in the Ways and Means Committee similar to that made in the Rules Committee in 1961. The incidents with the striptease dancer that led to Wilbur Mills's resignation as chairman of Ways and Means were also used as an opportunity to enlarge the committee, create four new subcommittees, and fill the new positions with more liberal members. The Democratic members of the Ways and Means Committee also lost their right to make House Democratic party committee assignments, which had been an important part of their power. (As mentioned, committee assignments are now made by the Steering and Policy Committee of the Democratic caucus.)

The Ways and Means Committee handles tax bills to raise money; the *Appropriations Committee* deals with how government *spends* that money. When the federal budget is presented to Congress by the president each year, it is sent to the House Appropriations Committee and its thirteen subcommittees as the first stage in congressional review. Because the power to tax and spend is the power to make or break policies, programs, industries, areas, and individuals, and because specialization and reciprocity ensure that Congress will tend to follow the lead of its committees, the importance of the Ways and Means and Appropriations committees and their subcommittees is clear. It is equally clear that the rise of the Budget Committee has cut into the traditional influence of these committees.

Major Committees in the Senate

The most important committees in the Senate (besides Budget) are Appropriations, Finance, and Foreign Relations. The Senate *Appropriations Committee* receives appropriations bills after they have been passed by the House. Its procedures are very much like those of its House counterpart, with the important distinction that the Senate committee tends to act as a "court of appeals," adding money to or subtracting it from the amounts granted by the House. If passed by the House, tax legislation then goes to the Senate *Finance Committee*, the Senate's equivalent to Ways and Means in the House.

The Senate *Foreign Relations Committee* is a watchdog over the president's dominant position in foreign policy. Its importance comes from the Senate's role in confirming appointments of ambassadors and approving or disapproving treaties. These issues are reviewed by the committee before the full Senate votes on them. It is also considered a helpful publicity forum for senators with presidental ambitions.

The Senate also has a Rules Committee, but it is much less important than its House counterpart. The Senate has fewer than one-fourth as many members as the House.

Thus, the problems of organization, coordination, and efficiency are not as great. Because each branch of Congress sets its own procedures, the Senate simply decided that it did not need to set up a strong traffic cop to screen legislation between committees and the Senate floor.

OTHER POWERS OF CONGRESS

So far we have discussed the *legislative* powers of Congress. Congress also has several *nonlegislative powers,* which of course can affect legislation. Among these are *oversight* of the executive branch and *investigation.* Through legislation, Congress created the various executive agencies and departments and specified their duties and powers. It can change them at any time. In addition, Congress appropriates the funds those agencies need to perform their jobs. These powers give Congress both an interest in what the executive branch is doing and the means to find out. For example, Congress can determine whether the government will regulate mail-order firms or not, decide who will and who will not receive food stamps and at what price, and judge whether environmentalists or oil drillers will decide on the uses to be made of federal lands. In short, the annual appropriations process gives Congress the chance to ask what the bureaucracies are doing; tell them what they ought to be doing; and, finally, give money for what Congress wants and withhold money for what it doesn't want.

The *General Accounting Office* (GAO) and the *Congressional Budget Office* are agencies created by Congress to help with its oversight function. Congress uses the GAO to examine certain government programs or departments. The Budget Office is intended to serve as a congressional counterweight to the president's Office of Management and Budget.

In addition, the Congress has the power to *investigate.* If Congress, or a committee (or committee chairman) decides that something is being done wrong, or not being done which should be, an investigation may be launched. The subject might be foreign-policy decision making in the executive branch, or price fixing by private industry, or the power and influence of organized crime. In other words, Congress can investigate whatever it wishes.

Congressional investigations are not welcomed by executive departments, for they allow Congress to influence executive behavior. The Senate Foreign Relations Committee's public hearings on the Vietnam War and the special Watergate Committee's investigation illustrated that power. The recent investigation by a House Committee of how President Carter's papers got into the hands of President Reagan's campaign prior to their debate in 1980 (the so-called "Debategate") provoked howls of outrage from the White House. Done for the wrong motives congressional investigations can be dangerous. In the 1950s, Senator Joseph McCarthy's Permanent Investigations Subcommittee and the House Un-American Activities Committee ruined the reputations of many innocent people, forced able persons out of government service, and whipped up fear and hatred throughout the country with their often unfounded charges of disloyalty and communist sympathies.

Just as the Constitution gives the president the right to make foreign treaties only with the approval of two thirds of the Senate (illustrated by the close approval of the Panama Canal Treaty in 1978), the Senate also has the power to approve or reject most presidential appointments, including ambassadors, cabinet members, military officers, and other executive-branch officials. The two-thirds majority needed for treaties and the simple majority for executive appointments are based on those members of the Senate present and voting when the issue arises, not on the entire hundred-person Senate.

Many presidential appointments within the executive branch are routine, and there is a tendency in the Senate to agree that the president has a right to have the persons he wishes working with him. Still, Ed Meese, President Reagan's nominee for Attorney General in 1984, ran into trouble after the Senate Judiciary Committee brought to light financial assistance he was given by friends later appointed to federal jobs. The "behind-the-scenes" pressure of Senate dissatisfaction undoubtedly causes presidents not to make certain unpopular nominations in the first place. Also, the Senate often takes a more active role in presidential appointments to the independent regulatory commissions and the Supreme Court, as when it rejected two of President Nixon's nominations to the Supreme Court.

Congress also has certain judicial functions. The House of Representatives can *impeach* (bring charges against) a federal official by a simple majority vote. Then, the Senate holds a trial on these charges. If two thirds of the Senate votes to uphold the charges and to convict the official, that official is thereby removed from office.

Impeachment is difficult, slow, and cumbersome. Several federal judges have been impeached and convicted in the past, but only one president was ever impeached, Andrew Johnson in 1868, and he was not convicted by the Senate. Richard Nixon resigned the presidency (the only president ever to do so) in the face of almost certain impeachment by the House and conviction by the Senate. Despite the difficulty of impeachment, the process does remain an ultimate power over the executive in the hands of the legislative branch.

Case Study: Congress and the Campaign Finance Reform Bill[1]

On June 17, 1972, five burglars hired by the Nixon reelection committee broke into Democratic party headquarters

[1] For more detailed analysis, see *Congressional Quarterly Weekly Reports*, 1974, pp. 1003, 2233, 2691, 2865–70, and 2927–28; 1977, p. 1294.

in the Watergate office complex in Washington, DC. They were caught by police while planting illegal listening devices in the office telephones. The investigations triggered by the Watergate break-in revealed the greatest scandal in American political history. Finally, more than two years after the Watergate break-in, faced with almost certain impeachment by the House and conviction by the Senate, Richard Nixon resigned the presidency in disgrace. Nixon's resignation did not, however, eliminate public anger and suspicion. Calls for large-scale reform of campaign practices were widespread.

Before 1972, there were few limits on American campaign practices, and the ones that existed were never effectively enforced. In 1972 Congress passed the Federal Election Campaign Act, which required candidates to report their campaign fund-raising, and set limits on the amounts they could spend on radio and television advertising. Although these disclosure provisions turned out to be helpful in unraveling the Watergate mess, the scandal itself showed a need for further reform.

It was public pressure that did most to force change. By 1974 Congress was looking at public opinion polls that showed it had even less respect than President Nixon. Groups like Common Cause, calling itself a "people's lobby," and newspapers across the country joined in criticizing the role private money had come to play in politics.

As the Watergate scandal continued to unfold, Congress began to act. As early as November 1973, the Senate passed a new campaign financing bill that would have provided federal funding for both presidential and congressional races. But the House refused to accept it, and action was stalled.

After Congress reconvened in January 1974, the Senate Rules Committee again began work on public campaign-funding legislation. The bill it came up with called for partial public financing of primary campaigns and full public funding of general elections for both president and Congress, and placed limits on private contributions and spending. When the bill reached the Senate floor, it touched off a filibuster by southern Democrats and conservative Republicans who opposed the public financing sections. It did so partly because southern Democrats often faced little electoral opposition from the weak Republican party in the South, and thus did not need such funding, and conservative Republicans in general have little trouble raising private funds. Thus, public funding of campaigns was more likely to benefit their opponents than themselves. They also argued that the bill was unfair to taxpayers, one more instance of big government getting into areas that ought to be left alone. Nevertheless, the filibuster was defeated and the bill passed.

In the House, the Administration Committee had been working on a similar bill. It moved slowly, no doubt because many conservative members of the House, who have little trouble getting reelected, preferred to leave things alone. The continuing Watergate revelations and the increasing likelihood of Nixon's impeachment, however, kept up public pressure on Congress. The bill cleared the Rules Committee and reached the House floor in late July. Public financing of congressional elections had been eliminated, however, and on the floor spending limits for House candidates were lowered. (Low spending limits may sound like an obvious reform; but in reality they may help incumbents, if challengers are kept from spending enough to make their names known or to keep up with the free publicity an officeholder gets.)

Now the bill was sent to a conference committee, where members where deadlocked for three weeks over the issue of public funding of congressional races. The Senate demanded it, but the House refused. Finally the senators gave in, in exchange for higher spending limits in House and Senate elections and a tougher, more independent elections board to administer and enforce the law. No overall limit on campaign contributions from organizations was included in the bill. This appeared to be a victory for organized labor, but since the law's passage many businessmen have chan-

neled even more money into campaigns through new "voluntary" organizations called political action committees
(PACs).

Another interesting feature of the bill was the "Common
Cause amendment," which requires any organization attempting to influence the outcome of a federal election to
file reports with the new elections commission. As part of
its lobbying, Common Cause had run an ad in *The Washington Post* that was critical of House Democrats. Later it
held a news conference devoted to special interests and the
Senate and House members who had substantially benefited
from them in the past. Wayne Hays, chairman of the House
Administration Committee, had not appreciated Common
Cause's pressure on the campaign financing bill, and the
requirement that the group disclose its spending and contributions was Hays's revenge. The conference committee also
settled on an annual limit of $15,000 on the fees members
of Congress can accept for speeches or articles. This was a
blow mainly to the better-known and more popular senators. House conferees may have pushed this provision to
make liberal Senate sponsors of the bill pay for their public
image as reformers.

The final bill included public financing of presidential,
but not congressional, elections. Private individuals were
limited to $1,000 per candidate per election and $25,000
total per year. Organizations may spend $5,000 per candi-
date with no overall limit. Limits were placed on how much
House and Senate candidates could spend on their campaigns, but these were removed by a later Supreme Court
decision. Presidential candidates may spend a maximum of
$10 million in all primary elections combined. After a cer-
tain minimum is reached, all contributions under $250 will
be matched by the federal treasury. In the general election,
federal funding up to $30 million is available, in which case
no private money is allowed. An elections commission will
oversee the law, although it must refer possible criminal
violations to the Justice Department.

President Ford signed the campaign finance bill (formally

titled the Federal Elections Campaign Act Amendments of 1974) into law on October 15. Former President Nixon had earlier threatened to veto the bill (Nixon, who had raised more than $50 million for his 1972 race, some of it illegally, called the bill a "raid on the public treasury"). Ford also expressed doubts about using federal money for campaigns as well as possibly violating First Amendment rights by limiting contributions. Ford's pardon of Nixon on September 8 had drawn widespread criticism, however, and the congressional elections were less than a month away. As he said, "the times demand this legislation."

But passage of the law did not end debate. The bill's opponents (led by two former senators, James Buckley on the right and Eugene McCarthy on the left) simply moved to the courts, where they challenged it on grounds of unconstitutional restriction on free speech, favoritism to incumbent members of Congress, and bias against all unknown challengers. In its January 1976 decision (*Buckley* v. *Valeo*) the Supreme Court upheld most of the bill, including the public financing section, but struck down several provisions. Perhaps the most controversial loophole created by the Court's decision was its removal of the limits on candidates' own contributions to their campaigns. The advantage this gave to wealthy candidates was shown by H. John Heinz (of the H. J. Heinz food company family), who contributed $2.5 million of his personal fortune to his successful campaign to become Republican senator from Pennsylvania.

An even more serious consequence of the bill was the encouragement it gave to business groups to form political action committees (PACs). These organizations have resulted in even larger amounts of special-interest money being channeled into elections — contravening the intent of the law. (For more on the rise of PACs, see pages 227–230). Apparently, despite the law, the influence of private money in public affairs will be with us for quite a while yet.

WRAP-UP

The United States Congress consists of two houses, the Senate and the House of Representatives. Two senators are selected from each state, and they serve for six years. Representatives are allocated to states according to population; they serve for two years. The Senate, with 100 members, is smaller, more informal, more prestigious, and less hierarchic than the House, with its 435 members.

The House and Senate operate separately, but before any legislation can be sent to the president for signing it must be passed in identical language by both branches. In the House, floor debate is controlled by the Speaker of the House, who is elected by the majority party. The Speaker works closely with the House majority leader and whips. The Senate has no speaker; floor debate is managed by the Senate majority leader. Each branch also has minority leaders and minority whips. At present the Republicans are the majority party in the Senate, and the Democrats hold a majority in the House. Both the House and the Senate rely heavily on committees and subcommittees, and members in both branches tend to follow the lead of their committees. The pattern of specialization and reciprocity supports the committee system. Although this arrangement gives committee chairmen (who are always of the majority party) considerable power in Congress, the recent increased uses of the majority-party caucus and of subcommittees has cut into their influence. Chairmen are almost always chosen on the basis of seniority — longest consecutive service on the committee.

All legislation other than revenue raising and appropriation bills (which must start in the House) can be introduced first in either the House or the Senate. It is then assigned to the relevant committee for examination. Witnesses may be called to testify, and the bill may be revised. If approved by committee, the bill is sent to the floor of the House or Senate (going in the House through the Rules Committee). If approved there, the bill goes to the other branch for a similar process. Any differences between the House and Senate versions will be ironed out by a conference committee. When both branches of Congress have approved the same bill, it is sent to the president. He may sign it, veto it, pocket veto it, or allow it to become law without his signature. If he vetoes it (other than by a pocket veto), Congress may try to override the veto by a two-thirds vote in each house.

Congressional procedures seem complex and confusing because they are complex and confusing. The Congress has often been criticized for being slow, unresponsive, and even unrepresentative. Certainly the procedures discussed in this chapter often involve much time-consuming duplication of effort. The seniority system, the filibuster in the Senate, and the overall fragmentation of power between committees and the floor may sometimes frustrate majority wishes. But these procedures also help to prevent a rash or unwise response to a momentary crisis or public passion. And they have not stopped Congress from quickly acting on legislation with broad and effective popular support.

The Congress has remained an arena for national debate since it began. Although many would say its accomplishments have been too slow in coming, Congress has produced large budget reductions, civil service reforms, voting-rights bills, and measures designed to protect the environment and conserve energy. If Congress is sometimes slow to respond to apparent national needs, it may be because the country itself does not agree on the nature of the problem or the way to fix it. If Congress sometimes bogs down in party disputes or struggles to reach a watered-down compromise solution, it may be because a country as large as the United States includes strongly opposing interests and attitudes that the Congress merely reflects. If special interests sometimes seem to receive special treatment from Congress, this preference may simply be an accurate reflection of the political power of these players.

Congress was not set up to make government run more efficiently. It was established to reflect the wishes of the people governed, to be the democratic center among the institutions of government. Congress acts best not when it acts least, but when it reminds the rest of the government where its monies and support ultimately rest.

THOUGHT QUESTIONS

1. In recent years, many commentators have argued that Congress is in decline relative to the executive branch. In what ways is Congress adequately organized and equipped to perform its role? What changes would you recommend?
2. Think about the "unwritten rules" of seniority, specialization, and reciprocity. How do these rules help Congress to operate? What are their drawbacks?
3. To what extent do political party leaders control what goes on in Congress? What factors encourage party leadership? What factors limit it?
4. Congress has been described as an arena of widely dispersed power centers faced with the constant threat of stalemate. Is this description accurate? Are there any advantages to such a system?

SUGGESTED READINGS

Adams, Gordon. *The Iron Triangle*. New York: Council on Economic Priorities, 1981.
  A critical description of the relationships among Pentagon officials, aerospace corporations, and congressional committees, showing how this "triple alliance" can make policy.

Dodd, Lawrence C., and Bruce Oppenheimer, *Congress Reconsidered*, 2nd ed. New York: Praeger, 1981. Pb.
  Articles by scholars on recent reforms and changes in Congress.

Drew, Elizabeth. *Senator*. New York: Simon and Schuster, 1979.
  A close-up look at how a junior senator pushes environmental legislation through committees and around lobbyists.

Fiorina, Morris P. *Congress: Keystone of the Washington Establishment*. New Haven: Yale University Press, 1977. Pb.
  A brief study of how Congress operates — and for whom.

Jacobson, Gary. *The Politics of Congressional Elections*. Boston: Little, Brown, 1983.
  How some people are nominated and elected to Congress and some aren't.

Kennedy, John F. *Profiles in Courage.* New York: Harper & Row, 1956. Pb.

The future president wrote these prize-winning profiles of members of Congress who stood up to the popular pressures of their time and sacrificed their careers to do what they thought was right.

Radler, Don. *How Congress Works.* New York: Signet, 1976. Pb.

A short, balanced introduction to Congress.

Redman, Eric. *The Dance of Legislation.* New York: Simon and Schuster, 1973. Pb.

An insider's engaging account of the messy realities of the legislative process, written by a twenty-one-year old staff aide to the chairman of the Senate Commerce Committee.

The Judicial Branch: The Supreme Court and the Federal Court System

5

The Constitution is brief and to the point in providing for the judicial player: "The judicial Power of the United States shall be vested in one supreme Court, and in such inferior Courts as the Congress may from time to time ordain and establish" (Article III, Section 1). Congress did set up two major levels of federal courts below the Supreme Court — federal district courts and courts of appeals. It has also established several special federal courts as the need for them has arisen. The federal court system is responsible for judging cases involving the United States Constitution and federal laws.

Parallel to this judicial structure is the state court system. Each state has its own judicial system to try cases that come under state law (though it may also deal with cases under the United States Constitution and laws). Issues involving the Constitution may be appealed to the United States Supreme Court. In this chapter we will focus on the federal court system and particularly the Supreme Court; state courts are set up in much the same way.

FEDERAL COURT SYSTEM

United States District Courts

At the base of the federal court system are the *United States district courts*. These are the courts of *original jurisdiction*. Except in a few special instances, all cases involving federal law are tried first in the district courts. There are ninety four district courts in the United States and its possessions, with at least one federal district court in each state. The larger, more populous states have more district courts. New York, for example, has four. Each district has between one and twenty-four judges, for a total of 516 district judges in the country. These judges preside over most federal cases, including civil rights cases, controversies involving more than $10,000, antitrust suits, and counterfeiting cases. The large volume of cases they handle (almost 200,000 in 1979–1980) has led to long delays in administering justice. At one time it took an average of almost four years to complete a civil case in the Southern District of New York.

Courts of Appeals

Above the district courts are the *courts of appeals* (sometimes called by their old name, *circuit courts of appeals*). These courts have only appellate jurisdiction; that is, they hear *appeals* from the district courts and from important regulatory commissions, like the Interstate Commerce Commission. If you took a civil rights case to your district court and lost, you could protest the decision and have the case brought before a court of appeals. The United States is divided into twelve *circuits* (eleven plus one in Washington, D.C,), each with one court of appeals. Each of the twelve courts has up to fifteen judges, depending on the volume of work. Usually three judges hear each case. In 1980, 132 circuit court judges were handling 23,200 cases. These are the final courts of appeal for most cases, but a few cases they consider are appealed further to the Supreme Court (see Figure 5.1).

Special Federal Courts

Special federal courts have been created by Congress to handle certain cases. The *United States Court of Claims* deals with people's claims against government seizure of property. The *United States Court of Military Appeals* (often called "the GI Supreme Court"), composed of three

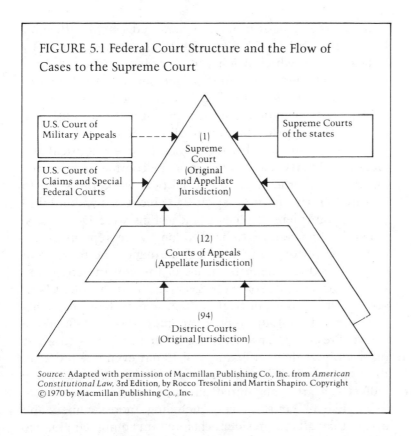

FIGURE 5.1 Federal Court Structure and the Flow of Cases to the Supreme Court

U.S. Court of Military Appeals

Supreme Courts of the states

U.S. Court of Claims and Special Federal Courts

(1) Supreme Court (Original and Appellate Jurisdiction)

(12) Courts of Appeals (Appellate Jurisdiction)

(94) District Courts (Original Jurisdiction)

Source: Adapted with permission of Macmillan Publishing Co., Inc. from *American Constitutional Law*, 3rd Edition, by Rocco Tresolini and Martin Shapiro. Copyright © 1970 by Macmillan Publishing Co., Inc.

civilians, is the final judge of court-martial convictions. The United States Supreme Court can review only certain types of military cases.

The Judges

All federal judges, including Supreme Court justices, are nominated to the bench by the president and must be approved by the Senate. Although it is usually given, confirmation by the Senate is not merely an empty ritual. In 1969 and 1970 two federal judges, Clement F. Haynsworth and G. Harrold Carswell, nominated to the Supreme Court by President Nixon, were rejected by the Senate.

Under the Constitution, all federal judges hold office for life "during good behavior" and can be removed only by impeachment, which has happened only ten times. To further protect them from political pressures, judges' salaries cannot be reduced during their time in office.

Despite these protections, the appointment of judges is a very political matter. Judges are almost always selected on a party basis and usually as a reward for their political services to the party. One professor of law commented that the judiciary was "the place to put political workhorses out to pasture." In this partisan spirit 93 percent of Lyndon Johnson's appointments to federal judgeships were Democrats, whereas 93 percent of Richard Nixon's were Republicans.

This power of the president to influence the makeup of one of the three major branches of the government is extremely important. Some observers feel that President Nixon's most lasting political influence may have been his appointment of four Republican judges to the Supreme Court. President Carter, on the other hand, was the first full-term president in history not to put even one judge on the Supreme Court. (Because of a new law expanding the judiciary, Carter appointed an unprecedented number of lower federal court judges, including more women and blacks than all the presidents before him combined.) Justice Potter Stewart's resignation enabled President Reagan to nominate the first woman to the Supreme Court, Arizona state judge Sandra D. O'Connor. With five of the justices over seventy-five years old, it is likely that the current president will have a great opportunity to shape the court to reflect his political outlook.

To further ensure local party influence, the Senate follows a custom called *"senatorial courtesy"* in confirming federal judges below the Supreme Court. This is the practice by which senators will not vote for nominees who are unacceptable to the senator from the state concerned. In the 1960s the results of this procedure made it difficult to find southern federal judges who would enforce locally unpopular civil rights decisions.

Jurisdiction

Jurisdiction refers to the matters over which a court may exercise its authority. The jurisdiction of the federal courts falls into two broad categories: In the first group it depends on the *subject of the case,* in the second on the *parties to the case,* no matter what the subject. The federal courts have jurisdiction over all subjects related to the Constitution, and over treaties of the United States. (Admiralty and maritime cases involving international law are also included.) Jurisdiction determined by parties includes cases involving ambassadors and other foreign representatives; controversies in which the United States is a party; and controversies between two or more states or between a state or citizen of the United States and a foreign citizen or state. The federal court system's last and largest source of cases is suits between citizens of different states.

This definition does not mean that the federal courts have the *only* jurisdiction over such cases. Federal courts have *exclusive jurisdiction* in some cases, such as cases involving crimes against the laws of the United States. But in other cases they have *concurrent jurisdiction,* shared with state courts. For example, some suits between citizens of different states may be heard by both federal and state courts.

UNITED STATES SUPREME COURT

The *Supreme Court of the United States,* composed of a chief justice and eight associate justices, stands at the head of the federal court system (see Table 5.1). Congress can set by law the number of justices on the Supreme Court. Although the number has varied from time to time, it has remained at nine since 1869. Though the Supreme Court has some *original jurisdiction* (some cases can be presented first to that court), most of the cases it hears are appeals of lower court decisions, which involve its *appellate jurisdic-*

TABLE 5.1 The Supreme Court, 1981

Justice	Date of birth	Appointed by	Date appointed
William J. Brennan, Jr.	1906	Eisenhower	1957
Byron R. White	1917	Kennedy	1962
Thurgood Marshall	1908	Johnson	1967
Warren E. Burger (chief justice)	1907	Nixon	1969
Harry A. Blackmun	1908	Nixon	1970
Lewis F. Powell, Jr.	1907	Nixon	1971
William H. Rehnquist, Jr.	1924	Nixon	1971
John Paul Stevens	1920	Ford	1975
Sandra D. O'Connor	1930	Reagan	1981

tion. If your civil rights case lost in both the district court and the court of appeals, you might be able to get it heard by the Supreme Court.

Actually, very few cases ever reach the Supreme Court. Of more than 10 million cases tried every year in American courts (federal and state), 4,000 to 5,000 petitions for review make it to the Supreme Court. Of these, the Court hears oral arguments in about 140 cases. The rest of the petitions are affirmed or reversed by written "memorandum orders."

Many cases that reach the Supreme Court involve constitutional issues. The majority of these 5,000 cases come to the Court in the form of petitions (written requests) for a *writ of certiorari* (certiorari means to be informed of something). A writ of certiorari is an order to the lower court to send the entire record of the case to the higher court for review. Someone who has lost a case in a lower court may petition for this writ. It is granted when four justices of the Supreme Court feel that the issues raised are important enough to merit a review. The Court denies between 85 and 90 percent of all such applications. This procedure keeps control over the appeal process in the hands of the Supreme

Court, allowing it to keep a maximum of decisions in the lower courts. It also enables the Court to influence the actions of lower-court judges by establishing guiding decisions on certain crucial cases.

The Final Authority?

The Supreme Court has been prominent in American political history because it has been thought to have "final" authority over what the Constitution means. Historically, however, a ruling of the Court has not always been the "final" word. The Court itself has reversed its decisions, as will be shown in the case study, "Separate but Equal?" (pp. 149–156). If the court interprets a law in a way Congress doesn't like, Congress will often overrule the Court simply by rewriting the statute. Amendments to the Constitution also have reversed decisions by the Court. The Court's pre–Civil War *Dred Scott* decision supporting ownership of slaves in all parts of the country was reversed by the Thirteenth Amendment outlawing slavery. An 1895 Court decision striking down the federal income tax was overcome by the Sixteenth Amendment in 1913, which allowed such taxes. More recently an unsuccessful attempt was made to reverse the Supreme Court's ruling severely restricting antiabortion laws by an amendment to the Constitution.

The strength of the Court's "final" authority is also affected by the other branches of government. Congress and the president, as well as the Supreme Court, have taken their turn in interpreting vague parts of the Constitution to meet the demands of the time and the needs of those in power. The president's right to involve the country in the Korean and Vietnam wars without a declaration of war would seem to fly in the face of the war-making powers given to Congress by the Constitution. Yet without a challenge by the courts and Congress, the president's interpretation of the Constitution stood.

Despite this shared role in changing the Constitution, the Supreme Court, by its constant interpretation and reinterpretation of the Constitution through its rulings, breathes life into two-hundred-year-old words. A brief history of the Court will show how this has been done.

Early Years of the Court

THE
CONSTITUTION

The Supreme Court has undergone many changes in the nearly two hundred years it has existed. For its first fifty years or so, suprising as it seems today, interest in the Court was slight. No cases at all were brought to the Supreme Court in its first three years. Many leaders, such as Patrick Henry and Alexander Hamilton, refused appointments to serve as judges; and court sessions were held in such places as basement apartments.

Two landmark decisions greatly increased the influence of the court during its initial period. The first established *judicial review*, the power not only to declare acts and laws of any state and local government unconstitutional but also to strike down acts of any branch of the federal government. The second major decision established the principle of *national supremacy*, that the United States laws and Constitution are the supreme law of the land and that state laws that are in conflict with federal laws cannot stand.

Judicial Review and National Supremacy

The principle of judicial review was established in the case of *Marbury* v. *Madison* (1803) in which the Supreme Court for the first time struck down an act of Congress. The case also illustrates how shrewd Chief Justice John Marshall was as a politician. Shortly before leaving office, President Adams (who had nominated Marshall to the court) appointed a number of minor judicial officials in order to maintain the influence of his party in the coming administration of his opponent, Thomas Jefferson. When Jefferson took office, he discovered that one of the commissions, that of William Marbury, had not actually been delivered. Jefferson ordered his secretary of state, James Madison, to hold it

CHIEF JUSTICE JOHN MARSHALL

John Marshall, the fourth chief justice of the Supreme Court (1801–1835), was a conservative and a Federalist. Although he attended only two months of law school, Marshall is often considered the Court's greatest chief justice. Two of the cases he presided over became landmarks. *Marbury v. Madison* (1803) established the principle of judicial review. *McCulloch v. Maryland* (1819) established the supremacy of the federal government within its constitutional limits, and in doing so confirmed the role of the Court in judging disputes between the states and the federal government.

up. Under a section of the Judiciary Act of 1789, Marbury sued in the Supreme Court to compel delivery of the commission. Marshall was then confronted with deciding a case between his political allies and his enemy, Jefferson, who was not only president but also intent on weakening the power of the conservative Supreme Court. What Marshall did was to dismiss Marbury's case, ruling that the section of the Judiciary Act under which he had sued was unconstitutional (the act allowed the Supreme Court original jurisdiction in a case not mentioned by the Constitution). By doing so he clearly asserted that the Supreme Court, on the basis of *its* interpretation of the Constitution, could set limits on the actions of Congress. The Court also supported Jefferson's argument that he did not have to deliver the commission. How could the president object?

Another early decision established clearly that states could not interfere with the functioning of the federal government. In this case, *McCulloch v. Maryland* (1819), the state of Maryland attempted to tax the Baltimore branch of the unpopular Bank of the United States, established by the federal government. Chief Justice Marshall, speaking for a unanimous court, ruled that the federal government "... though limited in its powers, is supreme within its sphere of action." He also found that although the Consti-

---

ON JUDICIAL REVIEW: JEFFERSON VS. MADISON

"Why should an undemocratically constituted body of nine elitists, who are not responsible to the people via the ballot box, be accorded the overriding power to strike down what the people want? Is not Congress, and is not the Executive equally capable of judging and interpreting the constitutionality of a proposed measure or course of action? Are they not equally devoted to the principles of government under law?" — Henry J. Abraham, on Jefferson's views, *The Judiciary*, 3d ed. (Boston: Allyn & Bacon, 1973), p. 128.

"Judiciary is truly the only defensive armor of the Federal Government, or rather for the Constitution and laws of the United States. Strip it of that armor and the door is wide open for nullification, anarchy, and convulsion." — James Madison, ibid., p. 129.

---

tution did not specifically allow Congress to create a bank, Article I, Section 8 gave Congress the power to make all laws "necessary and proper" for carrying out its authority. This statement of *implied powers* based on this clause was to be used later in broadly expanding the duties that Congress could undertake.

Then in 1857 came the famous *Dred Scott* case (*Dred Scott* v. *Sanford*). Here the Court ruled that a slave, Dred Scott, was not automatically free merely because his owner had taken him to a state not allowing slavery. Congress, the Court said, had no right to interfere with property rights guaranteed by the Constitution. The Court went on to say that the *Missouri Compromise* (1820), which had attempted to resolve the slavery issue by dividing the new western territories into slave and free parts, was invalid. In terms of constitutional development, this unpopular decision was the first time an act of Congress of any great importance was struck down by the courts. As such, the *Dred Scott* case marked a critical expansion of judicial powers.

The Court since the Civil War

The end of the Civil War was also the end of the major political conflict that had dominated the first seventy-five years of the Republic — *states rights* versus *federal powers.* With unity achieved, rapid national growth began. The resulting economic expansion and the unrestrained growth of giant monopolies created a new demand for government regulation of the economy. The Supreme Court became more active, and judicial power was greatly enlarged. In just nine years (1864–1873), ten acts of Congress were struck down, compared with only two acts in the previous seventy-four years.

Not only was the Court more active, it was also more conservative. In the view of many, the Court became an instrument for protecting the property rights of the rich and ignoring popular demands for government regulation.

In the twentieth century, the Court found itself up against the growing power of the executive branch. The presidency was widely felt to be the most effective place in the government to regulate the social and economic changes brought about by the post–Civil War industrialization. But the Supreme Court continued to resist the expansion of state and federal regulatory power, even though much of the legislation it struck down (such as minimum-wage and child-labor laws) was demanded by the American people. Between 1890 and 1936, the Court declared forty-six laws unconstitutional in full or in part.

It was President Franklin D. Roosevelt who caused the Court's policy to change. He countered the Court's opposition to his New Deal measures with a threat to pack the Court with new judges of his own choosing, the so-called *court-packing* bill. Although Roosevelt's plan was unsuccessful and aroused a storm of public and congressional opposition, in 1937 the Court nevertheless backed down and turned away from the arena of economic policy making.

The Modern Court

Since 1937 Supreme Court decisions have shown three major trends. First, the Court has invalidated much less federal legislation than it had in the previous fifty years. Since 1936 only a handful of federal laws have been held unconstitutional, and in most of these cases the legislation struck down was not very significant. In a second area, the Court has avoided protecting private property rights. Generally the Court in the present era has not been greatly concerned with guarding economic interests from government policy making.

A third area, in which the Court has shown more positive interest, is increased judicial protection for civil liberties. While reducing property rights in importance, the Court has sought to preserve and protect the rights of individuals against the increased powers of the government. First Amendment freedoms of speech, press, religion, and assembly have been developed and expanded by modern Supreme Courts. With Earl Warren as chief justice (1953–69), the Supreme Court moved in reapportionment, racial discrimination, and the rights of defendants in criminal cases.

In decisions dealing with *reapportionment,* beginning with *Baker* v. *Carr* (1962), the Warren court established the principle of "one man, one vote" for election districts. The Court ruled that districts should be drawn based on equality of population so that each citizen's vote would count as much as another's. In moving to eliminate *racial discrimination,* the Court has been a leading force in cutting away racism in schooling, voting, housing, and the use of public facilities.

Another major interest of the Warren Court's decisions, the rights of criminal defendants, has seen the Court throw the protection of the Bill of Rights around people accused of crimes by state and federal authorities. The Court has insisted on an impoverished defendant's basic right to a lawyer; declared that illegally seized evidence cannot be used in state criminal trials; and held that a suspect must be advised of his or her constitutional right to silence, and to have a lawyer, before questioning. This last area, summed up as the *Miranda* decision (*Miranda* v. *Arizona*, 1966), is familiar to all fans of television detective series.

The Supreme Court under Warren Burger, appointed chief justice by President Nixon in 1969, has been less activist than the Warren Court, but not as conservative as some had expected. On the liberal side, the Burger Court has legalized abortions except in the last ten weeks of pregnancy, declined to stop publication of the Pentagon Papers (official papers discussing the government's planning for the Vietnam War unofficially released to the press), and severely limited capital punishment. The Burger Court has also outlawed wiretapping of domestic groups without a court warrant and declined to interfere with massive busing designed to integrate schools in cities like Boston and Los Angeles.

This is not the whole story of the Burger Court. In more conservative directions, the Court has allowed local communities, within limits, to define obscenity and ban those works considered pornographic. It has also been rather sympathetic to states' rights, as shown when it struck down a 1974 law extending federal minimum-wage standards to millions of state and local government employees. Perhaps the most important changes the Burger Court has made in the precedents set under Chief Justice Warren are in the rights of the accused. Here the Court has allowed the police broader powers in searching without a warrant — deciding, for example, that persons detained on minor charges (like traffic violations) may be searched for evidence of more serious crimes (like possession of drugs). The Court has also permitted some illegally obtained information to be used at a trial and the police to continue their questioning after a suspect has claimed the right of silence. The *Miranda* decision still remains partly in effect.

Many of these rulings by the Warren and Burger Courts have aroused fierce opposition. But much of today's widespread attention to human rights may have started with the

PRESIDENTS AND THE COURT

Supreme Court justices have a way of disappointing the president appointing them. President Eisenhower was so angered at Chief Justice Earl Warren's rulings that he called Warren's appointment "the biggest damn-fool mistake I ever made." The controversy set off by the Warren Court's activism led President Nixon to appoint Warren Burger as chief justice to replace Earl Warren when he retired in 1969. Nixon hoped Burger would inspire greater political restraint in the Court. But the Burger Court, in *U.S.* v. *Nixon* (1974), ruled that President Nixon had to surrender the White House tapes, recording his often illegal conversations, to the special Watergate prosecutor. The President, who resigned shortly afterward, was certainly not pleased by this clear example of the strength and independence of the Court.

decisions of this supposedly most conservative of American political institutions — the Supreme Court.

STRENGTHS AND WEAKNESSES OF THE SUPREME COURT

The United States Supreme Court has often been called "the least dangerous branch of government." Despite its great power of judicial review, the Court is clearly the weakest of the three branches. It must depend on the other parts of the government to enforce its decisions. Its authority to cancel actions of the other branches of the federal government is in fact seldom used and strictly limited. These limits are found both within the Court and in the political system as a whole.

Internal Limits on the Court

Most of the limits on the power of the Court are found within the judicial system, in the traditional practices of the Court. For one thing, a long-held interpretation of the Constitution requires that an *actual case* be presented to the Court for it to exercise judicial review. The Court cannot take the lead in declaring laws unconstitutional. It cannot give advisory opinions. It must wait for a real controversy brought by someone actually injured by the law to make its way through the lower courts, meaning that years may pass after a law is put on the books before the Court can rule on it. (The Supreme Court's *Dred Scott* decision struck down the Missouri Compromise passed thirty-seven years before.)

Another important limit on the Court's actions is the practice that the Court will not attempt to resolve *political questions*. A political question is an issue on which the Constitution or laws give final say to another branch of government, or one the Court feels it lacks the capability to solve. Political questions often crop up in foreign relations. The justices of the Court lack important secret information; they are not experts in diplomacy; and they recognize the dominance of the presidency over the conduct of foreign affairs. Consequently the Court has generally rejected attempts to involve it in resolving disputes such as those over the Vietnam War.

The Court has narrowed or expanded its definition of a political question at various times. For many years the Court used this doctrine of political questions as grounds for refusing to consider reapportionment of state legislatures and congressional districts. In 1962, however, the Court reversed its position and forced state legislatures to draw boundaries to create districts with more nearly equal populations. A political question, then, can be whatever issue the Supreme Court wants to avoid.

Just as the Court attempts to avoid political questions, so too it often *avoids constitutional issues*. The Court will not decide a case on the basis of a constitutional question unless there is no other way to dispose of the case. The Court usually will not declare a law unconstitutional unless it clearly violates the Constitution. In general, the Court will assume that a law is valid unless proved otherwise. Although we have stressed the role of the Court in applying the Constitution, the vast majority of cases it decides deal with interpretation of less important federal and state laws.

A final internal limit on the Court is that of *precedent* or *stare decisis.* As we have seen, the Court generally follows previous Court decisions in cases involving the same issue. The Court has reversed past decisions in a number of cases, however.

What these and the other limits on the Court's power mean is that the Court actually avoids most of the constitutional questions pressed upon it. For both political and legal reasons the Court will often duck an issue that is too controversial, on which the law is uncertain or no political consensus has formed. It may simply not hear the case, or it may decide it for reasons other than the major issue involved. Knowing the difficulty of enforcing a ruling against strong public opinion, the Court generally seeks to avoid such a confrontation. This self-imposed restraint may make the use of judicial review scattered and often long delayed. But one can argue that the Court has maintained its great authority by refusing in most instances to use its power of judicial review.

External Limits on the Court

The Court is also limited by the duties the Constitution gives to other parts of the government, especially to Congress. Congress has the right to set when and how often the Court will meet, to establish the number of justices, and to limit the Court's jurisdiction. This last power sometimes has been used to keep the Court out of areas in which Congress wished to avoid judicial involvement. For example, the bill establishing the Alaska pipeline excluded the Court from exercising jurisdiction (on possible damage to the environment) under the Environmental Protection Act. Also, Congress may pass legislation so detailed that it limits the Court's scope in interpreting the law. Finally, the Senate

SUPREME COURT AND OBSCENITY

"The Justices take their obligation to research opinions so seriously that in one area of law — obscenity — the result has led to a lot of snickering both on and off the bench. Since 1957, the Court has tried repeatedly to define obscenity. The subject has become so familiar at the Supreme Court building that a screening room has been set up in the basement for the Justices and their clerks to watch the dirty movies submitted as exhibits in obscenity cases. Justice Douglas never goes to the dirty movies because he thinks all expression — obscene or not — is protected by the First Amendment. And Chief Justice Burger rarely, if ever, goes because he is offended by the stuff. But everyone else shows up from time to time.

"Justice Blackmun watches in what clerks describe as 'a near-catatonic state.' Justice Marshall usually laughs his way through it all. . . . The late Justice Harlan used dutifully to attend the Court's porno flicks even though he was virtually blind; Justice Stewart would sit next to Harlan and narrate for him, explaining what was going on in each scene. Once every few minutes, Harlan would exclaim in his proper way, 'By George, extraordinary!' " — From Nina Totenberg, "Behind the Marble, Beneath the Robes," *The New York Times Magazine*, March 16, 1975. Copyright © 1975 by The New York Times Company. Reprinted by permission.

has the duty of approving the president's nominations to the bench, and Congress has the seldom-used power to impeach Supreme Court justices.

These limits on the Court reflect the very real weaknesses of that body. With no army or bureaucracy to enforce its decisions, the court must depend on other parts of the government and all the political players to accept and carry out its decisions. (President Andrew Jackson, violently disagreeing with a Supreme Court decision, once remarked: "John Marshall has rendered his decision; now let him enforce it!") Yet with few exceptions, the Court's decisions have been enforced and accepted. And when opposed, this

weak and semi-isolated branch of government has been able
to overcome resistance. Why?

Strengths of the Court

The major political strengths of the Court lie in its enormous prestige; the fragmented nature of the American constitutional structure; and the American legal profession,
which acts in many ways as the Court's constituency.

The Court's *prestige* is unquestionable. Public opinion
polls have shown repeatedly that the position of a judge is
one of the most respected in our society. This respect is due
not only to the generally high quality of the people who
become judges, but also to the judicial process itself. Anyone who has seen a court in action is aware of the aspects
of theater in the legal process: the judge sitting on a raised
platform dressed in robes; the formal speeches addressed to
"your honor"; the use of Latin phrases; the oath on the
Bible. All create a heavy impression of dignity and solem-
nity, which often masks the fact that a judge is simply a
public administrator judging controversies. The Supreme
Court, which presides over this judicial system, has added
prestige because it is seen as the guardian of the Constitution and often is equated with that document in people's
eyes.

Another strength of the Court lies in the *fragmented nature of the American system of government*. With separation of powers dividing up power among the branches of the
federal government, and federalism dividing power between
the states and federal government, conflict is inevitable.
This division of power creates a need for an umpire, and the
Court largely fills this role.

In acting as an umpire, however, the Court is hardly neu-
tral. Its decisions are political (they determine who gets
what, when, and how), and to enforce them it needs political support. The other political players might not give this
support to decisions they strongly disagree with. Consequently, the Court's rulings generally reflect the practices

and values of the country's dominant political forces. As an umpire the Court enforces the constitutional rules of the game as practiced by the political game's most powerful players, of which it is also one.

A final source of support for the Court is the *legal profession*. There are only some 600,000 lawyers in the United States. Yet lawyers occupy all the major judicial positions, and more lawyers than any other occupational group hold offices in national, state, and city governments. The American Bar Association (ABA), with about half the lawyers in the country as members, represents the legal profession. The ABA reviews nominees to the bench, and its comments on a candidate's fitness have a great deal of influence on whether he or she is appointed. The legal profession, through the ABA, has generally supported the Court. For example, it opposed bills to curb the Court for its liberal civil liberties decisions. Because of their own commitment to law, as well as some similarity in educational and social backgrounds, members of the legal community generally back the Court.

THE COURT AS A POLITICAL PLAYER

It should be clear by now that the Supreme Court is a *political institution* that sets national policy by interpreting the law. In applying the Constitution to the cases before it, the Court clearly makes political choices. In arriving at decisions on controversial questions of national policy, the Court is acting in the political game. The procedures may be legal; the decisions may be phrased in lawyers' langauge; but to view the court solely as a legal institution is to ignore its important political role.

Judicial Restraint

"We are under the Constitution, but the Constitution is what the judges say it is," declared former Chief Justice Charles Evans Hughes. In interpreting the meaning of the Constitution, each Supreme Court must operate within the political climate of its time. Clearly the judges not only read the Constitution, they read the newspaper as well. The Court has no armies and must rely on others, especially the executive branch, to enforce its rulings. The Court cannot ignore the reaction to its decisions in Congress or in the nation, because, as a political player, its influence ultimately rests on the acceptance of these decisions by the other political players and public opinion. Nor, generally, are the Court's opinions long out of line with the dominant views in the legislative and executive branches.

Judicial Activism versus Judicial Restraint

The question of how the political and legal power of the Court should be applied has centered on the use of judicial review. Should judicial authority be active or restrained? How far should the Court go in shaping policy when it may conflict with other branches of the government? The two sides of this debate are reflected in the competing practices of *judicial restraint* and *judicial activism.*

Judicial restraint is the idea that the Court should not impose its views on other branches of the government or on the states unless there is a clear violation of the Constitution. Judicial restraint (often called self-restraint) calls for a passive role in which the Court lets the other branches of the government lead the way in setting policy on controversial political issues. The Court intervenes in these issues only with great reluctance. Felix Frankfurter and Oliver Wendell Holmes, Jr., are two of the more famous justices of the Supreme Court identified with judicial restraint. Frankfurter often argued that social improvement should be left to more appropriate parts of the federal and state government. The Court, he declared, should avoid conflicts with other branches of the federal government whenever possible.

Judicial activism is the view that the Supreme Court should be an active, creative partner with the legislative and executive branches in shaping government policy. Judicial activists seek to apply the Court's authority to solving eco-

Judicial Activism

nomic and political problems ignored by other parts of the government. In this view the Court is more than an umpire of the American political game: It is an active participant as well. The Supreme Court under Earl Warren for the most part practiced judicial activism. In its rulings on reapportionment, school desegregation, and the right to counsel, the Warren Court broadly and boldly changed national policy.

It is important not to confuse judicial activism versus restraint with liberal versus conservative. Although most of the recent activist justices, such as Earl Warren and Thurgood Marshall, have taken liberal positions on issues like school integration and toleration of dissent, this wasn't always so. John Marshall's court was both activist (in establishing judicial review) and conservative (in protecting private property rights). And it was the activist, *conservative* Supreme Court during the 1930s that attempted to strike down most of Franklin D. Roosevelt's New Deal program as unconstitutional. On the other side, justices Frankfurter and Holmes were political liberals. Yet both believed it was not wise for the Court to dive into the midst of political battles to support policies they may have personally backed.

Case Study:
Separate but Equal?

An example of the Supreme Court's role as a political player is the evolution of the "separate but equal" doctrine. In first approving this doctrine of racial segregation late in the nineteenth century and later abolishing it in the mid-twentieth century, the Court played a central role in establishing the national policy that governed relations between the races. The changing but always powerful position of the judiciary in the history of racial segregation shows how influential the Court's political role can be.

Political Background of Segregation

The end of the Civil War and the emancipation of the slaves did not give blacks the full rights of citizenship. Nor did the passing of the Thirteenth Amendment in 1865 (which outlawed slavery); or the Fourteenth Amendment in 1868 (which extended "equal protection of the laws" to all citizens); or the Fifteenth Amendment in 1870 (which guaranteed the right to vote to all citizens regardless of "race, color, or previous condition of servitude").

Between 1866 and 1877 the "radical Republicans" controlled Congress. "Reconstruction" governments were established in the South to put through reforms in the former Confederate states, and also to bring in votes for the Republicans. Although the sometimes corrupt period of Reconstruction partly deserves the bad name it has gotten in the South, it was a time when blacks won a number of both civil and political rights. The radical Congress passed five civil rights and Reconstruction acts aimed at granting blacks immediate equality and preventing states from curbing these rights.

Then in 1875 Congress passed a civil rights act designed to prevent any public form of discrimination — in theaters, restaurants, transportation, and the like — against blacks. Congress's right to forbid a *state* to act contrary to the Constitution was unquestioned. But this law, based on the Fourteenth Amendment, assumed that Congress could also prevent racial discrimination by private individuals.

The Supreme Court disagreed. In 1883 it declared the Civil Rights Act of 1875 unconstitutional. The majority of the Court ruled that Congress could pass legislation only to correct *states'* violations of the Fourteenth Amendment. Congress had no power to enact "primary and direct" legislation on individuals; that was left to the states. This decision meant the federal government could not lawfully protect blacks against most forms of discrimination. In other words, white supremacy was beyond federal control.

With this blessing from the Supreme Court, the southern states passed a series of laws restricting the freedom of black people. The so-called *Jim Crow laws* included all-white primary elections, elaborate tests to qualify for voting, and other laws and customs legitimizing segregation. Earlier, in 1877, the radicals had lost control of Congress and the Reconstruction Era came to an end. White southern political power in Congress increased, which meant that most of the post–Civil War rights laws were gradually removed.

Separate but Equal

Segregation was given judicial approval in the landmark case of *Plessy v. Ferguson* (1896). Here the Court upheld a Louisiana law requiring railroads to provide separate cars for the two races. The Court declared that segregation had nothing to do with the superiority of the white race, and that segregation was not contrary to the Fourteenth Amendment as long as the facilities were equal. The doctrine of "separate but equal" in *Plessy v. Ferguson* was allowed to become the law of the land in those states maintaining segregation.

In approving segregation and establishing the "separate but equal" doctrine, the Court was undoubtedly reflecting the temper of the time. To restore the South to the Union, the new congresses were willing to undo the radicals' efforts to protect blacks. It was the southern black who paid the price — exile halfway between slavery and freedom. And just as the Court was unwilling to prevent these violations of civil rights, so too were the executive and legislative branches.

Can Separate Be Equal?

Plessy v. *Ferguson* helped racial segregation continue as a southern tradition. For some forty years the "separate but equal" doctrine was not seriously challenged. "Separate" was strictly enforced; "equal" was not. Schools, government services, and other public facilities for blacks were clearly separate from tax-supported white facilities, but just as clearly inferior to them. One can argue that the Court did not even support its own doctrine during this period.

By the late 1930s, the Court began to look more closely at so-called equal facilities. In *Missouri ex. rel. Gaines* v. *Canada* (1938), the court held that because the state did not have a law school for blacks it must admit them to the white law school. Missouri's practice of paying the tuition of black law students at law schools in other states did not provide equal treatment for residents of the same state, the Court ruled. In *Sweatt* v. *Painter* (1950), a black (Sweatt) was denied admission to the University of Texas Law School on the grounds that Texas was building a law school for blacks. The Court carefully compared the facilities of the existing law school with those of the one being built. The Court found the new school would in no way be equal to the white one and ordered Sweatt admitted to the existing school. In other important rulings in the 1940s, the Court outlawed racial discrimination in political primaries and refused to uphold contracts with racial or religious restrictions.

HARLAN'S OPINION ON *PLESSY* v. *FERGUSON*

Justice John M. Harlan, dissenting in the Plessy case (1896), wrote prophetically:

"The destinies of the two races in this country are indissolubly linked together, and the interests of both require that the common government of all shall not permit the seeds of race hate to be planted under the sanction of law. What can more certainly arouse hate, what more certainly create and perpetuate a feeling of distrust between these races than state enactments which in fact proceed on the ground that colored citizens are so inferior and degraded that they cannot be allowed to sit in public coaches occupied by white citizens."
— *Plessy* v. *Ferguson*, 163 U.S. 537 (1896).

Thus the Plessy doctrine of "separate but equal" was increasingly weakened by judicial decisions. By stressing the "equal" part of the doctrine, the Court was in fact making the doctrine impractical. (Texas was not likely to build a law school for blacks equal to its white one.) These decisions also reflected the Court's change in emphasis after 1937 from making economic policy to protecting individual rights more fully.

Still, the Court did not overrule *Plessy* in this period. The Court was following precedent, a policy often called *stare decisis* ("to stand by the decisions"). Stare decisis is a common practice in which a court follows previous decisions made by other courts in cases involving the same issue.

We have seen that Supreme Court rulings tend to reflect the temper of the time. Paralleling the rulings of the Court were the actions of the executive branch and some northern states that were increasingly critical of racial segregation. In 1941 Roosevelt issued an executive order forbidding discrimination in government employment, and in 1948 Truman abolished segregation in the army. By 1953 eight northern states had passed fair-employment laws outlawing racial discrimination in hiring. In contrast to these developments, Congress, dominated by a conservative-oriented seniority system and blocked by southern filibusters, was unable to pass a number of civil rights measures that came before it. Nonetheless, political attitudes toward segregation in the public at large were changing, and the Supreme Court's rulings were reflecting that change.

The End of Separate but Equal

In 1954 the Supreme Court finally reversed *Plessy* v. *Ferguson* in *Brown* v. *Board of Education*. Here the Court held that segregated public schools violated the "equal protection of the laws" guaranteed in the Fourteenth Amendment. "Separate but equal" had no place in public education, the Court declared. Drawing on sociological and psychological studies of the harm done to black children by segregation, the Warren Court's unanimous decision stated that in fact

THE BAKKE CASE

"It is far too late to argue that the guarantee of equal protection to all persons permits the recognition of special wards entitled to . . . protection greater than that accorded others."
— Justice Lewis F. Powell, Jr.

"The dream of America as the great melting pot has not been realized for the Negro; because of his skin color he never even made it into the pot." — Justice Thurgood Marshall

On June 28, 1978, the Supreme Court ruled on the controversial "reverse discrimination" *Bakke* case (*Regents of the University of California* v. *Bakke*). Allan Bakke, a white engineer, had charged that he was denied admission to medical school while minority applicants less qualified than he were admitted because a quota of places had been set aside for them. Bakke challenged the university's affirmative action program as a violation of his constitutional right under the Fourteenth Amendment to equal protection of the laws.

In a complicated 5–4 ruling, with many justices giving separate opinions, the Court ordered the university to admit Bakke. The Court ruled that universities may not establish a quota for minorities denying whites the opportunity to compete for those places. The Constitution does, however, allow race to be considered as one of the factors in deciding who is to be accepted and who rejected. In other words, the Court seemed to say, strict quotas are unconstitutional, but affirmative action programs encouraging groups that have suffered from past discrimination are allowed. The *Bakke* case stands today as an example of the changing, and frequently confused, position of the Court on one of the most controversial questions of modern civil rights.

separate was "inherently unequal." This finding was the beginning of the end of *legal segregation*.

The Court backed up its new equal-protection stand in areas other than education. In the years following the *Brown* decision, it outlawed segregation in interstate transportation, upheld legislation guaranteeing voting rights for blacks, reversed convictions of civil rights leaders, and often protected civil rights demonstrations by court order. These decisions, though they stirred up opposition to the Court (including demands to impeach Earl Warren), helped a larger political movement apply pressures to wipe out racial discrimination. The NAACP's Legal Defense Fund was very active in these cases, which shows how results sometimes can be gotten from one part of government (the courts) if another part (the Congress) is unwilling to act.

Congress finally joined in by passing civil rights acts in 1957, 1960, and 1964. The 1964 act, coming after continuing pressure and agitation by blacks, was the first comprehensive legislation of its kind since 1875. The act prohibited discrimination in those public accommodations (hotels, restaurants, gas stations) involved in interstate commerce, and in most businesses, and more strictly enforced equal voting rights for blacks.

In most of these areas the Court acted both to encourage and to force all levels of the government — federal, state, and local — as well as the private sector, to move toward full equality. The Court's support of busing to end segregation of schools caused by housing patterns has aroused opposition in northern cities like Boston. Affirmative-action programs requiring institutions to recruit minorities and women also have produced conflict, as shown by the Bakke case.

Yet racism remains. And for this wrong the Supreme Court as well as the rest of the political system must share some responsibility. For it was the Supreme Court which struck down civil rights acts of the Reconstruction Era, and which failed to protect the rights of black people between 1883 and 1937 when they were most trampled on. And it was the Court that made "separate but equal" the legal justification for white supremacy and refused for far too long to reverse it. The Court's effort in the late 1950s to put equal rights before the eyes of the nation was in many ways merely an undoing of its past mistakes.

Throughout this history of the "separate but equal" doctrine, the Court has acted politically as well as morally. At times the Court held back efforts at social and political reform; at other times it confused the efforts; and at still others it forced political and social changes more rapidly than some would have preferred. Most recently the Court has stood as the one part of the government most responsive to the arguments of dissenters and minorities. Yet as the history of "separate but equal" makes clear, whether the Court's stand appears moral or immoral to us, it is never removed too far or for too long from the positions dominating the political game as a whole.

WRAP-UP

The federal court system consists of United States district courts, courts of appeals, special federal courts, and the United States Supreme Court. Although very few of the cases tried in the United States ever reach the Supreme Court, it has a unique position as the "final authority" over what the Constitution means. Yet the Court's decisions often are changed over the years, usually by the Court itself, in part reflecting the changing political climate. Our brief history of the Court showed this, as did the case study of "separate but equal," where the Court first allowed racial segregation and then gradually reversed its position.

The practices of judicial activism and judicial restraint are two sides of the debate over how far the political involvement of the Court should go. The Court is limited by a number of its own practices and, most important, by its dependence on other parts of the government to enforce its decisions. The Court's respect for these limits as well as its own great prestige have given it the strength to overcome most resistance. In recent years there have been frequent calls for reform of the Court. Critics of its decisions on civil liberties and desegregation have attempted to restrict the Court's involvement in these areas. All the attempts have run up against solid support for the Court and have failed.

Secure within its limits and resting on its supports, the Supreme Court of the United States remains a unique political player. No other government can boast of a long-held tradition that gives "nine old men" (and women, now) non-elected and serving for life, the duty of overturning the acts of popularly elected legislative and executive branches. Through this power of judicial review, the Court is deeply involved in influencing national policy, setting limits on how the political game is played, and bringing pressing social issues to the attention of the people and their leaders. Whether the Court continues to protect the rights of groups threatened by the most powerful players will depend on who the justices are and which political forces prevail in the country as a whole.

THOUGHT QUESTIONS

1. How is the Supreme Court protected from too much political pressure from the other political players? Why was it partly detached from the rest of the national government?
2. Is the Supreme Court too much influenced or not influenced enough by the executive and legislative branches of government and by public opinion?
3. Do the courts, rather than popularly elected officials of the government, generally appear to be more interested in defending constitutional rights? If so, why?

SUGGESTED READINGS

Baum, Lawrence. *The Supreme Court.* Washington, D.C.: Congressional Quarterly Press, 1981.
A good straightforward start for understanding the work and influence of the Court.

Goulden, Joseph C. *The Million Dollar Lawyers.* New York: Putnam, 1978.
These are behind-the-scenes stories of high-level lawyers involved in multi-million-dollar cases, practicing the kind of law that was never taught in law school.

Jacob, Herbert. *Justice in America*, 4th ed. Boston: Little, Brown, 1984.
  A necessary book for budding lawyers, which analyses the judicial system and the players in it.

Lewis, Anthony. *Gideon's Trumpet*. New York: Vintage, 1966. Pb.
  A short, readable story that traces the development of a case from a Florida jail to the United States Supreme Court.

Simon, James F. *In His Own Image*. New York: McKay, 1973. Pb.
  A revealing account of the politics surrounding the Nixon nominations to the Supreme Court.

Woodward, Bob, and Scott Armstrong. *The Brethren: Inside the Supreme Court*. New York: Simon and Schuster, 1979. Pb.
  Gossipy stories of the Burger court and the bargaining that goes on among the justices in reaching decisions.

Civil Rights and Liberties: Protecting the Players

6

Civil rights and liberties are among the most important rules used by the judicial branch to limit the players in the political game. They describe not only the means by which government and politics are to be conducted, but also the ends of the process. They tell us how to play, as well as why we ought to play. Americans like to think that they believe that all people are created equal, "with certain inalienable rights, that among these are Life, Liberty and the Pursuit of Happiness." America's government was created and limited so that certain rules govern the relationships between the citizens and their government, and other rules govern the relationships between groups of citizens. The two principles on which these rules rest are straightforward: The government must not violate the civil rights and liberties of the people; the government must protect citizens from the actions of others who would violate these rights.

In this chapter we focus on how the courts and other players protect people's liberties and rights and what these protections are. The history of these liberties will show how they have been widened as to whom they cover and deepened as to what they cover. Many different actors are involved in applying these protections, and a case study will illustrate some of them in action.

WHAT ARE CIVIL LIBERTIES AND RIGHTS?

One general way of looking at the two terms is to see *civil liberties* as those rights protecting citizens against government actions and *civil rights* as those protections given citizens against discrimination by other groups. Civil liberties can be seen as those protections given all citizens against the government infringing on rights such as freedom of speech. Civil rights, though granted to all citizens, usually refer to rules preventing discrimination against particular groups because of race, religion, or sex. Clearly the terms overlap. When a black leader is arrested for giving a fiery speech, his followers may claim that both his civil liberties (freedom of speech) and his civil rights (freedom from racial discrimination) are being violated. The differences, though helpful for understanding, may be difficult to apply in the real world.

Civil liberties mean those rights of freedom of speech, petition, assembly, and press which protect citizens against governmental actions that would interfere with their participation in a democratic political system. This definition includes various guarantees of due process of law in courtroom proceedings. The underlying principle here is that ours is a government of laws, rather than of arbitrary and unfair action. *Civil rights are the protections granted in the Constitution recognizing that all citizens must be treated equally under the laws.* No racial, religious, or economic group can claim or receive privileged treatment. Nor can any group be discriminated against by other groups or by majorities acting through state or national government.

Examples of these issues are present in all our lives. Civil liberties may involve your rights as a college student: Can school authorities censor the student newspaper? Suspend you for demonstrating or leafleting? Prevent you from wearing a political button to class? Others involve your rights as a citizen to be informed: Can the government prevent a newspaper from publishing a story? Can it require reporters to reveal sources to a grand jury? Can the government censor books dealing with the CIA, even when the material is unclassified?

Women, minorities, and everyone else may be affected by civil rights issues: Will you receive equal pay for equal work? Will you be discriminated against in hiring and promotion? And will affirmative-action programs designed to make up for past discrimination against another group lead to "reverse discrimination" against you?

These issues are also becoming more important in American politics. In recent presidential elections, prayer in the public schools, the Equal Rights Amendment, school busing, and censorship of pornography were major issues. To get a better grip on some of these current issues, we might first look at the past.

Expanding the Bill of Rights

When the Bill of Rights was added to the Constitution in 1791, it applied only to the activities of Congress and the president. The Founding Fathers had no intention of restricting the activities of state governments. Since then, the rights guaranteed to citizens under the Bill of Rights have been extended as to *whom* they cover and deepened as to *what* they cover. Perhaps the most significant expansion has been in their application to state governments and individuals.

How can federal courts today apply the Bill of Rights to actions of state officials or of private individuals? The answer rests in the Fourteenth Amendment, adopted after the Civil War. That 1868 amendment says in part, "nor shall any State deprive any person of life, liberty or property, without due process of law, nor deny to any person within its jurisdiction the equal protection of the laws." The two key, if vague, phrases are "due process" and "equal protection." They have been used by the courts over the years to both extend and increase the protections granted in the Bill of Rights.

The "equal protection" clause has been used to prevent state officials from engaging in racial or sex discrimination. It has also prevented discrimination by private individuals when that action: (1) is aided by state action such as a law; (2) furthers a state activity such as an election, or the activities of a political party; or (3) involves a fundamental state interest such as education or public safety. Therefore, though individuals may discriminate in whom they invite to their homes or associate with in private clubs, they cannot discriminate in associations like private schools, because education involves a fundamental state interest. Private clubs that continue to discriminate may, however, lose certain tax advantages under a recent court ruling.

The "due process" clause of the Fourteenth Amendment echoes similar language in the Fifth Amendment of the Bill of Rights and therefore extends the regulation of government from the national to the state sphere. But to say that states must act according to due process raises a basic question: What does due process mean? The debate over the meaning and application of due process illustrates the difficulty of expanding the coverage of the Bill of Rights.

On one side of the debate over due process are the *partial incorporationists.* They see the due process language of the Fourteenth Amendment as meaning that the states must obey *some* parts of the Bill of Rights, mainly those procedures guaranteeing a fair trial. First Amendment freedoms of religion, speech, and the press might also be included by partial incorporationists as applicable to the states. In other words, the language of the Fourteenth Amendment is a "shorthand" phrase that includes some of the protections of the Bill of Rights and applies them against actions of state officials. Which rights are incorporated? That is left for the courts to decide.

An opposing definition of due process is given by those judges and laywers who are *complete incorporationists.* They state simply that because of the Fourteenth Amendment, *every* provision of the Bill of Rights should be applied to the states. The complete incorporationists thus do not have to consider which rights to apply when a case comes before them — they apply them all. The partial incorporationists, however, must decide whether to break new ground by moving another right onto their list of those rights "incorporated" into the Fourteenth Amendment.

Consider the case of a prisoner held in a state penitentiary who is suing the warden in a federal court. The prisoner charges that two months of solitary confinement for a mess hall riot is a violation of the Eighth Amendment prohibition against cruel and unusual punishment.

The partial incorporationist would have to decide whether or not the Eighth Amendment should be incorporated into the Fourteenth Amendment as a limitation on state prison officials. He or she might argue that the "due process" clause of the Fourteenth Amendment applies only to criminal trials in the states. Because the prisoner has already been tried, he has no rights under the Bill of Rights once he is in a state prison. The full incorporationist would argue that the entire Bill of Rights was incorporated into the Fourteenth Amendment and therefore applies to the state prison warden. The judge would then decide whether two months of solitary confinement did indeed constitute "cruel and unusual punishment."

CIVIL LIBERTIES: PROTECTING PEOPLE FROM GOVERNMENT

The framers of the Constitution believed in limited government because they thought that the greatest danger to the citizens lay in the abuse of governmental power. For this reason the most important civil liberties are those which provide protection for players in the political game. Most of these are called *First Amendment freedoms* because they are derived from the First Amendment, which states that:

> Congress shall make no law respecting an establishment of religion, or prohibiting the free exercise thereof; or abridging the freedom of speech, or of the press, or the right of the people peaceably to assemble, and to petition the Government for a redress of grievances.

Without such freedoms, a government might trample opposition politicians. Those citizens in the minority after one election would have no opportunity to win future elections. Without the protection of the First Amendment's "rules of the game," there would be no way for democracy to work or for the institutions of government to be accountable to the people. The First Amendment freedoms enable people to obtain information and to communicate with their leaders without fear. Denial of free expression prevents those in government from learning about real complaints and problems and therefore delays solutions. As Professor Emeritus Thomas Emerson of Yale Law School pointed out, "freedom of expression, far from causing upheaval, is more properly viewed as a leavening process, facilitating necessary social and political change and keeping a society from decay."

A look at recent thinking about three of the most important civil liberties will make these points clear. The liberties are *freedom of speech*, which comes directly from the First Amendment; *rights of privacy*, which are found in the First and Ninth Amendments; and *due process*, which is stated in the Fifth and Fourteenth Amendments as a support of those liberties in the First. Taken together, they go far in describing the constitutional protections that keep government off the backs of its citizens.

Freedom of Speech

The First Amendment guarantee of freedom of speech has been extended to state governments under the Fourteenth Amendment. Its meaning has also been deepened by various court decisions. "Speech" now includes not only speaking, but also gesturing and mimicking, belonging to organizations, wearing buttons or raising signs, and leafleting passersby. The Supreme Court has upheld laws passed by Congress, designed to regulate the Communist party, which make it a crime to conspire to overthrow the government by force. But it has also struck down various convictions of Communists because the government was prosecuting them simply for membership in the party, and not for conspiracy to commit a defined act. Mere belief in the violent

HIGH SCHOOL CIVIL LIBERTIES

The 1984 yearbook of Brunswick High School in Brunswick, Maine was the unlikely focus of a fight over free speech. Graduating seniors get to choose a brief quotation to run along with their yearbook picture. One senior had been thinking long and hard about capital punishment. Rather than write "a standard butterfly quote," she chose the following from a *Time* magazine story on capital punishment: "The executioner will pull this lever four times. Each time 2,000 volts will course through your body, making your eyeballs first bulge, then burst, and then boiling your brains. . . ."

While not exactly a joyful farewell to her high school years, she intended to "provoke some of my classmates to think a little more deeply. . . . " The reaction the seventeen-year-old got was more than she could have expected. The students running the yearbook vetoed it as "bad taste," the school principal called it "disruptive," and the school board turned thumbs down on printing it. With the help of the Maine Civil Liberties Union, however, the stubborn student took the school board and the principal to court. The federal judge referred to the First Amendment as preventing the government (in this case, the school board) from interfering with peoples' ability to voice their ideas, no matter how unpopular. Then the judge issued an injunction prohibiting the yearbook from being printed until the case was resolved.

Faced with not being able to print the yearbook at all, the school system eventually reached a settlement with the student that allowed the quote to remain. A lone voice had stood up to the majority (her classmates, principal, and school system) and, with a little help from the Constitution, had won. — from Nat Hentoff, "One Student's Yearbook Quotation," *The Washington Post*, April 6, 1984.

overthrow of the government, even a speech about revolution, does not justify laws imprisoning the advocates of these positions. The courts insist that if the government wishes to put these people in prison, it must prove that they conspired to commit a crime. But the First Amendment provides no protection to speech that directly motivates listeners to illegal conduct.

The Supreme Court has given some protection to what is called "speech plus." This involves various symbolic actions, such as picketing or wearing buttons (but not burning draft cards). One case upheld the right of students protesting against the Vietnam War to wear black armbands in their junior high school. In another case, an antiwar student who entered a courthouse with the words "F—— the Draft" written on his jacket was held in contempt by a local judge, but the decision was reversed by the Supreme Court. As one justice pointed out, "while the particular four-letter word being litigated here is perhaps more distasteful than most others of its genre, it is nevertheless often true that one man's vulgarity is another's lyric." But in cases in which an individual addresses abuse and "fighting words" at someone, particularly a law enforcement official, the balance may swing the other way. The courts have upheld convictions of speakers for incitement to riot, disturbing the peace, and other criminal acts.

Rights of Privacy

To what extent do citizens have privacy rights against snooping by government officials or attempts to regulate their intimate social, sexual, and cultural behavior? The First Amendment, along with other parts of the Bill of Rights, is sometimes read by the courts as creating a "zone of privacy" that shields individuals from government intrusion into their thoughts, religious beliefs, and some forms of action. Just as parts of the First Amendment offer protection to individuals in public affairs, so too the amendment guards against involvement of the state in private matters. The First Amendment not only gives us the freedom to tell the government what we do believe, but also — because, for example, we need not recite prayers or the oath of allegiance in school — gives us the freedom not to have to say what we don't believe.

Some recent privacy issues have centered on personal sexual conduct between adults. The state, according to the Supreme Court, cannot prevent couples from using contraceptive devices. Nor can states forbid abortions in the first three months of pregnancy. The state cannot forbid sexual relations between individuals of different races. On the other hand, courts have ruled that individuals of the same sex are not protected from state action if they attempt to have sexual relations, and that homosexual marriages need not be recognized by states. Courts have also ruled that states are not required to fund abortions for those individuals who cannot pay for them.

Due Process Rights

As mentioned before, the Fifth Amendment prevents the national government, and the Fourteenth Amendment prevents the state governments, from depriving citizens of their lives, liberty, or property without "due process of law." Due process rights involve fundamental procedural fairness and impartial decision making by government officials, especially in courtrooms. In criminal cases the right to due process would generally include: adequate advance notice of the charge; representation by a competent lawyer; the right to confront and cross-examine the accuser; a written record of proceedings; a speedy and fair trial by an impartial judge and jury of one's peers; and the right to appeal the decision to a higher court.

These rights were granted in federal criminal trials by the Fifth and Sixth Amendments. Gradually, as a result of Supreme Court decisions over the years, many of these rights have been established in state criminal trials as well. In the 1970s the federal courts also began to require that some of these procedures be introduced into other settings. Students could not be transferred, suspended, or expelled from universities without certain kinds of hearings. People on welfare could not be purged from the rolls, or tenants in public housing evicted, without going through due process proceedings.

Consider the case of a student who has received a government loan for college tuition and is then told by some government officials that she is ineligible. Surely she would want all the due process guarantees she could obtain in order to prove to these officials that she had a "right" to the loan. Thus due process standards serve as a useful check against unfair actions by bureaucrats. Obtaining one due process right often leads to efforts to gain others. Once the

---

FREEDOM OF SPEECH

"I disagree profoundly with what you say, but I would defend with my life your right to say it." — Voltaire

"If all mankind minus one were of one opinion, and only one person were of the contrary opinion, mankind would be no more justified in silencing that one person than he, if he had the power, would be justified in silencing mankind." — John Stuart Mill

"Overthrow of the government by force and violence is certainly a substantial enough interest for the government to limit speech. Indeed, this is the ultimate value of any society, for if a society cannot protect its very structure from armed internal attack, it must follow that no subordinate value can be protected." — Chief Justice Fred M. Vinson

"The vitality of civil and political institutions in our society depends on free discussion. . . . It is only through free debate and free exchange of ideas that government remains responsive to the will of the people and peaceful change is effected." — Justice William O. Douglas

"The character of every act depends upon the circumstances in which it is done. . . . The most stringent protection of free speech would not protect a man in falsely shouting fire in a theater and causing a panic. . . . " — Justice Oliver Wendell Holmes

right to a "fair hearing" is obtained, the student might demand a lawyer to represent her. Once a lawyer is in the picture, he may demand a written transcript and the right to appeal. Often the existence of a fair hearing procedure and the presence of a lawyer will encourage officials to settle issues informally, without a hearing — a money-saving step usually welcomed by all parties.

These due process issues are directly related to First Amendment political freedoms. It does little good to give people the right to protest or to petition the government if officials can retaliate by cutting off essential services or funds to protestors. Students or workers who are politically involved need legal rights for protection from unfair actions by school officials or employers. Due process guarantees them protection.

CIVIL RIGHTS: PROTECTING PEOPLE FROM PEOPLE

So far we have been discussing relationships between government and the individual. But a large set of civil rights involves the treatment of minorities (including women) by majorities. Here the government becomes potentially a positive force for ensuring that the rights of minorities are protected against unjust actions by majorities and their elected representatives.

Civil rights issues involve discrimination based on classifications such as race, religion, sex, or national origin. A group that believes it is being discriminated against cannot always rely on the private arena for fair treatment. The minority group can try to obtain satisfaction from elected officials, or it may turn to the judiciary to end discrimination practiced against it. Some people could not purchase homes of their choice in the free market because sellers discriminated against their race. No matter how much they were willing to pay in the free market, they could not buy the housing they desired. These people tried to obtain a fair-housing law at the state level or a law passed by Congress banning such discrimination. They sought a presidential order banning discrimination in housing that involved federally financed mortgages. Travelers denied the right to eat in a restaurant or sleep in a motel room because of their color simply could not depend on the free market for redress. No matter how much they were willing to pay for a meal or a room, racial bigots refused to serve them. To obtain a remedy they went through the political system — in this case, congressional passage of the Civil Rights Act of 1964 with its provisions for an end to discrimination in public accommodations.

The civil rights issues of the past thirty years have involved the struggle for rights by a minority against discrimination by the majority. In the 1980s more complicated situations have arisen, at times pitting one group suffering from discrimination against others. The woman who supports affirmative-action programs in order to get a job is in conflict with the black man who thought affirmative action

would involve only race. Blacks who want quotas for admission to professional schools come into conflict with Jews who remember that two generations ago such quotas were used to keep them out of these schools. As one group after another receives the status of "protected class" (for which affirmative action goals apply), the meaning of affirmative action may be diluted. Dr. Kenneth Clark, a noted black civil rights leader, asked, "Are there now so many protected groups that none are protected?" Whether minority groups, each with an interest in affirmative-action programs, can form a coalition, or whether the groups will battle for scarce jobs and be unable to resolve their differences, only time will tell.

Which People Need Protection?
Suspect Classifications

The right to receive "equal protection of the laws" comes from the Fourteenth Amendment, adopted at the end of the Civil War in 1868. The government can, however, still pass laws applying to some citizens and not to others. The question is what limits are placed on the ability of national and state governments to classify citizens and enact legislation affecting them. One important limit placed by the courts on government actions is called a *suspect classification*. These are categories for which the burden of proof is on the government to show that they are necessary. Governments must, when the law or action touches a "suspect class," prove a compelling state interest for their action. A suspect category is one the courts will look at with the assumption that it violates the equal-protection guarantee unless it can be proved otherwise. Race has become a suspect category in recent times, and sex has verged on becoming one without quite having made it.

Race as a Suspect Classification

For many years the Supreme Court upheld racial segregation. The phrase "equal protection of the laws" was inter-

preted to mean that facilities (like schools and public transport) that were racially segregated, but equal, did not violate the Fourteenth Amendment. In practice, even facilities that were not really equal were permitted by the courts. Then, in the 1954 landmark case of *Brown* v. *Board of Education*, the Supreme Court held that schools segregated by race were always unequal, violated the Fourteenth Amendment, and were therefore unconstitutional. After *Brown*, courts eventually struck down all laws based on racial categories and made race a "suspect classification" when placed in state or national laws (see case study, page 149).

But do racial classifications always violate the Fourteenth Amendment? Or are there circumstances in which classification by race is a valid exercise of governmental power? Courts have decided that even though racial classifications are suspect, they may be used in laws or in court decisions when they serve to eliminate prior state-sponsored segregation. The courts may use their powers to consider the racial makeup of schools and to issue orders for assignment of pupils to new schools based on their race. In 1978, in *University of California Regents* v. *Bakke*, the Supreme Court upheld the principle of affirmative action in order to give admissions offices of universities some flexibility in admitting minority students. Courts have upheld employer affirmative action programs required by Congress that are based on race; in 1979, in the case of *Steelworkers* v. *Weber*, the Supreme Court upheld a company training program that reserved a number of places for blacks. In 1980 (*Fullilove* v. *Klutznick*), the court upheld a congressional law providing that 10 percent of funds for some public works be set aside for minority businesses. The Court thus upheld a law based directly on racial classifications. By 1984, however, the Court maintained in *Memphis Firefighters* that affirmative action relief should apply ". . . only to those who have been actual victims of illegal discrimination" (see box).

Supporters of "benign" quotas argue that there is a difference between a racial classification designed to discrimi-

---

FIREFIGHTERS BATTLE RACIAL
CLASSIFICATIONS

In a 1984 decision the Supreme Court put the entire question
of racial classifications in doubt. The *Memphis Firefighters*
case (*Firefighters Local Union #1784* v. *Stotts*) involved minorities who had been recently hired under an affirmative
action program and then laid off by budget cutbacks by the
city of Memphis. Under the "last hired, first fired" rules of
the firefighters' seniority system the new black officers lost
their jobs. This action undercut the purpose of affirmative
action, the black officers argued.

The Court, in a 6–3 decision disagreed, ruling in favor of
seniority rights. The majority declared that Congress did not
intend for affirmative action to interfere with a seniority
system that did not intentionally discriminate against
blacks. Further, and even more significantly, the majority
viewed affirmative action remedies as limited to specific victims of discrimination, not entire classes of people. As Justice Byron White wrote, "Each individual must prove that
the discriminatory practice had an impact on him." Although the eventual effect of this decision on racial classifications is not yet clear, it has brought into question the
future use of racial quotas in employment cases. *Memphis
Firefighters* may well mark the beginning of the end of their
use.

---

nate against a minority group and a classification designed
to help a group make up for past discrimination. But the
opinion of the Supreme Court has been evolving toward the
principles stated by Justice Harlan in 1896: "Our Constitution is color-blind, and neither knows nor tolerates caste
among citizens. In respect of civil rights, all citizens are
equal before the law."

Is Sex Suspect?

Until recently, most laws containing classifications
based on gender were justified because some supposedly
provided benefits or preferences to women. Under this rea-

soning, courts upheld state laws keeping women off juries, barring them from certain professions, and preventing them from assuming certain legal responsibilities involving property or contracts. As Supreme Court Justice Brennan observed, this "romantic paternalism" had the effect of putting women, "not on a pedestal, but in a cage."

In the 1970s women's groups began attacking these laws in federal courts, arguing that sex should be considered a suspect category. The Supreme Court has responded unevenly. Some laws have been upheld and others struck down. The Court has allowed state laws granting certain tax benefits to widows but not widowers, and permitting men but not women to serve as guards in maximum security prisons, and has let stand a lower-court decision permitting single-sex schools. On the other hand, the court has ruled that widows and widowers should get equal social security benefits, that men have equal rights to sue for alimony, that the drinking age must be the same for both sexes, and that unwed fathers have rights in deciding whether or not the baby is put up for adoption.

The Supreme Court has gone about halfway in making gender a suspect category. It has allowed the government to reasonably show that sex classifications serve important governmental objectives. Men but not women are required to register for the draft, for example, and the Supreme Court upheld this law in a 1982 decision. In employment, the Court has followed laws passed by Congress in viewing women as a "protected class" able to benefit from affirmative action programs.

The Court has also decided that victims of sex discrimination must prove that public officials intended to discriminate against them. Merely showing that the law had a different effect on one sex is not enough. This "rule of intention, not merely results" favors the government, because often it is hard to prove a deliberate intent to discriminate. The Equal Rights Amendment approved by Congress in 1972 would have outlawed gender classifications so that they would be struck down in much the same way as racial categories are under the Fourteenth Amendment. Although the ERA did not become part of the Constitution, it is likely that more sex-based classifications will fall as a result of the present standards applied by the courts.

ACTORS IN CIVIL LIBERTIES AND RIGHTS

Civil rights and liberties are applied and argued by various players in the political game. Within the government, the courts have been the most important player, although the legislative and executive branches may pass laws, issue executive orders, and monitor developments. Outside the government are a number of organizations that champion the rights of particular groups. The politics of civil liberties and rights involves struggles of group against group, and group against government, in a never-ending attempt to strike a balance among competing claims.

Judges

Many judges have played a leading role in expanding and deepening civil rights and liberties. These activist judges (who along with other supporters of civil liberties are called *civil libertarians*) usually support transferring civil rights cases from state courts to federal courts, where they generally receive more favorable attention. They back *class action suits*, in which people bring a case to court not only for themselves but on behalf of everyone in a similar situation — perhaps millions of people. Judges may rely on court-appointed experts and consultants to do the research needed to resolve complicated social and political issues. To decide a case, they may use not only previous cases and legislative laws, but also the concept of *equity*.

Equitable remedies are used to prevent future permanent damage in situations not covered by existing law. Suppose my neighbor, Jones, decides to cut down a tree in his yard. I

see that the tree will crash into my house. My legal remedy is to sue Jones after my house is damaged. My equitable remedy is to obtain an injunction that prevents Jones from cutting down the tree. Activist judges use equity to shape remedies that overcome the effects of discrimination. Take a school district that has been segregated by race because of state laws and administrative action. Merely requiring that the system desegregate may not have any real effect if neighborhood boundaries have influenced school districts so much that the schools remain segregated. Some federal judges and the Supreme Court have applied an equitable remedy: They have required that the school districts take into account racial imbalances and then come up with plans (some of which involve busing) to overcome the imbalances. The courts may even impose their own plans.

Other judges are more restrained in cases of civil liberties and rights. They are unsympathetic to class actions. They tend to follow past decisions made on a given subject rather than establishing new rights. They are likely to place great weight on the policies of Congress, the president, and state legislatures. These judges will presume that elected officials are acting rationally and legally unless proven otherwise. Because elected officials are directly accountable to the people, these judges hesitate to impose their own views. (See pages 148–149 for more on activist and restrained judges.)

The Justice Department

At times the Department of Justice has played a key role in protecting civil rights and liberties. Its lawyers in the U.S. Attorney's offices may prosecute persons, including state or federal officials, accused of violating people's civil rights. Justice Department lawyers may intervene in cases brought by civil rights groups and help argue them in court. They may draft guidelines for federal agencies to ensure protection of civil rights and liberties.

Recently the Department has opposed the goals of civil rights groups. The Reagan administration's attorney general

argued that some decisions had led to "some constitutionally dubious and unwise intrusions on the legislative do-
main." The Department began to intervene in court cases
against civil rights groups, especially in matters involving
court-ordered busing and affirmative-action hiring programs, preferring a "color-blind" rather than a "color-con-
scious" approach to ending discrimination.

"Private Attorneys General"

Various organizations have been created to support the
rights of individuals and groups. These are called *private
attorneys general* because they act, not on behalf of the
government, but for groups bringing court cases against the
government or against other groups. They are funded in part
by foundations and wealthy people, and in part by dues-
paying members.

The largest such group is the American Civil Liberties
Union. The ACLU has a national staff of about 350 in New
York City and has fifty state chapters. Its 5,000 volunteers
handle more then 6,000 cases each year. The ACLU was
organized in the 1920s to defend individuals against the
hysteria of "red scares" (a period when socialists were per-
secuted) and has played a part in almost every civil liberties
issue since. It also lobbies for changes in laws involving
wiretapping, surveillance, and "dirty tricks" of law enforcement agencies.

Another important organization is the NAACP Legal Defense and Educational Fund, Inc. (LDF). The LDF was created in 1939 and consisted originally of one lawyer,
Thurgood Marshall, who became the first black appointed
to the Supreme Court. In the 1950s the LDF concentrated
on school desegregation suits and in the next decade defended black students arrested in nonviolent demonstrations. Today its efforts are focused on discrimination in
employment and housing, voting rights for blacks, and
abuses in the judicial system.

Several organizations have been created along the lines

of the LDF. In 1968 the Mexican-American LDF, or MAL-DEF, was created. With a staff of fifteen, it has brought cases in bilingual education, voting rights, and employment. The Puerto Rican Legal Defense and Education Fund, Inc., was created in 1972 to deal with similar problems. The largest legal organization for women is the National Organization for Women (NOW) Legal Defense and Education Fund. It has a number of staff attorneys who work to protect women in gaining equal employment opportunity and compensation.

Legal Strategies

All these organizations use a variety of legal tactics. They conduct research on the problems of their clients, hoping to find a pattern of discrimination or lack of due process. They then write articles for law and bar journals in order to influence thinking in the legal profession and the law schools. They offer their services to individuals whose rights may have been violated. Such individuals cannot afford the hundreds of thousands of dollars that it takes to pursue a case all the way through the Supreme Court, so that the aid of the "private attorneys general" is essential. Civil liberties lawyers can choose from a large number of complaints until they find a *test case* for their arguments. Such a case offers the group its "best shot" because the violation is so obvious, the damage so great, and the person making the complaint so appealing.

The litigating organization hopes that its case eventually will wind up in the Supreme Court as a *landmark decision,* one that involves major changes in the definition of civil rights and liberties. Such a decision creates a new general rule, which is then enforced by lower federal and state courts. These organizations cannot rest after a landmark decision in the high court but usually must bring dozens of cases in federal district courts to make sure that rights affirmed by the Supreme Court are enforced. (For an example of a landmark decision, see *Brown* v. *Board of Education*, pages 153–154.)

Obeying the Courts

These private organizations may ask judges to do several things. First, they may ask that a national or state law, executive order, or private action be declared unconstitutional, or a violation of the laws of Congress. Second, they may ask that a right be protected by various kinds of judicial action. Of these, the most important are the *injunction*, which prevents someone from taking an action to violate someone else's rights, and the *order*, which requires someone to take a specified action to ensure someone else's rights.

In the event that someone does not comply with an injunction or an order, the judges may issue a citation for contempt of court. They can impose fines or jail sentences. The orders of a federal court are enforced by federal marshals, but if necessary these officials are backed up by the state's National Guard — brought into federal service by proclamation of the president — or by federal troops under the orders of the president as commander-in-chief. In 1957, when Governor Faubus of Arkansas refused to obey a federal court order to desegregate public schools, President Eisenhower took control of the Arkansas National Guard away from the governor and then used federal troops to protect black children being sent to white schools. In 1961 President Kennedy used regular army troops to desegregate the University of Mississippi, using his powers as commander-in-chief to uphold the law of the land against mob violence and resistance by the governor of the state.

In writing their orders, federal courts can act as administrators over state agencies. Their orders may allow judges to take control of agencies: At one time in the 1970s federal judges in Alabama were running the state highway patrol, the prison system, and the mental hospitals, because the governor refused to obey various federal court orders in his state.

Often state agencies do not wish to comply with the spirit or even the letter of the court orders. Consider the landmark decision of *Miranda* v. *Arizona* (1966), in which the Supreme Court held that once an investigation by police focused on someone, the person had to receive the following warning:

> You have the right to remain silent.
> Anything you say may be used against you in a court of law.
> You have the right to be represented by an attorney of your choice.
> If you cannot afford an attorney, a public defender will be provided for you if you wish.

At first, there was only limited acceptance by many police departments of the new rules of the "cops and robbers" game. After all, unless one could put a federal judge into every patrol car, voluntary agreement was the only way such a rule could be effective. Not all police supervisors or district attorneys insisted that arrests and questioning be conducted under these safeguards. Some departments ignored the order; others gave only part of the warnings. Eventually, after hundreds of lower-court cases were decided, most police departments complied with the rulings. But they did so only because the federal and state courts began to apply the *exclusionary rule:* throwing out evidence at trials, including confessions, obtained by unconstitutional means. Later the Supreme Court narrowed the exclusionary rule, sometimes allowing the use of evidence if police officers "acted in good faith" even if they did not follow all the due process rules laid down by the Courts.

Public Opinion and Civil Liberties

Clearly, public agreement with a landmark civil rights decision cannot be taken for granted. It is precisely *because*

UNCLE SAM: ENEMY OF CIVIL LIBERTIES?

Civil liberties in general have received broad support, but few people have come to their defense in unpopular cases. Throughout United States history there are uncomfortable reminders of government actions that many would now see as violating the Bill of Rights.

During the presidency of John Adams, not many years after the ink had dried on the Constitution, Congress passed the *Alien and Sedition Acts* of 1798. Aimed at the opposition party, these acts promised heavy fines and imprisonment for those guilty of writing or speaking anything false, scandalous, or malicious against any government official. Such a broad prohibition today would put an end to most political campaigns — which was also the intent then. The conviction of one congressman under the law led to a political uproar, and the acts ultimately helped the opposition party win control of Congress. The slavery issue in 1840 led Congress to pass the "Gag Rule" preventing antislavery petitions from being received by Congress (thus violating a specific First Amendment right). Not to be outdone, President Andrew Jackson called on Congress to pass a bill prohibiting the use of the mails to encourage slave rebellions. The bill didn't pass — not on grounds of free speech but because the states concerned were already censoring the mails.

Violations of civil liberties continued into the twentieth century. Within five months after the United States entered World War I, every leading socialist newspaper had been suspended from the mails at least once, some permanently. The *Espionage Act* of 1917 effectively outlawed Marxist parties; because of it a leader of the Socialist party was convicted for urging draft resistance. The *Smith Act* of 1940 forbade teaching or advocating the violent overthrow of the government. In 1951, eleven Communist party leaders were convicted under it for activities labeled "preparation for revolution." This "preparation" involved advocating and teaching major works of Marxist thought, like the *Communist Manifesto*, which today can be found in any college library. Ten defendants were each sentenced to five years in prison. The Smith Act remains a law to this day.

the majority has discriminated against a minority, or because the rights of politically unpopular groups have been violated, that the judicial decision has become necessary. One can assume that the public will oppose the changes that are being implemented and will seek to avoid complying with them. Surveys conducted between the 1950s and the 1980s show a dramatic increase in the number of people who support civil liberties positions and who oppose discrimination. At the same time, large majorities of the public oppose affirmative-action plans or court-ordered busing, and support prayer in the schools.

Where support by local political leaders does not exist and community sentiment runs against the decision, as with the ban on prayer in public schools, compliance can be spotty or nonexistent in many communities. Often a Supreme Court ruling signals the start — not the end — of political debate.

The rightness of judicial action never rests on its popularity with the public or its agreement with the beliefs or practices of the majority. The judiciary is not elected and is not directly accountable to the people. It is accountable to a Constitution that provided for limited government and secured the rights of the people against governmental action. The judiciary protects the rights of the minority against certain actions of the majority. Low levels of approval for some of its decisions are nothing to be alarmed about: If anything, this is evidence that the system is working as intended.

At the same time the courts function in the political game, and for their decisions to be effective they must be followed by other parts of the government as well as by the public. The following case study looks at an extreme case of civil liberties in the political process.

Case Study:
Nazis in Illinois

Early in 1977 the National Socialist Party of America (Nazis) announced plans for a May 1 parade through Skokie, Illinois. The American Nazis had some very weird ideas: persecution of Jews, forced return of blacks to Africa, supremacy of the white race around the world, and overthrow of the present form of government in the United States. They chose to march in Skokie because it contained 7,000 Jewish survivors of German Nazi concentration camps.

In response, Skokie officials passed several town ordinances to prevent the march. These included a requirement that organizations post a $350,000 insurance policy as a guarantee against property damage in the event of violence — a requirement that could cost the Nazis as much as $1,000 a day in insurance premiums, assuming that they could get a company to underwrite the policy. There were also prohibitions against public demonstrations by "members of political parties wearing military style uniforms" and distribution of material that "promotes or incites hatred, abuse or hostility" toward members of any racial, religious, or ethnic group. Also banned were marches likely to lead to breaches of the peace. Town officials then went to court and won an Illinois Circuit Court injunction banning the proposed Nazi march, for it would violate all these ordinances.

Because of the free-speech issues involved, the Illinois branch of the American Civil Liberties Union decided to defend the Nazis' civil liberties — an unpopular decision that cost them about 15 percent of their statewide and national membership. The ACLU argued that the laws were directed against freedom of speech and a symbol (the swastika), rather than at any illegal actions. Therefore the ordinances were violations of the First Amendment to the Constitution.

At first the Illinois courts refused to lift the injunction. Then they decided the march could take place, but only without public display of the swastika. They argued it might lead to violence because eighteen Jewish organizations were planning a large counterdemonstration against the Nazis if they dared to march in Skokie.

Eventually the Illinois Supreme Court ruled, in *Village of Skokie* v. *the National Socialist Party of America* that the Nazis could display their swastika when they marched. Later, in 1978, a federal district judge struck down the other Skokie ordinances, including the one that required insurance against property damage. This decision was affirmed by a federal court of appeals, and was left standing by the U.S. Supreme Court (which did not, however, issue its own decision).

After more than a year of court cases, the Nazis, aided by the American Civil Liberties Union, had won the right to march in Skokie. Village officials then reluctantly issued the leader a permit to march in June 1978. By this time, however, the Nazis had decided to move the march elsewhere because of the strong possibility of a violent reaction against their presence in Skokie. They agreed to march in a park in Chicago if given a permit. A federal district judge, over the opposition of Chicago officials, who also tried to ban the demonstration, ruled that the Nazis could march in the park. Eventually, the march took place without incident.

This case illustrates some essential points about civil liberties. First, they often involve highly unpopular groups, even those pledged to overthrow the government. Second, those who defend their rights, such as the ACLU and the state and federal courts, often do not support the political views of the groups. Third, such cases are likely to drag on through lower state and federal courts for months or even years. Fourth, the end result of the cases is often to establish or defend a principle. There may be little effect on the shape of American politics or government. The Nazis marched, and nothing happened.

Should the Nazis have been allowed to march? The
ACLU said yes. It argued that First Amendment freedoms
are universal, applying to everyone, no matter how unpopular the group or how disgusting its message. The sole function of state and local authorities, in this view, would be to
guard the line of march and prevent disruptions and violence.

Town officials took a different view. They wanted to safe-
guard the interests of the citizens of Skokie. They argued
that the town had an obligation to preserve the public peace.
The requirements that uniforms not be worn and swastikas
not displayed were simply reasonable regulations designed
to reduce tensions in the community. If the Nazis refused
to obey regulations designed to protect them, then they gave
up their right to demonstrate.

But if Nazis are forbidden the right to demonstrate today,
which group will be banned tomorrow? Would a town hostile to blacks then be able to ban a demonstration by a civil

rights group on the grounds that violence might erupt? Could a liberal college campus prevent demonstrations by the Moral Majority? Would Mexican-American farmworkers be held back by a town rule prohibiting them from raising flags and banners during their marches?

Others argue that the history of the rise of dictatorship is full of cases of uniformed bullies who seize control of the streets and engage in violence against their opponents. Should not local and state governments be able to defend their own streets against totalitarian movements?

Judges weighing these issues (and college students as well) must think about many factors when deciding whether or not to uphold limits on freedom of speech and assembly. The freedoms of the First Amendment are easier to support while the streets are being filled only by the rantings of a few dozen people. But things might seem different to the courts if a mass movement began to extend its activities in the streets to widespread excesses and violence. When groups move from the arena of protected *speech* to prohibited *action*, the First Amendment shield is unlikely to be applied. For whatever else it may be, the Constitution is not a suicide pact.

WRAP-UP

Civil rights and liberties are constitutional protections granted all citizens. They protect people against violations of their rights by other people and by the government. Civil liberties usually refer to rights such as freedom of speech and due process, which allow people full participation in a democratic political system. Civil rights guard minorities against discrimination by other groups of citizens. Historically both sets of rights have been both deepened as to what they cover and widened as to whom they cover. Using the vague phrases of the Fourteenth Amendment, the courts have expanded the First Amendment freedoms to apply not only to the federal government but to states and individuals as well.

A look at some of these rights shows how this extension has been achieved. The application of civil liberties such as freedom of speech, rights of privacy, and due process has been gradually expanded. Civil rights have similarly been expanded with the use of suspect classifications to deal with racial prejudice, although not yet with sexual discrimination. Helping the process along have been judges and private groups whose "test cases" have served to change public practices slowly. The case study of a Nazi march in Skokie, Illinois, illustrates how unpopular deeply believed rights can become when applied in particular instances.

Although we have spoken of these rights and liberties as protection for often unpopular groups and opinions, they also provide another sort of protection: they protect our system of government. These well-tested values give balance and restraint to the drives and ambitions of our leaders. They give us traditional standards by which to judge the actions of these players. They underline the historical truth that majorities can be wrong, that leaders can err. And if they don't help the United States government reach perfection, they at least save it — and us — from worse mistakes.

THOUGHT QUESTIONS

1. What do you think are the most important civil liberties you have as a citizen? What are the most important you have as a college student? Do you think due process rights of students should be extended? How?
2. What accounts for the fact that not all of the Bill of Rights applies against state officials? Do you think it should? Which approach do you think makes most sense: full incorporationist or partial incorporationist? Which would you apply in terms of the rights of college students?
3. Do you think the courts should be allowed to use racial quotas for "benign" purposes? Would you apply such quotas to women as well?

4. Would you have allowed the Nazis to march in Skokie? Do you
   think the village authorities had the right to ban the wearing of
   uniforms or display of the swastika in order to prevent possible
   violence? Why do you think the American Civil Liberties
   Union defended the Nazis? If you were a lawyer, would you
   have taken their case?

SUGGESTED READINGS

Abraham, Henry. *Freedom and the Court: Civil Rights and Liberties in the United States.* New York: Oxford University Press,
1982. Pb.
   *A scholarly look at the ways in which the United States meshes
   individual freedom with the rights of the community — with close-
   up views of due process, and freedom of speech and religion.*

Bradbury, Ray. *Fahrenheit 451.* New York: Ballantine Books, 1976.
Pb.
   *Sci fi novel describing a society so afraid of free speech it requires
   books to be burned — at 451°.*

Friendly, Fred W. *Minnesota Rag.* New York: Random House,
1982. Pb.
   *A journalist's story of the attempt to close down an unpleasant
   newspaper and the noted court case that followed.*

Hamlin, David. *The Nazi/Skokie Conflict: A Civil Liberties Battle.* Boston: Beacon, 1980.
   *A review of the "media-hyped" battle by the ACLU lawyer who
   defended the Nazis.*

Hentoff, Nat. *The First Freedom: The Tumultuous History of Free
Speech in America.* New York: Delacorte Press, 1980.
   *The exercise of free speech by students, teachers, journalists, and
   judicial and legislative responses.*

Voters and Political Parties

Now that we have looked at the formal constitutional players in the political game, it's time to look at some important players who were not established by the Constitution. In the next two chapters we will examine voters, political parties, interest groups, and the media, to see what they do and how they influence American politics. A case study of an election at the end of the next chapter will bring all these players together in an actual game. We will first look at voters — who they are, how they vote, and why many others don't. Then we will look at the political parties that organize voters and provide the link between them and the government. The history, the functions, and the structures of the party system provide the bones of the story. Their political consequences for us provide the meat.

VOTERS

Who Votes?

The answer to "who votes?" may seem like an obvious one. Citizens who are eighteen or older (because of the Twenty-sixth Amendment) and who have satisfied the residency requirements of their states *can* vote, but an increasing number of them do not. In the 1984 presidential election less than 53 percent of the voting-age population actually voted. Despite the efforts of both parties to register new voters, this was only a slight increase over 1980, and continued the pattern of low voter turnout since the 1960 election (see Figure 7.1). Voting rates are even lower in nonpresidential elections. In 1978, only 35 percent of eligible voters turned up at the election booths, although by 1982,

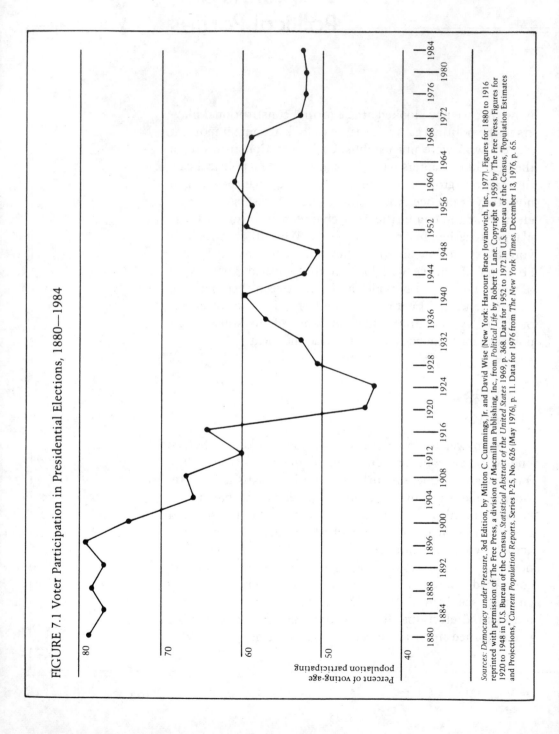

FIGURE 7.1 Voter Participation in Presidential Elections, 1880—1984

Sources: Democracy under Pressure, 3rd Edition, by Milton C. Cummings, Jr. and David Wise (New York: Harcourt Brace Jovanovich, Inc., 1977). Figures for 1880 to 1916 reprinted with permission of The Free Press, a division of Macmillan Publishing, Inc., from Political Life by Robert E. Lane. Copyright © 1959 by The Free Press. Figures for 1920 to 1948 in U.S. Bureau of the Census, Statistical Abstract of the United States 1969, p. 368. Data for 1952 to 1972 in U.S. Bureau of the Census, "Population Estimates and Projections," Current Population Reports, Series P-25, No. 626 (May 1976), p. 11. Data for 1976 from The New York Times, December 13, 1976, p. 65.

41 percent voted. The questions grow. What influences whether people become voters? What influences how they vote? And what has led to the great numbers of people who don't vote?

Political Socialization

Political socialization provides part of an answer to how, or if, people participate in politics. *Political socialization* is the *process of learning political attitudes and behavior.* The gradual process of socialization takes place as we grow up in settings like the family and the schools. In the home children learn about participating in family decisions — for example, the more noise they make, the better chance they have of staying up late. Kids also learn which party their parents favor, how they generally view politics and politicians, and what are their basic values and outlook toward their country. Children, of course, don't always copy their parents' political leanings, but they are influenced by them. Most people stay with the party of their parents. Schools have a similar effect. Students salute the flag, obey their teacher, take civics courses, participate in student politics, and learn that democracy (us) is good and dictatorship (them) is bad.

People's social characteristics also influence their participation in politics. Although it is difficult to weigh how important they are for each individual, whether a person is young or old, black or white, rich or poor, northerner or southerner will affect his or her political opinions and behavior. The views of a person's peer group (friends and neighbors), of political authorities ("The president knows what he's doing"), and of one's political party influence how people vote as well.

The influence of religion and ethnic background can be seen in most large cities where parties run "balanced tickets" with Irish, Italian, and Jewish candidates — and, more recently, blacks and women as well. Besides the well-known tendency for people to vote for "one of their own," they also share certain political attitudes. Catholics tend to vote Democratic more often than do Protestants. Blacks and Jews are generally more supportive of social programs. On specific issues religion may also play a role: many Catholics back aid to parochial schools, many Jews support arms for Israel, many fundamentalist Protestants favor prayer in the schools.

Class and Voting

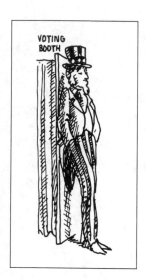

Class may be even more important in shaping people's political opinions and behaviors. The term *class* refers to a *group's occupation and income, and the awareness it produces of their relations to other groups or classes in the society.* In general we can speak of three broad overlapping categories: a working class, a middle class, and an upper class. The *working class,* including almost always the majority of people in a society, receives the lowest incomes and fills "blue-collar" jobs in factories and farms, as well as many "white-collar" jobs like clerical and secretarial jobs in offices. The *middle class* consists of most professionals (like teachers and engineers), small businessmen, bureaucrats, and some skilled workers (say, those earning more than $20,000 a year). The *upper class* (often called the elite or ruling class) is composed of those who run our major economic and political institutions and receive the highest incomes for doing so.

At least as important as these "objective" categories that political scientists use is the "subjective" way in which people in these classes view their own position. Whether union members or teachers or housewives see themselves as members of the working class or the middle class will also influence their political attitudes. An important fact about class in the United States is that class identification is quite weak. People either don't know what class they are in or don't think it's important. Most Americans see themselves as members of the middle class no matter what "objective" class they may be put into.

Class as reflected in income and occupation, however, does influence people's attitudes on a variety of issues. Studies have shown that people in the working class tend to be liberal in wanting greater economic equality and more social-welfare programs. This liberalism on economic issues contrasts strongly with their ideas on civil liberties. Here people of lower income and education tend to be intolerant of dissenters and not supportive of protection for minority views or new styles of behavior (such as homosexual rights). Members of the middle class tend to be more conservative in their economic views and more liberal on issues such as free speech and respect for civil rights. Class attitudes on political questions, then, tend to be both liberal and conservative depending on the type of issue.

The problem with figuring out how these various characteristics — race, class, religion — influence a person's political behavior is that so many of them overlap. If we say that blacks are more likely not to vote than whites, are we sure that race is the key category? We also know that poorer people, those with less education, and those who feel they have less effect on their government also are less likely to vote. All these categories include the majority of blacks. But we don't yet know which is more important in influencing behavior. And so even the "true" statement that blacks vote less may conceal as much as it reveals. We would also have to examine whether blacks with more income or education also vote less — which they don't. We might then conclude that race was not as important in voting turnout as, say, class.

WHO DOESN'T VOTE?

The problems just outlined illustrate the difficulty of answering the question of why people increasingly don't vote. Studies have shown that nonvoters are most often from the less-educated, nonwhite, rural, southern, female, poor, blue-collar, and very old or very young segments of the American population. Voters most often come from the white, mid-

dle-aged, male, college-educated, urban or suburban, afflu-
ent, white-collar groups. These are only broad tendencies,
with a great many exceptions in each case. One result of
these tendencies, however, is a middle- and upper-class bias
in voting. Another consequence is that although more
Americans are registered Democrats than Republicans, Republicans tend to vote in higher percentages, thus lessening
their disadvantage.

There are some other things, gathered from various opinion polls, of which we are sure: (1) Americans, in general,
are poorly informed about politics. Surveys have shown that
only about half the voters know the name of their representative in Congress and only 20 percent know how he or she
has voted on any major bills. (2) Distrust of government and
dissatisfaction with its leaders have grown in the last
twenty years. (3) People feel they have less influence on
their government. In 1966, a third of those surveyed agreed
that public officials didn't care much what people "like me"
think. By 1980 more than half agreed, and in 1982 the figure
dropped to 46 percent. There is, then, dissatisfaction with
and detachment from politics and government, as shown by
peoples' decreasing likelihood of voting.

Since 1980 there has been some rebound in public confidence in the government. Those believing the government
in Washington could be trusted most of the time rose from
23 percent in 1980 to 32 percent in 1982. This rise was
interpreted as coming from the widely held opinion that
the Reagan administration was effectively limiting the role
of the national government. Curiously, then, the slight rise
in public trust in government came from the effort to reduce that government's activities. Overall the American
people remain negative toward government and public
officials.

Part of the reason for these trends undoubtedly lies in the
turmoil of the late 1960s and early 1970s. Vietnam and Watergate, with the demonstrations and scandals they led to,
stood as symbols of government bungling, corruption, and
unresponsiveness. As more was revealed about how the gov-

ON VOTING

"The existence of the vote does not make politicians better as individuals; it simply forces them to give greater consideration to demands of enfranchised and sizeable groups who hold a weapon of potentially great force. . . . The ability to punish politicians is probably the most important weapon available to citizens." — Gerald Pomper

"I never vote. It only encourages them." — a woman polled by CBS news

"Even *voting* for the right is *doing* nothing for it." — Henry D. Thoreau

"Nobody will ever deprive the American people of the right to vote except the American people themselves." — Franklin D. Roosevelt

---

ernment operated, from the Pentagon Papers to the Nixon tapes, less respect and confidence were given to political leaders. Politicians became the constant butt of television jokes, and cynicism became an accepted approach to political analysis. Even with Vietnam and Watergate behind us, there has been only a limited recovery of public confidence. Although people seem satisfied with their personal lives and the basic organization of the government and the economy, the feeling is widespread that the shortcomings of their leaders are undercutting the strengths of the country.

Another explanation for voter apathy goes back to the question of class. There is no doubt that members of the working class are least likely to vote or participate in politics. One study found that in a recent presidential election 68 percent of working people reported no activity (such as attending a meeting or wearing a campaign button). Only 36 percent of those identifying themselves as "upper middle class" said they had done nothing. Voting figures say the same thing. In 1980, 39 percent of those with incomes below $5,000 voted, whereas 74 percent with incomes above $25,000 voted.

There are a number of reasons for these class differences. The most obvious is that low-income people with immediate personal problems like finding a job or paying bills will be more likely to view politics as a luxury they can't afford the time to follow. Class differences in political socialization also have an effect. Working-class children, whether because of their more rigidly structured families or because of the poor education they receive, are brought up to believe that they can have little influence on politics ("You can't fight City Hall"). At the same time, because of the disadvantaged reality they and their parents face, they tend to have a not-so-favorable image of political leaders like the president. These children, then, end up being both more resentful and more passive toward politics. Middle- and upper-class children have a higher regard for political leaders and are taught in their schools to value participation in politics. They are encouraged to participate and led to believe that the political system will respond favorably to their participation.

The political game itself is shaped to limit the participation of lower-income citizens. A belief in equality has always been central to American political thought. This myth of a "classless society" leads to class being downplayed as a basis for participating in, or even understanding, politics. The United States is the only developed democracy without a socialist or labor party to represent and organize the working class. As we will see later in the chapter, the two-party system that does exist tends to push both parties toward the moderate center in seeking support. The lower class, living in a society not recognizing class differences and not providing organizations to voice its interests, tends to have its issues ignored and is given little encouragement to participate politically. Of course, the less that low-income groups participate, the less they will find the political process responding to their interests, and vice versa.

The successful efforts of Jesse Jackson to register blacks

in the 1984 presidential race show a way out of this predicament. Reverend Jackson was able to unify and mobilize blacks around his candidacy. Although he lost his race for the Democratic nomination, he could present himself as representing the black electorate and bargain with party leaders on issues of concern to his bloc of voters. Because these leaders needed black support for the presidential election, they tended to listen. On a local level black mayors, like Chicago's Harold Washington, labor unions, and Hispanic leaders, have all succeeded in bringing increasing numbers of low-income groups to the polls — and thereby winning elections.

From another viewpoint nonvoting can also be seen as representing a basic satisfaction with how things are going. Supposedly, if people were upset enough by a depression or a war, they would vote. This argument, however, assumes that people see voting as an effective means of changing unpopular policies. Unfortunately, nonvoting indicates that many people no longer hold out this hope. Nonvoting has become a sign of both apathy and protest toward what many continue to view as an unresponsive political process.

POLITICAL PARTIES

The major established structures for organizing people to determine the makeup of the government through elections are political parties. The history of their development in America, how they are structured to seek political power, and how well they do it, are the major themes in the rest of the chapter.

The national government, as we have seen, is based on a system of dividing or *decentralizing* power. Political parties, on the other hand, are a means of organizing or *centralizing* power. The framers of the Constitution decentralized power in separate branches and a federal system partly to avoid the development of powerful factions that could take over the government. This very decentralization of power, however, created the need for parties that could pull together or centralize that power.

A *political party* is an organization that runs candidates for public office under the party's name. Although the framers seemed more concerned with factions and interests than with parties, they were well aware of the possibility that parties would soon develop. George Washington, in his famous farewell address, warned against "the baneful effects of the spirit of party." Nevertheless, the development of parties continued.

Origin of Today's Parties

The *Federalists* and *Anti-Federalists*, the factions that supported and opposed the adoption of the Constitution, were not organized into actual political parties. They did not run candidates for office under party labels, but they were networks of communication and political activity struggling on opposite sides of a great dispute — ratification. Although most of the Founding Fathers preached against political parties, they found them necessary almost as soon as the national government was operating.

After the Constitution was ratified, the Federalist faction grew stronger and more like a political party. Led by Alexander Hamilton, secretary of the treasury under President George Washington, the Federalists championed a strong national government that would promote the financial interests of merchants and manufacturers. After Thomas Jefferson left President Washington's cabinet in 1793, an opposition party began to form under his leadership. The new *Democratic-Republican* party drew the support of small farmers, debtors, and others who did not benefit from the financial programs of the Federalists. Under the Democratic-Republican label, Jefferson won the presidential election of 1800, and his party continued to control the presidency until 1828. The Federalists, without power or popular support, gradually died out.

At the end of this twenty-eight-year period of Democratic-Republican control, the party splintered into many factions. Two of these factions grew into new parties, the *Democrats* and the *Whigs* (first called the National Republicans). Thus our Democratic party, founded in 1828, is the oldest political party in the world. The early Democratic party was led by Andrew Jackson, who was elected president in 1828. It became known as the party of the common people. The Whigs, more like the old Federalists, were supported by the wealthier and more conservative classes in society: bankers, merchants, and big farmers.

In 1854, a *coalition* (a collection of groups that join together for a specific purpose) of Whigs, antislavery Democrats, and minor parties formed the *Republican* party. One of the common goals of the party supporters was to fight slavery. The Republicans nominated a "dark horse" (a political unknown), Abraham Lincoln, on the third ballot for president in 1860. The Democrats were so deeply divided over the slavery issue that the southern and northern wings of the party each nominated a candidate. Against this divided opposition, Lincoln won the election in the electoral college with less than a majority of the popular vote but more than any other candidate.

Maintaining, Deviating, and Realigning Elections

The Democratic and Republican parties have dominated American politics for the past 125 years. Their relative strength and the nature of their support, however, have shifted back and forth. We can see this shift by looking at three types of presidential elections: maintaining elections, deviating elections, and realigning elections. *Maintaining elections* keep party strength and support as they are. *Deviating elections* show a temporary shift in popular support for the parties, usually caused by the exceptional, popular appeal of a candidate of the minority party. *Realigning elections* show a permanent shift in the popular base of support of the parties, and usually a shift in the relative strength of the parties so that the minority party emerges as the majority party.

Most presidential elections between 1860 and 1932 were maintaining elections. The Republicans (often called the GOP, Grand Old Party) kept the support of a majority of voters, and controlled the executive branch, for all but sixteen of those seventy-two years. When the Democrats did gain control of the presidency, they held office for only short periods. The two Democratic elections of Woodrow Wilson in 1912 and 1916, for example, were caused by temporary voter shifts, or deviations in party support, and splits within the Republican party.

The great social and economic impact of the Depression of the 1930s destroyed the majority support Republicans had enjoyed for so long, and contributed to a realignment in the two-party system. Under Franklin Delano Roosevelt, the Democrats became the majority party and were known as the party of labor, the poor, minorities, urban residents, immigrants, eastern liberals, and the white South. Since 1952, however, the Republican party has gained substantial support in presidential and congressional elections among white voters in the once "solid South" and among the suburban middle classes.

After the 1984 election some political analysts foresaw a Republican realignment similar to the Democratic one of 1932. A conservative Republican was overwhelmingly re-elected president, which meant that in the last four out of five presidential elections the Republican nominee has won with an average of over 82% of the electoral college votes. Further, the southern and western states consistently voted for Republican candidates, the youth vote shifted to Reagan, and polls of party identification showed almost as many Republicans as Democrats.

There were arguments raised against the interpretation. One difference between the 1984 and 1932 elections was in voter turnout. Roosevelt's election and reelection in 1936 brought millions of new people to the polls, while 1984 continued a 20-year pattern of low voter turnout. In spite of the president's popularity, the 1984 Congressional races saw the Democrats losing only a few seats in the House and gaining two in the Senate. Democrats retained control of an estimated 75 percent of all elective offices in the country. Republican popularity remained hostage to their ability to maintain the health of the economy. Nevertheless, the Democratic majority coalition put together by Roosevelt seems all but gone, at least in presidential races, and this may mean the Reagan landslide will be seen in the future as a realigning election.

Tweedledee and Tweedledum?

Is there a real difference between the Republican party and the Democratic party? To answer this question we should look at both party image and party reality. The image of the parties is usually based on a stereotype of people who support the parties. A "typical" Republican is white, middle class, and Protestant; has a college education; and with the rise of the "gender gap" in the 1980s is less often a woman. He or she supports big business, law and order, limited government intervention in the economy and in our private lives, and a hard-line policy in foreign affairs.

The "typical" Democrat is a member of a minority ethnic or racial group, working class, non-Protestant, and an urban resident. He or she supports social-welfare measures to improve the status of the poor at home, government regulation of big business, more equal distribution of wealth and privilege, and more liberal foreign policies.

Of course, the reality is much more complex than the image. It has been found that leaders of the Democratic and Republican parties do disagree fairly consistently on major issues. But party followers who are not actively involved with the party tend to be much more moderate (or indifferent) than leaders on these issues. Democratic and Republican party followers, in fact, often agree more with each other than with their party leaders.

Another complicating factor in party differences is that each party is deeply divided within itself. The Democratic party includes, for example, liberal, black, urban, working-class supporters from the northern industrial cities, and conservative, white, wealthy farmers from the South. The GOP includes moderate-liberal business or professional people from the East, and small-town conservative shopkeepers or farmers from the Midwest. There has been a rise in split-ticket voting where voters favor candidates of another party but retain their party ties. In 1984, many conservative working-class Democrats voted for President Reagan while supporting their party's candidates for state and local offices.

This decline in partisanship has been reflected in the increase of voters identifying with neither political party. These *independents* compose about one-quarter of the voters, as opposed to one-fifth of the electorate twenty-five years ago. They also tend to be less well informed and less active in politics than those voters belonging to a party. Because their opinions are more likely to change during elections, most presidential campaigns are aimed at holding onto the party base and winning over the independent voter. The rise of independents has led some analysts to predict the further decline of political parties. Despite the weakening in party identification, the two major parties are likely to continue dominating elections.

Party Functions

What do political parties do? Political parties throughout the world try to organize power in order to control the government. To do so, American political parties (1) contest elections, (2) organize public opinion, (3) bring interests together (often called *aggregating* interests), and (4) incorporate changes proposed by groups and individuals outside the party system and the government.

First, parties *contest elections*. They organize voters in order to compete with other parties for elected offices. To contest elections, parties — or, more usually, their candidates — *recruit* people into the political system to work on campaigns. Parties *provide people with a basis for making political choices.* In fact, most people vote for a candidate because of the party he or she belongs to. In addition, when parties contest elections, they must *express policy positions* on important issues. To some extent this function of the parties serves to *educate* voters about the political process. Most people are not ordinarily involved in politics. They often rely on elections to keep them informed and active.

Second, parties organize *public opinion.* Despite the wide variety of opinion within them, parties give the public a limited channel of communication to express their desires about how government should operate. At the least, voters can approve the actions of the party that has been holding office by voting for it. Or they can show disapproval by voting for the opposition.

Third, the two major parties bring together or *aggregate various interests.* The Democratic and Republican parties aggregate the special interests of groups and individuals in society into large coalitions for the purpose of winning elections. Gathering special interests under the broad "umbrella" of a party label is an important function of American political parties.

Finally, the two major parties *incorporate changes* or reforms proposed by third parties or social protest movements. If third parties or political movements show that they have considerable support, their programs are often adopted, though usually in more moderate form, by one of the major parties. In the 1984 elections Ronald Reagan generally supported the position of "right-to-life" groups calling for an amendment to the Constitution making abortions in the United States illegal.

VIEW FROM THE INSIDE: PARTY ORGANIZATIONS

American parties have tended to be weak organizations. They have been most formally organized on a local and state level, and become even weaker as they approach the national level. But powerless parties have not always been the rule in this country, and it's a rule that may be changing now.

Particularly in the last half of the nineteenth century, American parties at the local level were so tightly organized that they were often called political *machines*. Party machines have a party *boss* (leader) who directly controls the political party workers at lower (usually city district or ward) levels. Local leaders obey the boss because he controls party nominations, patronage positions (jobs that can be given to loyal supporters), political favors, and party finances. Machines, many of which had a well-deserved reputation for being corrupt, lost much of their leverage early in the twentieth century when three things happened: (1) local, state, and federal agencies took over distributing benefits to the poor; (2) civil service reforms made most city jobs dependent on results of competitive examinations, and (3) direct primaries made competition for party nomination a contest anyone could enter.

American Party Structure

Today, we can picture American party structure as a pyramid. Local political organizations or clubs are at the bottom; county committees are above them; state committees are above the county; and the national committee of each party is at the top (see Figure 7.2). Though the strength of the party has traditionally been at the bottom, in most localities the foundation is not very strong.

As a result of the welfare, civil service, and primary reforms, most local party organizations have few goodies with which to maintain a strong organization. Local parties range from virtual disorganization to still-powerful machines, with most parties falling closer to the pole of disorganization. In much of America, especially the rural areas, a handful of officials meet occasionally to carry out the essential affairs needed to keep the party alive. They are largely without influence, raise little money, and create little public

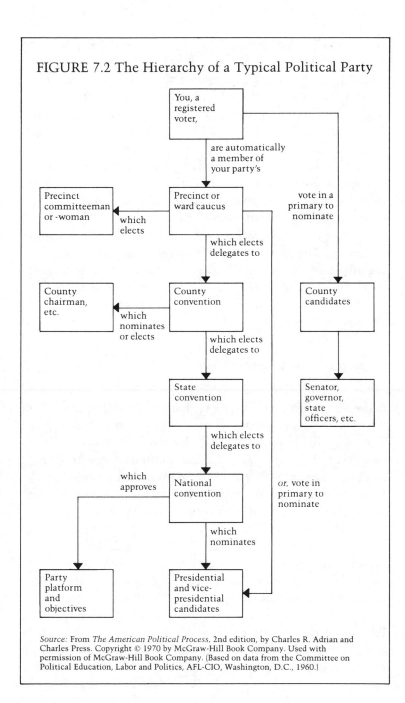

FIGURE 7.2 The Hierarchy of a Typical Political Party

Source: From *The American Political Process*, 2nd edition, by Charles R. Adrian and Charles Press. Copyright © 1970 by McGraw-Hill Book Company. Used with permission of McGraw-Hill Book Company. (Based on data from the Committee on Political Education, Labor and Politics, AFL-CIO, Washington, D.C., 1960.)

attention. The party comes alive only around elections to support a candidate who was generally selected by his or her own efforts. On the other end of the pole of organization, some party machines still exist. Until his death in 1976, Richard Daley, mayor of Chicago for more than twenty years, kept firm control of a strong Democratic party machine. Daley's machine acted as an informal government and social service agency, meeting the immediate needs of urban citizens. Chicago's political machine has declined in recent years and this type of party organization, in general, seems to be a leftover from the past.

State party organizations tend to be weaker than county or city organizations. State party committees run the party organization, but generally the state chairperson dominates party activity. State party organizations have some patronage to distribute and can give essential backing to candidates for state office.

National Party Organization

Between presidential elections, each party is governed by its *national committee.* The national committee consists of representatives chosen from each state party organization. The committee is led by the *chairperson,* who is usually chosen by the party's presidential nominee every four years. In the past decade the national party committees, led by the Republicans, have undertaken drastic reforms designed to strengthen and centralize the power of the parties.

Using money and technology, the Republicans have revived their national party structure. They have moved far ahead of the Democrats in fund-raising and organization. In 1983 the Republicans raised over $93 million, nearly six times the $16 million raised by the Democrats. In the 1981– 82 election cycle the GOP raised almost as much as the PACs and Democrats combined. The Republicans' postage bill alone — $7.5 million — almost equaled half of the entire operating budget of the Democratic National Committee. By the 1984 elections the Republican party had become the single most important source of money in American politics.

These funds were used to support the party's candidates and buy expensive campaign technology. The large amounts of money the Republicans gave to their candidates tended to concentrate power in the national organization and produced a great deal of loyalty in party members' votes in Congress on the president's program. Besides increasing party discipline, the funds were spent on sophisticated media and computerized mail campaigns to reach and register Republican voters. Although the Democrats remained the majority party, the Republicans clearly had the advantage in money and technology in getting their voters to the polls. In the years ahead the power of both national parties is likely to increase as the formerly weak parties strengthen their central organizations.

The National Convention

Most of the public attention the party receives comes at the *national convention* held every four years during the summer before the presidential campaign. The national convention is attended by delegates chosen by the states in various ways. In 1984 the Republican convention had 2,235 delegates, and the Democratic convention had 3,933. The delegates to the convention adopt a party platform and elect the party's presidential nominee.

The *party platform* is actually written by a Platform Committee and then approved by the convention. It is generally a long document that states the party's position on many issues and can be used as a basis for the party's electioneering. If the party is in power, the platform will boast of the party's achievements. If the party is out of power, the platform will criticize the policies of the other party. The platform will emphasize the party's differences with the other major party and minimize the divisions within the party.

Frequently, groups of convention delegates will organize

into factions in order to press for statements representing their minority political views to be included in the platform. In 1980 a minority group of women at the Republican national convention pressed unsuccessfully for *planks* (parts of the platform) supporting the Equal Rights Amendment and federal funding for poor women's abortions. As seen in the 1984 Democratic convention, platforms tend to be more important in reconciling groups within the party than in outlining what a president will actually do when in office.

The high point of the convention comes when the delegates vote for the party's presidential nominee. The candidates have been campaigning throughout the country to show their popularity with the voters and to influence convention delegates from each of the states to vote in their favor. Recent reforms have led to more popular participation in the nominating process while giving party leaders somewhat less control. Most states hold *presidential primaries* or *caucuses* in which candidates from the same party run against each other, competing for popular support and for the right to send delegates pledged to their candidacy to the national convention. For the first few days of the convention, candidates and their campaign workers try to line up unpledged delegates who will support them.

Toward the end of the convention, the names of the candidates are placed in nomination, with nominating speeches by famous party figures. A roll-call vote of the delegates is then taken. Each state, in alphabetical order, announces the tally of its delegate votes. The final party nominee for the office of president is elected by a simple majority vote. In 1924, the Democratic convention took 103 ballots before it was able to reach a majority decision. In recent decades the presidential nominee has been chosen on the first ballot, reflecting the votes in the state primaries and caucuses. Conventions today can be accurately described as *approving* or *ratifying* the candidate selected by the party voters. The delegates who are usually pledged to a candidate don't actually make the choice themselves.

The presidential nominee chooses a vice-presidential running mate who is then formally approved by the convention. Usually a main goal is to "balance the ticket." Walter Mondale, a moderate from the Midwest, chose Geraldine Ferraro, a liberal woman from New York, to be his running mate in 1984. Or the vice-presidential nominee may be a well-known competitor of the presidential nominee, as was George Bush when Ronald Reagan chose him in 1980. Sometimes he is a political unknown and therefore not going to offend anyone immediately, as was Spiro Agnew when Nixon chose him in 1968.

The national convention is the starting point of the fall presidential campaign. Party workers and party supporters, their enthusiasm sparked by the convention proceedings, set out to make their party's nominee the winner of the presidential election in November.

VIEW FROM THE OUTSIDE: THE TWO-PARTY SYSTEM

In the United States we have a *two-party system* on the national level, meaning that two major parties dominate national politics. In a *one-party system*, a single party monopolizes the organization of power and the positions of authority. In a *multiparty system*, more than two political parties compete for power and electoral offices.

From the Civil War until the election of Dwight David Eisenhower to the presidency in 1952, the eleven southern states of the Civil War Confederacy had virtually one-party systems. These states were so heavily Democratic that the Republicans were a permanent minority. The important electoral contests took place in the primaries, where blacks were systematically excluded. Multiparty systems have also existed in the United States. New York state has a four-party system today in which Democrats, Republicans, Liberals, and Conservatives compete in state and local elections. Nationally, however, the United States has a two-party system.

Causes of the Two-Party System

There are four main reasons for the continued dominance of two parties in America. The first is the *historic dualism* of American political conflict. The first major political division among Americans was dual, or two-sided, between Federalists and Anti-Federalists. It is said that this original two-sided political battle established the tradition of two-party domination in this country.

The second reason is the *moderate views of the American voter.* Unlike that of the European democracies, where radical political parties such as the Communists have legitimacy, American politics tends more toward the center. Americans may be moderate because their political party system forces them to choose between two moderate parties, or American parties may be moderate because Americans do not want to make more extreme political choices. As with the chicken and the egg, it's tough to know which came first.

Third, the *structure of our electoral system* encourages two-party dominance. We elect one representative at a time from each district to Congress, which is called election by *single-member districts.* The winning candidate is the one who gets the most votes, or a *plurality.* (A majority of votes means more than 50 percent of the votes cast; a plurality simply means more votes than anyone else.) Similarly, in presidential elections the party with a plurality in a state gets all the electoral votes of that state. This system makes it difficult for minor-party candidates to win elections, and without election victories parties tend to fade fast.

Many countries with multiparty systems elect representatives by *proportional representation.* That is, each district has more than one representative, and each party that receives a certain number of votes gets to send a proportionate number of representatives to the legislature. For example, in a single-member district; a minor party that received 10 percent of the vote would not be able to send its candidate to Congress. In a multimember district the size of ten congressional districts, however, that 10 percent of the vote would mean that one out of ten representatives sent from the district would be a minor party member.

Finally, the Democratic and Republican parties continue to dominate national politics because they are flexible enough to *adopt some of the programs proposed by third parties,* and thus win over third-party supporters. The Socialist party in America, even during its strongest period, always had difficulty achieving national support partly because the Democratic party was able to *co-opt,* or win over, the support of most of organized labor with prolabor economic programs. The Republican party lured voters away from Alabama Governor George Wallace's American Independent Party (AIP) by emphasizing law and order and deemphasizing civil rights in its 1968 presidential campaign.

Consequences of the Two-Party System

The moderate "umbrella" nature of our parties can be considered a plus or a minus. Our party system prevents the country from being *polarized,* or severely divided, by keeping factions with radical views from winning much power. But this also means that many dissenting opinions get little consideration by the voters. When a candidate does take a strong stand on issues, especially in a national campaign, he or she usually loses. Two of the most lopsided presidential elections in our history reflect this fact. Barry Goldwater, the conservative Republican candidate for president in 1964, and George McGovern, the liberal Democratic candidate for president in 1972, were both overwhelmingly defeated in their election campaigns. Ronald Reagan applied this lesson in 1984 by moderating his own positions (such as reducing social security) and making Walter Mondale's policies (such as tax increases) the issue rather than his own.

As we discussed earlier, the two parties competing for national office must appeal to a majority of voters to win, and thus both parties tend to shy away from taking extreme positions. Parties and their candidates avoid being specific about programs they might enact when in office, for discussing specific programs will win the support of some voters, but lose the support of many others. When they need majority support, politicians try not to commit themselves to positions on controversial issues. Politicians whose party is out of power also realize that they have more to gain by simply attacking the party in power than by proposing alternative programs. All these factors mean that when it comes to taking a public stand, politicians often must sound good, but say as little as possible.

WRAP-UP

Voters are the broadest, most representative player in the political game. Directly or indirectly they legitimate how the government is run and choose who is to run it. Many factors, like political socialization, party membership, religion, race, and class, influence how people vote or even *if* they vote. The continued growth of nonvoting poses serious questions about the representative nature of government and the responsiveness of people to their government.

The political parties provide a major link between voters and their elected officials. Historically the parties have evolved into a two-party system, with the Democrats and Republicans dominating elections for more than a century. Though the parties historically have been weakly organized on a national level and only slightly stronger locally, recent reforms, led by the Republicans, have considerably strengthened the national parties. Through a process of primaries, nominating conventions, and election campaigns, they put their labels on candidates for positions of national leadership. Both the party structure and the historical tone of American politics lead to moderate positions by the competing parties and, some contend, to little difference between the two.

Predictions of the decline and fall of the two-party system of Democrats and Republicans are undoubtedly overstated. Despite the increase in nonvoting, and the decrease in party loyalty among those who do vote, both parties still have a few cards left to play. They have shown great flexibility in the past in adapting to the demands of new political groups, whether blacks, women, or Christian fundamentalists. A similar flexibility in dealing with national issues, such as full employment, tax reform, budget deficits, and street crime, will allow them to continue as vital links between the people and their government. Directly confronting these issues of economic and political justice will allow the parties to remain the leading players in electoral politics. Not to do so will lead to the questioning of their own role as political players and to the continued indifference of turned-off voters to the political game.

THOUGHT QUESTIONS

1. If you voted in the last election, what influenced the way you voted? Can you relate your political views to your family, religion, or class background?
2. If you didn't vote, what led you not to vote? Was it a conscious decision? What would lead you to vote in the future?
3. How would the development of a multiparty system on the national level change the role and nature of our political parties? What would be the advantages and disadvantages of such a system?
4. Should our political parties be strengthened? If not, why not? If so, how?

SUGGESTED READINGS

Crotty, William. *American Parties in Decline*, 2nd ed. Boston: Little, Brown, 1984.
   An assessment of the current state of political parties and the difficulties facing them.

Mandel, Ruth B. *In the Running: The New Woman Candidate.* New York: Ticknor and Fields, 1981. Pb.
The special problems women face in running for office, such as projecting an image and crashing male political circles, and how they overcome them.

Nie, Norman H., Sidney Verba, and John Petrocik. *The Changing American Voter.* Cambridge, Mass.: Harvard University Press, 1976.
A close look at the opinions and behavior of the American people toward politics, and how they've changed.

O'Connor, Edwin. *The Last Hurrah.* New York: Bantam, 1957. Pb.
A classic novel of big city (Boston) party machines — how they worked and how they died. (Also a good late-night movie often shown on television on election nights.)

Reeves, Richard. *Convention.* New York: Harcourt, Brace Jovanovich, 1977.
The fast-paced story of the 1976 Democratic presidential convention, focusing on the spicy human-interest side of a political happening.

Riordan, William L. *Plunkitt of Tammany Hall.* New York: Dutton, 1963. Pb.
The witty confessions of a New York City political boss covering the politics of his party around the turn of the century.

Sabato, Larry. *The Rise of Political Consultants.* New York: Basic Books, 1981. Pb.
Somewhat dryly traces the increased power of all-important campaign consultants and recommends ways of improving their ethics.

Thompson, Dr. Hunter S. *Fear and Loathing on the Campaign Trail '72.* New York: Popular Library, 1973. Pb.
Rolling Stone's Outlaw Journalist writes a hip, slightly crazed journal of what it's like to be in the muddle of a presidential campaign.

Interest Groups and the Media 8

The Constitution does not take into account interest groups and the media. Except for the First Amendment's guarantee of freedom of the press, neither is mentioned in the document. The framers of the Constitution recognized various interests in society but not their role in government. And although they made wide use of the press in their efforts to get the Constitution adopted, they could not foresee the influence of modern media on politics. Indeed, what could the framers have said about these two political players? Their development has filled gaps left by the Constitution in the political process.

Both interest groups and media provide people with access to the political process. Interest groups provide the means for people with common concerns to make their views known to government officials. The media are a communications link (and an actor in their own right) through which people keep informed of political events. In providing instruments of power, the two can influence the political game they play and the people they serve, as shown in the case study of an election to the Senate. Who they are, what they do, and how interest groups and media shape and are shaped by politics in the United States are the questions at the heart of what follows.

INTEREST GROUPS

Alexis de Tocqueville, in his famous book *Democracy in America*, wrote in 1835 that Americans have a tendency to form "associations," and have perfected "the art of pursuing in common the object of their common desires."[1] One type of association is the *interest group* or *pressure group*, a group of people who organize to pursue a common interest by applying pressure on the political process. As we have seen, American parties are not organized very well for expressing specific interests or positions. Interest groups partly fill this gap.

How Do Interest Groups Differ from Parties?

Party organization and the electoral system are based on geographic divisions. Our senators and representatives represent us on the basis of the state or the district in which we live. But within one district there might be very important group interests that are not represented. People of different religions, races, ethnic backgrounds, income levels, or occupations may have different political concerns. Interest groups have developed to give Americans with common causes a way to express their views to political decision makers.

Interest groups may try to influence the outcome of elections, but unlike parties they do not compete for public office. Although a candidate for office may be sympathetic to a certain group, or may in fact be a member of that group, he or she nevertheless does not run for election as a candidate of the group.

Interest groups are usually more tightly organized than political parties. They are often financed through contributions or dues-paying memberships. Organizers communicate with members through newsletters, mailings, and conferences, Union members, for example, usually receive regular correspondence from the union leadership informing them about union activities, benefits, and positions they are expected to support.

[1] Alexis de Tocqueville, *Democracy in America*, Vol. 2 (New York: Vintage, 1945), p. 115.

Types of Interest Groups

The largest and probably the most important type of interest group is the economic interest group, including business, professional, labor, and farming groups. James Madison, in *The Federalist Papers,* expressed the fear that if people united on the basis of economic interests, all the have-nots in society would take control of the government. This has obviously not happened. The most influential groups in the political process are often those with the most money (see Tables 8.1 and 8.2).

Business groups have a common interest in making profits, which also involves supporting the economic system that makes profits possible. The Chamber of Commerce, the National Association of Manufacturers, and the National Small Business Association are well-known business groups. Large, powerful companies, like American Telephone and Telegraph (AT&T), United States Steel, and General Motors often act as interest groups by themselves.

TABLE 8.1 1982 Interest-Group Contributions to
Congressional Campaigns

Category	Contributions
Corporate PACS	$27,528,000
Labor PACs	$20,288,604
Ideological PACs	$10,988,963
Trade, Member, and Health PACs (AMA, NRA, Realtors)	$22,939,475
Cooperative PACs (Agriculture)	$ 2,199,443
Corporations without stock (Commodity exchanges, Life insurance companies, etc.)	$ 1,067,735
Total	$85,012,220

Source: Federal Election Commission Press Release, 11/29/83.

TABLE 8.2 Major Interest-Group Contributions in
          1981–82

Interest Group	Total Contributions
National Association of Realtors	$2,115,135
American Medical Association	$1,737,090
United Auto Workers	$1,623,947
International Association of Machinists and Aerospace Workers	$1,444,959
National Education Association	$1,183,215
National Association of Home Builders	$1,005,628
Associated Milk Producers	$ 962,450
American Bankers Association	$ 947,460
Automobile Dealers Association	$ 917,295
AFL-CIO Political Contributions Committee	$ 906,425

Source: Congressional Quarterly, July 16, 1983, p. 1452. Copyrighted material from Congressional Quarterly, Inc. Reprinted by permission.

Professional groups include the American Medical Association, the National Association of Realtors, and the American Bar Association, all of which have powerful lobbies in Washington.

Labor unions, like the International Brotherhood of Teamsters and the unions that make up the American Federation of Labor and the Congress of Industrial Organizations (the AFL-CIO), are among the most influential interest groups in the country. One of the charges Walter Mondale had to answer in 1984 was that he was under the thumb of the AFL-CIO, which backed his campaign for the Democratic presidential nomination. Labor leaders, who tend to stay in power longer than most politicians, are powerful political figures in their own right. Newer and smaller unions, like the United Farm Workers, an organization of mainly Chicano farm laborers, are less effective than older, wealthier unions.

Agricultural business interests have a long history of influential lobbying activity. The American Farm Bureau Federation, the National Farmers Union, and the National Grange are among the most powerful groups in Washington. Specialized groups, like the Associated Milk Producers, Inc. (AMPI), also have a large influence on farm legislation.

Some interest groups are organized around religious, social, or political concerns. Groups like the NAACP, the Urban League, and the Southern Christian Leadership Conference (SCLC) focus on economic interests as only one aspect of their efforts on behalf of blacks in America. Groups like the Sierra Club are concerned with legislation to protect the environment. Some interest groups, such as the liberal Americans for Democratic Action (ADA) and the conservative Americans for Constitutional Action (ACA), represent groups of people who share similar political ideas.

LOBBYING

When interest groups put pressure on the government to act in their favor, we call the activity *lobbying*. Interest groups today maintain professional staffs of lobbyists in Washington to protect their interests. These staffs often include former members of Congress or former employees of executive bureaucracies who are experienced in the techniques of political influence. According to the 1946 Federal Lobbying Act, interest groups must register with the clerk of the House and the secretary of the Senate if they want to influence legislative action, but this act is easy to get around and is frequently not enforced.

Direct lobbying usually takes place in congressional committees and executive bureaucracies. Although lobbying the legislature gets most of the publicity, lobbyists usually devote more attention to executive agencies in attempting to influence their regulations. It is sometimes said that the real decisions of government are made among lobbyists, bureaucrats, and congressional committees — the so-called "Iron Triangle." Lobbyists provide information about their industry or population group to committees and bureaucracies. In turn, lobbyists are given an opportunity to present their case for or against legislative proposals or executive programs.

Indirect lobbying may involve massive letter-writing campaigns run by lobbyists in Washington. The National Rifle Association successfully used this tactic to fight gun-control legislation. More subtle lobbying efforts involve "nonpolitical" public relations campaigns. Oil companies responded to criticism about increased prices with advertising showing their concern for the public welfare. Another form of indirect lobbying is for interest groups to persuade other interest groups to support their goals. If the American Automobile Association (AAA) favors new highway construction, it will try to raise support from other groups with similar interests, such as trucking companies, oil corporations, auto manufacturers, and construction unions.

Interest groups also use the courts to influence the political process. They may bring lawsuits and file *amicus curiae* ("friend of the court") briefs in suits initiated by others. Class-action suits are brought by interest groups in order to get a favorable court ruling on issues that affect a whole class or group of people in a similar situation.

Interest groups often use demonstration techniques to influence politicians. Strikes and boycotts are important techniques, particularly for labor unions. Some interest groups are skilled at using the media to spread propaganda about their interests. Mobil Oil Company, for one, publishes columns in advertising space purchased in major newspapers across the country. Some of these tactics were used by MADD (Mothers Against Drunk Driving) to gain attention for their campaign for stiffer penalties for driving while drunk (see box).

Campaign Contributions and PACs

The most controversial aspects of lobbying relate to elections. By contributing money to a political campaign, interest groups can reward a politician who has supported them in the past and encourage candidates to give support in the future. Often groups "hedge their political bets" by helping to finance the campaigns of two opposing candidates.

Interest groups can also work to defeat candidates they oppose. A recent well-publicized effort was that of a Christian fundamentalist organization called the *Moral Majority.* Founded in late 1978 by the Reverend Robert J. Billings and the Reverend Jerry Falwell (star of television's "Old Time Gospel Hour"), the Moral Majority claims chapters in all fifty states. In its fight against moral decay, the conservative group's goals include constitutional amendments to ban abortion and permit prayer in schools, and stiffer penalties for pornography and drug peddling. In the 1980 elections, the political arm of the organization raised money and targeted six liberal senators for defeat. All but one lost. Though the Moral Majority was not as successful in the 1982 elections, the group did register new voters and gain publicity for its efforts. Its campaigns also served as a warning to other moderate congressmen to watch how they stand on Moral Majority issues.

SPECIAL INTEREST GROUPS

One of the most important recent changes in the role of interest groups in elections has been the rise of *PACs (political action committees).* The PACs are organizations set up by private groups such as businesses or labor unions to influence the political process chiefly by raising funds from their members. These organizations are not new in American politics. Their model was created in 1955 when the newly formed AFL-CIO (American Federation of Labor and Congress of Industrial Organizations) started the Committee on Political Education (COPE). Through its national and local units, COPE not only contributed money to the pro-union candidates, but also organized get-out-the-vote drives and sought to politically educate its members.

MADD Lobbying

An example of a grassroots group that successfully mastered the techniques of lobbying in Washington emerged in 1984. MADD (Mothers Against Drunk Driving) was founded in 1980 by a California housewife, Mrs. Carrie Lightner, after her thirteen-year-old daughter was killed by a drunk driver. The group pushed for mandatory sentences for drunk drivers and for raising the minimum drinking age, pointing out that while teenagers made up 10 percent of the nation's drivers they accounted for 21 percent of alcohol-related deaths. By June 1984 MADD had gotten a bill before Congress that would reduce federal highway funds to states that failed to enact a minimum drinking age of twenty-one.

At first the measure was given little chance of passing. President Reagan opposed it and Senate conservatives saw it as an unnecessary federal interference in states' rights. MADD dramatized the drunk driving statistics in repeated appearances by victims and their relatives on television and before Congressional committees. The group gathered the support of twenty-six other organizations, including the national PTA, the American Medical Association, and Allstate Insurance. The groups met constantly, concentrated on key senators, and had their grassroots supporters write and telephone their congressmen.

In short order, the president reversed himself and the bill passed both houses of Congress overwhelmingly. Why? The president apparently saw a popular campaign issue on which he was on the wrong side. And in Congress it had become "an apple pie issue," which few dared oppose. MADD demonstrated it had changed popular and political opinion, and official Washington had little choice but to follow.

The big expansion in business PACs occurred in the late 1970s as an unintended result of campaign financing reforms (see pages 119–123). These laws, backed by labor, put strict limits on individual donations and provided for public disclosure. Before this legislation, money could legally go into campaigns in large amounts as individual donations from wealthy corporate leaders. There was thus little need for business PACs. The reforms backfired, however. Rather than reducing the influence of large "special-interest" contributions, they seem to have increased them. Corporations and trade associations organized PACs that more effectively channeled their money and influence into campaigns than individuals had been able to do. The number of PACs mushroomed, from 608 in 1975 to 3,525 by the end of 1983. By 1984 there were 1,500 corporate and trade association PACs, compared with 378 union PACs. Spending also skyrocketed. In 1974 interest-group donations to congressional candidates totaled $12.5 million. By the 1982 elections PAC contributions reached $83 million, a 50 percent rise from the 1980 elections. Whereas union PACs had outspent corporate PACs in the 1976 elections, by 1980 business and trade donations were far greater, and the gap was clearly growing. One estimate showed business groups outspending labor by two to one.

The 1982 congressional elections were the most expensive in history. Candidates for the House and Senate spent more than $342 million, a 43 percent rise from 1980. To win a seat in the Senate cost about $1.7 million, and getting to the House cost around $215,000. (Of course money doesn't guarantee victory. The biggest spender for a Senate seat — from Minnesota — spent $7.1 million and lost.) Although PACs gave about equal amounts to Republicans and Democrats, they gave a good deal more to incumbents than challengers. The increase in high-technology campaigns (computers and direct-mail efforts) reflected the availability of funds from PACs. As one expert said, "Whatever money is available to candidates, they'll spend."

Clearly this increasing spending has affected Congress. One congressman remarked, "It is a simple fact of life that when big money enters the political arena, big obligations are entertained." There also may be relatively little that can be done to block the impact of money and the creative ways campaigning politicians use to get it. As one lobbyist cynically concluded: "Trying to cleanse the political system from the evils of money is like writing a law ordering teenagers not to think about sex. . . . You don't need a law, you need a lobotomy."

Nonetheless, efforts have been made to restrain PAC influence. A bill first introduced in 1979 by 150 congressmen, the Campaign Contribution Reform Act, sought to limit the amount a candidate for the House of Representatives could receive from all PACs in an election and provided some public financing. The sponsors of the act worried that a number of corporations in the same industry (say, steel or energy) could separately contribute to a candidate. When combined, these contributions would be extremely large. Because they are likely to be lobbying on the same side of an issue, this "giving with a purpose" gives them great influence. Congressman David Obey (Democrat, Wisconsin) warned in introducing the bill that "the longer we wait, the harder it will be to kick the PAC habit" and concluded, "they may become too influential to curb in a few years." The bill has not passed.

The previous reforms designed to reduce the influence of wealthy interest groups have clearly failed. The role of such groups through PACs has increased. As long as these PACs are *a* factor in financing political candidates rather than *the* factor, they have a legitimate role to play. When they cross this narrow line, as many fear their rapid growth indicates, then more restrictions on their spending will be needed to keep democratic access open to the rest of us who lack abundant political dollars. Despite recent efforts by public-interest groups and grass-roots organizations, the interest-group system on the whole still has a strong bias in favor of those who have enough money to make their lobbying effective.

MEDIA

After an election year, few people would argue that the media are not powerful political forces. How we see politics and what we think is important are heavily influenced by the press and television. Politicians recognize those facts and act accordingly, often influencing the media at least as often as they are influenced by them.

An example of media influence over policy makers occurred in 1967 when, after a visit to Vietnam, CBS newsman Walter Cronkite turned against the war there. As the anchor for the evening news program. Cronkite was in no position to declare his opposition publicly. But thanks to the more critical approach he encouraged in the network's coverage of Vietnam, President Johnson reportedly concluded that all hope of uniting the public behind his war policy was lost. Evidently CBS's influence was a match for the president's.

The media have often been labeled "the fourth branch of government," rivaling the three official branches in political power. Although this power is overstated (the press can't actually *do* what the other three branches can), the way the media shape political attitudes makes them important to understand. In this part of the chapter we will attempt to come to grips with these questions: What are the media? What do media do? Who controls media? How do media influence politics, and how are they influenced by the other political players?

What Are the Media?

Media are *those means of communication which permit messages to be made public.* Media such as television, radio, magazines, and newspapers provide important links connecting people to one another. But these are links (unlike the telephone and the mail) with an important quality: they have the ability to communicate messages from a single source to a great many people at roughly the same time.

The major forms of media we will concentrate on are television and newspapers (see Figure 8.1). With more than 125 million television sets in the United States, television dominates the mass media. Its political influence is illustrated not only by an exceptional event, such as the presidential debates watched by more than 100 million Americans, but also by the networks' evening news pro-

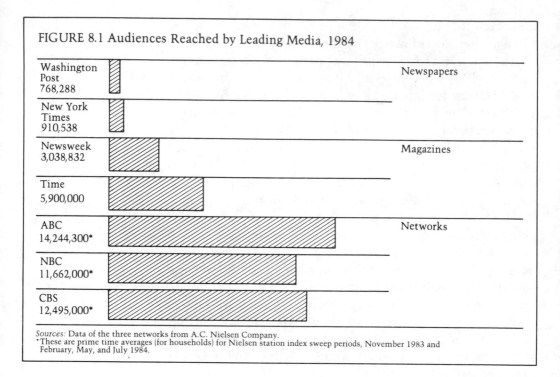

FIGURE 8.1 Audiences Reached by Leading Media, 1984

Washington Post 768,288 — Newspapers
New York Times 910,538
Newsweek 3,038,832 — Magazines
Time 5,900,000
ABC 14,244,300* — Networks
NBC 11,662,000*
CBS 12,495,000*

Sources: Data of the three networks from A.C. Nielsen Company.
*These are prime time averages (for households) for Nielsen station index sweep periods, November 1983 and February, May, and July 1984.

grams, which reach more than 45 million people each night. Television is in turn dominated by the three major networks, CBS, NBC, and ABC. These corporations each own seven television stations (the legal limit). But the *networks* function mainly as agencies that produce and sell programs with advertising to local broadcast stations called *affiliates.* (In 1980, NBC had 213 television affiliates; ABC, 204; and CBS, 203). The networks have contracts with their affiliates that enable them to buy or produce programs and to sell time to advertisers for the programs on a national basis. They then offer these programs, with ads, to the affiliates, who can sell time locally to advertisers — "and now a word from our local stations." The affiliates get the shows, and the networks get the national coverage, which allows them to sell time at $1 million for six minutes of advertising during prime evening viewing hours.

In recent years, the television networks have been challenged by a number of new technologies that are widening the choices available to media consumers. Almost 40 percent of the nation's nearly 84 million television households get their signals not over the air but through cables. News organizations, such as CNN (Cable News Network) and C-SPAN (Cable-Satellite Public Affairs Networks), have appeared to help fill the enormous appetite of a technology that already can provide upward of eighty channels per household. And nearly 100,000 American homes are connected to two-way cable systems, which allow them not only to *receive* television programs but to transmit messages as well. They can order goods from stores, transact business with their banks, and respond to opinion polls.

Newspapers are even more varied. They range in quality from the utterly respectable *New York Times*, which carries national and international news collected by its own reporters, to small-town dailies that relay crop reports and local fires but provide sketchy coverage of national events, reprinted from the wire services. (*Wire services* are specialized agencies like Associated Press (AP) and United Press International (UPI) that gather, write, and sell news to the media that subscribe to them.)

Newspapers are also getting less numerous and less competitive. At the turn of the century there were 2,600 daily papers in the United States. By 1984, though the population had tripled, there were only some 1,700. The same period has seen a decline in the number of cities with competing newspapers. In 1910 more than half the cities and towns in the United States had dailies owned by two or more companies. Today only 4 percent of United States communities have competing newspaper ownerships. Of our major cities only New York and Boston have three or more separately owned daily papers. We'll get to the reasons for this trend shortly.

What Do the Media Do?

The media provide three major types of messages. Through their *news reports, entertainment programs,* and *advertising,* the media help shape attitudes on many things — including politics.

In news reports, the media supply up-to-date accounts of what journalists believe to be the most important, interesting, and newsworthy events, issues, and developments in the nation and the world. But the influence of news reports goes well beyond relaying facts. The key to this power is *selectivity.* By reporting certain things (President Reagan's naps) and ignoring others (President Roosevelt's wheelchair) the media suggest to us what's important. Media coverage gives status to people and events — a national television interview or a *Time* magazine cover creates a "national figure." There are, of course, limits. Ohio Senator John Glenn, a former astronaut, was thought likely to benefit from the late 1983 release of a movie, *The Right Stuff,* based on the exploits of the early astronauts and featuring Glenn as a hero. The movie bombed, however, as did the Glenn campaign for president. And that was without the kind of intense scrutiny that is a part of media attention.

Perhaps the most important function the media perform has been called *agenda setting:* putting together an agenda of national priorities — what should be taken seriously, what lightly, and what ignored altogether. "The media can't tell people what to think," as one expert put it. "But they can tell people what to think *about.*" The attention the media give to the nuclear arms race, environmental pollution, or unemployment will largely determine how important most people think these issues are. How the problems are presented will influence which explanations of them are more acceptable than others, and which policies are appropriate as responses. Whether inner-city crime is associated with the need for more police or with cutbacks in urban welfare programs will help shape public debate. Likewise, if layoffs in the auto industry are linked to imports of Japanese cars — and not to the failure of U.S. automakers to modernize their factories — the result may be trade barriers rather than industrial aid.

Entertainment programs offer amusement and also give

FRED FLINTSTONE FOR PRESIDENT IN 2004?

An international study has shown that although only half the adults around the world could identify a picture of their national leader, 90 percent of American three-year-olds could identify a photograph of cartoon character Fred Flintstone.

Another survey asked four- to six-year-olds which they preferred, "television or daddy?" Forty-four percent replied, "Television."

---

people images of "normal" behavior. Certain standards are upheld by heroes, who are rewarded, and violated by outlaws, who are punished. In general, social and political conflict is changed into personal drama on these shows. The issue of black poverty is presented as whether a handsome young black actor can "go straight," stay in college, and turn his back on his violent street friends. People are rarely shown organizing to solve common problems. Instead they meet difficulties in their own homes or within their own consciences, even when these problems are shared by their friends and neighbors. Whether media are reflecting reality here is of course debatable.

Finally, the programs and news that media present are built around a constant flow of advertisements. Television programs are constructed to reach emotional high points just before the commercials so that the audience will stay put during the advertisement. Newspapers devote much more space to ads than to news, leading one English author to define a journalist as "someone who writes on the back of advertisements." The ads show generally well-off Americans enjoying the material rewards that come from conforming to the norms of society. Whether this image is true is again a very debatable and very political question.

MEDIA AND THE MARKETPLACE OF IDEAS

The framers of the Constitution believed that a free flow of information from a great many sources was basic to maintaining the system of government they set up. Ideas would compete with one another without restraint in the "marketplace of ideas." Fearing that the greatest enemy of free speech was the government, the framers added the First Amendment forbidding government officials from "abridging the freedom of speech, or of the press." The phrase has since been interpreted to include radio and television. The principle, however, remains the same, as Judge Learned Hand wrote:

> Right conclusions are more likely to be gathered out of a multitude of tongues than through any kind of authoritative selection. To many this is, and always will be folly; but we have staked upon it our all.

The ability of media to fulfill this goal of presenting a variety of opinion, representing the widest range of political ideas, has, to no one's surprise, been limited in practice. It is limited both by what the media are and by what the government does.

Media, such as television stations and newspapers, are basically privately owned economic assets bought and sold to make a profit. Profitability rather than public service has led to the increasing concentration of media ownership. The decrease in competition among newspapers mentioned earlier has been a reflection of the increase in *chains*, which are companies that combine different media in different cities under one owner. More than half the nation's newspapers today are owned by chains, as are many television and radio stations. Newhouse Publications, one of the largest chains, owns twenty-two daily papers, seven television stations, seven radio stations, its own wire service, and twenty national magazines including *Vogue* and *Mademoiselle.* Some people fear that chain ownership breaks the link between the owner (called the publisher) and the community that historically had helped maintain the quality of local newspapers.

The media industry is also very profitable. A 100 percent return on investment each year for a television station in a major city is not uncommon. One network affiliate in Miami changed hands in 1983 for $110 million. Network advertising revenues have climbed beyond $6 billion. Newspapers, though not as profitable, earn even more than the television industry — some $17 billion by the early 1980s. Although customers pay for newspapers, most of the papers' costs are covered by advertising.

Advertisers approach media with certain expectations. They want their ads to be seen or read by as many people as possible; they want the people seeing the ads to be potential customers; and they don't want the surrounding programs

or articles to detract from the ads. As a result, advertising encourages media content — whether news or entertainment — to be as conventional and inoffensive as possible in order to keep the customer satisfied. Tobacco companies have contracts that keep their ads away from articles linking cigarette smoking to health hazards. Airlines have standard arrangements with most newspapers that provide for their ads to be pulled from editions that carry news of commercial airline disasters. Television personality David Susskind once had a list of possible guests for his interview program cut by a third by his sponsor because of their political views. One of television's biggest advertisers, Proctor & Gamble, has a censorship code that reads in part: "Members of the armed forces must not be cast as villains."

Even newscasts, by attempting to be "objective," avoid antagonizing audience and advertisers but may deprive the public of the interpretation and debate needed to understand what's going on. In presenting two sides of an issue, the important questions the public should ask are: (1) *which* two sides are presented, and (2) what position is put forth as the point of balance — the "happy medium."

Media and Government

Government officials have a number of formal and informal means for regulating and influencing the media. Their formal powers include the requirement that radio and television stations renew their broadcast licenses with a regulatory commission, the Federal Communications Commission, every six years. Although this is usually a formality, the threat of losing a license can be an effective means of pressuring broadcasters hostile to a particular administration or policy. The FCC also tries to enforce certain standards in the industry. Its *fairness doctrine* requires that contrasting views on controversial issues be presented. If the stations do not give a balanced presentation, they may have to provide air time to correct the balance. In theory this requirement ensures that broadcasters do not use the valued public airwaves for propaganda. In practice it has sometimes been used against certain political views, as illustrated by President Johnson's use of it in 1964 to intimidate radio stations favorable to his Republican challenger, Senator Barry Goldwater. More important, the "fairness doctrine" has been criticized for encouraging media to steer clear of controversy — they make no money from providing free air time for dissenting opinions.

For campaigning politicians, the media are both opportunity and adversary. Between 50 percent and 60 percent of campaign money in the presidential races goes to advertising. Considerable effort also goes into engineering events that will be considered "newsworthy," and will capture free media coverage. Some of these activities have been called *pseudoevents* — not real events at all, but staged in order to be reported. Robert D. Squier, a Washington-based political consultant credited with putting Jimmy Carter in blue jeans

---

THE PRESS ON THE PRESS

"The duty of the press is to print the truth and raise hell."
— Mark Twain

"Newspapers start when their owners are poor, and take the part of the people and so they build a large circulation, and, as a result, advertising. That makes them rich and the publishers naturally begin to associate with other rich men . . . then they forget all about the people." — Joseph Patterson, publisher, *New York Daily News*

"If, over the last generation, the politicians and the bureaucrats in Washington have made such a mess of things with the press keeping some kind of watch over them, what would they have done with nobody watching?" — David Brinkley, television newsman

"The freedom to inform is now the counterpart of what was once the freedom to build castles." — Jean Sauvy, economist

DEALING WITH THE MEDIA

A Nixon aide's ideas for fighting media "bias" against the Nixon administration:

"Plant a column with a syndicated columnist which raises the question of objectivity and ethics in the News media. . . .

"Arrange for an article on the subject in a major consumer magazine authorized by Stewart Alsop, [William F.] Buckley or [James J.] Kilpatrick. . . .

"Have Rogers Morton [Chairman of the Republican National Committee] go on the attack in a news conference. . . . Have him charge that the great majority of the working press are Democrats and this colors their presentation of the news. Have him charge that there is a political conspiracy in the media to attack this Administration. . . .

"Arrange for an 'expose' to be written by an author such as Earl Mazo or Victor Lasky. Publish in hardcover and paperback. . . .

"Have outside groups petition the FCC and issue public statements of concern over press objectivity.

"Generate a massive outpouring of letters-to-the-editor.

"Have a Senator or Congressman write a public letter to the FCC suggesting the 'licensing' of individual newsmen . . ." — 1970 memo from Jeb Magruder to other White House staff members, in Thomas Whiteside "Annals of Television: Shaking the Tree," *The New Yorker*, March 17, 1975, p. 46.

and getting him to carry his own luggage during the 1976 presidential race, was hired by Senator Gary Hart's 1984 presidential campaign. Subsequently Senator Hart was seen chopping wood and imitating President John Kennedy's speaking style.

The examples of government leaders informally pressuring media are numerous. As seen in the box on "Dealing with the Media," the Nixon administration took a very hard line toward the media — with poor results. Most of the time presidents try to get on the good side of the media by giving favored reporters exclusive "leaks" of information and by controlling information going to the public through television, radio, and newspapers. This is called *news management*.

Press conferences have been used by presidents since Theodore Roosevelt to give the media direct contact with the chief executive. With radio, and then television, such conferences have allowed presidents to bypass journalists and present their views directly to the public. Franklin Roosevelt's radio "fireside chats" — which were briefly revived on television, with less success, by President Carter — were a skillful use of direct communication during the Great Depression. Television and presidents can also make uneasy partners. In 1960, presidential candidate Richard Nixon's streaky makeup, dull suit, and heavy beard made a poor impression in the first-ever televised debate with his opponent, John Kennedy.

Presidents generally have large staffs of media experts, speech writers, and public-relations people to perfect their images. As a former movie actor, professional speechmaker, and radio and television personality, Ronald Reagan understands the importance of television news to his image — and the importance of "visuals" to television news. His cheerful waves to the camera and smiling gestures to reporters have become common on newscasts, regardless of the substance of the report that the film illustrates. Says Sam Donaldson, ABC News White House correspondent: "If the visuals conflict with what I say, even sophisticated viewers will believe the visuals. If I say something that's negative and true, like, 'A shaken president, beset by dissent among his top economic advisers . . . ,' it won't be accepted by viewers who see Reagan happily kicking a patch of snow," Donaldson says. Similarly, if confronted with hard questioning from reporters, Reagan may "just jolly us along with a joke, point to his watch, or wave. The viewer sees a good-natured guy being nice about being pestered, but what Reagan's really done is duck another question," says Donaldson.

The president's polish in front of the cameras does not

come easy. Aides say he spends up to ten hours a week rehearsing speeches. Jimmy Carter, by contrast, averaged three hours or less. The result of Reagan's skill as "The Great Communicator" is an ability, unrivaled in recent presidents, to look and sound absolutely sincere, honest, and forthright. Says Bob Landers, a top commercial announcer since 1959: "You'll notice that when Ronald Reagan makes a mistake, he says the wrong word with the same sincere fervor as the right one. That's the skill of a professional communicator; it comes from years and years of 'being sincere.' "

Media and the Public

Political scientist E. E. Schattschneider pointed out that the "definition of alternatives is the supreme instrument of power." By "definition of alternatives" he meant the ability to set limits on political debates, to define what is politically important and what is not, and to make certain solutions reasonable and acceptable and others not. Media to a great extent have this power. Who influences the exercise of this power is another question.

Certainly the media managers (editors, newscasters, producers, reporters) have an important role in shaping political views. It was these managers whom former Vice President Agnew saw as too powerful and attacked as "the nattering nabobs of negativism." The owners of media, whether television networks or newspaper chains, play a part in selecting who will handle the day-to-day running of the press and what the general "slant" of the media they own will be. Advertisers, by buying space in some programs or papers and not in others, affect the messages the public gets. Government and politicians have a whole catalogue of laws and tactics to pressure media into conforming to their political priorities. And the public, by watching or not watching certain programs, by buying or not buying certain papers, by demanding or not demanding access to the *means* of free speech, can help shape the output of mass communications.

No matter who controls the media, the messages that the media provide usually reflect the power of those in the political game. The official players, through press conferences, paid public-relations experts, and news releases, can be fairly sure of reaching the public through the media. Through paid advertising those with wealth can claim media time to persuade the public to act in certain ways — usually by buying the goods they produce, but sometimes (like oil companies) simply by thinking well of them. The ability of nonelite groups to address each other, as well as their political representatives, is far more limited. The practice of giving air time to community groups has not gone very far in this country (certainly not as far as in the Netherlands, where any group with enough members is entitled to a certain amount of time on television each week to present its programs). Free speech without broader access to the *means* of free speech must remain a limited right for most people.

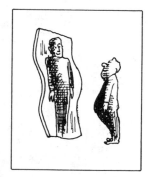

Case Study: Electing a Senator[2]

Elections provide an opportunity for the media and interest groups to influence who will be the players and what the policies of the political game will be. In Maryland Senator Joseph Tydings's 1970 campaign for reelection against J. Glenn Beall, the activities of these groups were vital. Not only did the voters and the two parties play a role, but interest groups and the media also were major factors in the outcome of the election.

[2] Adapted from John F. Bibby and Roger H. Davidson, "I Guess I Was Just Too Liberal: Joseph Tydings of Maryland," in *On Capitol Hill* (Hinsdale, Ill.: Dryden Press, 1972), pp. 25–51.

The Setting

The politics of Maryland are not that different from those of the rest of the country. Most of the voters in the state are found in the suburbs of Washington and in the urban areas of Baltimore. They are mainly Democrats and, when they are put together with conservative rural Democrats, one finds 70 percent of the voters declared Democrats and only 27 percent Republicans. This preponderance has meant a strong grass-roots Democratic organization able to dominate most local and state legislative offices. In statewide and national elections, however, where publicity and media campaigning are more important, the Maryland Republicans have done much better. In the eight elections for the United States Senate between 1945 and 1970, the Republicans won five times.

The Republicans didn't win one in 1964. Joseph Tydings easily triumphed over J. Glenn Beall, Sr., the incumbent Republican senator and father of Tydings's 1970 opponent. Tydings, whose father had also been a senator from Maryland, had run against the Democratic party organization's candidate in the 1964 primary and throughout his political career was not on close terms with the state party. As a young political reformer he continued his independent ways in the Senate. A strong supporter of civil rights legislation and urban programs, Tydings broke with the Johnson administration over the Vietnam War in 1967 and later endorsed his friend Robert Kennedy for the presidency. His opposition to the war and defense spending had labeled Tydings as a liberal.

Perhaps his most controversial action as a senator was in sponsoring gun-control legislation, which provided for federal registration of guns and licensing of gun owners. Although the bill did not pass, Tydings aroused the opposition of many gun owners, and in 1970 he was the "number-one target" of the national gun lobby. Trying to make this and other controversial stands a virtue, Tydings campaigned on the theme, "He never ducks the tough ones." Even though he lost 40 percent of the vote in winning the Democratic primary, the senator was considered a strong favorite for reelection in 1970.

So strong, in fact, that the Republicans had difficulty finding a candidate to run against him. Finally, following reports that the Nixon White House had urged him to run, Republican Congressman J. Glenn Beall, Jr., announced his candidacy. Beall had the advantage of his father's well-known name in the state and, having been in Congress only one term, was not strongly identified with any particular issue. As a pleasant, uncontroversial candidate, Beall could make Tydings and his record the main issue in the campaign.

The Campaign

Senator Tydings's first decision in seeking reelection was about whether to rely on the local Democratic party organization or build his own campaign structure. Given the party regulars' dislike of Tydings, he chose to create a volunteer organization. Along with some professional staff, the organization was made up of people who had worked in his first campaign, those whom Tydings had helped during his years in office, and others who stopped by to volunteer. At the same time, the Tydings campaign tried to stay on good terms with the party organization. The party was backing a popular governor running for reelection, and although most organization Democrats supported Tydings after he won the primary, few did much for him.

Campaigning followed the traditional route. Concentrating on the heavily populated areas, there was early morning handshaking at plant gates (workers are less eager to go to work than to go home in the afternoon), shopping-center tours accompanied by sports stars, coffees given by candidates' wives for women's groups, stops at local headquarters to meet volunteers and have pictures taken, and appearances at big events in the evening. As a campaigner Tydings was generally considered cold and aloof before large groups, whereas Beall was described by his ads as "a man you can walk up to and talk to."

Interest Groups. Interest groups played a prominent role in the campaign. Labor unions supported and gave money to Tydings, whereas more conservative business groups backed Beall. The most visible interest group, however, was the gun-control lobby whom Tydings had earlier antagonized.

Gun owners throughout the country poured money into a local group called Citizens Against Tydings (CAT). Some $60,000 was used for tens of thousands of bumper stickers and pamphlets, thirty full-page newspaper ads, and dozens of radio announcements. The National Rifle Association was not allowed to campaign directly because of tax laws, but the effort clearly had its blessing. Surveys had shown that the majority of Maryland voters supported gun control, but for the sizable minority who intensely opposed it, the issue was of prime importance.

Tydings took on the issue directly. Citing crime rates from firearms and statements by law enforcement officials, he accused out-of-state gun interests of "bullying" tactics and of lying about his bill. In one television ad the names and ages of Marylanders killed by guns were rolled slowly across the screen as Tydings appealed for his position on gun control. Although Beall benefited from the issue and opposed gun registration as useless ("criminals won't register their guns anyway"), he described himself as a middle of the roader. Beall was trying to avoid becoming a one-issue candidate, captured by an interest group.

Media. Media were used by both candidates to reach voters and also acted independently as an important player in the campaign.

Most of the $500,000 spent in each campaign went into media advertising. Tyding's ads stressed his experience, his independence, and his personal concern about people (to counter his image of being cold). Sixty-second television spots showed his contributions to the state and featured

Tydings with cops and kids. Media ads were also pinpointed to certain audiences: Appeals to working people were broadcast on country-and-western radio stations; the senator's wife made an ad aimed at housewives that was shown on daytime television; black politicians' endorsements ran on stations playing soul music. Press releases, endorsements, and challenges to opponents by both sides kept a constant stream of "news" going to the press.

Both candidates appeared for a series of television debates broadcast statewide. Because Tydings was better known, the debates probably aided Beall by giving the lesser-known candidate free exposure. Beall also benefited from the wide publicity given Vice President Agnew's hard-hitting attack on Tydings as a "radical liberal" and from President Nixon's campaigning in Baltimore. Beall saved most of his media money for the last week before the election. Concentrating on Tydings's record, he called him a "lackey" for "ultraliberal" groups.

But the press didn't act as a mere sounding board for the candidates. Most of the major newspapers of the region, like the Washington *Star* and the Baltimore *Sun*, endorsed Tydings. At least as important, however, was an article in *Life*, a photo-feature magazine, charging that the senator had helped a company he partly owned get a loan from the government. Tydings repeatedly denied the accusation and charged the Republican White House with pushing *Life* into running the story. The government agency involved cleared Tydings of any involvement in the loan decision, but the declaration of his innocence was not publicly released until after the election. Although it's not clear how many votes were changed, the Tydings staff devoted a tremendous amount of time to answering the charges, and once again Tydings was put on the defensive.

The Election

In spite of these setbacks, most of the polls throughout the campaign showed Tydings with a large lead. At the same time, he was widely disliked for his stands on partic-

ular issues and considered to be "not a personal senator."
Just as important, though only 27 percent of the voters considered themselves liberals, more than half considered Tydings one. Nonetheless, with two-and-one-half times more
Democrats in the state than Republicans, a popular Democratic governor running for reelection, and a spirited volunteer staff and adequate funding, Tydings still looked like a
winner.

He wasn't. Tydings lost by some 25,000 votes out of almost 1 million cast (48 percent to Beall's 51 percent, with a
minor candidate getting 1 percent). Perhaps the key factor
in his loss was the very light turnout in heavily Democratic
Baltimore, especially in the black and working-class districts. Only 46 percent of the registered voters showed up,
compared with 60 percent in previous non-presidential elections. A heavy rain and lack of enthusiasm for Tydings combined to make nonvoters significant in Tydings's defeat.

When the head of Tydings's campaign was asked why the
senator had lost, he replied, "Well, the left-handed Lithu-
anian vote didn't go for him." In a sense, he meant that the
margin was so thin and the deciding factors so numerous, it
would be impossible to point to any one cause. Tydings
blamed the gun lobby, which was quite willing to take the
credit. The senator's image of remoteness didn't help, nor
did the *Life* article or the party organization's indifference
to his candidacy. Tydings himself became the major issue
in the campaign. Pleasant J. Glenn Beall offered an uncontroversial alternative or, in Baltimore, an excuse to stay
home.

The fragility of Beall's victory was shown six years later
when the Democrats ran Congressman Paul Sarbanes and
easily retook the seat. Tydings, running again, was defeated
in the Democratic primary.

WRAP-UP

Both interest groups and media are links for people and
players to influence the political game. Interest groups provide the means for business, labor, professional, or citizens'
organizations to make their views known to government
officials. They unify people with common concerns to bring
pressure on decision makers through campaign contributions, lobbying, or publicity. Of course, those interest
groups with the most resources or wealth tend to be the
most effective. Reforms to limit the influence of wealthy
interests have been notably unsuccessful.

Media seem to be everywhere. Besides being both a communications link and a profitable economic asset, media
also influence politics. Through news reports, entertainment, and advertisements, media directly and indirectly
shape political attitudes. What is and is not broadcast and
printed establishes political figures, sets priorities, focuses
attention on issues, and largely makes politics understand-
able to most people. The media in turn are affected by the
corporations that own them, the advertisers that pay for
their messages, the managers who run them, and the public
that consumes what they offer. Government officials grant
them licenses (if they're television or radio), stage pseudoevents, and distribute or withhold information as it serves
those officials' interests. As both a political player and a
communications link, the media are among the most powerful, complex, and controversial influences in the American political game.

By providing access to the political game, interest groups
and media have the potential of allowing wide public influence over how the game is played. The rise of public-ori-
ented interest groups (consumers, environmentalists, and
others) and of media outlets for community groups (public
television stations) shows the possibilities of these instruments of power being used by a broader cross-section of the
public. But in the main the wide public use of interest
groups and media is more a potential trend than an actual

practice. These instruments of power remain in the hands of the powerful.

THOUGHT QUESTIONS

1. Which interests are represented best by American interest groups? How would you remedy the limits of interest groups so that groups that are now poorly represented would be guaranteed an equal voice?
2. Does the First Amendment right to free speech and a free press conflict with the commercial nature of media in the United States? Should the media be run to make a profit?
3. What are the arguments for and against changing the media to make them more available for differing political viewpoints? Must this change mean more government control and regulation?
4. Based on your study of voters and parties, and of Maryland's election of a senator, how would you run a political campaign like Tydings's? What issues would you stress? What voters would you focus the campaign on reaching? And what would you use (media, mail, personal contact) to get your message across?

SUGGESTED READINGS

Interest Groups

Berry, Jeffrey M. *The Interest Group Society*. Boston: Little, Brown, 1984. Pb.
   An expert gives an overall view of these groups, their organization, lobbying, and the political consequences of their activities.

Drew, Elizabeth. *Politics and Money: The New Road to Corruption*. New York: Macmillan, 1983.
   A new look at how campaign finance reforms have been evaded in practice, and the influence contributions of money give to the contributors of money.

Goulden, Joseph. *The Superlawyers*. New York: Dell, 1972. Pb.
   A good chat about the powerful world of the leading Washington law firms and the wealthy interests for whom they lobby.

Sinclair, Upton. *Oil*. New York: Washington Square Press, 1966.
   A well-known novelist's fiction about the corrupting influence of big money on politics.

Truman, David B. *The Governmental Process,* 2nd ed. New York: Knopf, 1971.
The classic examination and defense of interest-group politics in America.

Media

Crouse, Timothy. *The Boys on the Bus.* New York: Ballantine, 1974. Pb.
The amusing inside story of press coverage in the 1972 presidential campaign, with character studies of the major reporters.

McGinnis, Joe. *The Selling of the President, 1968.* New York: Pocket Books, 1968. Pb.
An entertaining acocunt of how Richard Nixon used the media to create and sell a "New Nixon" image to the American voter.

McLuhan, Marshall, and Quentin Fiore. *The Medium Is the Message.* New York: Bantam, 1967. Pb.
This is the only predominantly picture book in the lists of suggested readings. It is also the easiest place to start in understanding McLuhan, a guru of the 1960s, who has important things to say about the media today.

Ruben, Richard. *Press, Party, and Presidency.* New York: W. W. Norton, 1981.
Shows how the decline of party and the increased power of the media have affected the presidency in modern times.

Westin, Av. *Newswatch.* New York: Simon and Schuster, 1982. Pb.
A top producer of a network evening news show tells how the news is gathered and edited, and with what consequences for the political game.

Who Wins, Who Loses: Pluralism versus Elitism

Is it clear now what American politics is about? Or, in describing the players and rules, the terms and institutions, have we lost sight of the game? This chapter will give us a chance to step back a bit and ask a few basic questions: Who's running the game? Who (if anyone) has control? Who wins, who loses? Who plays and who doesn't play?

It should not surprise you much that there is no accepted answer to these basic questions. Rather, there are two major competing approaches to an answer. The dominant one, supported to some degree by most political scientists and most of the players in the political game, is *pluralism.* Its competitor, the *power elite* school of thought, has attracted a growing number of supporters on both the Right and Left who are critical of the American political game.

PLURALISM

Pluralism is a *group theory of democracy.* Pluralism states that society contains many conflicting groups with access to government officials, and that these groups compete with one another to influence policy decisions. Although people as individuals can't have much influence over politics, they can get influence through their membership in various groups. These groups bargain both among themselves and with government institutions. The compromises that result become public policy.

Several key concepts make up the pluralist argument: fragmentation of power, bargaining, compromise, and consensus.

Fragmentation of power is the pluralists' way of saying

that no one group dominates the political game. Power is divided, though not equally, among a large number of groups — labor unions, corporations, citizen groups, and many others. To gain their goals, the groups must *bargain* with each other. Within this bargaining process the government, though it may have its own interests, acts essentially as a referee. The government will make sure the rules of the game are followed and may intervene to help groups that consistently have less power than their opponents. It is also to the advantage of all the groups to follow the "rules of the game," for the bargaining-compromise method is the most effective way to win changes.

The result of this many-sided bargaining process is inevitably a series of *compromises*. Because no group has dominant power, each must take a little less than it wants in order to gain the support of the others. This accommodation is made easier because both the interests and the membership of the groups overlap. Groups disagreeing on one issue must keep in mind that they may need each others' support in the future on another issue on which they agree. An individual may even be a member of two groups with different views on an issue. His or her membership in both will tend to reduce the conflict between them. A black doctor may be a member of the American Medical Association (AMA), which opposes an expanded program of government-directed medical care, and also a member of the National Association for the Advancement of Colored People (NAACP), which supports such a program. As a member of both, he or she may influence the groups to reach a compromise with each other.

Underlying this bargaining-compromise process is a *consensus*, an agreement on basic political questions that most of the groups are reasonably satisfied with. This agreement on the rules of the game, and also on most of its results, is the basic cooperative cement that holds society together. Aspects of this consensus in American society are things like the general agreement on the importance of basic liberties, on the goal of equality of opportunity for all citizens,

on the necessity for compromise, and on the duty of citizens to participate in politics. The pluralists maintain not only that there is widespread participation in political decisions but also that the decisions themselves, and the procedures by which they are reached, have the general agreement (or consensus) of society behind them.

What we have then in the pluralist view is a process of bargaining among organized groups, and also between these groups and various agencies of the government. The bargaining results in a series of compromises that become public policy and determine who gets what, when, and how. A widespread consensus on the rules and results of this process keeps the political game from degenerating into unmanageable conflict.

Examples of Pluralism

Examples of the whole bargaining-compromise process, pluralists claim, are easy to find in American politics. When Ralph Nader, the consumer advocate, proposes that automobile makers be required to install more safety devices, such as air bags, in their cars, numerous interests get involved in turning that proposal into law. The car manufacturers worry about the increased costs resulting in fewer sales and reduced profits, and they may try to limit the safety proposals. Labor unions may want to make sure that the higher costs do not result in lower wages. Insurance companies may be interested in how greater safety will affect the claims they have to pay out. Oil companies may worry about the effect on gasoline consumption if fewer cars are sold because of their increased cost. Citizens' groups like Common Cause may try to influence the legislation so that it provides the greatest protection for the consumer. The appropriate committees of the House and Senate and the relevant parts of the bureaucracy will weigh the competing arguments and pressures as they consider bills covering automobile safety. The resulting legislation will reflect the relative power of the competing groups as well as the compromises they have reached among themselves.

One of the best-known studies attempting to support the pluralist model is Robert Dahl's book on politics in New Haven, Connecticut, *Who Governs?* Dahl tried to find out who actually has influence over political decisions in an American city. He examined several important issues, such as urban development and public education, to see who made the key decisions in these areas. He concluded that different groups influenced decisions in the different areas. The people who had the most influence over education policy were not the same as those influencing urban development or political nominations. There was, Dahl concluded, no one economic and social elite wielding political power in New Haven.

THE PLURALIST VIEW

"The fact is that the Economic Notables operate within that vague political consensus, the prevailing system of beliefs, to which all the major groups in the community subscribe. . . . Within limits, they can influence the content of that belief system; but they cannot determine it wholly. . . ." (p. 84)

"In the United States the political stratum does not constitute a homogeneous class with well-defined class interests." (p. 91)

"Thus the distribution of resources and the ways in which they are or are not used in a pluralistic political system like New Haven's constitute an important source of both political change and political stability. If the distribution and use of resources gives aspiring leaders great opportunities for gaining influence, these very features also provide a built-in throttle that makes it difficult for any leader, no matter how skillful, to run away with the system." (p. 310) — Robert A. Dahl, *Who Governs?* (New Haven: Yale University Press, 1961).

Criticisms of Pluralist Theory

Who Governs? and other studies supporting pluralist ideas have run into numerous criticisms. One major argument condemns pluralism for emphasizing *how* the political game is played rather than *why* people play it. Critics say that pluralism does not give enough importance to how benefits really are distributed. A consensus that equal opportunity is good is not the same as actually having equality. A system of democratic procedures may simply be a cover for the most powerful interests' getting their way. The argument often goes on to say that there can be no political democracy without social and economic conditions also being equal for all. Critics of pluralism often ask: What good are the rules of the game to the majority of people who never get a chance to play?

Critics of studies like Dahl's have pointed out that those with power cannot always be identified by examining key decisions. Powerful elites may *prevent* certain issues from ever reaching the public arena for a decision. Whether housing in New York City should be taken over by the local government or whether public transportation should be free are not the types of issues on which people get a chance to vote. The interests of the many are not necessarily reflected in the decisions of the few. The pluralistic appearance of politics may merely mask domination by a small number of powerful elites.

POWER ELITE

Many of pluralism's critics believe the power elite approach more realistically describes the American political game. Supporters of this approach see society as dominated by a unified and nonrepresentative elite. This elite secures the important decision-making positions for its members while encouraging powerlessness below. Those in power do not represent the varied interests in society. Instead they look after their own interests and prevent differing views from surfacing. American politics is not a collection of pluralist groups maintaining a balance of power among themselves, but an elite of economic, political, and military leaders in unchallenged and unresponsive control of the political game.

How the Power Elite Rules

This elite rules the country through the positions its members occupy, according to this view. Power does not come from individuals but from *institutions*. Thus, to have power you need a role of leadership in a key institution of the society — you have to be a full admiral in the navy, or the chairman of the board of directors of General Motors. These leadership roles are not open to everyone. They are open only to the rich and the powerful, the *ruling class* of the country, whose names can be found in the social register and whose children go to the "right" schools. This influential class controls the country's economy and is in basic agreement that political power should be used to preserve the economic status quo.

The results of this elite control, needless to say, are different from the pluralist outcome. Political decisions, rather than representing a consensus in the society, merely represent the *conflict* within it. Society is held together not by widespread agreement but by force and control: the control the elite has over the majority. The only consensus that exists is everyone's agreement that some have power and others do not. From this pessimistic viewpoint politics is a constant conflict between those with power, who seek to keep it, and those without power, who seek to gain it. The policies that result from the political game reflect the conflict between elite and majority and the domination of the latter by the former.

Examples of the Power Elite

A favorite recent example of power elite rule is the *Trilateral Commission*. Founded in July 1973 by David Rockefeller, among others, the organization consists of 300 "distinguished citizens" from North America, Western Europe, and Japan (hence the name *trilateral* for the three regions). Members are drawn from government, academia, business, and labor. Americans compose a quarter of the membership, whose elite coloring is strengthened by names like those of Democrats Jimmy Carter and Robert Mc-Namara, former head of the World Bank, and Republicans Vice President George Bush and Secretary of Defense Caspar Weinberger. To those within the Trilateral Commission, it is a policy-oriented group analyzing issues such as energy and world trade that face all three regions, and developing proposals for joint action. To some critics it looks more like a partnership of world ruling classes set up to manage an international system among themselves. Either way, it of-

fers an inviting target as a visible example of elite cooperation.

The best-known study of elite control in America, *The
Power Elite*, was written in 1959 by a sociologist, C. Wright
Mills. Mills maintained that American politics is dominated by a unified group of leaders from the corporations,
the military, and the political arena. They make most of the
important policy decisions, and they cooperate among
themselves because they need each other. Mills pointed to
the frequent movement among the three areas, with business leaders taking jobs in high levels of government, military leaders getting positions in corporations, and so forth.
He also discussed the similarity in background, education,
and social class, of the leaders in these different arenas.

Supporters of Mills's ideas often point to President Eisenhower's farewell address, in which he warned of a vast "mil-
itary-industrial complex" whose influence "is felt in every
city, every state house, every office of the federal government."

Criticisms of the Power Elite Theory

Critics have been quick to do battle with the power elite
theory. Although they may agree that only a few people
participate in politics, they argue that this minority of activists is much less unified than Mills maintains. They point
to Watergate, or Vietnam, or any presidential election, as
examples of how some elites check others. These elites
compete, and democracy consists of people choosing among
them through the vote. Besides, the critics argue, the political ideals of democracy are probably carried out better by
these elites than they would be by the uninformed majority.
Public surveys, these critics contend, have repeatedly
shown a lack of democratic ideals among members of the
working class. Hence greater participation by the people
might, curiously enough, mean less liberty and justice, not
more.

Another criticism aimed at some of the less careful power
elite theorists is that they are supporting a conspiracy theory. The argument of these theorists becomes circular:
American politics is governed by a secret conspiracy that
can't be proved because it is a secret conspiracy. The existence of such a unified, frequently evil, elite, critics charge,
is thus an unprovable assumption that serves only to remove politics from analysis and thereby allow the lazy to
hold on to their biases.

THE DEBATE

The debate between supporters of the pluralist and the
elite theories does not usually come down to *whether* a

THE POWER ELITE VIEW

"The power elite is composed of men whose positions enable them to transcend the ordinary environments of ordinary men and women; they are in positions to make decisions having major consequences. . . . They rule the big corporations. They run the machinery of the state and claim its prerogatives. They direct the military establishment. They occupy the strategic command posts of the social structure, in which are now centered the effective means of the power and the wealth and the celebrity which they enjoy." (pp. 3–4)

"Within American society, major national power now resides in the economic, the political, and the military domains." (p. 6)

"The men of the higher circles are not representative men; their high position is not a result of moral virtue; their fabulous success is not firmly connected with meritorious ability. . . . They are not men held in responsible check by a plurality of voluntary associations which connect debating publics with the pinnacles of decision. Commanders of power unequaled in human history, they have succeeded within the American system of organized irresponsibility." (p. 361) — C. Wright Mills, *The Power Elite* (New York: Oxford University Press, 1959).

small number of people dominate the political game. Even in the pluralist model, the bargaining among the groups is carried on by a relatively few leaders representing their groups. Clearly only a minority of people directly participate in politics, and this small group has more influence than the majority of people. The central questions are how *competitive* and *representative* these elites are.

To what degree do elites compete rather than cooperate with one another over who gets what, when, and how? How much conflict is there between, say, heads of government agencies and corporations over regulation and taxes? Or how much do they share views on major questions of policy and cooperate among themselves regardless of the "public good"? Certainly anyone reading the daily newspaper can point out numerous examples of conflicts over policy taking place among various groups in the political arena. Are these conflicts to be dismissed as mere bickering among a small unified group on the top? Or are vital issues being resolved in fairly open free-for-all contests?

Then there is the question of how *representative* these elites are of the broader public. Do powerful elites reflect, however imperfectly, the wishes of the majority? In recent years elite circles of our society have opened their doors, not always voluntarily, to minorities and women. Hasn't this made these institutions more representative or at least more aware of the wishes of formerly excluded groups in our country? Is this just tokenism, or have these elites fairly adequately "changed with the times" to represent public opinion?

Is there, in fact, a "public opinion," or has that been manipulated beyond recognition? Take, for example, the question of what we see on television. It is frequently charged that, in general, television programs are a "cultural wasteland." But do we know why? Some say it's because an elite seeking its own profits controls what we see. Others argue that the abundant violence and silly commercials reflect what the majority wants, as shown by numerous opinion polls. But do these polls reflect what people actually want or what they are conditioned to want? Is there a real public opinion, or just one produced by an elite to further its own interests?

There may well be no "right" answer to the argument between pluralists and the power elite school. It may depend on which political conflict we are talking about. Sometimes, as in the town meetings held in many New England towns, we can see a number of views being expressed on an issue and a fairly democratic decision being reached by the community. In other areas, such as the making of foreign policy, a small number of high officials meeting secretly decides policies that will affect the lives of millions. We might conclude that the issue being decided is likely to affect how decisions will be made. Pluralism may be most appropriate in describing a small community's politics, but the power elite approach may help us understand how foreign policy is made.

The concepts we adopt as most accurately reflecting political reality are bound also to reflect our own ideals. The pluralists and elitists are asking and answering not only what *is* but what *should be.* The pluralists state that politics in America is democratic, with widespread participation in decisions that most people agree with. The elitists say that politics is dominated by an elite that controls and manipulates the rest of us in its own interest. The elitists contend that basic changes in the American system are needed to create a pluralist democracy, whereas the pluralists argue that we have one and that the means for change are available within it.

What do you think? The position you take will be based not only on your understanding and study of politics, but also on your ideals and experience in politics. Further, the position you take will guide your political choices.

WRAP-UP

Throughout the book we have spoken about politics as a game. We have discussed the nature of the political game and what the competition is about. We talked about the rules of the conflict, many of them set forth in the Constitution, and how they have changed. Most of the book has been devoted to the governmental and nongovernmental players, their history, structures, and powers. And in this last chapter we have looked at two schools of thought that try to sum up and analyze who wins and loses and how the game is really played. But we're not quite finished.

We said in the beginning that most of us are spectators of the game — nonparticipants. But just as politics is a very special kind of game, so too are we a very special kind of audience. We *can* participate in the game and, by participat-

ing, change the way the game is played as well as its outcome. As a respected scholar of politics has written:

> Political conflict is not like a football game, played on a
> measured field by a fixed number of players in the presence
> of an audience scrupulously excluded from the playing field.
> Politics is much more like the original primitive game of
> football in which everybody was free to join, a game in which
> the whole population of one town might play the entire pop-
> ulation of another town moving freely back and forth across
> the countryside.
>
> Many conflicts are narrowly confined by a variety of de-
> vices, but the distinctive quality of political conflicts is that
> the relations between the players and the audience have not
> been well defined and there is usually nothing to keep the
> audience from getting into the game.[1]

We should not expect the powers that be to encourage us
to participate. Our participation will change their power,
and they cannot be expected to welcome that. But their
resistance should only strengthen our determination.
"Power to the people" need not be only a slogan and a goal.
It can be a fact as well.

THOUGHT QUESTIONS

1. Which of the case studies in the other chapters tend to support
   the pluralist approach? Which support the power elite approach?
2. Pluralism has been described as essentially "liberal," whereas
   elitism can be either "radical" or "conservative." Do you agree?
3. Which approach, pluralism or elitism, do you feel best describes
   the political game in your community? Give examples.

SUGGESTED READINGS

Broder, David S. *Changing of the Guard.* New York: Simon and
   Schuster, 1980. Pb.

---

[1] E. E. Schattschneider, *The Semisovereign People* (New York: Holt,
Rinehart and Winston, 1960), p. 18.

A noted political reporter examines the turmoil of the 1960s and 1970s and the new groups emerging from it, such as women, Hispanics, the New Right, labor, and business.

Dahl, Robert A. *Who Governs?* New Haven: Yale University Press, 1961. Pb.
A case study showing pluralism operating in New Haven's city government.

Hodgson, Godfrey. *America in Our Time.* New York: Vantage, 1976. Pb.
Written by a British journalist, this is a clear, intelligent history of what happened to America and why in the 1960s and 1970s.

Mills, C. Wright. *The Power Elite.* Oxford: Oxford University Press, 1959. Pb.
The well-known attempt to show that an elite governs America in its own interest.

Silk, Leonard, and Mark Silk. *The American Establishment.* New York: Basic Books, 1980. Pb.
A witty survey tracing the evolution of the American elite from a religious faction to today's keepers of the flame, with peeks at Harvard, The New York Times, *and the Ford Foundation.*

APPENDIXES

The Declaration
of Independence

THE UNANIMOUS DECLARATION OF THE THIRTEEN UNITED STATES OF AMERICA

When in the Course of human events, it becomes necessary for one people to dissolve the political bands, which have connected them with another, and to assume among the powers of the earth, the separate and equal station to which the Laws of Nature and of Nature's God entitle them, a decent respect to the opinions of mankind requires that they should declare the causes which impel them to the separation. — We hold these truths to be self-evident, that all men are created equal, that they are endowed by their Creator with certain unalienable Rights, that among these are Life, Liberty and the pursuit of Happiness. — That to secure these rights, Governments are instituted among Men, deriving their just powers from the consent of the governed, — That whenever any Form of Government becomes destructive of these ends, it is the Right of the People to alter or to abolish it, and to institute new Government, laying its foundation on such principles and organizing its powers in such form, as to them shall seem most likely to effect their Safety and Happiness. Prudence, indeed, will dictate that Governments long established should not be changed for light and transient causes; and accordingly all experience hath shown, that mankind are more disposed to suffer, while evils are sufferable, than to right themselves by abolishing the forms to which they are accustomed. But when a long train of abuses and usurpations, pursuing invariably the same Object evinces a design to reduce them under absolute Despotism, it is their right, it is their duty, to throw off such Government, and to provide new Guards for their future security. — Such has been the patient sufferance of these Colonies; and such is now the necessity which constrains them to alter their former Systems of Government. The history of the present King of Great Britain is a history of repeated injuries and usurpations, all having in direct object the establishment of an absolute Tyranny over these States. To prove this, let Facts be submitted to a candid world. — He has refused his Assent to Laws, the most wholesome and necessary for the public good. — He has forbidden his Governors to pass Laws of immediate and pressing importance, unless suspended in their operation till his Assent should be obtained; and when so suspended, he has utterly neglected to attend to them. — He has refused to pass other Laws for the accommodation of large districts of people, unless those people would relinquish the right of Representation in the Legislature, a right inestimable to them and formidable to tyrants only. — He has called together legislative bodies at places unusual, uncomfortable, and distant from the depository of their public Records, for the sole purpose of fatiguing them into compliance with his measures. — He has dissolved Representative Houses repeatedly, for opposing with manly firmness his invasions on the rights of the people. — He has refused for a long time, after such dissolutions, to cause others to be elected; whereby the Legislative powers, incapable of Annihilation, have returned to the People at large for their exercise; the State remaining in the meantime exposed to all the dangers of invasion from without, and convulsions within. — He has endeavored to prevent the population of these States; for that purpose obstructing the Laws for Naturalization of Foreigners; refusing to pass others to encourage their migrations hither, and raising the conditions of new Appropriations of Lands. — He has obstructed the Administration of Justice, by refusing his Assent to Laws for establishing Judiciary powers. — He has made Judges dependent on his Will alone, for the tenure of their offices, and the amount and payment of their salaries. — He has erected a multitude of New Offices, and sent hither swarms of Officers to harass our people, and eat out their substance. — He has kept among us, in times of peace, Standing Armies without the Consent of our legislatures. — He has affected to render the Military independent of and superior to the Civil power. — He has combined with others to subject us to a jurisdiction foreign to our constitution, and unacknowledged by our laws; giving his Assent to their Acts of pretended Legislation. — For quartering large bodies of armed troops among us: — For protecting them, by a mock Trial, from punishment for any Murders which they should commit on the Inhabitants of these States: — For cutting off our Trade with all parts of the world: — For imposing Taxes on us without our Consent: — For depriving us in many cases, of the benefits of Trial by Jury: — For transporting us beyond Seas to be tried for pretended offenses: — For abolishing the free System of English Laws in a neighboring Province, establishing therein an Arbitrary government, and enlarging its Boundaries so as to render it at once an example and fit instrument for introducing the same absolute rule into these Colonies: — For taking away our Charters, abolishing our most valuable Laws, and altering fundamentally the Forms of our Governments: — For suspending our own Legislatures, and declaring themselves invested with power to legislate for us in all cases whatsoever. — He has abdicated Government here, by declaring us out of his Protection and waging War against us. — He has plundered our seas, ravaged our Coasts, burnt our towns, and destroyed the lives of our people. — He is at this time transporting large armies of foreign Mercenaries to complete the works of death, desolation and tyranny, already begun with circumstances of Cruelty & perfidy, scarcely paralleled in the most barbarous ages, and totally unworthy the Head of a civilized nation. — He has constrained our fellow Citizens taken Captive on the High Seas to bear Arms against their Country, to become the executioners of their friends and Brethren, or to fall themselves by their hands. — He has excited domestic insurrections amongst us, and has endeavored to bring on the inhabitants of our frontiers, the merciless Indian Savages, whose known rule of warfare, is an undistinguished destruction of all ages, sexes and conditions. In every stage of these Oppressions We have Petitioned for Redress in the most humble terms: Our repeated Petitions have been answered only by repeated injury. A Prince whose character is thus marked by every act which may define a Tyrant, is unfit to be the ruler of a free people. Nor have We been wanting in attentions to our British brethren. We have warned them from time to time of attempts by their legislature to extend an unwarrantable jurisdiction over us. We have reminded them of the circumstances of our emigration and settlement here. We have appealed to their native justice and magnanimity, and we have conjured them by the ties of our common kindred to disavow these usurpations, which would inevitably interrupt our connections and correspondence. They too have been deaf to the voice of justice and of consanguinity. We must, therefore, acquiesce in the necessity, which denounces our Separation, and hold them, as we hold the rest of mankind, Enemies in War, in Peace Friends. —

We, therefore, the Representatives of the United States of America, in General Congress, Assembled, appealing to the Supreme Judge of the world for the rectitude of our intentions do, in the Name, and by the Authority of the good People of these Colonies, solemnly publish and declare, That these United Colonies are, and of Right ought to be Free and Independent States, that they are Absolved from all Allegiance to the British Crown, and that all political connection between them and the State of Great Britain, is and ought to be totally dissolved; and that as Free and Independent States, they have full Power to levy War, conclude Peace, contract Alliances, establish Commerce, and to do all other Acts and Things which Independent States may of right do. — And for the support of this Declaration, with a firm reliance on the protection of divine Providence, we mutually pledge to each other our Lives, our Fortunes and our sacred Honor.

The Constitution
of the United States

We the People of the United States, in Order to form a more perfect Union, establish Justice, insure domestic Tranquility, provide for the common defence, promote the general Welfare, and secure the Blessings of Liberty to ourselves and our Posterity, do ordain and establish this CONSTITUTION for the United States of America.

ARTICLE I

Section 1. All legislative Powers herein granted shall be vested in a Congress of the United States, which shall consist of a Senate and House of Representatives.

Section 2. (1) The House of Representatives shall be composed of Members chosen every second Year by the People of the several States, and the Electors in each State shall have the Qualifications requisite for Electors of the most numerous Branch of the State Legislature.

(2) No Person shall be a Representative who shall not have attained to the Age of twenty-five Years, and been seven Years a Citizen of the United States, and who shall not, when elected, be an Inhabitant of that State in which he shall be chosen.

(3) [Representatives and direct Taxes[1] shall be apportioned among the several States which may be included within this Union, according to their respective Numbers, which shall be determined by adding to the whole Number of free Persons, including those bound to Service for a Term of Years, and excluding Indians not taxed, three fifths of all other Persons.][2] The actual Enumeration shall be made within three Years after the first Meeting of the Congress of the United States, and within every subsequent Term of ten Years, in such Manner as they shall by Law direct. The Number of Representatives shall not exceed one for every thirty Thousand, but each State shall have at Least one Representative, and until such enumeration shall be made, the State of New Hampshire shall be entitled to choose three,

---

[1] The Sixteenth Amendment replaced this with respect to income taxes.
[2] Repealed by the Fourteenth Amendment.

Massachusetts eight, Rhode-Island and Providence Plantations one, Connecticut five, New York six, New Jersey four, Pennsylvania eight, Delaware one, Maryland six, Virginia ten, North Carolina five, South Carolina five, and Georgia three.

(4) When vacancies happen in the Representation from any State, the Executive Authority thereof shall issue Writs of Election to fill such Vacancies.

(5) The House of Representatives shall choose their Speaker and other Officers; and shall have the sole Power of Impeachment.

Section 3. (1) The Senate of the United States shall be composed of two Senators from each State, [chosen by the Legislature][3] thereof, for six Years; and each Senator shall have one Vote.

(2) Immediately after they shall be assembled in Consequence of the first Election, they shall be divided as equally as may be into three Classes. The Seats of the Senators of the first Class shall be vacated at the Expiration of the second Year, of the second Class at the Expiration of the fourth Year, and of the third Class at the Expiration of the sixth Year, so that one-third may be chosen every second year; [and if Vacancies happen by Resignation, or otherwise, during the Recess of the Legislature of any State, the Executive thereof may make temporary Appointments until the next Meeting of the Legislature, which shall then fill such Vacancies].[4]

(3) No person shall be a Senator who shall not have attained to the Age of thirty Years, and been nine Years a Citizen of the United States, and who shall not, when elected, be an Inhabitant of that State for which he shall be chosen.

(4) The Vice President of the United States shall be President of the Senate, but shall have no Vote, unless they be equally divided.

(5) The Senate shall choose their other Officers, and also a President pro tempore, in the Absence of the Vice President, or when he shall exercise the Office of President of the United States.

(6) The Senate shall have the sole Power to try all Impeachments. When sitting for that Purpose, they shall be on Oath or Affirmation. When the President of the United States is tried, the Chief Justice shall preside: And no Person shall be convicted without the Concurrence of two thirds of the Members present.

(7) Judgment in Cases of Impeachment shall not extend further than to removal from Office, and disqualification to hold and enjoy any Office of honor, Trust or Profit under the United States: but the Party convicted shall nevertheless be liable and

[3] Repealed by the Seventeenth Amendment, Section 1.
[4] Changed by the Seventeenth Amendment.

subject to Indictment, Trial, Judgment and Punishment according to Law.

Section 4. (1) The Times, Places and Manner of holding Elections for Senators and Representatives, shall be prescribed in each State by the Legislature thereof; but the Congress may at any time by Law make or alter such Regulations, except as to the Places of choosing Senators.

(2) The Congress shall assemble at least once in every Year, and such Meeting shall [be on the first Monday in December,][5] unless they shall by Law appoint a different Day.

Section 5. (1) Each House shall be the Judge of the Elections, Returns and Qualifications of its own Members, and a Majority of each shall constitute a Quorum to do Business; but a smaller Number may adjourn from day to day, and may be authorized to compel the Attendance of absent Members, in such Manner, and under such Penalties as each House may provide.

(2) Each House may determine the Rules of its Proceedings, punish its Members for disorderly Behavior, and, with the Concurrence of two thirds, expel a Member.

(3) Each House shall keep a Journal of its Proceedings, and from time to time publish the same, excepting such Parts as may in their Judgment require Secrecy; and the Yeas and Nays of the Members of either House on any question shall, at the Desire of one fifth of those Present, be entered on the Journal.

(4) Neither House, during the Session of Congress, shall, without the Consent of the other, adjourn for more than three days, nor to any other Place than that in which the two Houses shall be sitting.

Section 6. (1) The Senators and Representatives shall receive a Compensation for their Services, to be ascertained by Law, and paid out of the Treasury of the United States. They shall in all Cases, except Treason, Felony and Breach of the Peace, be privileged from Arrest during their Attendance at the Session of their respective Houses, and in going to and returning from the same; and for any Speech or Debate in either House, they shall not be questioned in any other Place.

(2) No Senator or Representative shall, during the Time for which he was elected, be appointed to any civil Office under the Authority of the United States, which shall have been created, or the Emoluments whereof have been increased during such time; and no Person holding any Office under the United States, shall be a Member of either House during his Continuance in Office.

Section 7. (1) All Bills for raising Revenue shall originate in the

[5] Changed by the Twentieth Amendment, Section 2.

House of Representatives; but the Senate may propose or concur with Amendments as on other Bills.

(2) Every Bill which shall have passed the House of Representatives and the Senate, shall, before it becomes a Law, be presented to the President of the United States; If he approve he shall sign it, but if not he shall return it, with his Objections to that House in which it shall have originated, who shall enter the Objections at large on their Journal, and proceed to reconsider it. If after such Reconsideration two thirds of that House shall agree to pass the Bill, it shall be sent, together with the Objections, to the other House, by which it shall likewise be reconsidered, and if approved by two thirds of that House, it shall become a Law. But in all such Cases the Votes of both Houses shall be determined by Yeas and Nays, and the Names of the Persons voting for and against the Bill shall be entered on the Journal of each House respectively. If any Bill shall not be returned by the President within ten Days (Sundays excepted) after it shall have been presented to him, the Same shall be a Law, in like Manner as if he had signed it, unless the Congress by their Adjournment prevent its Return, in which Case it shall not be a Law.

(3) Every Order, Resolution, or Vote to which the Concurrence of the Senate and House of Representatives may be necessary (except on a question of Adjournment) shall be presented to the President of the United States; and before the Same shall take Effect, shall be approved by him, or being disapproved by him, shall be repassed by two thirds of the Senate and House of Representatives, according to the Rules and Limitations prescribed in the Case of a Bill.

Section 8. (1) The Congress shall have Power To lay and collect Taxes, Duties, Imposts and Excises, to pay the Debts and provide for the common Defense and general Welfare of the United States; but all Duties, Imposts and Excises shall be uniform throughout the United States;

(2) To borrow money on the credit of the United States;

(3) To regulate Commerce with foreign Nations, and among the several States, and with the Indian Tribes;

(4) To establish an uniform Rule of Naturalization, and uniform Laws on the subject of Bankruptcies throughout the United States;

(5) To coin Money, regulate the Value thereof, and of foreign Coin, and fix the Standard of Weights and Measures;

(6) To provide for the Punishment of counterfeiting the Securities and current Coin of the United States;

(7) To establish Post Offices and post Roads;

(8) To promote the Progress of Science and useful Arts, by securing

for limited Times to Authors and Investors the exclusive Right to their respective Writings and Discoveries;

(9) To constitute Tribunals inferior to the supreme Court;

(10) To define and punish Piracies and Felonies committed on the high Seas, and Offenses against the Law of Nations;

(11) To declare War, grant Letters of Marque and Reprisal, and make Rules concerning Captures on Land and Water;

(12) To raise and support Armies, but no Appropriation of Money to that Use shall be for a longer Term than two Years;

(13) To provide and maintain a Navy;

(14) To make Rules for the Government and Regulation of the land and naval Forces;

(15) To provide for calling forth the Militia to execute the Laws of the Union, suppress Insurrections and repel Invasions;

(16) To provide for organizing, arming, and disciplining the Militia, and for governing such Part of them as may be employed in the Service of the United States, reserving to the States respectively, the Appointment of the Officers, and the Authority of training the Militia according to the discipline prescribed by Congress;

(17) To exercise exclusive Legislation in all Cases whatsoever, over such District (not exceeding ten Miles square) as may, by Cession of particular States, and the Acceptance of Congress, become the Seat of the Government of the United States, and to exercise like Authority over all Places purchased by the Consent of the Legislature of the State in which the Same shall be, for the Erection of Forts, Magazines, Arsenals, dock-Yards, and other needful Buildings; — And

(18) To make all Laws which shall be necessary and proper for carrying into Execution the foregoing Powers, and all other Powers vested by this Constitution in the Government of the United States, or in any Department or Officer thereof.

Section 9. (1) The Migration or Importation of such Persons as any of the States now existing shall think proper to admit, shall not be prohibited by the Congress prior to the Year one thousand eight hundred and eight, but a tax or duty may be imposed on such Importation, not exceeding ten dollars for each Person.

(2) The Privilege of the Writ of Habeas Corpus shall not be suspended, unless when in Cases of Rebellion or Invasion the public Safety may require it.

(3) No Bill of Attainder or ex post facto Law shall be passed.

(4) No Capitation, or other direct, Tax shall be laid, unless in Proportion to the Census or Enumeration herein before directed to be taken.[6]

---

[6] Changed by the Sixteenth Amendment

(5) No Tax or Duty shall be laid on Articles exported from any State.

(6) No Preference shall be given by any Regulation of Commerce or Revenue to the Ports of one State over those of another; nor shall Vessels bound to, or from, one State, be obliged to enter, clear, or pay Duties in another.

(7) No Money shall be drawn from the Treasury, but in Consequence of Appropriations made by Law; and a regular Statement and Account of the Receipts and Expenditures of all public Money shall be published from time to time.

(8) No Title of Nobility shall be granted by the United States: And no Person holding any Office of Profit or Trust under them, shall, without the Consent of the Congress, accept of any present, Emolument, Office, or Title, of any kind whatever, from any King, Prince, or foreign State.

Section 10. (1) No State shall enter into any Treaty, Alliance, or Confederation; grant Letters of Marque and Reprisal; coin Money; emit Bills of Credit; make any Thing but gold and silver Coin a Tender in Payment of Debts; pass any Bill of Attainder, ex post facto Law, or Law impairing the Obligation of Contracts, or grant any Title of Nobility.

(2) No State shall, without the Consent of the Congress, lay any Imposts or Duties on Imports or Exports, except what may be absolutely necessary for executing its inspection Laws: and the net Produce of all Duties and Imposts, laid by any State on Imports or Exports, shall be for the Use of the Treasury of the United States; and all such laws shall be subject to the Revision and Control of the Congress.

(3) No State shall, without the Consent of Congress, lay any duty of Tonnage, keep Troops, or Ships of War in time of Peace, enter into any Agreement or Compact with another State, or with a foreign Power, or engage in War, unless actually invaded, or in such imminent Danger as will not admit of delay.

ARTICLE II

Section 1. (1) The executive Power shall be vested in a President of the United States of America. He shall hold his Office during the Term of four Years, and, together with the Vice-President, chosen for the same Term, be elected, as follows:

(2) Each State shall appoint, in such Manner as the Legislature thereof may direct, a Number of Electors, equal to the whole Number of Senators and Representatives to which the State

may be entitled in the Congress; but no Senator or Representative, or Person holding an Office of Trust or Profit under the United States, shall be appointed an Elector.

[The Electors shall meet in their respective States, and vote by Ballot for two persons, of whom one at least shall not be an Inhabitant of the same State with themselves. And they shall make a List of all the Persons voted for, and of the Number of Votes for each; which List they shall sign and certify, and transmit sealed to the Seat of the Government of the United States, directed to the President of the Senate. The President of the Senate shall, in the Presence of the Senate and House of Representatives, open all the Certificates, and the Votes shall then be counted. The Person having the greatest Number of Votes shall be the President, if such Number be a Majority of the whole Number of Electors appointed; and if there be more than one who have such Majority, and have an equal Number of Votes, then the House of Representatives shall immediately choose by Ballot one of them for President; and if no Person have a Majority, then from the five highest on the List the said House shall in like Manner choose the President. But in choosing the President, the Votes shall be taken by States, the Representation from each State having one Vote; A quorum for this purpose shall consist of a Member or Members from two-thirds of the States, and a Majority of all the States shall be necessary to a Choice. In every Case, after the Choice of the President, the Person having the greatest Number of Votes of the Electors shall be the Vice-President. But if there should remain two or more who have equal Votes, the Senate shall choose from them by Ballot the Vice-President.][7]

(3) The Congress may determine the Time of choosing the Electors, and the Day on which they shall give their Votes; which Day shall be the same throughout the United States.

(4) No person except a natural born Citizen, or a Citizen of the United States, at the time of the Adoption of this Constitution, shall be eligible to the Office of President; neither shall any Person be eligible to that Office who shall not have attained to the Age of thirty-five Years, and been fourteen Years a Resident within the United States.

(5) In case of the Removal of the President from Office, or of his Death, Resignation, or Inability to discharge the Powers and Duties of the said Office, the same shall devolve on the Vice-President, and the Congress may by Law provide for the Case of

[7] This paragraph was superseded in 1804 by the Twelfth Amendment.

Removal, Death, Resignation or Inability, both of the President and Vice-President, declaring what Officer shall then act as President, and such Officer shall act accordingly, until the Disability be removed, or a President shall be elected.[8]

(6) The President shall, at stated Times, receive for his Services, a Compensation, which shall neither be increased nor diminished during the Period for which he shall have been elected, and he shall not receive within that Period any other Emolument from the United States, or any of them.

(7) Before he enter on the Execution of his Office, he shall take the following Oath or Affirmation: — "I do solemnly swear (or affirm) that I will faithfully execute the Office of President of the United States, and will to the best of my Ability, preserve, protect and defend the Constitution of the United States."

Section 2. (1) The President shall be Commander in Chief of the Army and Navy of the United States, and of the Militia of the several States, when called into the actual Service of the United States; he may require the Opinion in writing, of the principal Officer in each of the executive Departments, upon any subject relating to the Duties of their respective Offices, and he shall have Power to Grant Reprieves and Pardons for Offenses against the United States, except in Cases of Impeachment.

(2) He shall have Power, by and with the Advice and Consent of the Senate, to make Treaties, provided two-thirds of the Senators present concur; and he shall nominate, and by and with the Advice and Consent of the Senate, shall appoint Ambassadors, other public Ministers and Consuls, Judges of the supreme Court, and all other Officers of the United States, whose Appointments are not herein otherwise provided for, and which shall be established by Law: but the Congress may by Law vest the Appointment of such inferior Officers, as they think proper, in the President alone, in the Court of Law, or in the Heads of Departments.

(3) The President shall have Power to fill up all Vacancies that may happen during the Recess of the Senate, by granting Commissions which shall expire at the End of their next Session.

Section 3. He shall from time to time give to the Congress Information of the State of the Union, and recommend to their Consideration such Measures as he shall judge necessary and expedient; he may, on extraordinary Occasions, convene both Houses, or either of them, and in Case of Disagreement between them, with Respect to the Time of Adjournment, he may adjourn them to such Time as he shall think proper; he shall

[8] Changed by the Twenty-fifth Amendment.

receive Ambassadors and other public Ministers; he shall take
Care that the Laws be faithfully executed, and shall Commission all the Officers of the United States.

Section 4. The President, Vice President and all civil Officers of
the United States, shall be removed from Office on Impeachment for, and Conviction of, Treason, Bribery, or other high
Crimes and Misdemeanors.

ARTICLE III

Section 1. The judicial Power of the United States, shall be vested
in one supreme Court, and in such inferior Courts as the Congress may from time to time ordain and establish. The Judges,
both of the supreme and inferior Courts, shall hold their Offices
during good Behavior, and shall, at stated Times, receive for
their Services a Compensation which shall not be diminished
during their Continuance in Office.

Section 2. (1) The judicial Power shall extend to all Cases, in Law
and Equity, arising under this Constitution, the Laws of the
United States, and Treaties made, or which shall be made,
under their Authority; — to all Cases affecting Ambassadors,
other public Ministers and Consuls; — to all Cases of admiralty
and maritime Jurisdiction; — to Controversies to which the
United States shall be a Party; — to Controversies between two
or more states; — [between a State and Citizens of another
State];⁹ — between Citizens of different States; — between Citizens of the same State claiming Lands under Grants of different
States, and [between a State, or the Citizens thereof, and foreign
States, Citizens or Subjects].¹⁰

(2) In all Cases affecting Ambassadors, other public Ministers and
Consuls, and those in which a State shall be Party, the supreme
Court shall have original Jurisdiction. In all the other Cases
before mentioned, the supreme Court shall have appellate Jurisdiction, both as to Law and Fact, with such Exceptions, and
under such Regulations as the Congress shall make.

(3) The trial of all Crimes, except in Cases of Impeachment, shall
be by Jury; and such Trial shall be held in the State where the
said Crimes shall have been committed: but when not committed within any State, the Trial shall be at such Place or Places
as the Congress may by Law have directed.

⁹ Restricted by the Eleventh Amendment.
¹⁰ Restricted by the Eleventh Amendment.

Section 3. (1) Treason against the United States, shall consist only in levying War against them, or in adhering to their Enemies, giving them Aid and Comfort. No Person shall be convicted of Treason unless on the Testimony of two Witnesses to the same overt Act, or on Confession in open Court.

(2) The Congress shall have Power to declare the Punishment of Treason, but no Attainder of Treason shall work Corruption of Blood, or Forfeiture except during the Life of the Person attainted.

ARTICLE IV

Section 1.   Full Faith and Credit shall be given in each State to the public Acts, Records, and judicial Proceedings of every other State. And the Congress may by general Laws prescribe the Manner in which such Acts, Records and Proceedings shall be proved, and the Effect thereof.

Section 2. (1) The Citizens of each State shall be entitled to all Privileges and Immunities of Citizens in the several States.

(2) A Person charged in any State with Treason, Felony, or other Crime, who shall flee from Justice, and be found in another State, shall on demand of the executive Authority of the State from which he fled, be delivered up, to be removed to the State having Jurisdiction of the Crime.

(3) [No Person held to Service or Labor in one State, under the Laws thereof, escaping into another, shall, in Consequence of any Law or Regulation therein, be discharged from such Service or Labor, but shall be delivered up on Claim of the Party to whom such Service or Labor may be due.][11]

Section 3. (1) New States may be admitted by the Congress into this Union; but no new State shall be formed or erected within the Jurisdiction of any other State; nor any State be formed by the Junction of two or more States, or Parts of States, without the Consent of the Legislatures of the States concerned as well as of the Congress.

(2) The Congress shall have Power to dispose of and make all needful Rules and Regulations respecting the Territory or other Property belonging to the United States; and nothing in this Constitution shall be so construed as to Prejudice any Claims of the United States, or of any particular State.

[11] This paragraph has been superseded by the Thirteenth Amendment.

Section 4. The United States shall guarantee to every State in this Union a Republican Form of Government, and shall protect each of them against Invasion; and on Application of the Legislature, or of the Executive (when the Legislature cannot be convened) against domestic Violence.

ARTICLE V

The Congress, whenever two-thirds of both Houses shall deem it necessary, shall propose Amendments to this Constitution, or, on the Application of the Legislatures of two-thirds of the several States, shall call a Convention for proposing Amendments, which, in either Case, shall be valid to all Intents and Purposes, as part of this Constitution, when ratified by the Legislature of three-fourths of the several States, or by Conventions in three-fourths thereof, as the one or the other Mode of Ratification may be proposed by the Congress; Provided that no Amendment which may be made prior to the Year One thousand eight hundred and eight shall in any Manner affect the first and fourth Clauses in the Ninth Section of the first Article; and that no State, without its Consent, shall be deprived of its equal Suffrage in the Senate.

ARTICLE VI

(1) All Debts contracted and Engagements entered into, before the Adoption of this Constitution, shall be as valid against the United States under this Constitution, as under the Confederation.
(2) This Constitution, and the Laws of the United States which shall be made in Pursuance thereof; and all Treaties made, or which shall be made, under the Authority of the United States, shall be the supreme Law of the Land; and the Judges in every State shall be bound thereby, any Thing in the Constitution or Laws of any State to the Contrary notwithstanding.
(3) The Senators and Representatives before mentioned, and the Members of the several State Legislatures, and all executive and judicial Officers, both of the United States and of the several States, shall be bound by Oath or Affirmation, to support this Constitution; but no religious Test shall ever be required as a Qualification to any Office or public Trust under the United States.

ARTICLE VII

The Ratification of the Conventions of nine States, shall be sufficient for the Establishment of this Constitution between the States so ratifying the Same.

DONE in Convention by the Unanimous Consent of the States present the Seventeenth Day of September in the Year of our Lord one thousand seven hundred and Eighty seven and the Independence of the United States of America the Twelfth. In Witness whereof We have hereunto subscribed our Names.

Go. WASHINGTON
President and deputy from Virginia

ARTICLES IN ADDITION TO, AND AMENDMENT OF, THE CONSTITUTION OF THE UNITED STATES OF AMERICA, PROPOSED BY CONGRESS, AND RATIFIED BY THE LEGISLATURES OF THE SEVERAL STATES, PURSUANT TO THE FIFTH ARTICLE OF THE ORIGINAL CONSTITUTION.

AMENDMENT I[12]

Congress shall make no law respecting an establishment of religion, or prohibiting the free exercise thereof; or abridging the freedom of speech, or of the press; or the right of the people peaceably to assemble, and to petition the Government for a redress of grievances.

AMENDMENT II

A well regulated Militia, being necessary to the security of a free State, the right of the people to keep and bear Arms, shall not be infringed.

AMENDMENT III

No Soldier shall, in time of peace be quartered in any house, without the consent of the Owner, nor in time of war, but in a manner to be prescribed by law.

[12] The first ten amendments were adopted in 1791.

AMENDMENT IV

The right of the people to be secure in their persons, houses, papers, and effects, against unreasonable searches and seizures, shall
not be violated, and no Warrants shall issue, but upon probable
cause, supported by Oath or affirmation, and particularly describing the place to be searched, and the persons or things to be seized.

AMENDMENT V

No person shall be held to answer for a capital, or otherwise infa-
mous crime, unless on a presentment or indictment of a Grand
Jury, except in cases arising in the land or naval forces, or in the
Militia, when in actual service in time of War or public danger;
nor shall any person be subject for the same offense to be twice put
in jeopardy of life or limb; nor shall be compelled in any criminal
case to be witness against himself, nor be deprived of life, liberty,
or property, without due process of law; nor shall private property
be taken for public use without just compensation.

AMENDMENT VI

In all criminal prosecutions, the accused shall enjoy the right to a
speedy and public trial, by an impartial jury of the State and district wherein the crime shall have been committed, which district
shall have been previously ascertained by law, and to be informed
of the nature and cause of the accusation, to be confronted with
the witnesses against him; to have compulsory process for obtaining witnesses in his favor, and to have the Assistance of Counsel
for his defense.

AMENDMENT VII

In Suits at common law, where the value in controversy shall
exceed twenty dollars, the right of trial by jury shall be preserved,
and no fact tried by a jury, shall be otherwise reexamined in any
Court of the United States, than according to the rules of the common law.

AMENDMENT VIII

Excessive bail shall not be required, nor excessive fines imposed, nor cruel and unusual punishments inflicted.

AMENDMENT IX

The enumeration in the Constitution, of certain rights, shall not be construed to deny or disparage others retained by the people.

AMENDMENT X

The powers not delegated to the United States by the Constitution, nor prohibited by it to the States, are reserved to the States respectively, or to the people.

AMENDMENT XI[13]

The Judicial power of the United States shall not be construed to extend to any suit in law or equity, commenced or prosecuted against one of the United States by Citizens of another State, or by Citizens or Subjects of any Foreign State.

AMENDMENT XII[14]

The Electors shall meet in their respective states and vote by ballot for President and Vice-President, one of whom, at least, shall not be an inhabitant of the same state with themselves; they shall name in their ballots the person voted for as President, and in distinct ballots the person voted for as Vice-President, and they shall make distinct lists of all persons voted for as President, and of all persons voted for as Vice-President, and of the number of votes for each, which lists they shall sign and certify, and transmit sealed to the seat of the government of the United States, directed to the President of the Senate; — The President of the Senate shall,

[13] Adopted in 1798.
[14] Adopted in 1804.

in presence of the Senate and House of Representatives, open all the certificates and the votes shall then be counted; — The person having the greatest number of votes for President, shall be the President, if such number be a majority of the whole number of Electors appointed; and if no person have such majority, then from the persons having the highest numbers not exceeding three on the list of those voted for as President, the House of Representatives shall choose immediately, by ballot, the President. But in choosing the President, the votes shall be taken by states, the representation from each state having one vote; a quorum for this purpose shall consist of a member or members from two-thirds of the states, and a majority of all the states shall be necessary to a choice. [And if the House of Representatives shall not choose a President whenever the right of choice shall devolve upon them, before the fourth day of March next following, then the Vice-President shall act as President, as in the case of the death or other constitutional disability of the President.][15] — The person having the greatest number of votes as Vice-President, shall be the Vice-President, if such number be a majority of the whole number of Electors appointed, and if no person have a majority, then from the two highest numbers on the list, the Senate shall choose the Vice-President; a quorum for the purpose shall consist of two-thirds of the whole number of Senators, and a majority of the whole number shall be necessary to a choice. But no person constitutionally ineligible to the office of President shall be eligible to that of Vice-President of the United States.

AMENDMENT XIII[16]

Section 1. Neither slavery nor involuntary servitude, except as a punishment for crime whereof the party shall have been duly convicted, shall exist within the United States, or any place subject to their jurisdiction.

Section 2. Congress shall have power to enforce this article by appropriate legislation.

AMENDMENT XIV[17]

Section 1. All persons born or naturalized in the United States, and subject to the jurisdiction thereof, are citizens of the United

[15] Superseded by the Twentieth Amendment, Section 3.
[16] Adopted in 1865.
[17] Adopted in 1868.

States and of the State wherein they reside. No state shall make or enforce any law which shall abridge the privileges or immunities of citizens of the United States; nor shall any State deprive any person of life, liberty, or property, without due process of law; nor deny to any person within its jurisdiction the equal protection of the laws.

Section 2. Representatives shall be apportioned among the several States according to their respective numbers, counting the whole number of persons in each State, excluding Indians not taxed. But when the right to vote at any election for the choice of electors for President and Vice-President of the United States, Representatives in Congress, the Executive and Judicial officers of a State, or the members of the Legislature thereof, is denied to any of the male inhabitants of such State, being twenty-one years of age, and citizens of the United States, or in any way abridged, except for participation in rebellion, or other crime, the basis of representation therein shall be reduced in the proportion which the number of such male citizens shall bear to the whole number of male citizens twenty-one years of age in such State.

Section 3. No person shall be a Senator or Representative in Congress, or elector of President and Vice-President, or hold any office, civil or military, under the United States, or under any State, who, having previously taken an oath, as a member of Congress, or as an officer of the United States, or as a member of any State legislature, or as an executive or judicial officer of any State, to support the Constitution of the United States, shall have engaged in insurrection or rebellion against the same, or given aid or comfort to the enemies thereof. But Congress may by a vote of two-thirds of each House, remove such disability.

Section 4. The validity of the public debt of the United States, authorized by law, including debts incurred for payment of pensions and bounties for services in suppressing insurrection or rebellion, shall not be questioned. But neither the United States nor any State shall assume or pay any debt or obligation incurred in aid of insurrection or rebellion against the United States, or any claim for the loss or emancipation of any slave; but all such debts, obligations and claims shall be held illegal and void.

Section 5. The Congress shall have power to enforce, by appropriate legislation, the provisions of this article.

AMENDMENT XV[18]

Section 1. The right of citizens of the United States to vote shall
not be denied or abridged by the United States or by any State
on account of race, color, or previous condition of servitude.
Section 2. The Congress shall have power to enforce this article
by appropriate legislation.

AMENDMENT XVI[19]

The Congress shall have power to lay and collect taxes on incomes,
from whatever source derived, without apportionment among the
several States, and without regard to any census or enumeration.

AMENDMENT XVII[20]

The Senate of the United States shall be composed of two Senators
from each State, elected by the people thereof, for six years; and
each Senator shall have one vote. The electors in each State shall
have the qualifications requisite for electors of the most numerous
branch of the State legislatures.

When vacancies happen in the representation of any State in
the Senate, the executive authority of such State shall issue writs
of election to fill such vacancies: *Provided,* That the legislature of
any State may empower the executive thereof to make temporary
appointments until the people fill the vacancies by election as the
legislature may direct.

This amendment shall not be so construed as to affect the election or term of any Senator chosen before it becomes valid as part
of the Constitution.

AMENDMENT XVIII[21]

Section 1. After one year from the ratification of this article the
manufacture, sale, or transportation of intoxicating liquors

[18] Adopted in 1870.
[19] Adopted in 1913.
[20] Adopted in 1913.
[21] Adopted in 1919. Repealed by Section 1 of the Twenty-first Amendment.

within, the importation thereof into, or the exportation thereof from the United States and all territory subject to the jurisdiction thereof for beverage purposes is hereby prohibited.

Section 2. The Congress and the several States shall have concurrent power to enforce this article by appropriate legislation.

Section 3. This article shall be inoperative unless it shall have been ratified as an amendment to the Constitution by the legislatures of the several States, as provided in the Constitution, within seven years from the date of the submission hereof to the States by the Congress.

AMENDMENT XIX[22]

The right of citizens of the United States to vote shall not be denied or abridged by the United States or by any State on account of sex.

Congress shall have power to enforce this article by appropriate legislation.

AMENDMENT XX[23]

Section 1. The terms of the President and Vice-President shall end at noon on the 20th day of January, and the terms of Senators and Representatives at noon on the 3rd day of January, of the years in which such terms would have ended if this article had not been ratified; and the terms of their successors shall then begin.

Section 2. The Congress shall assemble at least once in every year, and such meeting shall begin at noon on the 3rd day of January, unless they shall by law appoint a different day.

Section 3. If, at the time fixed for the beginning of the term of the President, the President elect shall have died, the Vice-President elect shall become President. If a President shall not have been chosen before the time fixed for the beginning of his term, or if the President elect shall have failed to qualify, then the Vice-President elect shall act as President until a President shall have qualified; and the Congress may by law provide for the case wherein neither a President elect nor a Vice-President elect

[22] Adopted in 1920.
[23] Adopted in 1933.

shall have qualified, declaring who shall then act as President, or the manner in which one who is to act shall be selected, and such person shall act accordingly until a President or Vice-President shall have qualified.

Section 4. The Congress may by law provide for the case of the death of any of the persons from whom the House of Representatives may choose a President whenever the right of choice shall have devolved upon them, and for the case of the death of any of the persons from whom the Senate may choose a Vice-President whenever the right of choice shall have devolved upon them.

Section 5. Sections 1 and 2 shall take effect on the 15th day of October following the ratification of this article.

Section 6. This article shall be inoperative unless it shall have been ratified as an amendment to the Constitution by the legislatures of three-fourths of the several States within seven years from the date of its submission.

AMENDMENT XXI[24]

Section 1. The eighteenth article of amendment to the Constitution of the United States is hereby repealed.

Section 2. The transportation or importation into any State, Territory, or possession of the United States for delivery or use therein of intoxicating liquors, in violation of the laws thereof, is hereby prohibited.

Section 3. This article shall be inoperative unless it shall have been ratified as an amendment to the Constitution by conventions in the several States, as provided in the Constitution, within seven years from the date of the submission hereof to the States by the Congress.

AMENDMENT XXII[25]

Section 1. No person shall be elected to the office of the President more than twice, and no person who has held the office of President, or acted as President, for more than two years of a term to which some other person was elected President shall be

---

[24] Adopted in 1933.
[25] Adopted in 1951.

elected to the office of the President more than once. But this Article shall not apply to any person holding the office of President when this Article was proposed by the Congress, and shall not prevent any person who may be holding the office of President, or acting as President, during the term within which this Article becomes operative from holding the office of President or acting as President during the remainder of such term.

Section 2. This article shall be inoperative unless it shall have been ratified as an amendment to the Constitution by the legislatures of three-fourths of the several States within seven years from the date of its submission to the States by the Congress.

AMENDMENT XXIII[26]

Section 1. The District constituting the seat of Government of the United States shall appoint in such manner as the Congress may direct:

A number of electors of President and Vice-President equal to the whole number of Senators and Representatives in Congress to which the District would be entitled if it were a State, but in no event more than the least populous State, they shall be in addition to those appointed by the States, but they shall be considered, for the purposes of the election of President and Vice-President, to be electors appointed by a State, and they shall meet in the District and perform such duties as provided by the twelfth article of amendment.

Section 2. The Congress shall have power to enforce this article by appropriate legislation.

AMENDMENT XXIV[27]

Section 1. The right of citizens of the United States to vote in any primary or other election for President or Vice-President, for electors for President or Vice-President, or for Senator or Representative in Congress, shall not be denied or abridged by the United States or any state by reasons of failure to pay any poll tax or other tax.

[26] Adopted in 1961.
[27] Adopted in 1964.

Section 2. The Congress shall have power to enforce this article
by appropriate legislation.

AMENDMENT XXV[28]

Section 1. In case of the removal of the President from office or of
his death or resignation, the Vice-President shall become President.

Section 2. Whenever there is a vacancy in the office of the Vice-
President, the President shall nominate a Vice-President who
shall take office upon confirmation by a majority vote of both
Houses of Congress.

Section 3. Whenever the President transmits to the President pro
tempore of the Senate and the Speaker of the House of Representatives his written declaration that he is unable to discharge
the powers and duties of his office, and until he transmits to
them a written declaration to the contrary, such powers and
duties shall be discharged by the Vice-President as Acting President.

Section 4. Whenever the Vice-President and a majority of either
the principal officers of the Executive departments or of such
other body as Congress may by law provide, transmit to the
President pro tempore of the Senate and the Speaker of
the House of Representatives their written declaration that the
President is unable to discharge the powers and duties of his
office, The Vice-President shall immediately assume the powers and duties of the office as Acting President.

Thereafter, when the President transmits to the President
pro tempore of the Senate and the Speaker of the House of
Representatives his written declaration that no inability exists,
he shall resume the powers and duties of his office unless the
Vice-President and a majority of either the principal officers of
the executive departments or of such other body as Congress
may by law provide, transmit within four days to the President
pro tempore of the Senate and the Speaker of the House of
Representatives their written declaration that the President is
unable to discharge the powers and duties of his office. There-
upon Congress shall decide the issue, assembling within forty-
eight hours for that purpose if not in session. If the Congress,
within twenty-one days after receipt of the latter written declaration, or, if Congress is not in session, within twenty-one

[28] Adopted in 1967.

days after Congress is required to assemble, determines by two-thirds vote of both houses that the President is unable to discharge the powers and duties of his office, the Vice-President shall continue to discharge the same as Acting President; otherwise, the President shall resume the powers and duties of his office.

AMENDMENT XXVI[29]

Section 1. The right of citizens of the United States, who are 18 years of age or older, to vote shall not be denied or abridged by the United States or any state on account of age.

Section 2. The Congress shall have power to enforce this article by appropriate legislation.

PROPOSED AMENDMENTS:
(EQUAL RIGHTS AMENDMENT)[30]

Section 1. Equality of rights under the law shall not be denied or abridged by the United States or by any State on account of sex.

Section 2. The Congress shall have the power to enforce, by appropriate legislation, the provisions of this article.

Section 3. This amendment shall take effect two years after the date of ratification.

(D.C. VOTING RIGHTS)[31]

Section 1. For purposes of representation in the Congress, election of the President and Vice President, and article V of this Constitution, the District constituting the seat of government of the United States shall be treated as though it were a State.

[29] Adopted in 1971.

[30] Approved by Congress in 1972 and sent to the states for ratification. On October 6, 1978, Congress voted to extend the deadline for ratification from March 29, 1979, to June 30, 1982, marking the first time the ratification period was ever extended. The ERA was approved by 35 out of 38 states necessary for ratification.

[31] Proposed Amendment passed by Congress and sent to the states for ratification on August 28, 1978.

Section 2. The exercise of the rights and powers conferred under this article shall be by the people of the District constituting the seat of government, and as shall be provided by the Congress.

Section 3. The twenty-third article of amendment to the Constitution of the United States is hereby repealed.

Section 4. This article shall be inoperative, unless it shall have been ratified as an amendment to the Constitution by the legislatures of three-fourths of the several States within seven years from the date of its submission.

Index

AGAINST
THE LAW

AGAINST THE LAW

A JOE THE BOUNCER NOVEL

DAVID GORDON

THE MYSTERIOUS PRESS
NEW YORK

AGAINST THE LAW

Mysterious Press
An Imprint of Penzler Publishers
58 Warren Street
New York, N.Y. 10007

First Mysterious Press paperback edition, 2022

Interior design by Maria Fernandez

Library of Congress Control Number: 2021904774

ISBN: 978-1-61316-293-4

eBook ISBN: 978-1-61316-227-9

10 9 8 7 6 5 4 3 2 1

Printed in the United States of America
Distributed by W. W. Norton & Company

For Matilde

PART I

1

JOE WAS IN HELL. Or close enough. The suburbs of hell. And he was stuck there with a kid who was bugging the shit out of him.

"I'm hungry," Hamid said, sprawled face down in the dust, in the middle of nowhere, staring at nothing.

"Have one of those protein bars," Joe told him. Joe was lying beside him, holding the gun.

"Those shits taste like sawdust. Or actually, they taste like dirt. The same dirt that we're lying in, and that I already got in my mouth and nose and eyes and ass crack. I don't need any more. I want a chicken parm sub from Defonte's. And a hot shower. And a bed with clean sheets."

"Sounds good," Joe said. "You can buy me one too, with your share of the money. Meanwhile protein bars and bottled water are free. Pretend like you're working at Google."

Hamid snorted derisively but started chewing a protein bar, which shut him up for a minute at least. Joe wasn't used to chatter on this kind of mission. But he couldn't really blame Hamid either. He wasn't exactly thrilled himself. This was the last place he'd ever choose to be, though he found that he visited often enough, in his nightmares. It was a place whose memory he tried to erase, first with alcohol and later with opium and heroin. It was a place that had nearly killed him, and left him wounded, physically and mentally, wounds that had finally begun to heal. And now he was back. By choice. In hell.

Joe was prone, on a low ridge, in camouflage clothing, holding a rifle, and staring through a sniper's scope at a patch of desert road. All around him, poppy fields spread, their brilliant red and pink and purple petals open like eager mouths, smiling at the orange sun, which blazed and bled into the hills as it sank and dusk gathered between them. This was the province of Helmand in Afghanistan. He was waiting for a heroin deal to go down, and for a bandit to come out of hiding and steal it. No one Joe knew had ever met or even seen this bandit unmasked, but his name was Zahir al Zilli, Zahir the Shadow, and Joe was here to kill him. That was what brought him back to this place he never wanted to see again. That and a half million dollars.

❖

There was a time when Joe did this sort of thing for a living, full-time—as a Special Forces operative dispatched on top secret missions around the world. Then he retired, or the government retired him, erasing his records and sending him home with a bad case of PTSD and some substance abuse issues. Now assassinating drug lords with terrorist ties was more like a hobby, something he did part-time when he wasn't busy with his regular gig, as a bouncer at a strip club in Queens, not too far from the airport. However, this strip club (which was technically owned by an eighty-something widow) belonged to Gio Caprisi, a Mafia boss and Joe's childhood friend, and when the heads of New York's underworld—Russian, Dominican, Black, and Chinese gang leaders among others—decided they had to organize and fight any terrorist cells in the city, to protect their domains and keep the government off their backs, Gio had tapped Joe, and the bosses made him their sheriff, empowered to pursue his quarry throughout their territories. He was 911 for people who don't call the cops.

His last job for them had involved blocking a heroin shipment that was being used to fund terror overseas. Joe had stopped it and, with the help of his crew, had also stopped the smugglers, permanently.

But the mastermind behind it, a mysterious figure named Zahir, was still at work, hijacking heroin shipments bound for established US and European dealers and funneling the money to terror cells. Zahir's New York pipeline was still operational but no one knew how the heroin got in. And everyone back in this corner of the world, the source of the highly-sought-after "Persian" dope, was terrified of Zahir, though no one knew his last name, or what he looked like. Or those who did know were dead.

So Little Maria, a major player in the New York dope trade despite being less than five feet tall, had put a bounty on Zahir's head and implored Joe to find that head and cut it off. Generally speaking, not even a half million dollars would tempt Joe to pop over to Kandahar for a weekend of sunbathing and souvenir shopping but, despite grave misgivings, he felt a certain nagging obligation to close out this business once and for all. Not to mention, friends like Gio Caprisi and Little Maria are hard people to deny when they come asking a favor. And enemies like Zahir and his New York connections, whoever they were, are dangerous enemies to leave alive.

Joe's last caper had left some loose ends. For one thing, Maria had really wanted to get her hands on that Persian heroin, which had ended up literally in the wind, four million dollars' worth tossed out of the car window by Joe's colleague Yelena, who didn't approve of dope. And speaking of Yelena: an ace thief and deadly fighter, she and Joe were a good team at home and on the field, but her own past had caught up to her. A child of the Russian prison system and a natural-born criminal, the Russian secret service, the SVR, had set her free on the condition that she spy on the Russian mob in New York. Now, thanks largely to helping Joe, her life was in danger from both Moscow and Brighton Beach and she had vanished, most likely, Joe figured, never to be seen again. Then there was Donna Zamora. Donna was an FBI agent with whom Joe had repeatedly crossed paths, and while their relationship had been strictly professional—she was law, he was crime—she had ended up shooting a terrorist, Heather Kaan, to save Joe, under circumstances

the FBI might not understand. Joe had returned the favor by getting rid of the body. And so on . . .

Let's just say Joe's life, the simple life of a strip club bouncer who lived with his grandmother in Jackson Heights and liked to read and watch *Jeopardy*, had suddenly gotten very complicated, and the idea of settling it all with one quick trip to Afghanistan, and one well-placed bullet in the brain, had seemed to make sense. The money didn't hurt either. A half million dollars in cash could finance his very simple life for a very long time.

❖

"Look," Hamid said, interrupting Joe's thoughts. "Here they come."

At the end of the last job, Joe had taken a cell phone off the corpse of a dope smuggler, Felix Habibi, and though it hadn't contained much data, Juno had managed to trace a few calls and emails to a nondescript office building in Kandahar. However, all Joe discovered was a bland import/ export office owned by Wildwater Corporation, US military contractors. That didn't mean much. Maybe someone who worked there was involved. Maybe just someone who used their Wi-Fi. Maybe nothing at all.

Then Maria got a tip from her local sources. There was a big exchange going down; a large shipment of heroin processed from these opium fields would be sold to traffickers, who would smuggle it to Albania, then on to Italy and the rest of Europe. It was just the sort of target Zahir chose, so Joe and Hamid had driven out in their Range Rover Defender and set up here, Hamid with a pair of high-powered binoculars and Joe with the rifle. Joe was white and lean, in his thirties, in worn desert camo pants and jacket, an old black T-shirt and brand-new sunglasses, his last pair having gotten smashed in a fight at the club. His hair was a bit ragged and he had a few day's scruff on his chin. Hamid, short and boxy, with a heavily muscled upper body, was in jeans, Nikes, and a black hoodie, his hair and goatee freshly trimmed.

Hamid was his translator. He was a fluent speaker of Farsi, known locally as Dari, but he wasn't local. He was from Brooklyn, and a tough,

somewhat troubled kid, though not by Kandahar standards. He'd dropped out of school, gotten into some minor scrapes with the law, mostly just fighting and dealing weed or molly, but enough to make him the black sheep of his high-achieving family. This was his chance to make them proud, as proud as they were of his older sister the doctor or his brother the social worker. Joe was well-liked in the Muslim community, where he was known, or at least rumored, to have stopped a large-scale terror attack, sparing New York thousands of deaths, and sparing New York's Muslims the inevitable reprisals they'd suffer, despite the fact that many of them, like Hamid's own Persian parents, had come to New York fleeing religious extremism and violence. When Joe took on this new mission, his young friend Juno, a tech genius and delinquent from Bed-Stuy who often worked with Joe, had recruited Hamid, whom he knew from the clubs. Juno told him he'd make enough to open his own club, and get to roll with a kick-ass secret-agent type. Instead he was bored to death, lying in the dirt or staring at buildings all day and night, or watching Joe read from the paperback that was poking from his back pocket now: *Selected Poems*, the cover said; selected, Hamid guessed, by some guy named Rilke. What kind of person reads poems for fun?

But now, sure enough, a small caravan of two SUVs, one open and one closed, was making its way over the tracks that led through the hills. The open one held armed men in *khet*—the long, tunic-like top—and *partug*—the loose-fitting pleated trousers, folded at the waist. Some wore vests or military jackets and all had *kufi* or turbans on their heads. The second vehicle would have the dope, plastic-wrapped kilos packed into boxes or sewn into sacks.

Adjusting his scope, Joe scanned the landscape, and spotted a rising dust trail coming the other way, from the nearest small village. There was a closed Jeep and behind that a surplus military truck. The buyer. This would be the dope trader Maria knew about, an established supplier who would repack the goods and, through bribes or deceit, send them on to their next stop, the price doubling each time they changed hands. Depending on the quality, the bricks in those trucks might be selling

for three to six thousand dollars each, less for a large purchase of course. By the time they hit New York, they'd be worth fifty to eighty thousand a piece. Opium production dwarfed all other sectors of the Afghani economy and war had been good for business. Lack of government control had led to a surging crop, which would lead to a flooded market, which meant lower prices, higher quality, and eventually, dead junkies.

But Joe wasn't here about any of that. The way you survived in this world was to mind your own business and watch your own ass. His job was to kill Zahir, if he showed. What difference did it make if one or two more trucks full of dope got through or not?

The dust trails converged and, as dusk crept over the raw landscape, the earth shifted between shades of brown and tan, rust and red. Below him was the road, then another lower ridge, and beyond that, the poppy fields, a sea of flowers, the fat petals like soft, sleepy heads, drooping atop their stalks, like an army of angels descended to earth. He'd seen men die in these fields. He'd seen US soldiers patrolling between the flowers, and children tending the crops. He'd seen civilians blown up accidentally by American ordnance and his fellow soldiers tortured by insurgents. He knew that 42% of the world's opium came from this one province, more than all of Burma, the number two supplier after Afghanistan. He knew that opium fed the worldwide drug epidemic and financed the Taliban who made life hell for so many of those who lived here. But it was still a beautiful sight. That was the thing about hell; it could look a lot like heaven.

Then, as the two parties met and halted, Joe caught a glimpse of something else, a small dark shape moving on the horizon. It was just a flicker, with the sun behind it, and then it was gone, but Joe knew; someone else was there.

"Don't move," he told Hamid, who was fidgeting. "This is it."

The exchange happened fast. Two men stepped from the lead vehicles, and Joe watched through the scope as the money changed hands, a leather grip that the seller unzipped, checked and then re-shut. He yelled a command and his men began quickly unloading, handing off the packages to

the buyer's men, who quickly loaded it onto the truck. Other men stood guard, standing in a loose perimeter, weapons drawn. In a few minutes it was done. They climbed back into the trucks and, in a cloud of dust, turned around and raced off the way they'd come.

"Shit . . ." Hamid muttered. "That's it, I guess."

"Shhh . . ." Joe silenced him. "Just wait."

He remained still, moving only enough to refocus the scope, because the black speck he'd seen before, or almost seen, was on the move. Really that was all he saw, movement, a gray shape moving in the gray air, now that the sun had disappeared behind the horizon. But something was moving fast now, and he heard a faint buzz as well, like a mosquito. The mosquito darted along the far ridge, then down a winding path to the road in the direction the seller had gone. Joe focused: it was a figure on a motorbike, dark clothes and scarf billowing, rifle strapped to its back.

"Let's go," Joe said and rolled back, then got to his feet. Hamid followed, shouting questions, but Joe didn't answer as he scrambled down the steep hill to where the Defender was parked out of sight. They got in and Joe pulled out, wrestling the wheel as they plunged down the rutted path, then hitting the gas as they reached the road. He sped until he heard the whine of the motorcycle and then eased back. Now they were following the biker, who was in turn, it seemed, following the money.

"Is that Zahir?" Hamid asked, catching his breath between guzzles of water.

"Maybe," Joe said. He opened a water and drank. The MO was all wrong. Zahir stole the dope not the dough. There might be a hundred or hundred and fifty thousand dollars of whatever currency in that bag. Not a bad score, but nothing compared to what that product was worth on the streets of New York. And what was the point of having a network like Zahir's if you weren't going to use it? Plus, Zahir wrote his name in blood and terror. Take the dope and the money, leave a pile of corpses and burning trucks. That was the way to get people's attention in this neighborhood. One armed man on a bike wasn't especially impressive. Though, Joe supposed, it depended on the man.

Night fell as they reached the village, just a few buildings around a market square, with homes and small shops staggered along the dirt streets from there. There was no one in sight. He moved slowly, cruising around the square at walking speed. Just then a man came running, sprinting right past the truck without a glance. Joe nosed the truck into the lane he'd come from. Two more young men ran by.

"Zahir!" one yelled. *"Zahir darad meeyayad!"*

Now Joe saw a café, lit from within. The bike was parked out front, beside the dust-covered Jeep the seller had been driving. Men rushed through the door and scattered.

"Zahir!" one screamed as if warning the town about a fire.

"Al Zilli! Al Zilli!" another yelled as he bolted past. The shadow. Joe parked.

"Wait here," he told Hamid.

"Don't you need me to translate?"

"Zahir!" an old man yelled as he quickly hobbled by on a cane. A younger, wider man raced past him, tripped and fell flat, then jumped up and fled.

"I think I get the gist," Joe told him. "The keys are in it. If I'm not back in ten minutes, drive back to the hotel. If I'm not back there by tomorrow, go home."

"What if you don't come back at all?" Hamid asked, suddenly quieter.

Joe smiled and patted his arm, reassuringly. "Then at least you got those free protein bars." Leaving the sniper's rifle, he took his Beretta M9 pistol and jumped from the truck. "See you soon, kid."

Then he crossed the road to the café. He removed the safety on his gun and positioned it in front of him, proceeding carefully, though the men who ran by him, all heading the other way, barely gave him a glance. He approached the door, just a curtain hung in the archway, and went in low, thrusting the curtain aside. The café was deserted. Glasses of tea and hookahs sat abandoned. Stools were overturned. A cat wandered by, unconcerned. A sudden whistle made him swing left, pistol aimed. It was just a kettle boiling. More tea. Joe quickly checked behind the bar, turned

the heat off under the kettle, and then made his way to the back door. He suspected there was another room where opium was smoked, a scene with which he was all too familiar. He eased the door open slowly with his free hand, then stepped into the dimness. Immediately he smelled it, that odd but distinctive scent, somewhere between gooey brownies and rotting fish. The perfume that the poppy only releases in smoke. The scent of dreams and slow, happy death. A few men lay on their backs, sprawled on thin mats, their heads propped on pillows, eyes closed or seeing nothing in the gloom. They hadn't run when Zahir came through. They were beyond care. That was what you paid for here: to not give a shit for an hour or a night. Joe crossed the room, leaving the lotus-eaters undisturbed, and crept through the exit, which led to an alley in the rear.

There was Zahir. A figure all in black, black tunic, loose black trousers, a black turban, and over his face, a cotton ski mask. He wore gloves and held a rifle pointed at the seller, a bearded man in his forties, who kneeled now, hands clasped together, as if earnestly praying and offering up the gift of the zippered bag, which was on the ground before him. Just as Joe entered, Zahir reacted, leaping like a cat, and somersaulting out of his line of fire. But Joe didn't fire. There were windows behind Zahir, and he was afraid of his bullets entering the neighboring building. Instead he moved too, ducking right, trying to take cover against the wall while training his pistol on Zahir, whose gun pointed back at him. The kneeling man trembled between them, with both guns leveled right at his skull. They were in a standoff. If either moved, even to take a shot, they'd be exposed to the other. Joe stayed perfectly still.

That's when Zahir, while keeping his gun on Joe, began to slowly lift his left hand, palm out, as though holding traffic. "Don't shoot me, Joe," the figure said in a familiar voice, peeling away the mask and turban. Blond hair tumbled out.

Smiling, Joe lowered his gun.

"Hi Yelena."

2

DONNA WAS IN HELL. But at least she had her pal Andy there with her. He was the one who, as they walked into the training center that morning, had quoted Dorothy Parker, and whispered in her ear, "What fresh hell is this?"

Hell, at least for today, was FBI Terror Response Training. Important of course, and extremely serious business, but they'd been getting sent to new sessions every time the alert level bumped up to orange, which was rather often lately. And while it was supposed to be mandatory for all agents, those on active field assignments could postpone it indefinitely, which only reconfirmed how inactive her own career was, if she was back down here again, stuck in school while her teammates were out playing, catching, and scoring in the field.

Special Agent Donna Zamora worked the tip line in the basement of the FBI's New York office, sorting through the avalanche of information that poured in every day and sifting for gold. Special Agent Andrew Newton was her best friend in the office, and as a gay Black agent and a Latina they felt the need to support each other in what often felt like the Fraternity of Boy Investigators. Even worse, Donna's ex-husband, a devious CIA agent, had deliberately undermined her, planting doubts about her integrity, suspicions that she might be in league with mobster Gio Caprisi and sleeping with Gio's known associate, Joe Brody. None of which was true. But what even Andy didn't know was that Gio had,

in his cockeyed scheme to protect New York from terror and keep it safe for crime, handed her key information in two investigations, and that she was, against her better judgment, entangled with Joe—emotionally, if not physically or legally. Even her mom had become pals with Joe's grandmother. Their last interaction had led to several dead terrorists and a destroyed heroin shipment, all evidence of which Joe had conveniently made disappear. So she was clean—in her record and conscience. But still, confirming that you are *not* working for the Mafia is hardly the ticket to promotion. Which is how she ended up back at Terror Response Training. Again. Today's topic? Neutralizing Explosive Devices.

Wearing safety goggles and gloves, with a small tool kit beside her, Donna was seated at a long table with her fellow trainees, each preparing to defuse a make-believe bomb. Hers was a cluster of wires, pipes, and electronics packed into a Hello Kitty rolling suitcase. Donna peered suspiciously at the clean-cut men around the table, earnestly bent over their suitcases, wondering if they'd deliberately given her the pink one.

"One minute . . ." the instructor clicked his stopwatch. "Go!"

As it happened, even if they did stick her with the girly-bomb, they'd done her a favor: she recognized this device as almost identical to one she'd worked on in her last course. She quickly unscrewed the cover from the timing mechanism, a cheap digital clock set for thirty seconds, and rewired it to keep it from knowing how much time had really elapsed, then located the main wire set to trigger the ignition. Her stomach grumbled. She'd been too busy feeding her daughter Larissa that morning to eat herself.

"Was that a bomb I heard?" Andy asked in a whisper.

"Shhh . . ." Donna answered.

"Ten seconds . . ." the instructor said. "Counting down to . . ."

"Lunch," Andy whispered beside her, and this time she couldn't help giggling.

"Something funny, Zamora?" the instructor barked.

"No, sir!"

"Okay then, two seconds . . ."

Suddenly flustered, Donna snipped the wire. Her bomb buzzed loudly.

"Trip wire, Zamora," the instructor said. "You killed us all. At least you died laughing."

"Sorry, sir."

"And Newton . . ."

"Yes, sir?"

"At least you were right about one thing today. It is time for lunch."

❖

"I'm sorry, Donna, lunch is on me," Andy told her as they walked to the choose-your-own-salad place.

"I'm getting salmon. Serves you right. Now I've got to retake that class next month."

"I know, I know. Ari hates it too, always asking how come I have to be such a wiseass."

"Exactly, listen to your husband. The secret to a happy marriage is less wisdom. More ass."

Andy chuckled as they entered the powerfully air-conditioned deli. It was still hot enough outside to raise a little sweat walking here, at least in his suit, despite the hint of autumn in the early September air.

"Speaking of which," he said as they got on line. "Ari has someone he wants to set you up with. A journalist."

"Are you crazy? I'd be better off working for the mob than sleeping with a reporter."

"Not a real reporter. He's like a culture critic. You know, analyzes TV shows or whatever. Anyway, he showed me a picture. Handsome. And . . ." Andy touched her shoulder as if making his key point, ". . . he told Ari he likes strong women."

"So? What am I, a wrestler now?"

"He means strong in character, dummy." They were at the counter now and the cook was waiting. "Go ahead, order your salmon."

❖

Back in the office after lunch, sipping a plain black double espresso—Donna usually had Sameer, the coffee cart guy, make her a latte with two sugars, but all that talk about asses and possible dates got to her—Donna settled into work, scanning the logs she kept of calls and emails received and turning over something she'd been thinking about for the past few weeks. Finally, she stood, downed the last of her coffee, and marched into her boss's office.

"Excuse me, sir, can I ask you something?"

"Shoot," Agent-in-Charge Tom Foster answered without lifting his eyes from the report on his desk.

"What do we know about White Angel?"

He looked up, frowned, and removed his reading glasses. "That a trick question? I get enough riddles from my kids. What's next, knock-knock jokes? They love those."

"I'd call it more of a rhetorical question," Donna said, sitting across from him. "The answer is nothing. But we should. It's a brand of dope. Apparently very powerful, very pure, and whoever's behind it is taking over a lot of territory, muscling in on the usual crews."

"So?"

"I'd say we have a major new player in town. And the rumor on the street is that junkies are calling this dope Persian."

"What do junkies know?"

"About junk? A lot. And that case we just closed? The heroin smuggling? Also Persian."

"As I recall, all we recovered was a couple grams of stuff, right?"

"Yes, sir."

"And the ring are all dead or missing?"

"Right."

"That sounds like a closed case to me. Congratulations."

"I'm just saying, it feels like there could be a connection. Maybe I should arrange an undercover buy, get a sample, and compare it."

Tom stood up, sighing dramatically. "Donna. What is today's date?"

"Sir?"

"The date. Today's date."

"September second?"

"Good." He swept his hand over the window that looked out onto the crowded, bustling square. "And what major event is about to turn this whole area into a giant pain in my ass in exactly nine days?"

"September eleventh, sir."

"Right again. And just like every year, every federal, state and local agency from the NSA, CIA, and Homeland Security down to the MTA, sanitation, and parks department are squeezing my balls about one thing—terror threats. Is this a terror threat?"

"Not yet," Donna admitted.

"Not at all," he corrected. "It's a drug case. And not even a federal one, as far as I can see." He looked out the window, peering bitterly at the people walking, talking, eating snacks, sitting on benches, and taking photos of each other, as if he were angry at them for providing such nice soft targets. "If they start selling that Blue Angel or whatever to tourists in Ground Zero, let me know. Otherwise, refer it to local PD." He glanced back. "Anything else?"

Donna shrugged. "Knock, knock."

He frowned. "What?"

"Knock, knock."

He sat down with another sigh. "Who the hell is there?"

"To."

"To who?"

Donna pointed a stern finger at him. "To whom!"

He blinked a couple times then grinned widely. "Hey that's pretty good."

Donna saluted and left.

3

DETECTIVE GERALD PARKS WAS in hell. Or close enough. He was stuck in a filthy unmarked car, baking in the sun, with a partner who not only had BO but insisted on smoking, which was clearly against regs, explaining that being on stakeout constituted exigent circumstances, since he couldn't take a cigarette break. Not only that, but after ordering a double beef burrito for lunch, which stank the car up even more (Parks was vegan and competed for the department in long-distance races), he had clearly farted, despite ardent denials. Then he claimed that the smoke from his cigarette would help cover the smell.

"Isn't that what they say?" Detective Fusco, his senior partner, asked. "To light up after you rip one?"

"That's a match. And you just denied farting anyway. If this was an interrogation you'd be caught contradicting yourself."

"Match, cigarette, it's the same idea—you actually need smoke. And if this was an interrogation, my lawyer would argue the first law of evidence: he who smelt it dealt it."

"Whatever," Parks said, rolling his eyes. He was trapped in hell with a gross fat infant. "You want to talk about dealing it. Tell me why we're here." He nodded at the scene unfolding down the street, which Fusco and he had been discretely observing from afar. It was a corner in Sunset Park. A couple of teenagers in drooping, pegged jeans and hoodies were standing on the corner. Most folks walked right by. But a steady string

17

of more scraggly characters approached the youths, who directed them into a nearby alley. A minute later the same person would emerge and quickly rush away.

"Because," Fusco said, unbuckling his belt. "My gut tells me something isn't right here."

"Yeah it tells me that too. I'd say it's the burrito and coffee for starters."

"Out there, genius." Fusco nodded at the usual hustle playing out. Parks shrugged.

"Looks like a pretty standard cop spot and some friendly neighborhood dope fiends to me."

"Yeah but who are the guys working it?"

"I don't know. Nobodies. Kids."

"Chinese kids."

"So?" Parks braced himself for some racial shit. Not that he was Chinese. He was African-American, from Fort Greene. His father was a retired high school principal, his mother a nurse and community activist. A lot of his friends wondered how he could be a cop, considering all the conflicts it raised for a politically-conscious Black man, but Gerald had always wanted to be a detective. It sounded simple, but seeing his sharply dressed father head out to work each morning, tie and pocket square and polished shoes, and come home drained and exhausted gave him a simple goal: he wanted to wear nice suits to work, but he didn't want to sit in an office. He liked being out in the fresh air, in the street. Though not in a car inhaling some fat-ass's farts. He also had a gift for solving puzzles, for analytical thinking. And he was brave. So he excelled on the force, rose quickly, and landed this assignment, as junior partner with Fusco in Major Case as a prize. Because despite everything—the bad jokes, the bad breath, the farts and cigarettes, and even the suspicious phone calls from what sounded like angry bookies—Fusco was a top investigator and a legendary detective. He was the real deal and Parks was determined to learn from him, if there was anything left in him but gas.

"Chinese neighborhood, Chinese drug dealers. Standard," he told Fusco.

"And the last spot I took you too? In East New York? Who was selling there?"

Parks gritted his teeth. "Black kids."

"Right," Fusco said. "Black neighborhood, Black kids. Also standard. Selling what though?"

"Dope, man. Heroin. What is this?"

"What brand?"

"The touts were yelling White Angel. It's the bomb, apparently."

"Right." Fusco checked his gun and took the keys from the car. "Come on, let's take a walk. Get some fresh air. That cologne you wear is driving me nuts."

Chuckling, Fusco lumbered from the car and started walking down the street, while Parks followed, trying to control his temper and, yes, taking some deep, cleansing breaths. Maybe this was Fusco's brand of ball-busting. And okay, he was new on the squad. But he was no rookie, and he didn't plan to sit still for any hazing. He'd knock him right on his ass.

But Parks's attention shifted quickly, and he jumped into high alert when he realized where his new partner was leading him—right into the bustling little operation they'd been observing.

"Five-O, Five-O."

"Cops yo!"

"Police coming!"

The lookouts and touts—immediately recognizing that a heavy white guy in a rumpled, blue suit, food-stained white shirt, and creased red tie walking with a well-built, six-two Black man in a glen plaid with a subtle dark green woven in the gray, with a crimson tie and matching pocket square, could be nothing but cops—vanished, as did the customers, scurrying off like roaches in the light.

"What the fuck?" Parks asked as Fusco walked into the alley. It was empty. "You really think they were going to hang around, answer your questions?"

"Don't need them to," Fusco said. Eyes on the ground, he walked to the end of the alley and downstairs into a stairwell. He drew a utility

combo knife from his pocket then bent over, grunting a little, and came up smiling. "Here," he said, holding a small, torn glassine envelope by the corner with the knife's tiny tweezers. "Got a small evidence bag?"

Parks took one out and held it open. Fusco dropped in the envelope, then held it up. It was stamped with a small, poorly reproduced image: an angel, wings spread.

Fusco grinned. "A Chinese crew in Sunset Park and a Black crew in East New York, both selling the same brand of dope? That, my tofu-eating, nonsmoking, perfume-wearing young friend, is not standard. Is it?"

"No," Parks said, examining it more closely. "It definitely is not."

"Interested now?" Fusco asked, lighting a cigarette as they headed back to the car, a chorus of whistles alerting the block to their progress.

"Very interested," he said, and grinned.

❖

Unfortunately, their boss, Captain Maureen O'Toole, didn't share their interest.

"Who cares?" she asked, looking at the small collection of used baggies they'd laid on her desk.

"Captain," Fusco said, "this White Angel crew is all over. Not just Brooklyn. They're in Harlem. On the West Side. Maybe the Bronx too. They're organized. And the product is strong. Junkies are dropping right and left."

"He's right," Parks added. "I checked around, and everyone on the street is saying White Angel is the bomb." It was a bleak truth of the dope business—killing off some of your customers was the best advertising there was. Junkies heard about ODs and knew that meant the brand was legit.

"I repeat, who cares?" O'Toole repeated. "I'm asking. Literally. I know I don't. Junkies OD'd? In other news, drunks threw up and pigeons shit on a statue."

"But you have to admit," Parks added, "for a gang to be crossing ethnic lines like this, taking on different groups in different neighborhoods. It's highly unusual."

"But this isn't the highly unusual case squad, is it? This is the Major Case squad. And what they meant by Major Case is a case where anyone with a rank of major or up is going to catch shit from the press or the politicians."

Fusco glared. "So you're saying come back when some rich white kid or celebrity dies."

The captain pointed at him. "Now that is inappropriate and discriminatory, right detective?" She winked at Parks. "Teach your new partner some manners." She pushed the baggies toward them. "And file this crap under NHI."

As they walked back to their adjacent desks in sullen silence, Parks muttered to Fusco. "What's NHI again? I don't remember it in the manual."

Fusco snorted. "It's not in the fucking manual. Dealers killing junkies? NHI means No Humans Involved."

4

GIO WAS IN HELL. As boss of a Mafia crime family, one of the youngest in memory, he was used to having people fear him. And since he was the one who had organized the city's other organized crime bosses in a joint effort to stop terrorists, much of the credit for thwarting a recent attack and for blocking a dope shipment that would fund a terror network had gone to him, at least in his world. Not to mention that in the process, two rats who'd been talking behind his back were eliminated, one a powerful Irish boss named Pat White who'd now been replaced by the Madigan Brothers, his allies. Gio's power and glory had never burned so bright.

So why had he woken up with a groan, full of dread at opening his eyes today? Why was his stomach in knots? The truth was he was heartbroken. And he was scared.

He was heartbroken because the other rat, the second government snitch talking about his business behind his back, had been his accountant and his secret lover, Paul. Since his early teens, Gio had nursed and smothered a hidden desire, a need to take a break from being a man and, as a woman, to be dominated, abused really, by a handsome young man, ideally blond and blue-eyed, like Paul. With him, he'd fulfilled that desire and more, he'd found intimacy and love. Until his love betrayed him and had to die. But Gio hadn't killed him. His wife had.

Carol, Gio's college sweetheart, his partner and the mother of his children, was his other true love and the other half of his broken heart.

Discovering the truth of their affair as well as the fact that Paul had been pressured into feeding the government information on Gio's crimes and hidden fortune, his wife, a harmless civilian afraid of guns, a child therapist for Christ's sake, had shot Paul, and Gio had disposed of the body. Since then things had been a little weird around the house. Finally, after a few failed attempts to talk it all over, Carol had come up with this plan—the worst idea Gio had ever heard—but Carol reminded him he'd said he'd do *anything*, which is why he was sitting here now, scared shitless. Gio Caprisi, feared mob boss and deadly criminal, was heading into couple's counseling.

The waiting room was nice enough—patterned carpet, fabric couch, lots of pillows, flowers in a vase and more flowers in the paintings on the walls and the embroidery on the back of the wooden armchair—like the granny's cottage in a kid's cartoon. But the cozy, soft vibe vanished when the door to the inner office opened and another couple came out, a big guy in a tracksuit and a thin woman in white slacks and loose silk top. The guy looked crushed. The woman looked furious.

Gio squirmed. Carol squeezed his hand and whispered in his ear. "Just be honest and it will be fine."

Gio nodded, squeezing her hand back as a tiny woman in her seventies stood in the door. She wore denim overalls over a T-shirt, sandals, big glasses, and had a thick head of gray curls. Earrings and necklaces dangled. She smiled warmly and held out a bangled hand.

"Mr. and Mrs. Caprisi?"

Nodding, Gio stood formally and buttoned his jacket over his tie, as if in court. Carol popped up and shook hands.

"I'm Carol and this is Gio."

The old lady beamed, taking Carol's hand in both of hers. "So nice to meet you. I'm Dr. Meg Stein. Please come in."

She ushered them in, Carol leading the way, and shut the door behind them. Five minutes later they were rushing back out, Carol in the lead again, and Gio mumbling apologies. Neither spoke till they were in the car, her car, the Volvo wagon. She put the key in but didn't crank it.

Instead they sat, both with their belts on, and stared. Finally, Gio spoke in a low tone.

"Not so easy being honest is it?"

Carol stiffened, and gave him some sharp side-eye, but said nothing.

In fact, Gio had been honest, more or less: When Stein, or Dr. Meg, as she preferred, had asked what the main problem that had brought them to therapy was, Carol had said, "infidelity," and when Dr. Meg asked whose, he'd raised his hand. Avoiding specifics, like gender and flogging, he nevertheless explained that he'd been seeing someone, that it was a purely sexual arrangement (which wasn't entirely true), and that, for him, it was completely separate from his marriage, a need he simply had to fulfill. And when the shrink asked why he assumed his wife couldn't fulfill it, he cleared his throat and said, "Well, it's a kink thing I guess."

"Oh . . ." she said, still smiling blandly. "And Carol, that's not in your wheelhouse? Sometimes we can incorporate these desires into the marital sex life, find ways to fulfill each other's fantasies."

Carol squirmed and Gio spoke: "More specifically . . . a kink thing with a man."

"Oh . . ." the shrink shrunk a little. "I see. And where is this man now?"

Silence. Gio shrugged. "It's over. He's gone. For good."

"And Carol," Dr. Stein asked, turning to her, "how does that make you feel, hearing Gio say he's gone for good? Does that make you feel better? Do you believe it? Do you believe he's really gone forever?"

That's when Carol stood up. "I'm sorry," she said. "I can't talk about this." And she ran.

And now, in the car, she finally spoke, turning to Gio and saying, "I guess I'm like you now, full of secrets and lies and crimes I can never speak of. But I'm new at this, so sorry if I have a hard time swallowing my guilt. Not that you ever feel any."

"How do you know that?" Gio asked, anger flaring for a moment, then looked at her. "Is that honestly what you feel? You feel guilt? You wish you hadn't killed Paul?"

Carol shook her head. "No . . . actually. I don't."

"I didn't think so," Gio said. "And neither did I. Until now. I feel guilty about putting you in that position." He touched her shoulder. She stiffened, staring straight ahead, but didn't pull away. "But I don't blame you either."

"The honest truth? I'd do it again. And that's why I feel guilt."

He squeezed her tighter. "You just did what you had to do."

Now she glanced at him. "So did you."

Gio's phone beeped. He shifted but didn't reach for it. Carol nodded. "Go ahead. Check it."

"It's work," Gio said and checked it. A text: *Diner When? F.* "It can wait," he said.

Carol shook her head. "You might as well go. I have to get back to the office anyway."

"Okay," Gio told her. "Drop me outside the Parkview Diner on your way. I can call Nero or someone for a ride later."

As she started the engine and pulled out, Carol smiled ruefully. "Do you know how jealous I would have been before, worried about who you were meeting?"

"You wouldn't be if you knew, believe me," Gio said, picturing the sweaty face breathing stale smoker's breath on him. "But then again, you don't really want to know."

❖

Carol dropped Gio in front of the diner and he went in, stopping by the men's room to splash water in his face, then got a take-out coffee at the counter before leaving again by the back door. Fusco was in the rear of the parking lot, by the dumpsters, smoking, with his city-issued black Chevy Impala nearby. Knowing how Gio felt about smoking, he stomped on the butt as he approached. He'd lost heavily on last week's games and needed Gio's goodwill, his protection when the bookies started to call.

"So?" Gio asked, stepping out of view, into the space between the dumpsters. He sipped his coffee. "You look into this dope thing for me? This White Angel?"

Fusco shrugged. "I tried, Gio. I staked out the spots. I even got baggies. But my captain doesn't give a shit. She won't approve an investigation."

"She doesn't give a shit about a new heroin operation taking over New York? That's a sad commentary on the state of law enforcement today." In fact, Gio wouldn't normally give a shit either. His own involvement in the drug world was minimal—some weed and coke along the routes his family's Italian Ice and Soft Serve trucks worked on the Long Island beaches in season, and a general oversight over the trade in speed, molly, and so forth in his territories. A dispute among heroin dealers uptown and in Brooklyn was not his problem. But a big new operator with a superior product and organized enough to take over territory could upset the whole ecosystem. That worried him.

"I'm sorry, Gio," Fusco was saying. "What about that other friend of yours? You know, the guy they call sheriff. Put him on it."

"He's not a real sheriff, Fusco. He can't arrest people. That's what I have you for."

"I didn't mean . . ."

"Anyway he's out of town on business. What would get this captain of yours interested?"

Fusco shrugged. "She's interested in whatever the bosses tell her to be. Like if the mayor's office starts bitching. Or the feds."

Gio snapped his fingers. "Good idea. Make that call."

Fusco wasn't aware he'd had an idea. "The mayor won't take my call, Gio. He doesn't even know who I am, thank God."

"Not to the fucking mayor, you big mook. The FBI."

"I need more evidence that it's a federal case. Can you tell me more?"

"I can tell you that there's no opium fields in Brooklyn. Or Queens. Or even Staten Island last time I checked. So that means the shit comes in from somewhere out of state. Probably someplace far away where they wear turbans. And that's federal, right?"

"Sure, Gio . . ."

"So, you're a detective, get out your magnifying glass and go find some clues and shit, Sherlock." Gio finished his coffee and tossed the cup into the dumpster. "Or else pay what you owe."

"Right," Fusco said. "I understand. I'm on it."

"Good. I have every confidence in your abilities." As he turned to go, walking back to the diner, pulling out his phone to dial Nero, he shouted back: "You have a week."

5

AGENT MIKE POWELL WAS in heaven. Or maybe that was a stretch, he admitted: no one, even those born there, could quite describe the Helmand region of Afghanistan as heaven these days. A rugged environment, it had its own harsh beauty and a graceful, ancient culture, but had been riven by constant warfare since 2001, under Taliban control for years, and torn by conflicts over the opium crop for who knows how long back into history. It was considered to be the most dangerous province in Afghanistan—which is saying something. But for Powell it was a chance at redemption and maybe a shot at much more.

He'd been a rising young CIA agent, a smart analyst and a tough, effective operative, but his marriage, to an FBI agent, Donna Zamora, derailed him—or maybe even deranged him. He was intensely jealous and controlling, an impulse that was itself, ironically, beyond his control. He couldn't help it. He found himself spying on her and eventually even using agency resources to try and snoop, all of which bit him right in the ass when they divorced. He lost custody of his daughter, Larissa, and came close to losing his job. But the agency decided it was less embarrassing—to itself—to just bury him, so he was parked in a secure New York office, running interference with the locals and feeding information to his luckier colleagues overseas. Then Joe Brody entered the picture. Convinced that something was up between him and Donna, both romantically and criminally, and forgetting at times that even if

she was seeing Joe (which he had no evidence of) that wasn't exactly "cheating" now that they were divorced, Powell tried to implicate them both in a recent case involving a diamond heist and heroin being brought into New York by terrorists. Instead, when the case broke, he was the one who ended up on the losing end: two of his informants vanished or dead, the FBI and NYPD recovering the stones, and, he suspected, Joe Brody eliminating the terrorists. Powell was screwed and expecting to really be fired this time when his phone rang, and his life changed.

The voice on the phone had identified itself as Zahir, a somewhat mythic figure in intelligence circles, known as the Shadow. Zahir offered to help Powell, to act as an asset more or less, in exchange for unspecified favors. Why did Powell believe him? He didn't. After ten years in the CIA he didn't believe anything. Not only did everyone, and he meant *everyone*, lie, even when someone told the truth, it was for a reason, and that reason was often secret, a lie of the heart hiding behind the facts. But Zahir made him curious. For one thing, he'd called on Powell's secure office line, which wasn't supposed to be possible. Then, as soon as he'd told him he was at least interested in talking, Powell found himself transferred. Not, as he'd feared, to sit and stare at the Bering Straits in some ice tower for the next year, watching Russians scratch their frozen balls, but to Athens, an active station overseas. Did his superiors wonder why the fuck-up of the month was suddenly operational instead of getting punished? Probably, but they didn't question it. After all, they too believed nothing except that everyone lies—it's an occupational hazard. So who knows? Maybe the higher-ups had a use for Powell. Maybe this *was* a punishment in some inscrutable way. Or maybe the whole catastrophe had been part of some bigger, better lie and so not really a failure at all.

In any case, when he arrived in Athens, Powell was handed a fake passport and a plane ticket to Kabul and told to rendezvous in Kandahar with one Rick Toomey, formerly a black ops commando for the army, presently a military contractor. Powell's new assignment? To offer assistance and expertise to the people Toomey worked for, the Wildwater Corporation, a company that did business with the US military and intelligence forces

in the Middle East. In other words, after a season on the bench, he was back in the game.

But the real joy didn't kick in until later. He had gotten to the hotel, taken a shower, and changed when there was a knock on his door. Toomey. He was, Powell had to admit right off, a good-looking man: blue eyes, close-cut blond hair, easy smile. He was also, he quickly learned, excellent company. Asking if Powell had eaten, he immediately dismissed the idea of dining in the hotel and took him to a small, comfortable, homey place where they sat in a lovely courtyard and, as soon as he stepped in and smelled the roasting lamb, he knew the food would be excellent. It was. And over dinner, coffee, and the drinks he surreptitiously supplied from a bottle of scotch he poured under the table, Toomey kept up an easy, funny patter, regaling Powell with stories about the time he came under fire while in the latrine and had to take cover in the waste tank, the time he had to crawl in silence under the legs of some tied-up camels and remain still while one pissed on his head, and the time he broke into the wrong villa in a South Asian city, thank God he was only there for recon, and had to flee after accidentally catching a US diplomat in bed with a Chinese diplomat.

"What a relief to be talking to someone with top security clearance," he said, as Powell laughed. "Normally I have to redact my best material." He poured them both more scotch under the table and handed Powell his. "But what I'm going to tell you now is outside the parameters completely. It has no level of classification because it doesn't even exist."

"You're going to tell me who Zahir is," Powell said. He sipped his drink; really he just touched it with his lips. He was on high alert and wanted to stay that way.

"If you still want to know. Only a half dozen people in the world do, and if you become one of them, there's no going back. Now's your chance to walk away."

Powell shook his head. "I came too far to leave without answers."

"Good," Toomey said, and smiled that craggy, movie-star smile. "I'm glad to hear you say that. But first, a couple of questions. Then some

answers." He pulled a folder from his satchel. "Since you've been tapped to join us, a few new faces have shown up around here. I wonder if you can identify any of them."

He slid the folder across and Powell looked: surveillance shots of varying quality, taken from odd angles with a long distance lens. The first few were of someone he didn't recognize, a young guy, Middle-Eastern looking but in a Supreme hoodie and jeans so probably American or Western European. "Him I don't know." The next were of a blond woman in her mid to late twenties. He couldn't name her, but it was easy to picture her with a gun on a dark Brooklyn street. "Her I've seen. But I don't know much."

"That's okay," Toomey said. "We do. Another associate of ours has known her since she was a little Russian brat stealing candy." He tapped the third set of photos. "What about contestant number three?"

Now Powell smiled, as he flipped through the photos of the lean, hard-looking man in the sunglasses and the black T-shirt. "Oh, him I know very well. That's Joe Brody, aka the bouncer, aka the sheriff, aka a big pain in everybody's ass back home."

"A pal of yours?"

"Hardly."

"Good," Toomey said, closing the file. "Because he's just expanded into ass pain over here as well. And they cure that with a bullet in Afghanistan."

"Suits me," Powell said, and that was the moment when he realized this new job was going to be more like a vacation.

Toomey finished his drink and stood, holding out his hand. "Then let me be the first to say welcome aboard, Mike."

Mike stood and shook. "Thanks, Rick."

Toomey shouldered his satchel and threw some cash down on the table. "Now let's go upstairs and meet Zahir."

6

YELENA FOLLOWED JOE AND Hamid on the highway back
to Kandahar, Joe mostly deflecting Hamid's eager questions about
Yelena—yes, he knew her and they had worked together before, yes,
she was the badass Russian chick Juno had told him about—though Joe
didn't answer when Hamid asked if Juno had really dusted her butt for
handprints (he had, but he should have shut up about it)—and wondering
about questions of his own, like how the hell did she get from Queens,
where he last saw her, fleeing a room strewn with corpses, to a dope deal
in deep Afghanistan?

Back at the hotel where Joe and Hamid were staying, all three went to
the restaurant, found a quiet corner, ordered, and, while Hamid gorged,
Yelena talked and Joe listened.

"I knew when I left New York that I couldn't go anyplace where I am
known for a while. First I tried France, the Riviera. The beach was nice.
But I got bored. And I needed money."

"Bored?" Joe asked. "It was only a few weeks. Why didn't you just rob
the fancy hotel safes? Take it easy for a while?"

Hamid snorted as he scooped humus into a pita. "Wow you think
robbing hotel safes is easy?"

Joe smiled at Yelena. "For her it is."

She shrugged. "Stealing old lady's jewelry is more something for when
I retire maybe."

Hamid laughed. "That's awesome. You're like the pink panther."

Yelena frowned. "Pink? Because I am a girl?"

Joe waved it off. "It's a movie. Believe me she's more of a black cat. So then what?"

"I got recognized. Some Russian oligarch's mistress knew me so I had to go before word got to my enemies in Moscow. I heard about the bounty on Zahir. I decided, why not come here and kill him?"

Hamid laughed again, his mouth full, waving a shish kebab skewer. "Just like that? That's cool as shit."

She narrowed her eyes at him. "Shit?"

Joe explained. "It's a compliment. He's impressed. He's okay; Juno knows him."

She nodded at that. She liked Juno.

"You're totally awesome," Hamid told her. "Cat burglarizing. Killing overlords. Like a Marvel hero."

Yelena looked doubtful. "Thank you," she said politely.

Joe handed him a napkin. "Stop drooling and eat with your mouth closed." Then to Yelena: "So what happened? No luck finding Zahir?"

Yelena laughed. "There is no Zahir. How do you say, the myth you use to scare children so they behave?"

"The boogeyman?"

"Yes. Zahir is the bourgeois man that scares smugglers, so they give up their loads." She shrugged. "No one has seen him. No one even knows anyone who has seen him. Finally I decide, it's easier to just be the shadow than to find him."

Hamid laughed again. "Sorry," he said, hands up. "I'll be quiet. It's just . . ." He leaned toward Yelena, "Hanging with this guy's been pretty dull. Juno said he was a badass, but all he does is read poems and, like, silently brood, lurking in the dust. You know?"

Now Yelena laughed. "See?" she told Joe. "He thinks I am cooler than you. And a badder ass."

Joe nodded. "I'm not arguing. You win. Especially in the ass department."

"Yo, let's a get a hookah," Hamid suggested. "It's called a chillum here I think."

"Maybe later," Joe said. "I want to check out this first." He pulled a folded page from his pocket: the printout of a map and a photo of a nondescript five-story building. "Juno couldn't get much off of Felix's cellphone," he told Yelena as he handed her the papers, "but some of his messages are from an IP address that connects back to here."

"We already drove by yesterday," Hamid complained. "It's just a regular office building."

"He's right," Joe admitted. "Nothing to do with politics or fundamentalists. Just shipping and receiving for a company called Wildwater. Some kind of contractors. But . . ." He grinned at Yelena. "As long as you're in the neighborhood, I bet they have a safe."

She laughed. "This is Joe's idea of a date," she told Hamid.

"Oh man, I'd love to see you work," he gushed.

"Easy," Joe said. "You need to stay in the room, get in touch with Juno, and be ready to relay whatever we find."

"Don't worry," Yelena told him. "I know a good hookah place in Kabul. And also one back in Astoria."

The Wildwater office in Kandahar was in a nondescript five-story office building close to what the local paper optimistically called "the famous" Shaheedan Square. Joe and Yelena took her motorbike, with her driving, still in black but minus the mask and turban, and Joe behind her, one arm snaked around her ribcage, his chest against her, a bag with their weapons and her tools on his back. It was late, and there was not much in the way of nightlife. A few cars and bikes rolled through the traffic circle in the center of the square. Taxis and motorized, open-backed carts cruised for passengers or loitered by the cafés. They parked in the alley behind the building, walked into the loading bay where, during the day, trucks came and went, and

while Joe kept watch, Yelena got in the door in less time than most people took with keys.

The building was drab, concrete and steel, dusty and filled with import/export firms and companies supplying the military. Finding their way upstairs with flashlights they'd covered with tape, leaving just a small beam, they headed swiftly and silently to the top floor, where the lock on the office door was even less serious than downstairs.

And at first glance, there wasn't much to protect. It was an office much like any other, a little less modern than the New York equivalent—desks, chairs, filing cabinets, old desktop computers, a watercooler. In a back room, with a bigger desk, a bigger chair, and a much-napped-on leather couch, Yelena spotted an old freestanding safe.

"You work on this," Joe whispered, handing her the bag. "I'll deal with the stuff in the office."

Joe went to a desk with an old computer, just a step or two above floppy disks, and turned it on. While it slowly booted up he got out the iPhone Juno had given him—his own phone was a basic flip—and called the only number on it, Hamid's.

"Hey," Hamid said immediately.

"It's me," Joe said.

"I know."

"Do you have Juno patched in?" Joe asked.

"Hey, bro," Juno shouted into Joe's ear. "I'm right here, back home in the studio. How's Afghanistan? You hit the beaches yet? I hear you met an old friend too."

"Afghanistan is landlocked, Juno. And let's be cool on the phone, right?"

"Sorry. You're right. You ready to transmit?"

"In a minute," Joe said. He set the phone on the desk and pulled a cord from his pocket. The screen now asked for a password, but Joe ignored that and plugged his cord directly into a port on the rear of the machine. He plugged the other end into the phone. "Okay," he told Juno and Hamid, "you're hooked up."

"I'm on it," Juno said. "Hamid, just chill and monitor the signal."

"Right," Hamid said. "I'm chilling."

The computer screen flickered with a stream of numbers as Juno hacked in remotely, and Joe began inspecting the papers on the desks, using his flashlight and, with a small camera, snapping photos of anything that seemed remotely interesting. There wasn't much: purchase, shipping, and customs documents, packing lists and invoices for shoelaces, water bottles, sunglasses, tires, and blankets—all the mundane crap that it took to run a war, most of it harmless except as trash in a landfill, and as a waste of tax money. No extremist tracts or receipts for heroin. Hopefully, Yelena would have better luck. Meanwhile he snapped away without much enthusiasm, pausing only when he saw, from the documents flashing by on the screen, that Juno was in and downloading the contents of the hard drive. He picked up the phone, which was still connected to the computer.

"Hey guys. How's it going?"

"It's going," Juno said. "But I don't know where. Looks like a bunch of bookkeeping crap to me."

"Yeah same here . . ." Joe began, but then dropped the phone, as Yelena came running out of the office, bag in her hand.

"Go!" she yelled as she slammed the office door behind her, but she didn't need to say anything. Joe knew from the look on her face. They bolted across the room, throwing the hall door shut behind them, and were just turning a corner of the hallway when an explosion ripped through the building, obliterating the office they were just in and rattling the entire place. They dove to the floor, instinctively clutching each other. The sound was deafening. Plaster dust poured down. The whole structure groaned like an old ship, but it held. After breathing in the dark for a second, and registering that he was alive and, except for the ringing in his ears, unharmed, Joe found his flashlight and clicked it on.

"You okay?" he asked Yelena, still whispering, though it hardly mattered. The whole neighborhood was awake.

"Yes," she said. "Just my pride is hurt."

"We can bandage that later," Joe said. "Let's go."

They began to make their way downstairs, a bit slower than before, stepping carefully over fallen signs and toppled trash cans, though for the most part, the rest of the building seemed intact.

"Booby trap?" Joe asked as they hurried down.

"A very good one too," she told him. "Better than the shit safe."

She explained that the old safe had been wired with a high-tech explosive device, set to destroy the contents of the safe if it was opened, along with anyone nearby.

"Guess working here isn't as boring as it looks," Joe said.

"But we won't know why," Yelena said as they reached the street level and went back out the alley door. "Sorry, Joe."

"Don't worry about it," Joe told her. "At least we got out clean."

But he spoke too soon, because shortly after they got back on the bike, and Yelena started to drive, a Humvee with floodlights and a machine gun mounted on the roof came straight down the alley at them.

7

Toomey led Powell up a dark staircase and knocked on the door. A moment later, it drew back and he entered a large private dining room, opulently furnished with cushions and drapes, dim lights and filigreed, openwork panels filtering the night air. No one was dining, however. The table held an ornate tea service—from the scent he knew it was chai green tea brewed with ginger and walnuts—as well as a bowl of fruit and dishes of sweets. A ruddy-faced, heavyset old man in a pink dress shirt and khakis sat at the head, ignoring the tea and treats and holding a glass of rosewater and lemonade over ice. He wore a wedding band, a Rolex, and an excellent toupee, and the blazer draped over the back of his chair had an American flag lapel pin. He looked familiar. He could have been a senator, except that then Powell would have recognized him.

To his left sat a tougher, harder-looking man with close-cropped salt-and-pepper hair and a seamed, tanned face. He wore an expensive white silk shirt and expensive navy silk trousers and a gold Russian cross around his neck. Russian then. There was an unlit Cuban cigar and a gold lighter on the table before him, next to his tea. Across from him, on the American's right, sat a younger, heavily muscled man, his hair grown out but still neat, in a camouflage T-shirt and jeans, with a USMC tattoo and an open laptop on the table. An ex-Marine, working no doubt for the senatorial American.

The fourth person in the room was a mystery. For one thing she was female. Also younger than the others, probably in her twenties, though she could have passed for a teenager, still with a layer of baby fat, her chubby cheeks dotted with pimples. She had a striking look, reddish auburn hair expensively chopped into a decidedly unmilitary, artful mess, very fair skin that could not have seen much Afghan sun, and striking green eyes. She wore a thin vintage Grateful Dead T-shirt cut high to reveal a few inches of soft belly, torn jeans, and a black biker jacket. Was she the Russian's mistress? No. Not flashy enough—she wore a black leather choker and an Apple watch but no gold or makeup, expensive high-top designer sneakers but no heels, and why would he have her here anyway? She was young enough to be the American's daughter, but first of all, Powell didn't sense she was American, at least not all-American like the older man, and she was languidly sprawled on some cushions smoking a chillum, tobacco mixed with hash, and sipping Sharbat-E-Rayhan, a cold drink made with basil seeds, staring at them all with a look of total impudence and indifference, as if they had mildly disturbed her private party—hardly the type for take-your-daughter-to-work-day. Plus she was armed; from the way she sat, and the way her jacket draped, it was clear to Powell that there was a handgun strapped beneath it. But all that was beside the point: the sharp, cold look in her eyes made it clear she was not here on anyone else's arm. She was no pet. She was a predator.

The other mystery was who was not here. No Afghanis. No Arabs or Middle Easterners of any sort. No one who could plausibly be Zahir.

"Gentlemen," Toomey said to the table, pointedly ignoring the woman, who blew steamed smoke into the air. "Let me introduce you to Mike Powell, CIA."

All three men turned to him. The older American stood. "Mike, I'm Bob Richards, CEO of Wildwater. Thanks for coming out." He reached across the table and gave Powell a CEO-quality handshake. Of course: Bob Richards was ex-NSA, from before Powell's time, and now headed up a company of military contractors, operating worldwide, handling

everything from logistics, supplies, and construction, to training and security, to, some said, mercenary warfare and covert ops with which official agencies didn't want to be connected. "This is Jensen, my assistant," he added.

"It's an honor, sir," Powell said, then turned to Jensen who rose, shook, and sat back down, hands on the keyboard.

"And this is Nick," Richards said, settling back in his chair.

The Russian smiled but did not stir or shake. "I prefer Nikolai. But first names only for now, I'm afraid," he said in fluent but accented English. "You understand."

Powell smiled back. "SVR?" he asked, guessing he was with the Russian Intelligence Service, the successor to the KGB.

"I am here unofficially like you. To advise and observe." He shrugged. "So not even really here at all."

"Have a seat, Mike," Toomey said, pulling a chair out and taking one himself. "Let's talk." He turned to the others. "Mike has already been pretty helpful, confirming the ID on Brody."

Now Jensen spoke, looking up from his screen. "You say he was ex-Special Forces, but I can't find a record. Not even high security."

Powell nodded, realizing now that of course they'd been listening to him and Toomey downstairs. "There is none. His records have been erased. Make of that what you will."

"Black ops," Jensen said.

"Pitch black. That's all I know."

"And now he's gone rogue, you say? Doing hits and pulling jobs for a Mafia family?"

Powell shrugged. What did rogue even mean, in his present company? "He grew up with Gio Caprisi. But maybe, before I say more, you should tell me why I'm here."

"You're here because there's a war going on, Mike. Same as us," Toomey said, but Richards waved him down.

"What Rick means is, some of our likeminded colleagues in the company thought you were our kind of people, and that you'd fit in."

"Fit in with what?"

"War is expensive, Mike. You know that. Everyone does. But what the public doesn't realize is that it doesn't just cost money and lives, it takes time. And it takes will. Iron will. Politicians haven't got the stomach for that; they're too worried about reelection. They're cowards by nature. And the public doesn't have the patience. They want, as they said back in Vietnam, to declare victory and go home. Have a parade and be done with it. Go back to sleep." He shrugged. "So a group of us, people in the military and intelligence communities, professionals like yourself, along with some members of the present administration, decided to step in and sort of . . . guide things along. Make sure the will didn't weaken, as we see this thing through to victory."

"Whatever that takes," Toomey added.

"You mean Al-Qaeda? ISIS? The war on terror?"

"We mean the war for the future of the world," Toomey told him.

Richards spoke again, leaning back in his chair. "Like Rick said, we are, as you know, embroiled in a conflict. The war on terror, of course, but that's just part of it. It's a clash of civilizations, of value systems, east versus west, freedom versus slavery."

"Christian versus Islam," the Russian, Nikolai, said. "For us too. We even fought right here, in this same place."

"It's been going on since 9/11," Richards said. "Longer really."

Toomey laughed. "Try a thousand years."

"And it won't be settled in my lifetime either," Richards said, with a wave of his hand.

"And Zahir?" Powell asked, taking this all in.

"A useful fiction," Richards said. "A way to stir the pot. Or stoke the fire, you could say. When will falters, and interest flags, we use Zahir to keep the voters—or should I say viewers—focused back home, which keeps the politicians on point, which keeps the right parties on the ground here off balance or in need of our help."

Powell nodded. "And all of which keeps the arms and money flowing."

Richards smiled. "Like I said, war is expensive. And victory takes men who aren't afraid to get their hands dirty, and to apply pressure when necessary. Men like us. And you."

Toomey leaned over and squeezed Powell's arm. "Men with a will of iron."

All eyes were on Powell, gauging his reaction, but Jensen broke in, addressing Richards.

"Sorry sir, but we've had a break-in at the Kandahar office." He turned to Powell. "It looks like your pal Brody and the Russian girl are sticking their noses in. Almost got them blown off too."

Toomey stood to see the screen and, for the first time, Nikolai seemed concerned. Richards explained to Powell while Jensen spoke into his earpiece. "We have the office booby-trapped. They won't find anything." He turned to Toomey: "But what about the latest shipment?"

"It's already en route," he said. "I handled it personally. Nothing can stop it now."

"Good," Richards nodded. "Then all they've done is destroy our evidence for us."

Jensen reported: "Our security team is on the way to intercept them now. And I scrambled the chopper."

"Let's go," Toomey said. Nikolai stood too and prepared to move.

"Care to observe from the air?" Richards said. "Might be your last look at Joe Brody."

"I'll pass sir," Powell said. He'd been given a lot to think about, and although he knew he was already involved, even by listening, he was hesitant to commit to action. And, happy as he would be to see Joe's head on a stick, he also knew that operations involving Joe Brody tended to get out of hand. "It's been a long day, and I'm just getting my bearings."

"We'll talk later then," Richards said and left in a hurry, flanked by the other men. Suddenly Powell found himself alone with the young woman who was now staring right him with an odd smile and blowing fragrant smoke like a Cheshire cat.

8

YELENA TURNED THE BIKE around when she saw the Humvee coming, and sped back the opposite way, just as the gunner opened fire. Bullets whistled invisibly past Joe's ears and flattened themselves into the concrete. Then another truck, carrying more men, came around the corner of the alley, blinding them with roof lights and sealing that exit as well. It did, however, have the immediate benefit of halting the gunfire, since the gunners on both vehicles knew they were likely to hit each other. Cursing under her breath, Yelena stopped and spun the bike around again, touching her boot to the ground for balance. She drove them back into the loading bay of the building.

"So?" She looked back over her shoulder at Joe, who was pulling a machine pistol from his pack. "Fight here or go back upstairs?"

"Keep going," Joe told her, and as the first truck turned into the bay behind them, he was ready. Aiming carefully from the rear of the bike, he shot at the gunner, who dropped down into the interior of the Humvee, then sprayed the front, shattering the windshield and the lights. In the momentary dark, as the men inside took cover and began to scramble out, Yelena drove the bike through the doorway and, revving the engine, began to take them up the stairs, nosing the front tire slowly over the steps while Joe hung on. They rode up, taking the turns slowly and then pushing it on the flights, bouncing up, moving at about the pace of a quick jog. Looking down into the stairwell, Joe could see flashlights playing

over the stairs, and make out the sound of men yelling or squawking over the radios. They weren't far behind. Then, at the top landing, Yelena jerked to a stop.

"Hey, what's up?" Joe asked, putting his feet down for balance and standing as the bike bucked, braking hard, but before she could answer he saw: the blast had taken out the supports for the stairs and a big chunk of the landing, leaving bits of twisted rebar and broken concrete. In essence, it had cracked the top floor of the building in two. One side, where the office had been, was wrecked, with collapsed interior walls and a sagging ceiling. The other, which had the roof access, was messy but intact. And between them was a jagged gap several feet across.

"Now what?" Yelena asked. "I don't have enough room to jump it. I can't get the speed."

Joe looked around. "I have an idea. Take this."

He gave her the bag and slung his gun over his shoulder, then went to the bombed-out office. The metal door had been blown clean off its hinges, but was otherwise undamaged. He squatted down and began to drag it over to the open gap. Meanwhile, Yelena removed an automatic assault rifle from the pack and focused on the stairs. The top of a head appeared and she fired, dinging the helmet like a bell. The man fell back with a yelp.

"They're coming," she called to Joe.

"Give me a minute," he grunted as he hoisted the door to a standing position against a wall then walked it a foot or so further. Yelena fired a burst, keeping the attackers downstairs. Now Joe had the door standing at the lip of the open gap, and he let it fall, landing with a thud on the other side, and forming a small, precarious bridge. Immediately gunfire erupted from below, as the men in the stairwell saw and heard Joe moving above. Joe jumped back as the bullets shot up, while others ricocheted off the door, causing panic among the shooters below.

"Okay," he told Yelena. "Take it across. Carefully."

She handed him her rifle and he took up a stance, watching for movement and firing the occasional burst down the stairs or through the open

gap into the dark stairwell, more to hold them back than because he expected to hit anyone. At the same time, as Yelena edged the bike over the door, shots came up from below her, hitting the ceiling above, which showered dust, or ringing against the metal under her wheels. Once she was across, Joe took a deep breath and darted after her. He could see that all the gunfire had weakened the damaged ceiling even more, plaster and bits of ceiling tile were dropping away, so while she drove slowly out the exit onto the roof, he fired up at the ceiling while pushing the edge of the door with his foot. A beam fell, raining metal and concrete into the stairwell, and Joe could hear men shouting as the door clattered into the gap, falling on them. Firing across the now-reopened moat, he backed out onto the roof exit and shut that door behind him.

It was actually a lovely night out. Not that Joe had time to savor it, but the sudden quiet and the cool, dry air, the sleepy town around him and the thick swirl of stars out over the impenetrable dark of the desert made him wish, momentarily, that he was out on a blanket under the sky. Or better yet, home in noisy, stinky, never dark, and practically starless Queens.

Now they were on the roof, and safe for the moment, but where did they go next? Staying on the more stable, undamaged side of the building, Yelena cruised the bike slowly around and Joe ran to the edges. The front and one side faced a street corner, where he saw another truck full of men unloading, and ducked back as one took a quick shot at his head. The rear was the alley they had just fled. The remaining side overlooked a narrow airspace, and then another building, two stories shorter. Beyond that, Joe could see a single-story structure that housed a row of shops during the day.

"Do you think you can make the jump?" he asked Yelena.

She was about to ask him if she had a choice but noticed something and pointed instead. It was a helicopter, cruising above the city and headed for them. "Guess we will find out."

Joe took his belt off, passing it through the front loops of his pants and then got on the bike behind Yelena and buckled it around her waist.

Now they were strapped together. The chopper approached, the sound and wind growing as it lowered itself like a black beetle from the night sky. He adjusted the scope on the rifle. "Let's go," he said.

Yelena circled slowly back toward the wrecked part of the building, taking it to the furthest point she could safely bring the bike, giving her the longest runway for takeoff. She cranked the throttle, revving the engine as high as she could while holding the brake. As the helicopter arrived over the roof, it hit them with a spotlight. Yelena released the brake and the bike shot forward.

As they raced toward the edge and the alley below, Joe raised the rifle, bracing the stock against his body and turning up toward the chopper, which blinded him with its glare. He opened fire, blasting into the light, trying to stay centered while the bike carried them across the roof. Now the chopper opened fire too, bullets hitting the roof around them as the gunner in the air found his range. As the chopper shifted, trying to get a better angle of fire, the glare shifted momentarily too, and Joe was able to see the origin of the beam of light, spilling from a lamp attached to the bottom. He fired again. With a pop, the light went out. They were plunged back into the darkness. The gunner kept firing, but he was aiming blindly now, staring into shadow and with the thunderous roar of the chopper hiding any sound from the bike.

Joe grabbed Yelena with his free arm, holding on tightly as they reached the flat edge of the roof and went over, soaring across the alley. Joe held his breath as, for a moment, they were airborne, floating through space. He could feel Yelena's heart pound under his hand. Then they landed with a thud on the lower roof next door. The bike wobbled, swerving crazily as Yelena fought for control, and Joe put his feet down a couple times to help balance it. More shots rang out as the helicopter came from behind.

"Keep going," he shouted into her ear. The roar was deafening. As the tires bit, gaining traction on the roof, she cranked the throttle and they took off, crossing the building in seconds and flying over the far edge while bullets shot over their heads.

Now they were on top of the shops. A long gallery with shop fronts facing a square, this roof was more uneven, comprised of plaster and wood, and with covered seating areas, barrels of water, laundry hanging on lines. Ducking low to avoid getting clotheslined, they plowed through some sheets and took cover under a patched-together sheet metal roof that ran along one side of the building. While Yelena idled, Joe unbuckled himself and reloaded the rifle.

"We're never going to outrun that chopper on open ground," he told Yelena.

"So we make a stand here," she said.

He handed her the machine-pistol from his pack. "Here, fire off some rounds to get their attention."

She nodded and began cruising slowly, staying under the cover of the roof. When she heard the chopper approaching, coming around from the side, she took a few shots in its general direction. Gunfire fell like hail on the metal roof, some bullets zinging away while others punched through weak spots and hit the surface around her as she sped out of range.

Joe ran back to where the roof began, climbed onto a table and slowly peeked over the edge. In the moonlight, he saw the chopper lowering itself like a spider, trying to find a position that would let the gunman, who sat beside the pilot at an open panel, aim under the metal roof and sweep the area with gunfire. Yelena fired another burst from a spot further down and the chopper shifted a bit more to try and reach her. Bullet holes appeared in the roof around her as she zoomed up and down.

Joe, who knew they were facing away from him, trying to see under the shelter, stood and propped himself on the metal sheeting, aiming carefully at the chopper, waiting for his shot, while the pilot adjusted his position.

"No hurry Joe," Yelena yelled out. "Just relax and take your time." Moonlight poured in around her as the machine gunner turned her shield into a colander.

Now Joe could see them, the pilot and the gunner, with a few more figures in the seats behind them, all yelling over their headsets as they

tried to home in on Yelena. But still he waited, totally still, breathing carefully, eye on his scope.

"Come on," he whispered to himself. "Just a little more."

"I'm running out of roof here Joe," Yelena called out. She fired again, one lucky bullet clanging off the rotors, then quickly sped back down the gallery toward him.

The pilot turned too, trying to find the source of Yelena's fire, and exposed the open panel to Joe. He pulled the trigger.

In a flash, the gunner crumpled, killed instantly as gunfire entered the interior of the chopper. Joe kept firing, sending a stream of lead into the chopper, which swerved away like a fly from a swatter. At this low altitude, just four or five meters off the ground, the chopper quickly lost stability. It spun wildly over the square, stirring up a small storm of dust and paper, scattering the few souls present—mostly taxi drivers, late night café goers, cats and dogs—and then landing with a thud, banging headfirst into a wall. The rotors hit the concrete with a terrible wrenching sound and broken machine parts shot off like shrapnel as the aircraft came to rest.

With a grin, Joe ran over and got on the back of the bike, where he could see Yelena smiling too. "Good shot," she told him

"Thanks," he said, slinging the gun onto his back and grabbing hold of her. "But I think I only killed the gunner. We better go."

"Next stop, ground floor," she said, revving up. "Everybody off."

She hit it and they sped along the roof, picking up speed and, as the edge approached, she yanked the handlebars up, popping the bike into a wheelie that took them over the side. Letting the bike go as they fell, they dropped into the back of a cart that sat parked in a row with others, waiting for a late-night fare. The bike, with greater momentum, overshot the cart, hit the ground hard, and crashed.

For a couple of seconds, Joe, Yelena, and the driver were all completely disoriented, as the fabric awning over the rear of the cart collapsed and they tumbled into the bed of his truck, which contained only two empty side-benches for passengers. Yelena was the first to recover her balance,

leaping up with her usual agility and pointing a gun at the stunned driver. Joe freed himself from the fabric and stood, pulling a US hundred-dollar bill from his pocket and showing that to the driver too, as he began to yell at Joe in Dari.

"The gun or the money," Joe told him, pointing at each. Finally the driver nodded, and reached for the bill. Yelena lowered her gun. "Good. Thank you," Joe said, repeating it in Dari. *"Kheili khoob. Moteshakeram!"*

The cart took off, speeding down a side street and into the dark town, while Joe tried to remember the name of his hotel.

9

TOOMEY LIKED THIS GUY Joe. Or he would have, under other circumstances, where they didn't need to kill him. Like if they'd just been in a bar somewhere, trading stories over a beer. At first, he hadn't thought much about him. The only reason they even went up in the chopper was to observe: Richards because he liked to play general, sit there and watch his money at work; Nikolai because he had to report back to Moscow; and Toomey because he needed to be sure that everything went off like it should. His mission was too important to leave to amateurs. It was only when he saw them riding that bike across the roof, the girl jumping it expertly, and then Brody taking out the searchlight, doing what he himself would have done, that he began to think he was finally dealing with some pros. Then they pulled some shit that really impressed him.

First they took cover under a metal shed that shielded them from the bullets that their gunner, Tony, a kid who'd done a tour shooting insurgents before he signed on with Wildwater as a merc, was raining down on them indiscriminately. Then, as he deduced later, the Russian woman drew their fire, tricking the pilot, Trey, into exposing their flank, the open panel by Tony. A skilled sniper, Brody must have been lying in wait. He took that kid out like he was winning a teddy bear in an amusement park. Outstanding shot.

His next shot stunned Trey, bouncing off his helmet and ricocheting into the fuselage. Another hit the bulletproof plexi, which was great

when Brody had been shooting at them before, but now the bullet struck the plexi from inside and bounced back, grazing old Richards himself in the leg and ruining those nice pants. Richards yowled, Trey took evasive action and rapidly ditched, Nikolai cursed in Russian, and Toomey grinned, bracing himself for the crash.

They went down in a corner of the square. The chopper was totaled of course, but strapped in and helmeted, they were all fine, just a little battered and whiplashed. Except for Richards, moaning and carrying on, never having been shot before. It was nothing, a scratch, but the blood was spreading through his khakis. Toomey used Nikolai's handkerchief to bind the wound. Trey took off his helmet and let down that ponytail that he insisted on, a trademark gesture that he thought let the world know he was a free man, but that really just showed he was at least a decade out of fashion. Actually, both were true: he was one of Toomey's best men, a brave and ruthless fighter who, much like Toomey, was more at home in a warzone than in any of the places—Florida, where he grew up, the Marines, where he'd learned his skills, or Colorado, where his one-time fiancée now lived—that might have passed for "home." As for family, it was his team that mattered. And now, head still ringing, he was cursing and swearing vengeance on Brody for taking out Tony, his pal. Nikolai just shook his head at the mess and lit a cigar. Toomey called for help to come fetch them, patted Trey on the shoulder, and silently congratulated Brody in his head. He'd look forward to crossing paths with him again some time, and to buying him a beer. Or killing him. Or both.

10

JOE AND YELENA RODE back to the hotel in the motor-cart, lounging on the wadded fabric that had once been the roof, watching the night sky flow over them like a river of stars between the buildings.

"Sorry, Joe. All I did tonight was get you in trouble."

"And get me back out," he told her. "Anyway, I think I learned something important."

"Watch out for booby-traps."

"That there was something there worth booby-trapping. And sending a small army of mercenaries with a chopper to protect. I think you were right all along. Zahir is just a front. And now we know it's a front for a US corporation. Wildwater."

"So what will you do?"

"Catch a plane. Why chase the shadow around here? Especially now that they're onto us. Let's go back home. Start looking at Wildwater and see what we find."

She turned to face him. "You say we and let's. But New York is not my home."

"And Kandahar is? If you want to retire, fine. Go to Tulum or someplace. If you want to get into trouble and help earn this half million, come back with me."

She smiled. "Trouble and money are always tempting. But don't forget, I already made some money today. Not half of a half million, but enough for a nice slow trip around the world."

The cart came to a stop by the hotel. "Sorry. *Mote'as-sefam.*" Joe told the driver again as they climbed down. The driver shrugged. A hundred US dollars for a short ride more than covered some repairs. For him at least, it had been a good night. The small hotel was silent and dark. Joe used the key he'd been given, and they went quietly upstairs to where Joe and Hamid had adjoining rooms. A light shone from under Hamid's door.

"I will think about it tonight," Yelena whispered. "Meanwhile, we should take turns on watch until we leave for the airport. Tell Hamid to rest first." She squeezed his hand in the dark. "And we will try not to wake him up."

Smiling, Joe found the right key and was already saying, "Hamid, you missed a real party," when he swung the door open and found him, sprawled across the bed, dead eyes staring up at them, blood from his slit throat staining the white sheets red.

❖

Joe and Yelena moved immediately and in silence, automatic responses taking over, drawing their weapons and checking the other room and the bathrooms, which were all empty. There was, sadly, no reason to check Hamid; even a glance at his body, marked with slashes and burns, twisted with breaks and bruises, revealed that he'd been tortured before he was killed. The rooms had been ransacked, but all that was missing seemed to be Hamid's phone and laptop, as well as the satchel containing Yelena's money from the earlier exchange. They packed fast, pausing only for a moment over Hamid.

"I can't just leave him," Joe said. "I'm the one who brought him here. I owe his family more than that."

"You know you can't bring him," Yelena said. "The people here are very religious. They will know what to do. They'll treat him properly, and say the prayers."

Joe nodded. "That's more than I can do." He reached out and closed his eyes. Then they shut off the light and left.

❖

Powell felt like he was in hell. He felt damned. He'd met the devil and he, or in this case, she had just sucked out his soul. And the devil's name, which we know is Legion, was, surprisingly, Vicky. He didn't know her last name and didn't want to. He already knew too much, more than he could ever forget.

After the others rushed out to investigate the break-in and explosion at the local Wildwater office, the only person remaining in the private lounge besides himself was the striking but feral young woman in the torn black jeans and black leather jacket. Powell's intention had been to say goodnight and retreat to his hotel room, but she had other plans. She stood, set down her hookah, and grabbed her small leather backpack.

"Come along, company man," she said in a posh British accent, as she led the way out. "I've another errand to run for the boys. You can observe and advise me."

At first, Powell was frankly excited. The revelation of the Zahir group's true makeup and purpose had troubled him, but he was prepared to accept a certain amount of troubling; he was, after all, in the CIA. They had a long history of making murky alliances with sordid parties in the hope of achieving sometimes dubious goals, always, of course with the country's best interests in mind. That same history begged the question of how well this strategy usually turned out—in Cambodia for instance, or Iran or Cuba—but that, to Powell, was academic. Doing nothing while the world rushed into chaos and horror wasn't an option. And maintaining some sort of James Bond–like, or even better, Superman-esque moral purity and detachment was, literally, a fairy tale. The only thing to do was play the dirty game as best as you could, and the very fact that they'd sent him here demonstrated that he, and they, had some of his superiors' tacit approval. The CIA had been mixed up in the heroin trade at least since

Vietnam. They'd armed and funded warlords and opium traders in these very same valleys back when the Soviets were their common enemy. If intervening in the dope trade now saved some American lives later, so be it. It was all part of the usual game.

But this woman was not usual. Powell followed her downstairs to where a young, dark-skinned man, fine-featured and exquisitely muscled, in jeans and a white T-shirt, was standing beside a black Range Rover. He jumped to open the rear door, shut it after them, and drove.

"I'm Mike Powell, by the way," Powell said, as they moved through the evening traffic, extending a semi-ironic hand. "I wonder if you'd like to tell me where we're going?"

"Victoria," she'd said, her eyes facing out the window, his hand ignored. "Though I prefer Vick or Vicky. We are en route to ask someone a question or two."

Powell smiled to himself. Here he was, riding in an expensive car through an exotic city, accompanying a strange woman to a mysterious rendezvous. This really was like a scene from a movie and he had to admit, to himself if never to anyone else, he was delighted. For the first time in a long time, he was excited to be a spy.

❖

They pulled up in front of a small, nondescript hotel, with a tiny, thread-bare foyer rather than a proper lobby. The driver approached the old man behind the counter, speaking rapidly and drawing a wallet from his pocket. He waved some sort of credential, and then, after the cringing old man handed over a key, began to count out money, while Vicky, without further ado, took the key and proceeded quickly upstairs. Powell followed, starting to have more questions, but before he could formulate them, she stopped in front of a door, turned to him with a finger over her lips for silence, and handed him the key. Then she drew her gun.

Powell had no gun. And this wasn't the sort of meeting he'd been expecting. But there was no way to call a time-out now, so he carefully

slid the key into the simple lock set in the doorknob, turned it, and stepped aside as he pushed it open. Victoria went in first.

There was only one man in the room. A dark-skinned kid in western clothes, a hoodie, jeans, and sneakers, with closely buzzed hair and a neat goatee. Powell realized he'd been in the photos Toomey had shown him. Now he was wearing headphones and staring so intently into a laptop that he only noticed them when it was too late, eyes going wide in terror, and hands rising, as Victoria put her gun in his face.

❖

Powell had seen people tortured before. He'd even participated in beatings or waterboardings. He'd put people in hoods where they couldn't see or hear, or kept them awake with blinding light or noise. He'd worked with creepy CIA interrogators and ruthless Mossad experts. He'd even seen plain old cops smack suspects around. But he'd never seen anything like Vicky, he'd never seen a true sadist go to work on a victim and take the kind of pleasure in pain that he saw that night. By the time she was done, the poor kid was praying for death, and when—after extracting all the information she could about his mission in Afghanistan, about Joe Brody and the Russian woman he knew only as Yelena and the bounty that New York gangsters had offered for the head of Zahir—she finally took his life, she did it with an expression he could only describe as joyful, smiling, eyes aglitter, as she brushed his head soothingly with one hand, telling him he was a good boy, and then releasing him from his broken body and from a world of pain by expertly slicing open his throat.

Then she turned to Powell, as thrilled as if she'd just been on a fun-house ride: her pupils were dilated, her breathing rapid. Her fair skin was flushed and the pulse beat in her own throat. She ran her tongue over her parted lips. She was, he realized, aroused, sexually, and to his horror, he realized, so was he. He was also disgusted.

"You didn't have to do that," he said. "He would have talked. He's just a kid. You didn't have to kill him."

She smiled. "Don't worry. One more dead boy doesn't add up to much in Afghanistan. There's a war going on, remember?"

"But he's not Afghani, is he?" Powell argued. "He's American. He's from Brooklyn, for God's sake."

"Well then," Vicky said with a shrug, "he should have stayed home, shouldn't he, where it's safe? Now then . . ." She casually reached between his legs, feeling where, without his own consent or control, he responded to her touch. "Are you going to continue to bore me? Because if so, you can find a cab, and I'll ask my handsome driver to escort me safely home."

That was when Powell understood that, like some character in an old folktale, he had met the devil and without even knowing it, had traded away his soul.

❖

Joe and Yelena were on the highway. When they came down from the hotel, they'd found their driver still out front, taking a smoke break after bundling up the torn fabric from his truck's awning. "Kabul?" Joe asked him, gesturing to Yelena and himself. He pulled out another hundred. "The airport in Kabul? *Beh fooroodgah?*"

The driver hesitated. It was more than four hundred fifty kilometers; it would take all night. And he already knew these foreigners were armed and in some kind of trouble. Then again, trouble was not unusual in Kandahar, nor were armed foreigners, and this one was holding out another hundred-dollar bill. He added yet another, two hundreds, making three for the night. The driver shrugged and pocketed them, then got his engine going while his passengers settled in the back, using the fabric to improvise cushions.

And so, Joe and Yelena got to take in the view after all, riding through the desert at night, watching the ancient landscape pass, the moon rise and fall, staring up from their makeshift bed at the infinite stars, which had outshone all the names they'd been given and the countless prayers they'd heard, until, alive for one more day, both finally drifted into sleep, holding each other under the silence of heaven.

PART II

PART II

11

PARKS WAS AMBIVALENT: DISGUSTED by what it must be like to live in Fusco's body, but intrigued by his mind. Here he was, on his own time, spending the night in a van he cashed in a favor to unofficially borrow, working an off-the-books stakeout on a Brooklyn cop-spot, while Parks, admittedly, was home eating veggie burgers with his wife and kids. He might have been less impressed if he knew that Fusco was twice-divorced, that his kids didn't speak to him, and that if he hadn't been here, surrounded by soda bottles, candy wrappers, McDonald's bags, and, good Lord, were those Funyuns, his night off would have been spent losing at blackjack, but still . . . he'd put in the work, followed his hunch, and now he'd called in his partner to show him what he'd found: an honest-to-God clue. Classic detective work that Parks had to respect. This was why, as he discreetly shut the van door, and crept into the spare seat, he was feeling proud to be partnered with Francis "Fartso" Fusco. Then he kicked over the piss bottle.

"Oh Jesus fuck!" Parks called out as his foot, shod in an expensive soft leather boot that he was wearing with clean, new jeans and a button down shirt on his night off, kicked over a one-liter soda bottle that he realized, with horror, was full of urine and not very well sealed. Liquid gurgled out.

"What's wrong?"

"You disgusting pig!" Parks jumped up, pointing.

"Oh shit . . ." Fusco reached down and grabbed the bottle, moving it to a more stable spot. "Watch where you step."

"Watch where I step?" Parks was furious. "Watch where you empty your diseased bladder you gross animal."

"It's a stakeout," Fusco wheedled, in the same tone Parks's kids used when they wanted to skip flossing on a camping trip.

"Look, why the hell am I even here to witness this horror?" Parks asked, keeping well away.

Fusco checked his watch. "Because the show's about to start. Sit down and quit bitching." He patted at the chair and Parks gingerly sat so that he could see out the rear windows, filled with one-way glass. "And if you're thirsty," Fusco added, "help yourself to some soda."

"Fuck you, Fartso."

Fusco chuckled, then reached for his camera as he saw something. "Okay, here it is. Look."

They were in a dusty, graffiti-covered old van, parked up the block from the projects, with a good view out the back of an entrance between two brick towers. Young lookouts steered customers around the corner and into one of the buildings while civilians came and went, minding their own business. A car approached, slowing as it reached the spot.

"Black Mercedes?"

"Exactly. It's the re-up. But never mind the dope, watch the guys." He put the camera to his face and began shooting. Parks watched as the Mercedes, black metal gleaming and chrome glaring in the streetlights, rolled to a stop at the corner. The driver, with slicked-back hair, a thick gold chain, and a lot of ink showing under his white sleeveless T-shirt, peered out his window, watching for cops. The front passenger, a big man dressed in a tracksuit, with a shaved head and also a lot of black, prison-style tattoos, stepped out as a young kid rushed up from the closest doorway. The big man grabbed a paper grocery bag and handed it to the kid, who immediately scurried back over the sidewalk and vanished into the projects. The big guy jumped back in and they rolled.

"So kid, tell me what you see," Fusco said, still snapping away, getting the plates, till the car turned the corner.

"Nothing. A typical re-up. But we already know they're selling dope here. Maybe if you followed them."

"Not in this. They'd spot us in five minutes. We need a real team to do that. But what else did your keen detective mind notice?" He showed him the screen of the digital camera and scrolled through pictures he'd just shot. "Or are you one of those jerk-off liberals who claims not to see skin color?"

Now Parks grinned. "They're white."

Fusco grinned back. "Exactly."

"White gangsters dropping off the stash at a Black cop spot, in the projects."

"Not something you see every day is it?"

"Not something you see ever."

"So the plot thickens."

"No doubt, we got ourselves a bona fide mystery here."

"See," Fusco said, patting his shoulder. "I knew you had a detective's mind behind that pretty face."

"And I always knew you had some wisdom buried in all that fat and bad breath," Parks answered, happily. "But now what? I mean, you had me at heroin. You really think this is going to make the boss fall in love with this case?"

"Nope. I'm playing the long game here. But the next move is yours. That's why I called you in."

"Oh yeah?"

Fusco peered into the interior of the projects. "I need you to go in there and cop us a bag of this bomb dope everyone is talking about."

"Why me? Cause I'm Black?" Parks asked, incredulous.

"Exactly," Fusco said. "Look at me. I'm an old fat white guy who looks like a cop, as you never get tired of pointing out."

"And I'm dressed better than you, motherfucker. You think I look like a junkie?"

Fusco shrugged. "You look like a pansy. But pansies get high too sometimes. I'm not prejudiced."

Parks shook his head. Then he noticed something. "Here we go. Give me that camera." He took the camera and started shooting, as an emaciated white boy with stringy hair, dressed in rags, came loping along. "Now that's what a junkie looks like."

The junkie passed the van and went up to the lookout, a Black teenager, who nodded him in, then waved and whistled to his cohorts.

"Yeah okay, so what?" Fusco asked.

"So you wanted dope, I'm getting you dope," Parks said. "For free." The junkie disappeared around a corner and emerged seconds later, a new spring in his step. "Let's give him a block or two before we roust him."

Two blocks later, as the junkie turned a corner, Fusco pulled up sharply, and Parks jumped out, grabbing him up. They cuffed him, patted him down, took his dope and dragged him back to the station, where to his great relief, they told him they would turn him loose in exchange for surrendering his drugs and signing a statement about when and where he'd obtained them. He eagerly agreed. The dope was in a small wax paper envelope, taped shut and stamped with a crude design: an angel, wings outstretched as though in blessing or mid-flight.

"Now what?" Parks asked as they finished the paperwork and added this newest piece of evidence to the growing file on the case they were definitely not supposed to be working.

"Now," Fusco said, with a belch as he guzzled a Diet Coke (*I mean, really*, Parks thought, *Diet? Why bother?*), "I call a guy I know at the FBI and ask a favor."

12

DONNA WAS THINKING THAT maybe she kind of liked this guy.
Sort of. Gary was handsome—dark wavy hair and deep brown eyes and
more built up than most guys she dated, with the big shoulders and arms
of a gym rat. Smart too. According to Ari, he made big bucks in finance
but had grad degrees in math and computer technology rather than the
usual MBA. The dinner was lovely. Donna couldn't recall the last time
she had such delicious wine, or drank so much of it, or laughed so much
and felt so free, of work, stress, everything. He neither bragged about
himself and his career nor made her feel weird about her own: why would
a nice girl like her be wearing a gun and chasing villains? Did she have
some kind of issue? Some unresolved, repressed anger she wasn't in touch
with? *Not at all*, she always wanted to say, *my anger's getting in touch right
now. And it has a message for you: Fuck off.*

But Gary was different. He seemed genuinely interested, impressed,
even fascinated by what she did, listening raptly as she talked about her
training and experience. By the time they got to dessert, she even found
herself revealing how she'd been the best shot in her class at Quantico and
kept up at the range weekly, about her martial arts training, and about
the course in disarming bombs she'd just done—though she fudged the
part about failing it. Before she knew it, the panna cotta was gone and
she'd been blabbing for twenty minutes. She felt embarrassed suddenly,
rambling on like this, even bragging, but when she stopped herself she

realized that Gary was not bored or staring in shock, he was smiling warmly and his narrowed eyes were gleaming, the pupils enlarged. He was totally engaged, even, she ventured, aroused. Interesting. The check appeared and he reached for it and she let him. She smiled at him, her sexy smile, the one with the parted lips and melting chocolate eyes, took a last sip of wine, and, as he put his card in the binder, reached out to give his wrist a quick squeeze.

"Thank you," she said, keeping eye contact, "for a wonderful evening."

"The first of many I hope," he said; then, "It's so nice out tonight. Shall we walk?"

❖

It was just as they were having their first kiss that the fight started.

Gary had been right. It was indeed a nice night. The restaurant he'd chosen was in Tribeca, so they ended up walking by the river. They wandered along, side by side, first chatting, then in comfortable silence, as other folks drifted by on foot or wheels. The trees and grass seemed to filter and diffuse the city light and noise into something softer—the glare into moonlight, the yelling and honking into soft laughter and warm conversation. The traffic on the West Side Highway became another river, whispering behind them as they leaned on the railing, shoulders touching, hers bare and smooth, and stared across the Hudson toward New Jersey. The river was never really still of course (she was an Uptown girl, from Washington Heights, and the river was in the background of all her memories, its smell wafting over the rooftops in the summer, the biting winds chapping her hands and face in the winter), but tonight it looked polished, gleaming, a black lacquered surface held taut over the currents that stirred beneath it, like a sleeping body under a black silk sheet. That was when she felt Gary cover her hand with his, and squeeze it, and she squeezed back, like a little message passing back and forth. She felt him move, turning to her profile and she turned to face him and there they were, eye to eye, holding hands,

and they leaned together, as her eyes shut, and their mouths softly met. A perfect first kiss.

"Fucking bitch!"

Lips still touching, her eyes opened, and she saw Gary's also open wide. The voice was coming from behind them.

"Where the fuck do you think you're going?"

Some big loudmouth white guy, or red guy really—he had the telltale blush and sweat of an angry drunk—in a half-unbuttoned shirt and khakis, was yelling at a woman, also white and blonde. She was dressed to go out in a red dress and heels, but her hair was falling out of its ponytail and her makeup was streaked with tears.

"I said, where the fuck do you think you're going?" The guy was close to her now, no doubt breathing booze in her face. She turned away.

"Home," she said and started walking. The drunk reached out and grabbed her hand.

"Do not," he screamed now, "do not fucking walk away while I'm talking to you!"

While this drama played out, Donna had silently flipped a mental switch and was back in work mode. She checked discreetly for her gun (ankle holster), badge (purse), and phone (back pocket), and got ready to intervene if necessary, already assessing how she would take down this big bag of guts. But her training also made her hesitate, be sure a crime was actually happening before she took action—since just being a loud drunken slob was technically still legal in New York State, unfortunately. A lot of the local economy depended on it. And that's when she realized that Gary, the civilian she'd just been kissing, was already getting involved.

"Hey," he called out, stepping away from her and toward the blowhard, blocking her view, which was bad. "Excuse me."

The drunk turned on him. "What the fuck do you want? Directions?"

"If the lady wants to go, let her go," Gary said, stepping closer, his wide back to Donna now.

"Mind your own goddamn business," the drunk said and turned after the woman again. She was walking away fast, trying to just exit the whole

scene. The drunk reached for her, she pulled away, and the strap of her dress tore. She screamed. Gary grabbed the guy by the arm, yanking him back, which was no problem, because he was pretty strong and relatively sober, but also left his body wide open and with his weight all on one foot, off balance, which became a problem when, with the sudden focus and viciousness mean drunks are prone to, the guy whirled around, breaking free of Gary's grip and pulling a switchblade from his back pocket. Gary now jumped back, stumbling, and fell to the ground as the drunk came at him, blade first.

That's when Donna moved. Gary, by exacerbating the situation and also placing his body between herself and the drunk, had left her with only two real options. The first was to draw her weapon and order the suspect to freeze. The problem with that was he was really close to carving Gary open and so, if he didn't freeze, like instantly, she would most probably have to shoot him. Having a random encounter escalate from yelling and a torn dress to lethal force in ten seconds was not something she looked forward to explaining.

So she went with option two: she jumped over Gary, kicking the knife from the assailant's hand, then swiveled, her other foot coming up to catch him hard in the belly and knock the wind out of him. As he bent forward, gasping, she stepped to the side, tripping him by kicking his ankle and then using all her weight to force him down, so that he flopped onto his face, right beside Gary, who was just getting his bearings. She ground a knee into his back to keep him in place, bent his arm back to keep him in pain and under her power, and then drew her weapon, pressing the barrel against his neck so he could feel it in his alcohol-and-rage-sodden brain.

"FBI," she yelled, standing up now, gun in two hands. "Do not move, or I will shoot and kill you."

"Okay, okay," the guy yelled into the concrete against which his face was being smushed by her foot.

"You okay miss?" she asked the woman, who was watching all this in a daze, one hand holding up her dress. She nodded.

Then she turned to Gary, who was now on his knees, unharmed but stunned. "Gary, can you do me favor?" she asked. He looked up at her, his expression one of amazement. "Can you get your phone and call 911?"

❖

Actually one of the passersby who had witnessed the fight had already called 911 and some cops, who'd been patrolling the park nearby, appeared almost immediately. Donna identified herself and showed them her ID, then explained what had gone down. The older, male partner cuffed the suspect and led him off. His younger, female partner dealt with the victim, or victims if you counted Gary. But once she took down all their info, and the woman was safely in the back of a patrol car that had arrived meantime, Donna pulled her aside. She was an Asian woman in her mid-twenties with bobbed hair.

"Listen," she asked her in a low voice. "I know you have a ton of paperwork to do, but I was kind of on a date here. You mind if I come by and finish all this tomorrow?"

The officer shrugged. "I don't see why not. He's so drunk, by the time we book him and dump him in a cell he's going to be passed out anyway. You enjoy the rest of your evening." She glanced at Gary and smiled. "He is pretty cute."

"Isn't he?" Donna agreed, regarding Gary, who was back on his feet and looking fine, if still a little dazed. "Thank you so much."

"It's a pleasure," the cop said. "And Agent Zamora?" She extended her hand. "Nice work."

"Thank you, officer," she answered and shook. "I appreciate that."

Then she went over to Gary.

"Hey how you feeling? Are you okay?" she asked, her voice low and soothing, though she herself actually felt pretty great. She gave him a hug and he squeezed her back with real feeling.

"Wow," he said, "that was something. I'm a little nauseous. You were amazing back there."

She hid her grin. "I'm just glad no one got hurt. Especially you. And nausea is normal. It's the adrenaline and the shock. It will pass. But you're okay otherwise? Feeling fit?"

"Sure," he said. "Thanks to you."

"Great," Donna said, taking his hand, and leading him away from the crime scene. "Because when you were giving your statement, I couldn't help overhearing that your address is very close by."

13

"**You are a no** good, lying, cheating, adulterous bastard!"

"I know . . . I'm sorry . . ."

"You betrayed me, our family, everything . . ."

"I know . . . you're right . . . I deserve to be punished . . ."

"You deserve to be beaten, whipped . . ."

"Yes! Please! Punish me . . ."

In a rage, Carol swung the belt up high and then brought it down, hard, across her husband's back. The buckle knocked hard on the side of his head.

"Ow! Damn it, Carol . . ." He grabbed his head and rubbed the spot where no doubt a small contusion would rise.

"What happened? What happened?" Carol bent over him, suddenly frantic.

"Don't use the buckle end, Jesus . . ." Gio said, pissed.

"Oh my God, I'm so sorry, I didn't even think about it."

"Obviously not."

"I'm really sorry. Do you want me to get you some ice for it?"

"No, no, it's okay. Maybe after. Just hold it the other way and try again. Double it up. Gives you better control."

"Okay. That's a good idea."

"And whip my ass, not my head for Chrissakes."

"Yes, Gio. Sorry. I'll try."

Carol tried. She doubled up the thick leather of Gio's belt, the casual one he wore with jeans, gripped it tightly in her fist, and tried to focus, but she felt like maybe the moment had passed. It had, she admitted, been all her idea. After their attempt at couple's therapy failed spectacularly, she was depressed, but one point the therapist made stuck with her: she'd asked why Gio's special needs couldn't just be incorporated into their marriage. At first, she'd been defensive—he was the betrayer, the violator, the weirdo. Why should she adapt? But then she began to think that maybe this would promote deeper understanding and communication and eventually healing. It could be a breakthrough.

So she brought it up, and though he seemed irritated and embarrassed by the idea at first, totally dismissive, she told him they had to do something, so tonight, with their son out at a movie and their daughter eating dinner at a friend's, they decided to try. It was super awkward at first, and sexually it did nothing for her, but once she got into it, Carol had to admit it was a release. Just as, according to Gio, being dominated like this was a chance to give up control, to be free of the tension and responsibility he carried all the time, so for her, it was kind of liberating to let out all the anger and outrage she'd been holding in (well, not exactly holding it all in, she did shoot that man) but which she had not been able to voice directly to Gio in this way, and with him in a posture of supplication and surrender, accepting it.

It was amazing, she thought, her mind drifting for a second, how much we therapists could learn from our supposedly "sick" patients, how people instinctively found their own solutions, their own strategies for psychic survival. Maybe this could be theirs.

She lifted the belt again, high up, and was bringing it back down with all her might, when her hand, a bit sweaty, slipped, and the end of the doubled belt snapped out of her grip, catching her in the eye. She squealed in pain and Gio jumped up from the floor, standing over her solicitously.

"What's wrong, baby? Are you all right?"

"My eye . . ."

"Let me see." He took her face gently in his hands. She blinked up at him, tears flowing from that one eye. "Looks okay," he told her.

"Guess I'm a pretty crappy dominatrix," she said.

"The worst," he told her with a smile.

"Sorry . . ."

He started laughing.

"What?"

"Stop apologizing! I mean it's hard enough to just keep a straight face . . ."

"Oh right, sorry!" And with that, hearing herself, she burst into laughter too. Then she caught her own image in the mirror: there she was in her best stockings, garters, and a bustier she hadn't worn in ages, holding a belt and laughing. And there was Gio, her husband, squeezed absurdly into her largest pair of cotton panties, which were still basically choking him. It made her laugh harder. "You can't keep a straight face?" she yelled, pointing in the mirror. "Look at you!"

He saw himself and started to howl, clutching his stomach as he laughed. He lay down on the bed and she flopped beside him. It felt so good to be laughing together like this. It had been forever. She felt all of her tension and anger, all of her grief and bottled up fear exploding out of her. She was purging, they both were, as they rocked back and forth laughing, and suddenly, as one emotion after another passed uncontrollably through her body, she felt an overwhelming lust, an animal horniness that seemed to erupt out of the wild, primitive laughter that contorted their bodies. She rolled on top of Gio, straddling him, and furiously, they began to make love.

"Mom! Dad! Anybody home?"

It was Nora, their daughter, stomping up the stairs and yelling. Both Gio and Carol froze. "Did you lock the door?" he asked.

No. In a panic she jumped up and ran for her robe. But where was it? She'd flung it somewhere when first revealing her role-play outfit.

"Hey, you guys . . ." Nora's voice rang out from the hall. Realizing he had no time, Gio just put a pillow over his groin, hiding the flowered panties and the erection that distorted them, and then clutched at the blankets as the door opened. Carol simply turned to face her daughter in a fake casual pose, hands absurdly on her hips.

"Oh my God," Nora blurted as she stormed in.

"Haven't you heard of knocking?"

"It's like 7:30," Nora replied, somewhat off topic. "Who's in bed or undressed at 7:30?" Her eyes widened. "You guys weren't doing it were you?" Her face was a mask of horror.

"Don't be silly," Carol said.

"We were just talking," Gio added, having now got most of his body under cover.

"In your underwear?" Nora asked.

"Why not?" Carol asked, sitting on the bed and crossing her legs casually. "We're comfortable with our bodies."

"Gross," Nora decided.

"Anyway," Carol said, "Why are you home at 7:30?"

Nora shrugged and sat on the bed beside her. "I don't know. Mr. and Mrs. Turner are nice but sooo boring. And they're vegan, which is totally cool and like commendable, but the food had no taste, so . . ." She shrugged. Carol rubbed her back.

"Want me to heat up some sausage and peppers?"

"Nah . . ."

"I've got an idea," Gio said, glancing at his watch. "I've got to pick your brother up at the movies. What do you say we go by the warehouse after?"

"Yes! Can we?" Nora jumped around on the bed and Gio made sure to hold his covers down.

"Sure. It's a hot night. Just let me get dressed and we'll go. We can catch the last run before it goes out."

❖

And so, Gio and Carol threw on some clothes, decidedly nonfetish, though he did grab the belt and loop it through his jeans, picked up Jason, and headed to the warehouse where his family's fleet of Italian Ice and Soft Serve Frozen Custard trucks were headquartered. In a tradition that had begun when his kids were small and that, he realized suddenly, they would soon be too old for, he requisitioned one of the trucks, giving the driver a paid night off, and drove the route himself, with his kids handling sales, scooping ices, dispensing ice cream into cones, and squirting whipped cream and syrup onto sundaes, under Carol's supervision.

The truth is, that ice cream truck song can turn you into a psycho after a while, but otherwise it was pretty perfect, steering the old truck along the road, pulling in at beach parking lots and boardwalks, in the square white box with Caprisi's painted on the side in red cursive. He'd done this with his grandfather, who liked to personally take a truck out now and then and give out free ices to the neighborhood kids, who ran to line up when they saw his kindly face behind the wheel. Good memories. He'd kept up the tradition with his own kids as a lesson in hard work and in the family's working-class immigrant roots. Though he'd decided to spare them the lesson he'd learned another time when, on a different run late at night, with his father and grandpa, he'd had to dig in the freezer under the cartons of ice cream bars and retrieve the plastic bag which contained two hands, both rights, which they'd saved when disposing of a couple of rivals months before and used to plant misleading prints at a crime scene. The experience almost turned him off toasted almond bars, his favorite.

His family were complicated people. No wonder he had issues. But for now, for tonight, those issues seemed far away, and he felt calm, happy, and grateful, feeling the ocean breeze touch his skin, the sultry night air mingling with the frozen drafts from the ices, hearing his children laugh and the happy shouts of the customers ordering, and beyond that the sound of the ocean, crashing softly on the sand. He parked facing the beach, so he could hear the kids while watching the

water, a dark wave under a dark sky, lit here and there by the moonlight, ceaselessly appearing and disappearing on the shore. While she talked to their kids, Carol reached over and stroked his head affectionately from behind, playing absently with his hair. Unknowingly, she kept touching the place where she'd hit him, which was now bruised and tender. But he didn't say anything or let himself flinch: the perfect joy he felt was more than worth the pain.

14

THAT NIGHT, WHEN HIS brother died and returned from the dead, Liam was more grateful than ever to have Josh there with him.

They'd first met working for Joe, on his last caper: Liam as the youngest of the Madigan brothers, up-and-coming Irish hoodlums, Josh, freshly arrived from Israel, as a new member of Rebbe Stone's crew. When Josh was shot, Liam had transported him to safety, and the unspoken attraction between them had bloomed. They'd been a couple ever since.

This day had started early, with a hijacking: a load of digital cameras, Chinese-made cellphones and fancy vacuum cleaners, the kind you strapped to your back. A guy Liam's middle brother, Sean, drank with had tipped him off to it. He worked in the port of Newark and for a fee would let Sean know when the truck was leaving. The tricky part was how to take it: though more than one gangster had vanished into the surrounding swamplands, there was no way to guarantee that the truck would be heading down an empty road at a conveniently quiet hour. In fact, as it turned out, it was early morning, when the whole area was bustling.

Luckily, Liam had come up with a clever scheme and Josh, with his army training, had been able to implement it quite easily. Brandishing a fake manifest for a missing shipment, they walked onto the shipping company's yard before the truck ever even left to pick up the container. They found the right vehicle and, while Liam stood lookout, Josh had

crept under a wheel well and attached a small explosive device with a tiny radio transmitter.

Next, they got back in their own truck, a tow they had borrowed from their pal Cash, a highly successful car thief from the Chinese section of Flushing, who used a large junkyard called Reliable Scrap as his cover to strip and move stolen cars. They'd painted over the Reliable logo and switched the plates. Then, while the semi they had rigged was inside the port being loaded, they waited, drinking coffee and watching day break over the reed-filled wetlands, looking at the sun glint on the silver towers of chemical plants and burn through the wavering fumes while planes from Newark Liberty Airport passed, leaving jet trails overhead, listening to the songs of whatever strange birds could thrive in this wasteland and still find something to sing about.

"There it is." Josh pointed.

"I've got it," Liam said. "Let's give him a little more rope."

He put the tow truck in gear and slowly rolled out, while Josh got ready with the radio control. They let the truck get about fifty yards ahead on the road that led to the interstate, and then, as it cruised along between fenced-in waste ground, Josh pressed the button and the truck's front right tire blew. The whole rig shimmied, as the driver fought to steady it. Air brakes huffing, he slowly pulled over. That's when Liam drove up, honking, and stopped alongside.

"Hey," he yelled to the driver. "I just saw that blowout. You need some help?"

"Good timing!" the driver called back.

"Let's pull off over here," Liam told him, and guided him slowly onto a broken asphalt side road that ran into the high weeds, screened from the traffic.

"Now then," he said in his bright Irish accent, as he and Josh got out and met the driver as he climbed down from the cab. "Let's see if we can be of some assistance."

❖

A few hours later, Liam and Josh drove the truck into a South Williamsburg warehouse owned by Menachem "Rebbe" Stone. It looked like any of the other Hasidic-owned warehouses that stretched along the street: a brick hulk with a fenced-in yard, weeds sprouting in the cracked concrete. A pimply young man in a wide-brimmed black hat, white shirt, and long coat, with a sparse reddish beard, pulled the gate back, and they backed in, parking with the rear of the truck at the loading dock. Another thickset fellow looked down from the roof and nodded at Josh as he climbed from the cab. He too was in black, and heavily black-bearded, as were most of the men here. A few younger men had short, trimmed beards like Josh and were in regular clothes—jeans and polo shirts or button-downs—but still with yarmulkes and tzitzit, the knotted threads, dangling from their undershirts. They opened the truck and quickly began unloading, passing cartons to a forklift that was likewise operated by a skullcap-wearing bearded man in a white shirt and black trousers—his missing jacket the only accommodation made to the oppressive heat inside the dusty warehouse. Josh sat on the truck fender and lit a cigarette and Liam sat beside him and watched: for a lad from Belfast this was exotic indeed. Then a stout, older man with a stringy gray beard that hung like a tie over his shirt passed by, muttering something that Liam couldn't understand but that included the words "goyim" and "fagalah," at least one of which he could guess at. He let it pass, figuring it wasn't his place to intrude, but Josh felt different. As the mutterer passed, Josh reached out and grabbed his beard, hard, yanking him down so that he was bent nearly double and groaning. "What did you say?"

"Nothing, nothing . . ." the mutterer mumbled now, struggling but too scared to raise a hand.

Josh began singeing off strands of his beard with his lit cigarette. The man squealed and squirmed. Liam smelled burnt hair.

"You know what I did in the army don't you? Do you know how many ways they taught me to hurt you just with this cigarette? Do you?" He yanked harder.

"No . . ." the man shook his head, still straining as the beard pulled at his flesh.

"I'm not sure either. Let's count and see . . ."

"Yoshua!" a voice with an old-world lilt to it reached them from inside. Josh looked up. It was Rebbe, who had emerged from an inner office. "Stop fooling around and come here."

Josh let go immediately and the man gasped, stumbling back as if released from a tether, and then scurried off. Josh handed his cigarette to Liam, who took a drag then stomped it out, grinning.

Rebbe put his arm around Josh and led him off to a corner. "*Luzzem*," he said. "Don't bother with that *meskite*. He's a nobody. A nudnik. Not worth your time."

"Yes sir," Josh said.

"Your family back home, they're okay?"

"Yes, everyone is fine, thank you."

"And the job, no troubles?"

"No. Smooth."

"Good work, boychick." He squeezed his cheek, hard enough to leave an impression, then called to another tough-looking man in a long black beard and black suit. "Shlomo, get a couple cameras and one of those vacuums and put them in my trunk."

❖

In no time the goods were unpacked and distributed to camera and electronics stores run by Orthodox Jews as well as other dealers further down the pipeline: Black-owned appliance stores in Bed-Stuy, an Italian hardware shop in South Slope, even a discount place along Atlantic run by two Palestinian brothers. This was New York. Meanwhile, Liam and Josh disposed of the truck, leaving it under the BQE, had dinner at a Mexican place, and then circled back to pick up their share of the proceeds. It was a nice score, not at all bad for a day's work, and Liam knew Sean would be pleased with how things turned out. He'd been

complaining about money and had called a couple times to ask about the dough, so Liam was surprised when he finally called to say he had it and Sean didn't even pick up. But then again, that was Sean. Jack, the eldest, was the grown-up, steady brother. He was married already with a second kid on the way, and the kind of tough guy who had no trouble using a gun but would rather try his fists first. The scar tissue on his knuckles testified how often that was sufficient.

Sean was the wild middle brother. The one who got into scrapes as a kid, dropped out of school, who got drunk and fought now, and who, Liam suspected, might have developed a taste for other substances as well. And Liam? He was the baby, the spoiled one, pretty and clever, who got top grades at school but still preferred the life of crime to the life of the mind, and found, when the time came, that violence, when necessary, caused him no bother at all. They'd been brought over from Ireland by Pat White, a distant relative and then the boss of what was left of the Westies, the Irish mob who once ran Hell's Kitchen and still ran a share of bookmaking, extortion, robbery, political influence, and murder. But Pat had sold them out, and the Madigan brothers, with an assist from Gio, were in charge now.

"Mind if we swing by me brother's?" Liam asked Josh now. "I know that eejit too well. Even if he's dead drunk, he'll wake up yowling for his money like a babe for a tit."

"Of course not," Josh said, squeezing his hand. "It's a nice night for a drive."

So they cruised up the West Side to the rent-controlled walk-up that Sean had taken over when the former occupant, a one-time bank robber turned FBI snitch named Harry Harrigan, had been disposed of. Now the Madigans controlled the building, along with most of Pat's other assets, like the parking lot where they left Josh's Volvo convertible.

They buzzed. No answer. Was he drinking at a local bar? If so, he would have answered his phone. A neighbor came out, opening the street door, and they climbed the stairs and rang. Still nothing, but he could hear the TV.

"Come on, wake up, you moron!" Liam yelled, banging the door. It swung open. At this both men froze. Liam reached down and pulled the revolver he had in his ankle holster. He glanced at Josh, who nodded, and carefully stepped in. The lights were on. The TV was playing. Sean was alone, spread on the couch. His face was white. His lips were blue. His eyes were staring up at nothing. Drool curled from his slack mouth. And a needle dangled from his arm.

❖

It was Josh who knew what to do. He'd had medic training and it kicked into action. He immediately checked Sean's pulse and breathing and then got him on the floor where he performed CPR. Liam watched, frozen in horror.

"Liam! You need to focus," Josh yelled at him, as he pumped Sean's chest. He tossed him his keys. "There's a bag in the trunk of my car."

Snapping out of it, Liam caught the keys and sprinted frantically down to the lot, running right past the attendant to fetch the small first aid kit, and came back, breathing hard. By then Liam had him breathing shallowly, alive, if just barely. He tore the kit open, found the Naloxone, and injected Sean. Instantly, he was back, rejoining the living with a scream that made it seem more like a nightmare than a joy, perhaps similar to the scream he'd uttered at birth.

Later, after they'd made sure Sean was all right, and he'd cried and apologized, and Liam had cried and cursed him out and then forgiven him, and they'd gotten Sean to bed (though not before he remembered to ask for his money), they shut the bedroom door, and Liam put his arms around Josh, his eyes still shined with tears. "You saved his life. I don't know what to say. I was useless. Thank God for you, Josh."

Josh smiled back. "You saved mine too, remember? And risked your own for me."

Liam shook his head. "That's shite. We were partners on a job and you were just wounded. This is different. He was dead. Dead."

They gripped each other then, tight, and Liam, as if sharing a secret, whispered to him: "I love you."

Josh whispered back, "I love you too."

Before they left, Liam picked up the syringe and broke it with an expression of disgust. He threw it in the trash with the tarnished spoon Sean had used to cook the shot that had nearly killed him. That *had* killed him, Liam corrected himself, since his brother had died before Josh brought him back. And there on the coffee table beside it was a torn little envelope, coated with a trace of bitter powder, and stamped with the image of an angel, wings up, as though still poised to fly off with your soul.

15

USING ALL HER TRAINING and stealth, Special Agent Donna Zamora carefully turned the doorknob and entered the premises at 7:15 A.M. Taking care not to alert the occupants, she crept into the living room, silently shutting the door behind her.

"Morning, hon. Have a fun date?"

Donna froze in shock, regarding her accoster with horror. She did not, however, draw her weapon, as much as she might have liked to. Watching her from the kitchen doorway, with a cup of coffee in her hand (it was Donna's favorite mug, the one her daughter Larissa had painted for her with rainbows and suns), was Gladys Brody, Joe Brody's grandmother and, to Donna's extreme discomfort, her own mother's new best friend.

"Gladys! Why are you here?"

"I'm waiting for your mom. We're going to AC."

"Oh right. I forgot. Did you hurt yourself?" Gladys had a therapeutic cuff Velcroed around her lower arm.

"It's for the slots hon."

Her mom came in, from Donna's bedroom, where she slept when staying with Larissa overnight, already dressed and carrying a bag. She broke into a warm smile and came to kiss Donna. "Good morning, *mija*. You had a fun night I guess?"

Mortified, Donna glared at her. "If stakeouts are fun. I told you I was working."

Her mom shrugged.

"Gladys . . ." Donna changed the subject. "How's Joe these days?"

"He's working a lot too, like you. Out of town business trip."

"Really? I didn't know bouncers went on business trips. Did he have to go throw a drunk out of a strip club in another state?"

Now her daughter came out rubbing her eyes, looking heartrendingly adorable as she did every morning, in her pink Disney nightgown, her long hair floating like a cloud around her. "Mommy!"

She ran over for a hug. "I dreamed about pancakes."

"You did?"

She nodded. "Daddy came to take me and brought a bear."

"Sorry sweetheart. Daddy's at work, I told you. He had to go away. But I'm sure he will bring you something when he gets home. Now come on, let's make you some pancakes."

As she led her daughter toward the kitchen, she wondered if what she'd just told her was true. Her ex, Mike Powell, was CIA and, as far Donna knew, had suddenly been reassigned to a top-secret mission overseas. Abusive and controlling during their brief marriage, he had become obsessive, almost a stalker, during their divorce. But he had always been a loving and dutiful father, visiting Larissa often, attending school events, paying his share. Recently, however, he had revealed himself to be a real creep, the kind of creep who thought that undermining her career might somehow paradoxically win her back or teach her a lesson. The kind of creep who thought that rejecting him was something she needed to be punished for. This made dealing with him and arrangements for their daughter go from tense and awkward to full-on toxic, so when he suddenly announced that he was leaving and that where and why and how long were all classified, she was, frankly, relieved. But she couldn't explain that to Larissa. So she kept saying that Daddy was away, and would be back soon, though she fervently hoped that was not true.

She poured orange juice and handed it to Larissa, then poured coffee for herself.

"Donna!" her mom called out. "The van is here. We're going." Larissa ran over. "Come kiss Grandma goodbye. And give Aunty Gladys a hug."

Aunt Gladys? Donna sighed. She had to admit that she was fond of Gladys herself, and her friendship did seem to be brightening her Mom's life up a bit, though when she referred to Gladys as her "partner in crime," did she get that Gladys was an actual criminal with a rap sheet longer than most of the suspects Donna investigated at the FBI? It was one more complication in her already too mixed-up life. Speaking of which, there was Gary to think about now as well. She'd crept out while he slept, having told him in advance she needed to get home and relieve her mom from babysitting duty.

As if on cue, Donna's phone buzzed. It was a text from Andy. *So???*

Frowning, she texted back: *It was fun. Nice guy.*

Just fun? She felt Andy jumping down her throat from over the phone. *When Gary never called Ari for the post game briefing we thought—score!*

Um . . . she considered, then typed. *It got a little complicated. I will tell you later.*

I'm meeting Blaze for a beer later. Come and tell me all about it!

Blaze was Deputy Federal Marshal Blaze Logan. She and Donna had worked together, ending up in a couple of tight spots, and had become pals. Then, as an openly gay federal agent, Blaze had found she had a lot to talk to Andy about as well.

Great, she texted with one hand as Larissa, having distributed her kisses and hugs, took the other, chirping "Mommy! Pancakes!" *Just pick someplace quiet where we can actually talk please.*

Done, he answered, though Donna didn't believe it. She went in to start the batter, and while her daughter loudly requested bananas, and her mom and "Aunt Gladys" left to party in Atlantic City with their van full of old biddies, she found herself wondering, where in hell did Joe really go on his supposed business trip, and why?

❖

Joe woke up from a nightmare as they landed. Or rather, Yelena woke him.

"Joe," she said, "Joe," shaking his shoulder lightly and speaking softly into his ears.

"Huh?" His eyes popped opened. "What?"

"You're scaring these people."

He sat up and looked around. A flight attendant was crouching over them and, across the aisle, a woman a sweat suit with a blanket wrapped around her was staring in alarm. The heads of two small children, a boy and girl, peeked over the seats in front of him, their mustachioed hipster father hovering with a look of stern disapproval from behind his cool glasses.

"Sir . . ." The flight attendant leaned in, scolding him. "You can't yell and use foul language. You're disturbing the other passengers."

"Sorry," Joe said, nodding and rubbing his eyes. He'd thrown his own blanket on the floor and his Rilke paperback lay twisted on his lap, as though he'd tried to strangle it.

"Now please return your seat to the upright position," the flight attendant said. "We will be landing soon."

She moved on. The lady across the aisle kept glaring. "Disgusting," she muttered to no one.

"Sit down," the dad told his kids, then told Joe, "Chill out, all right, dude? You're scaring my kids." They didn't look scared, as it happened. They were grinning.

"You sit down and put your belt on," Yelena told him, flatly. She looked him the eye. "Imagine how upset they'll be if you get injured. Badly."

His eyes widened at her. Then he sniffed and sat back down.

"What was I saying?" Joe asked Yelena.

"Nothing. Just yelling fuck and shit like usual."

"Oh . . . sorry . . ." He saw the kids still peeking at him, now with their eyes pressed to the cracks between the seats. He winked at them. They giggled. Then he turned to look past Yelena and out the window. They were descending rapidly. The engines roared. Moisture

streaked the glass like tears as they tore through the atmosphere. Mist clung to the plane's wing in shreds. New York City was emerging from the clouds. He was home.

❖

Toomey heard the ruckus coming from where Joe and Yelena were sitting. He happened to be up, stretching his legs, before returning to his seat in business class. Those two, of course, were back in coach. That figured. Like Joe, he was sure, Toomey had flown many times in military planes, choppers, and private CIA jets, but on commercial flights, which soldiers took more than most civilians realized, coming or going from leave, reporting to new posts, they were strictly consigned to the cheap seats. He'd never sat up-front with the rich folk until he became a consultant. That was one of the things he'd point out to Joe if he were trying to recruit him. Which he would be happy to do if destiny hadn't set them on different paths, paths that were now converging.

That's how Rick Toomey thought of himself: a man of destiny, a warrior, like a samurai or a knight. He fought for a cause and lived by a code, and he would, he fully expected, die by it one day as well. But not today, so why not fly business class, put his feet up, sip champagne and flirt with the flight attendants? He'd earned it. That was the problem with society today, no code, no purpose and it was as bad, or worse, among the rich up here than among the poor. The poor had an excuse. The rich had an obligation. But now only poor boys fought wars, those who couldn't buy a way out, or those who saw the military as their one way out. Like Joe, who, he knew from his research, had been offered a choice of jail or army: either way he'd serve. Say what you like about the aristocrats in the olden days, however much wealth and luxury they had, they still sent their sons to die for king and country. It was what they were bred to do. Now that was over. The military too had its own aristocracy, and that was where Toomey was bred. His father had been a

colonel in the Marines and then an instructor at West Point. Choosing to go into the Special Forces meant Toomey himself would never rise to top brass, be a general, and sit around the Pentagon drinking coffee, but that was okay, the old man understood. Like Joe they were born to serve.

That's why Toomey was on this flight to New York. With Felix and Heather, their New York people, out of action, Toomey decided to shepherd this shipment himself, and be there to meet it when it came through. It was too important. Especially this one. It was carrying his destiny. And though he worked with Richards and his cronies at Wildwater (worked *for* them they would say, since they were paying for this plane ride and the steak he had consumed) he didn't respect them or trust them; they shared his values but not his code. They were rich but not aristocratic warriors, not samurai or knights.

That was why when Toomey saw Joe and Yelena in action, he smiled, and when they took down the chopper he was in, he laughed: it was a laugh of recognition. He had known immediately what Joe was: a warrior like him. And it seemed especially fitting when he learned that it was Joe Brody and his Russian cohort Yelena Noylaskya who had taken out Felix and Heather. He had found a worthy adversary, someone it would be a pleasure, an honor, to fight with, whether as comrade or foe. And if it had to be foe, so be it. That's why, when he heard Joe yelling and realized what was up, he grinned. Now he knew his opponent's weakness as well as his strengths. He was wounded. It was just in a place no one could see.

Yelena too was a warrior, and Nikolai had spotted her right away; he knew her, apparently from back when. All he would say was that she was well-known in the underworld in both Moscow and the Russian parts of New York, that she had worked for them but now seemed to be working for herself, and that she could be handled.

"Handled by who?" Richards had barked at Nikolai, still smarting, his ass and ego both bruised by that bumpy ride in the chopper. "You?"

"Why not?" Nikolai had smiled slyly, in that spook way—CIA or SVR, they were all the same. "I was her handler after all. I trained her."

But now, it seemed she'd gone feral again, snapped her leash, and Nikolai was spreading the word to his people. She was on the endangered list with Joe. Toomey chuckled at the thought, that while they snoozed uncomfortably in their cramped, hot, stinky seats, they were in fact in the cattle car that would take them to slaughter. The flight attendant, who was helping return his seat to its upright position, thought the grin was for her. She smiled back, bright white teeth, bright blue eyes, and glistening blonde hair.

"You seem happy to be in New York. Business or pleasure?"

"Both, I hope," he said, giving her his dimple. "What about you?"

He was just her type, he knew: clean-cut, handsome, strong-jawed, with a military bearing even in his navy blazer and khakis. Plus sitting in the expensive seats. A catch. She made a pout and let her Southern drawl ooze out, sweet as syrup. "I love New York but gosh it's so big. I never know what to do or where to go for fun."

"Sounds like you had the wrong tour guide."

She giggled. "Maybe so. Can you recommend one?"

He chuckled. "As it happens, I might be available. But I'm all out of brochures."

Now she gave him a real laugh and a real smile. "Then why don't I just give you my number?"

❖

The problem with Toomey, Victoria thought to herself as she watched him from afar, is that he takes all the fun out of being a sociopath. Just look at him, towing his luggage from customs into the chaos of JFK airport, frowning at the common rabble everywhere, hunting for the driver with his name on a sign. So uptight. So stiff and constipated. Always droning on about duty and destiny and all that boring bullshit.

When she found herself, as a kid, in a therapist's office, hearing herself described as "an extreme antisocial personality with poor impulse control, aggressive and narcissistic tendencies, and no capacity for empathy, guilt or remorse," she thought, *Hooray! Sounds like a right party for me! I can do anything I want!* And that was what she did, anything she wanted, or anything they paid her enough to do.

Victoria Dahlia Amalia St. Smythe was the last rotten fruit to drop from an exhausted, shriveling branch of a once proud and aristocratic family tree. She never met her father but was told he'd gotten married to get his hands on his trust fund, despite being exclusively interested in men and drugs. He had duly died of his pleasures. Her mother had been the schizophrenic descendent of an ancient, inbred, and now totally broke family, married off to get a piece of that same trust fund, and, for most of Victoria's life, had been locked up in a very posh loony bin. The cost was about that of a luxury spa, and the fund having been rather diminished by Daddy's bad habits, there wasn't much left for little Vicky. At first, old family friends arranged for her to get a scholarship to the public school her forebears attended, but paying for Cambridge was out of the question. Plus there was that girl whose eye she'd put out in a badminton dispute, whose family were still, unlike hers, quite rich. So Vicky was cut loose, and for a couple of years she floated from the squats, where she hung with the punks, to the high-end clubs, where she seduced the sons (and daughters) of her family's former friends, who were terrified she might carry on the family trade and trick one of them into marrying her. Finally, a black car picked her up and whisked her off to a fancy office, where she was asked if she might not like to serve her Queen and country.

"Whatever do you mean? Run for parliament?" she had asked. Not quite. They had something more off the books in mind. Like a spy.

A spy? She considered it. At first it seemed even crazier than running for parliament, all that code-talking and stuffing microfilm up her bottom, but then she thought, *Actually, when you think about it, James Bond is really a sociopath, isn't he?*

But that wasn't quite what they meant either. MI-6 was definitely not looking for her type. They meant really off the books. So she was sent to a school that suited her much better than Cambridge would have, and learned martial arts, weaponry, shooting. She was even sent abroad for courses in torture. Then she was sent to take care of a prostitute who was blackmailing a very wealthy and powerful man. Next an Irish nationalist, once a big man in the IRA, who was considered to be a threat to the new order of things. Since she was strictly freelance, with employers who didn't want to know or see her between jobs, she quickly found there were other people eager to pay very well for her services. Soon she was one of the world's most highly paid assassins. That was how she met Richards, as a referral through some of the powerful parties who were backing him, and he had more or less put her on retainer. Which was why she was here, in New York, keeping an eye on things, and ready to solve the problems these more gung ho, know-it-all macho types were prone to create. Essentially, that was what she did: rich, powerful people, mostly men, made disastrous mistakes and she cleaned up the mess. And she loved it.

That's why, unlike Toomey, she'd put a bit of effort in, and met this flight in a long black wig, trendy oversized glasses, a Yankees cap, a tight sports bra–like top with a padded bra under it, tight jeans, and sparkly high-top sneakers, looking, she thought, just like some trashy American here to meet her dumb boyfriend or pathetic little relatives. She even had her nails done in multiple colors and a little glass jewel in her belly button. While Toomey found his driver, barked at him for not holding the sign that said "Toomie" high enough, and marched off, still wheeling his own bag, she was enjoying herself. And that's why, when she saw Joe and Yelena come by next, carrying only a backpack and a small gym bag, less luggage than Vicky used for makeup and wigs, Yelena with a cigarette in her mouth ready to go, and Joe, unshaven with his hair sticking up and talking on a flip phone, Victoria actually stepped up and in her best New Yorkese (her sponsors had sent her to acting classes too, and she could do a number of accents) asked: "Excuse me, Miss. Can I get a cigarette?"

Yelena turned to her quickly, as though startled, then gave her a stare so piercing that Vicky somehow expected her to see through her disguise to the truth. Thoughtfully, she plucked the cigarette from her lips and handed it over.

"Thanks babe," Vicky said, winking as she placed it in her mouth.

"The cabs are this way," Joe said, striding off, and Yelena turned and followed.

Now, Vicky thought to herself, those two look like fun.

16

WHEN HE GOT HOME from the airport, Joe was relieved to find his grandmother out. He had Yelena with him, and while the old time grifter in Gladys recognized and appreciated a fellow pro, and Yelena had even brought vodka and caviar to their first meeting, the grandma side of her nature suspected that this girl wasn't a healthy long-term romantic choice for her Joey. So he was happy to find the note she left—*gone to AC*—on top of the fresh laundry she left on his bed. He also dipped into the stash of money she kept squirreled away from Joe's previous earnings, which he mostly passed on to her. They showered, changed—Joe took a clean black T-shirt and jeans to replace the ones he'd been wearing—and stopped in at his favorite Thai place for a big lunch before getting on the train to Bed-Stuy to break the news about Hamid to Juno.

❖

Juno took it hard.

"What the fuck did I do?" he asked Joe, distraught, as they sat on the couch in the studio/bedroom/high-tech lab he ran from his Mom's basement. His eyes were full of tears. "I knew that kid for years, man. Now I got him killed."

"You didn't get him killed, Juno," Joe told him now. "This is on me. I was supposed to take care of him."

Yelena shook her head at them both. "Are you two finished?"

"Sorry?" Juno asked, in shock.

"You are both wrong. Neither one of you is responsible."

"So who then?" Juno asked her.

"I don't know. And I didn't really know Hamid, like you did. But we worked together and I liked him. So I am going to find out who did this, and I am going to make them pay. If you are done wallowing in guilt and self-pity, then you can help me."

Joe frowned at her. She had a point, but she could have used a lighter touch with Juno, whom he still thought of as a kid. But Juno burst into a laugh.

"Damn I missed you, Yelena. I've never seen such an ice-cold bitch with so much heart."

She smiled. "Thank you, Juno. I missed you too."

Juno sniffed. "Okay, then, let's do this. What's the play? Get strapped and go hunting? I'm ready to get heavy on this one."

A tech wizard, Juno was definitely on the brains side of the business, and Joe wanted to keep him there. He didn't need another Hamid on his conscience. "For now I want you to start going through all the data we managed to send back before the bomb in the safe blew." He handed him the camera as well. "I know we lost the phone and the laptop, but maybe there's something in what we do have. Some clue."

"Clue to what?" Juno reached for his own laptop and pulled up the files. "Yeah Hamid sent me a ton of stuff, thousands of pages. All of it total bullshit: shipping records, boring ass emails about defective canteens, bills of lading, invoices. I never though being a terrorist dope smuggler could be so lame."

"But they are smuggling it in, somehow. That's the point. And you're the only one I can think of who can figure it out."

"Aye aye, captain," Juno said, saluting. "I'm on it."

"Thanks," Joe said, clapping his shoulder as he stood. He pulled out a thick roll of cash. "You need any dough right now?"

"Nah this is for Hamid."

Joe peeled off some bills for Yelena. "Get whatever you need. And maybe look around for a safe place to stay."

"What's the matter Joe?" she asked as she folded the bills and tucked them into her pocket. "Grandma won't let you have a girl sleep over?"

Juno snickered, then waved at Joe. "Hey I understand. My ma's strict too. She's at church right now. Baptist."

Joe smiled. "She's kidding. My grandmother's in Atlantic City right now. Blackjack."

❖

Joe went to the YMCA to meet Frank. He was midway through his own Sunday ritual, working out and then taking a steam. Frank Jones was a painter of some repute, a Black man in his seventies, who had been a Marine in Vietnam. He'd met Joe at the VA hospital, when Joe had just kicked dope and was feeling crazy, and Frank had invited him up to the studio to talk. He too had managed his nightmares and flashbacks with alcohol, drugs, and denial, and then found a more workable long-term solution: he painted them. Frank hadn't known Joe very long, but he gathered he wasn't the type to phone up just to say hi. So when Joe had called from the airport, asking if he could come by later, Frank told him where he'd be.

"So where you been?" Frank asked as the men sweated, side by side, wrapped in towels, Frank sprawled comfortably with his back against the wall, Joe sitting up, hands on his knees. Around them the room filled with hissing steam. Droplets ran down the walls. A few old men sat across from them, vague sweating lumps in the thick clouds, and a big guy, with a towel over his head, was bent forward as though concentrated intently on sweating as hard as he could.

"Afghanistan," Joe told him.

"Shit, man, what were you doing there?" He waved it off. "Never mind. I don't want to know."

The big man got up, poured a bucket of water over his naked flesh and left.

Joe waited for the door to shut. "I lost someone. A team member. I guess I feel responsible. Anyway, since then the nightmares are back."

"Yeah well what did you expect? You see me hopping over to Da Nang for a weekend?" He laughed. "Who am I kidding, I haven't even been to Brooklyn in years. Speaking of war zones, I hear Bed-Stuy is full of white hipsters now. Is that true?"

"Pretty much."

"Damn." He shook his head, then sat up and faced Joe. "Look, you woke up your devils right? I checked in a dictionary once, when I couldn't sleep. Nightmare comes from Old English. Mare was an evil goblin, like a demonic bitch that attacks in your sleep. Now you stirred her up. That's all. Let it pass."

Joe glanced at him. "Did yours?"

He shrugged. "Well I ain't going to lie to you. It's like this old scar . . ." He fingered a small knobby patch on his thigh that Joe could see was once a bullet wound. "Used to be so noticeable I was embarrassed to wear shorts. And of course it hurt like a motherfucker when it was healing. Now I forget it's there. Sometimes in the cold I feel it. And heat helps. The steam. That's one good thing about getting old, all your scars fade. Course by then, a bunch of new shit has gone wrong. But then the VA pays for it. So you're all set."

"You're not really reassuring me here."

"My point is . . ." Frank pointed to a couple of Joe's own scars, a white line that ran along his calf, a small patch of discolored skin above his elbow. "These looked worse, I'm sure, back when you got them. Twenty years from now they'll be hard to find. Same with the inner scars. The ones on your soul. Are you the same as before? No. But it fades." His eyes narrowed as he located the star-shaped brand on Joe's chest, up above the ribs on the left, off to the side of his heart: "Not that though. That's fresh."

"Yeah," Joe said, touching it reflexively, then sitting up so it was less noticeable.

"And it's not a scar is it?"

"No," Joe admitted. "Not exactly."

"Yeah well, it's like they told you when you were a kid. Nightmares aren't real, man. They can't hurt you." He nodded at the star again, or in its direction. "It's reality that will kill your ass."

An old man got up, naked, and began doing a series of squatting exercises in the steam. "Talk about nightmares." Frank muttered as he stood, tightening his towel around his waist. "I'm going to grab a cold shower and a hot steak. You coming?"

❖

Yelena went back to Brighton Beach with mixed feelings. She was definitely looking forward to the food. And where else was a Russian girl supposed to fade into the background? On the other hand, it was where her enemies were strongest. So her plan was to get what she needed, weapons, ID, and delicacies, and then go back to Queens to stay with Joe and Gladys, at least for the night. First stop was the Grandmaster Chess Shop, run by an old-timer everyone called Grandmaster, though no one had ever seen him play chess. He sold weapons from the basement, and she immediately felt better as she strapped a 9 mm Beretta to her ankle and stashed another, smaller .22 in a clip-on holster in the small of her back. Finally, she slid a knife in a sheath into her boot.

Then she went to see Vova. Vova was another old man, who didn't even speak English but who made a good living preparing expert false IDs in a cluttered apartment overlooking the boardwalk, every inch stuffed with books, Cyrillic newspapers, and huge antique pieces of furniture, armoires, leather armchairs, and heavy, padded couches. The first time Joe and Yelena worked together and found themselves on the run, they had hidden at Vova's and he'd given them IDs and credit cards on credit. This time Yelena had cash. But it didn't matter, Vova always greeted her the same way: he removed the ever-present cigarette from the corner of his mouth to give her a hug and kisses on each cheek, followed by a toast with vodka.

"Where's your boyfriend?" he asked her in Russian. "You know, the American from last time, who said he didn't drink." Vova chuckled at the memory of what he assumed was an absurd joke.

"Joe? He's not my boyfriend." She told him what she needed—a complete set: passport, cards, the works—and he took some digital photos of her against a white wall. Then she went shopping while he worked. She went to Gourmanoff's and spent the rest of Joe's cash on caviar, blinis, duck, blintzes, and a host of other treats, then returned to Vova's and laid the spread out after clearing the heaps of newspaper, books, and overflowing ashtrays from his table. He provided vodka, tea, and—by the time she was done with desert—her documents, which he brought out to the terrace, where she'd gone to escape the smoke, which even by her standards was getting to be too much.

"*Krasivaya!*" she'd declared, thanking him with a kiss on each cheek. He blushed happily and lit another smoke. He was proud of his work. He had used a real blank Russian passport, obtained God knows where, forged a few entry stamps for authenticity, and threw in an international driver's license and a couple of credit cards as well.

She tucked them away in a pocket and turned to gaze out at the beach. It was a warm night and the boardwalk was buzzing. Everywhere below them Russians talked, ate, laughed, smoked, drank, and ate more. They filled the cafés and bars, the restaurants and the benches. Kids ran back and forth over the planks of the boardwalk and, in the moonlight, you could see teenagers clustered together on blankets on the beach. Off to the right, the lights of Coney Island pulsated as the rides spun and the roller coaster snaked back and forth. Snatches of conversation reached them with bits of random music. And behind it all, the ocean came and went, a constant whisper, forever arriving on the beach and forever falling away, back to the edge of the horizon, where the world ended and infinite darkness began.

"You understand, Vova, they are looking for me?"

"Who?"

"Bratva."

He smiled, showing his hodgepodge of metal Russian and gold American dental work, with some fake white teeth and a few real ones, stained the color of smoke and tea. "Let them look. One trouble they have with us old-timers from the Soviet days? We've already been tortured by the best. I learned how to lie in Siberia." Then he pulled out a key. "You need a place to stay too, Lenushka?"

She smiled sweetly. "Thank you but not tonight. I'm going to Joe's."

"Ha! The one who's not your boyfriend?"

Yelena shrugged. "He's a friend. Anyway, his grandmother is there too."

"All together in one apartment? Like back in Moscow! What kind of Russian girl are you? Can't you find a rich American with a good job?"

"He has a job," Yelena told him.

"What job?"

She grinned. "He throws drunks out of a strip club."

"What?" Vova shouted. "And he doesn't even drink!" He laughed so hard the cigarette fell out of his mouth and dropped like a falling star to the beach.

❖

Donna ordered a round. By the time her mom got home from AC, ahead by thirty bucks after eight hours of work but happy so whatever, and they got Larissa to go back to bed, and then Donna got downtown to the, of course, roaring gay bar, Andy and Blaze had had a few. Donna fetched them refills and a beer for herself.

"Okay, so spill it," Andy said.

"Let her at least taste her beer first," Blaze put in, calming Andy with a steady hand and leaning back in her chair. "Then spill it."

"What is this," Donna asked, "good cop, drunk cop?"

Blaze shrugged. "You left for your dinner date at seven P.M. and came home, according to witnesses, at seven A.M. The evidence speaks for itself."

"Fine. I got laid," Donna said, toasting them and then taking a long drink. "About time too."

"Hallelujah," Andy said. "My husband is a genius. He's definitely getting laid tonight too."

"How was it?" Blaze asked, clinking bottles with her.

"Nice."

"Uh-oh," Blaze said. "Nice isn't good."

"Nice sucks," Andy said.

"No. Nice is fine," Donna said. "It's nice."

"What was wrong?" Andy asked. "Too fast? He was probably overeager."

"No . . . no . . . I mean he was eager all right . . ."

"Too small, right?" Blaze asked with a knowing nod.

"Now why would you say that?" Andy asked her. "You don't even like dick."

"No but if I did I'd sure want a lot of it."

"Well I can't argue there," Andy said and they toasted again.

Donna laughed and shook her head. "I'm glad you two agree. Just leave me out of it."

"Okay, let's rewind. How was dinner?"

So Donna told them the story, the lovely dinner, the warm vibes, the after-dessert walk, the perfect first kiss, and then the drunken asshole and the fight, followed swiftly by Agent Zamora's intervention and arrest.

"Well that explains it," Andy said. "You threw his game off. Civilians aren't used to seeing that shit."

"You emasculated him," Blaze said. "You practically cut his balls off."

"I had no choice," Donna said. "That drunk was about to cut something off for real. And for the record his balls were very much intact. Actually . . ." She shrugged. "The whole thing turned him on."

Andy nodded. "I've seen you kicking guys' asses and it is pretty hot."

"Works for me," Blaze agreed. "She's great in a bar brawl."

"So you went back to his place . . ." he prompted.

"And everything was fine. More than fine. Terrific."

"He like tore your clothes off and . . ." Blaze suggested.

"What? No. Jesus. He, you know . . ."

"What?" Blaze asked, clearly a little buzzed now.

"He went downtown, right?" Andy said. Donna nodded and he frowned at Blaze. "What kind of dyke are you anyway?"

Blaze shrugged. "So okay, he's a man who knows his place. So far so good."

Donna sighed. "Fine. So yeah that was great. And then when we were, you know . . ."

"Fucking?" Andy suggested.

"Right, thank you Andy, when we were fucking, that was great too, but he kept talking about seeing me take down that dude, how powerful it was and all that."

"Uh-oh," Blaze said.

"And then after," Donna said, plunging ahead, relieved now that she was getting it all out there, "he asked if I'd like, reenact that with him, like role-play arresting him, and even asked me to take out my gun, you know, without the clip, and . . ."

"Fuck him with it?" Blaze suggested.

"Make him suck it."

"I knew it." Blaze slapped the table. "The guy's a bottom."

"Total bottom," Andy said, shaking his head. "I should have known. Typical Ari. When he said the guy liked strong women I thought that meant he liked Meryl Streep movies. Not shrimping."

"What's shrimping?" Donna asked.

"Ask him and see," Blaze said. "But finish the story first. What did you do?"

"I said I was tired and we went to sleep. Then as soon as it was light I snuck out."

"Typical top." Blaze shrugged. "So what's the problem? Sounds like a pretty good date."

"I didn't say problem," Donna phumphered. "I just. I mean, no judgment. It's just not my thing."

"You're not looking for a bottom bitch," Andy said.

Donna wrinkled her nose. "Not specifically, no."

Andy nodded. "Okay, fine, you want a top. That figures."

"Sure," Blaze agreed. "Someone who makes *you* kneel and suck the gun."

"No." Donna set her beer down with a thud, like a gavel. "I mean, are those the only choices?"

"Then what do you want?" Andy waved beseechingly.

"I want an equal! I want passion and love! And great sex! With a partner!"

Andy and Blaze looked at each other. Andy shrugged.

"Straight girls . . ." he said.

"Don't get me started," Blaze told him.

It took a couple more beers and an order each of calamari and fried mozzarella sticks before, having finally exhausted the topic of Donna's sex life, Andy remembered the call.

"Oh right, I almost forgot," he said, when the subject of Monday being the next morning came up, "I got a call from the NYPD. Fusco. He's Major Case Squad."

"I know the name, sort of," Donna said. "He was on that last thing, the smugglers."

"Exactly. He still is, sort of. He has some evidence, a sample of this new heroin going around and he wants our lab to test it. He's hypothesizing that it's from the same supplier as your Zahir."

"What?" Donna sat up and focused. "Really? What did you say?"

"I said send it over. I asked the lab to compare it to the dope you so bravely obtained last time. And Janet said she'll run it tomorrow."

"And you waited till now to tell me this? This is major news. This is a case breaking wide open. Possibly. Maybe."

Andy smiled. "Honey, cases possibly maybe break open all the time. Now you getting laid, that is major news."

❖

When Joe got back to the apartment, his grandmother was in her chair, counting her winnings.

"Joey!" she beamed at him. "I knew this was going to be a lucky day."

He kissed her and sat on the couch. "How'd you do in AC?"

"How do you think?" She fanned out her money. "How about you?"

"Crapped out," he said. "Let's not talk about it."

"Fine."

"But I did want to tell you. You remember Yelena?"

"The Russian."

"She needs a place to stay."

"When?"

"Tonight. She will be here any minute. Sorry."

"What sorry? I've always encouraged you to bring home friends."

"I get the feeling you maybe don't like this friend so much."

"I didn't like that hyper one from third grade, what was his name?"

"Danny."

"Who broke the lamp. Melinda is very nice."

"Yelena."

"I'm just not sure I like how you end up when you play with her."

Joe smiled. "Fair enough. Though I remember you drank your share of that vodka. But she's not coming over to play. That's what I have to tell you. She's on the run."

"Law?"

"Maybe. And Russian mafia. She's out getting guns and a new passport now. But it could get dangerous."

Gladys frowned at her grandson. She folded the money and tucked it into her bra. "Then what are we talking about? Of course she can stay."

17

"IT'S A MATCH."

Donna and Andy were in the lab, which was down the corridor from her cramped little tip-line office, getting the results on the heroin sample from Janet, the forensic scientist.

"It's the same supplier?" Donna asked, feeling the tingle of excitement pass up her spine: her hunch was becoming a legit case. "It's Zahir?"

"Give me a break," Janet said. "I'm good but I'm not that good. I can't tell you the name of who bagged it up. It's from the same region. SWA."

"Southwest Asia."

"Right. The chemical composition is completely different from samples that come from, say, Mexico or South America. I can even say it probably came from the same country. Afghanistan. One big difference, though. That original sample, from the crime scene? That was like ninety-nine point nine percent pure. This is street ready." She peered through her glasses at the report on her table. "Contains lactose and cornstarch." She shrugged. "But it's still really good. Just about fifty percent pure. If good is the word I want." She pulled her vape pen from a pocket of her lab coat and peeked down the hall before taking a hit and blowing it at the air vent.

"Good dope means a lot of junkies dying out there," Donna said.

"Dying happy," Andy added.

"Cynic," Donna told him, then to Janet: "You, however, are better than good. You're the best. Lunch is on me."

"K-town?" she asked. "Turntable Chicken Jazz?" Janet was Korean-American and while she usually ate every day in the choose-your-own-salad place, she'd been craving spicy fried chicken. She was also a serious jazz nerd.

"I was thinking of the choose-your-own-salad place, to be honest," Donna told her.

"That chicken is really good," Andy noted. "And I have the car."

"Come on, vinyl and spicy chicken, it's like two of my biggest fetishes in one," Janet said.

"Fine," Donna said. "Now I'm craving it too. Okay, here's the plan. I pay. You order," she told Janet. "You drive," she told Andy. "And if we run late, we use the siren."

But they never made it out to lunch at all that day because when Donna stopped by her office to grab her bag, there was a message from Zahir.

❖

If you're looking for a nice spot to grab lunch and catch up with an old friend, not many would choose a strip club, but it suited Gio and Joe: it was quiet (they didn't open till six when the after-work crowd started drifting in), private (it was Gio's place), and oddly cozy without the noise and sweat and lust in the air; a cool, dark place for two old pals to split two heroes—one sausage and broccoli rabe, one prosciutto and mozzarella—washed down with Manhattan Special Coffee Soda. Gio had picked the order up on the way.

"So you think this Wildwater corporation is behind it? Why?"

Joe shrugged. "Why not? Soldiers smuggled dope back from Vietnam. So in our new corporate age, it's the contractors. Even the crime is outsourced."

"Sure. My dad knew some of those soldiers. From Frank Lucas's crew. But you're saying the top people in the corporation are in on it."

"I'm not saying anything yet. But someone in that office was connected to Zahir. Someone who also just happened to have a combat-ready squad

and an attack chopper to send after us. That's no grunt with a balloon full of dope up his ass."

"Okay, but we still don't know how they get the shit into the country," Gio said. "Or who is moving it for them here. Or why a bunch of American businessmen, corrupt or not, would be financing terrorists. What I do know is what's up our own ass. Our heads."

"You're right," Joe said. "Sorry, Gio. If you want someone else to handle it . . ."

"Who the fuck else is there?" Gio waved it off. Then he sat back in the booth and took a breath. "No. I'm sorry. I wasn't mad at you. It's just . . . let's just say, I'm pretty comfortable outside the law. Sex, drugs, gambling, corruption, even violence when necessary . . . that's my . . . what's the word?"

"Career?"

"Métier is the word I was looking for but okay, fine. My meat. I admit it. But this other shit: religion, politics, nationalism, or whatever. People blowing up each other's children. That I have no fucking idea what to do with." He smiled sheepishly. "Except send you. Which isn't fair. So I'm sorry."

Joe nodded once and drank his soda. Gio took a breath and went on: "Also." He shrugged. "I guess things have been a little tense at home too. You know, since Paul left us."

"A little?"

"A lot."

"I can imagine."

"I mean, we're working on it, Carol and me. Trying . . . things. But it's like . . ." He held up two sandwich halves, one sausage, one prosciutto. "My life had these two sides, dark and light. And now they're getting mixed up."

Joe grinned at the sandwiches. "But they're both still pork."

Gio laughed. "Well I don't have a vegan side, I admit."

"Actually," Joe said. "I do know what you mean. That trip kicked my dark shit up too. It ain't easy pushing it back down."

"I guess that's also my fault. And I'm sorry about the kid Hamid. But at least you're back, safe, in the light." He waved his sandwich at the gloomy bar where topless women would soon be laboring for horny stiffs. "Then again, there are those who would say our light side is pretty dark too."

"I guess it's relative. Different cuts of pork," Joe said and went back to his lunch. Gio's phone rang. He set his food down and wiped his mouth and hands with a napkin.

"It's my cop," he said, and answered. "Yeah? Interesting. Thanks." He shut the phone. "So . . . that new brand of dope on the scene? The one undercutting Maria and the rest?"

"Yeah?" Joe asked.

Gio reached for his sandwich. "Fusco had the FBI test a sample and it matches the shit you took off of that smuggler you whacked. So, Zahir or Wildwater or whoever the fuck they are, one thing we do know?" He took a big bite of sausage and bitter greens and chewed. "They're here."

18

WILDWATER'S CORPORATE HEADQUARTERS WERE in Midtown, in a glass and steel tower that was somehow both grandiose and anonymous, like a red carpet full of supposed celebrities you've never heard of. Robert Richards, the founder and CEO, was holding a press conference that day, and since it was open to the public, Joe decided this was as good a place as any to begin. Dressed like a tourist, in cargo shorts, Yankees cap, sunglasses, and a T-shirt that said "NYC Fuhgeddaboutit," and with a camera slung around his neck, he passed through a metal detector, then entered the building's giant atrium, where chairs and a small stage had been set up. The floor was of the same textured stone as the walls, which soared above them. Beyond a row of desks, elevators and escalators rose. There were cameras, lights, and a fair-sized crowd comprising bored reporters, enthusiastic employees, and a mix of people interested in politics and business and those just looking for an air-conditioned place to sit and eat lunch. Joe took a seat in back.

On his chair, on every chair, was a brochure with a picture of Bob Richards climbing aboard a helicopter much like the one Joe had shot down. He was giving the camera a thumbs-up, his coiffure suspiciously blond and still in the wind. It also contained a bio—Harvard business school, investment banks and hedge funds, then NSA for fifteen years—before he branched out into the war-biz to build an empire of his own. The following pages showed Wildwater's vast operations around the

world, though the office in Kandahar was overlooked. Then music played over the loudspeakers, a screen lowered over the back of the stage, and they ran a short movie that showed everything Joe had just read in the brochure. Next the host was introduced, a shill who would ply Richards with planned questions, and Joe didn't bother to catch his name. He introduced Richards, giving a more personal, warm version of the same bio yet again. By the time the great man stepped on stage, Joe was ready to nod off from boredom. It was about five minutes into the "conversation" that his ears finally perked up.

"Look, government has its function but that is being redefined in our time. You want a package to get there quick? Do you mail it? No way. You send it via FedEx or UPS. Funny things is, in their own way, these are paramilitary-style operations, with their attitude toward logistics and chain-of-command. They learned from the military. If you want technological innovation, do you go to the government or to Apple? If you want to buy something and get it on time at the best price? Amazon. Again and again, in every sector, we've proven that professionals are the way to go. Medicine. Communications. Even space exploration. Everything except the most important thing. Security."

"Well that's an interesting point, Bob," the interviewer opined, lamely trying to come off as if he hadn't heard it yet. "But can you explain just what you mean?"

"It's simple, Jim. Today we have a vast, bloated, inefficient military, with politicians at the top, who are amateurs after all, career bureaucrats in the middle management, and volunteer soldiers on the front lines. Now, no one honors those troops more than I do."

"Of course, Bob. One hundred percent."

"But do we really want our sons—and increasingly our daughters—out there? Let me ask you a question, Jim. Would you send your kids off to catch a burglar or put out a fire in the neighborhood?"

"No way, Bob. That's crazy. I'd call the police. Or the fire department."

"Exactly, Jim. That makes good common sense. Call the professionals. Well all I'm saying is, it's time for us to leave war to the professionals. By

utsourcing operations to an organization like Wildwater, our nation will be safer, while also saving lives and money long-term."

"Sounds great to me, Bob? What do you folks think?"

The front half of the audience, full of employees who'd been shepherded down from the offices upstairs, cheered on cue. The rest clapped half-heartedly. A few continued eating sandwiches and looking at their phones. As reporters started calling out questions, the less-invested audience members began to disperse, and Joe stood as well. He wandered the lobby, taking photos: there was no reason to hide it here, though he was more interested in the security cameras and elevator banks than most tourists.

The press conference ended and there was applause, though less than at the opening, as people were eager to make their way out, and Joe joined the flow, chewing gum and following the line to the revolving doors. That's when he found Yelena.

She too was in disguise, and, considering how hard it had been for him to spot her ponytail among the others, she'd done an excellent job of camouflage. She wore an oversized pink sweatshirt that said PINK on it (which he thought was just naming the color until she explained it was a brand), black running shorts, pink running shoes, gigantic dark sunglasses, and a black wig under a Mets cap. They'd arrived separately, and had agreed to rendezvous in the park, so he just walked by without a second glance. Then he got her text: *Saw someone. Following. Tell you later.*

❖

Upstairs, in the executive conference room, Mike Powell sat staring at a row of screens.

As a career government employee, he wasn't sure how he felt about Richards's speech as it played on one, but he was certainly impressed with the technology deployed on the others, particularly the facial recognition software.

"Freeze four," he told the tech, who hit a key. "Close in on that guy, the one in the ball cap. No, the other one in the other ball cap. There . . ." he

turned to Jensen, Richards's right hand, who was overseeing operation from here while the boss was on stage. "That's Joe Brody."

"Track him," Jensen told the tech, and the camera zoomed in tight, following Brody as he took photos of the building. Jensen turned to Powell. "I take it he's not an architecture buff."

"Nope. He's casing the joint." He watched as Brody, smiling innocuously, flowed with the crowd, through the revolving door, out of the building and off camera.

The door opened and Richards came in, without his sidekick and media handlers, but still with makeup on his face. Jensen jumped up.

"Terrific job, sir."

"Thanks. Damn those hot lights." He grabbed a water from the table and sat in the biggest, best seat at the table. "I think it went well. Crowd could have been bigger but Fox and CNN both said they'd cover it. The *Times* asked a question. What did you think?" he asked Powell.

"About the *Times*, I have no opinion. But I am interested in why Brody was there." He pointed at the frozen image of Joe on the screen. "This means he's connected Zahir to Wildwater."

"Because of the office? There was no evidence there for him to find. It's a dead end. The question is what led him there in the first place."

"And what he is looking for here," Powell told him. "Money? Dope?"

Richards laughed. "Not in this building. We piss test the janitors for Chrissakes." He finished his water. "Zahir's business is conducted completely outside of Wildwater. By very capable professionals."

"Toomey," Powell said.

"And as we speak he is moving to make that operation more secure, and more profitable, than it has ever been. As for unwanted guests like your friend Brody . . ." He shrugged. "We have a professional to handle that too."

Vicky, Powell thought, but did not say the name, as if it were a curse word. He just nodded.

"I will retest all our security, sir, but I don't see us as vulnerable to intrusion," Jensen said.

"Don't worry," Richards said, wiping his forehead with a hankie and taking off a swatch of orange. "We run a tight ship here, Powell. And a clean one."

"I hope so," Powell said, still dwelling on Brody in his getup. "Just remember, Joe Brody is a thief first and foremost. So ask yourself, what did he come to steal?"

❖

"Zahir is coming, America. You have been warned." Donna paused, letting the ominous email sink in. She was in the office of her boss, Tom, reading him a printout while Andy and Janet listened.

"That it?" Tom asked, taking a big bite of his sandwich. It was ham and Swiss on rye, with mustard and a pickle, as Andy and Janet both noted. They were hungry.

"The dots connect," Donna said.

"What dots?" he asked, mouth full.

"Thanks to Janet's tests and the info we have from NYPD, we now know that Zahir has moved from smuggling heroin to distribution at the street level. We also know that the funds are flowing back to terror operations overseas. And now we have a threat, their first operation on US soil."

"Goddamn it, I got mustard on my tie," Tom said. He grabbed a napkin and wiped while he talked. "You're right, Donna. It could be terrorists slinging dope in Brooklyn. It could also just be a crew of normal, patriotic All-American heroin dealers who scored some Afghani dope. And that money could be going to terror . . . according to a CIA snitch who promptly disappeared and an old Irish mobster who ended up in a Jersey swamp. You think Zahir did him too?"

"No, sir."

"Me neither. And as for this threat." He crumpled his napkin up and tossed it toward the trash. "Add it to my pile. You know how many we get a day?"

"Yes, sir. I read them all. We get a lot."

"Exactly. Plus there's what Homeland gets. And the CIA." He lifted his pickle. "Here's what I think. So far this still smells local to me. So give it to the locals. Andy, who's the detective who sent the sample?"

"Fusco."

"Give it to Fusco. Let him chase the shadow if he wants. Now then, can I finish my lunch?"

On the way out, Andy checked his watch. "So much for chicken and jazz," he told Donna. "You owe us."

19

THAT NIGHT, THEY HIT Alonzo first. Along a quiet street, in a sleepy part of Flatbush, a van pulled up to a plain two-bedroom house on a block of plain houses. Perhaps a sharp-eyed neighbor had noticed the security cameras or that the weedy lawn was a bit overgrown. Or maybe the mailman had realized that, aside from junk addressed to Our Neighbor and the electric bill, there was no mail. Black SUVs slid in and out of the automatic garage, lights burned dimly behind the always-drawn shades, but there was no trouble, and no noise, aside from faint music, if anyone had bothered to listen. Though he had never set foot in it, and his name appeared nowhere on any paperwork, this house belonged to Alonzo.

Alonzo controlled a big piece of the organized crime in the African-American neighborhoods of Brooklyn, a managerial feat that involved overseeing and disciplining his own unruly troops and protecting his territory and assets from others while also building his legitimate business profile, which included restaurants, clubs, car services, janitorial and landscaping companies, as well as a music label and a boxing gym.

This house was special though: it was the main stash. This was the central warehouse for Alonzo's dope and coke operation, though it had been years since he himself was in the same room with the drugs, or any mind-altering substance, beyond a cigar or a cognac. Or the edibles and

vapes that his younger brother, Reggie, insisted were the future but that sounded like some silly bougie shit to Alonzo.

The dope came from Little Maria, a Dominican drug overlord—or was it overlady?—who had maintained and expanded her late husband's empire, mainly in Spanish Harlem and the Bronx. His coke came from Colombians and Mexicans in Queens. The product was brought to this stash house, where it was cut, bagged up, and then sent out to the network of lieutenants who in turn ran the crews that sold the drugs from corners and alleys, storefronts, project courtyards, and tenement buildings all over Brooklyn. Of course there were always other players, independent crews who set up shop on an unclaimed corner or vacant lot, smalltime dealers who peddled drugs from their apartments via word of mouth or in the back rooms at clubs (not his clubs of course), and even established figures who held their own small patch of territory; but none of that really bothered Alonzo. As long as he had the best real estate and the best product, he sold all the shit he could possibly get his hands on and made more money than he could count. And it was his supply connections as well as his relationships with Anton the Russian, Rebbe, Gio, Uncle Chen from Flushing, and others, that allowed day-to-day business to proceed smoothly and with minimal friction. Until now.

Now a dirty gray van was cruising up to his stash house and parking in front of the house next door, under a tree, out of range of the cameras. Inside the van were four men, all in black fatigues and wool caps that pulled down to ski-masks. Silently, in the darkness, two slipped out and crept, crouched low, across the neighbor's lawn and through a missing board in their fence to take cover against the aluminum-siding-covered wall of the house. Lights glowed in the windows and hip-hop played within the walls. One man quickly jimmied the dark basement window while the other kept watch, then slid in. Except for some crap left by the previous tenant, it was empty. He waved his partner in.

They put on their night vision goggles and drew their AR-15 rifles. Then they proceeded carefully up the stairs. The basement door was only

locked with the doorknob mechanism, which the first man easily popped with the jimmy. They could hear the music and voices inside. The second man whispered into his headset.

"Set."

The answer from the van came: "Stand by."

Another man got out of the van, also armed but carrying a small hatchet as well. He jogged across the lawn, keeping low in the shadows, but less worried about the cameras now, because as soon as he reached the main power cable that ran up the wall of the house, he swung the hatchet hard, twice, and the cameras died, along with the lights and music. He then dropped the hatchet, which was tied to his belt, and raised his own rifle while moving to guard the door. The van now rolled forward, to stop right in front of the house and block the view.

"Go," the voice said over the earpiece. "Proceed right about three meters to the kitchen. Three persons."

The two men in the basement went through the door, into the main house.

"What the fuck? This a blackout?" they heard a rough male voice bark, though the gunmen saw a hallway in the underwater green of their goggles.

"You got any candles?" another voice asked.

"Why would I have candles, motherfucker? You got a birthday cake?"

The gunmen entered the kitchen, where they saw three men sitting around the kitchen table, weighing dope on a digital scale and bagging it up for sale. They opened fire.

"Two more in the room to your right," the voice from the van said. The driver was watching the feed from an infrared camera, mounted on top of the van, that registered the body heat in the house. Two other men had been on the couch, watching TV. Both drew their own weapons when they heard the gunfire, but in the darkness, one ran right into the gunmen coming from the kitchen and was shot dead. The other, a local kid named Reverb, ran for the door. He opened it to find a black-clad man in a black mask pointing a rifle at him.

"Oh shit," he said, raising his hands.

The man pushed him in as the two other gunmen joined him, having cleared the house. They lowered their goggles and flicked on their headlamps as the third man shut the door.

"Don't shoot, officer," Reverb said, dropping his pistol. "I'm unarmed."

"I am not officer, not anymore," the gunman told him, speaking in some kind of accent, German or Russian or French or something.

"You ain't? I thought you all were SWAT or some shit. With those outfits." He nodded toward the kitchen. "Well then the stash is in there. Take it."

"We don't want your crap shit," the guy said in his awkward English. He waved his gun at Reverb and the flashlights bounced off his face. "Your phone. Quick."

"Y'all want my phone?" Reverb shrugged. It was a new iPhone, but he'd bought it stolen anyway. He held it out. "Here."

"Call your boss. Tell him what happened here."

Now Reverb was really confused. "You want me to call *my* boss and tell him you just boosted his stash, is that right?"

They nodded, headlamps bobbing. Reverb shrugged. "All right, it's your funeral."

He called. "Hey it's Reverb," he told whomever answered. "I need to get word to the big man. We just been hit . . . just now, motherfucker! They still here, like chilling in the living room . . ." He was about to go on, but his call was cut short, with a bullet through the chest. He fell dead. The gunman stepped on the phone, crushing it under his boot, then set a small incendiary device while the other two moved quickly through the house, dousing the sparse furnishings with accelerant. They left the dope on the table.

"Ready," the gunman said over his mic to the van driver, who responded: "Clear. Come on out." He slid the door of the van open and put it in drive, watching the still-quiet street.

They left, shutting the door behind them and hurrying to the van. The fire started immediately but they were long gone before the neighbors noticed that the house was engulfed in flames.

❖

Alonzo was watching a western. It was *Tombstone*, one of his favorites, and he was in his recliner, sharing a bowl of gourmet salted caramel popcorn with Barry, his bodyguard and go-to man, since his kids preferred *Star Wars* movies and what they now called the Marvel Universe—it was just regular superhero comics in his day—and his wife didn't like movies with violence. So they were all upstairs. He was in his family room, in his house, in a leafy, calm, prosperous, and very safe suburban New Jersey town. He had a dentist for his left-side neighbor, and a tax attorney across the street, though with his corner lot on high ground, his house was nicer than either. They were just getting to the best part of the movie, the famous shoot out at the OK Corral, when the phone rang. The work cell.

"Fuck. Hit pause, will you?" Alonzo asked Barry, who had a handful of popcorn. Frowning, he stuffed it in his mouth and chewed while he searched for the remote among the cushions on the couch. "Yeah?" Alonzo said into the phone, and then barked at Barry, "Pause, I said! We're missing it."

"Immooking . . ." Barry mumbled with his mouth full, checking on the floor.

Then, as the voice on the phone spoke, Alonzo held a hand up for silence. "You fucking with me? Really? All right you better get down there and see. I'm rolling now."

He closed the phone and turned to Barry. It was his brother, Reggie, on the phone. The guy who ran their dope operation had called to say that a kid named Reverb had called him and said the main stash got hit.

"Who would rob you LZ?" Barry asked, finally swallowing. "What are they, crazy or stupid?"

"I don't know," Alonzo said, standing up. He was in track pants, T-shirt, and slippers. "I plan to ask them that just before I kill them." He found his car keys on the coffee table and tossed them to Barry. "Get the car out. I gotta tell my wife I'm leaving and find my shoes."

So Barry wiped his hands, pulled on his sneakers, and headed out to the driveway, where Alonzo's BMW was sleeping, absently picking popcorn from his teeth. Alonzo ran upstairs, rapped on the bedroom door, and called to his wife, who was reading in bed. She nodded, used to this, the way a doctor's wife is. He kicked off his slippers and stepped into sandals, then came back downstairs. No one paid any more attention to the gunfight that was now raging on screen. He was out the door and halfway down the drive when Barry started the engine and the bomb went off.

❖

Next they hit Little Maria's stop and cop spot. She was the Queen of Washington Heights and this operation was the jewel in her crown, a smooth-running operation catering to the commuters and the suburban trade who rolled back and forth across the George Washington Bridge, as well as cars coming down from the Bronx or up the West Side Highway. Basically it was like a drive-thru. You cruised slow down the block and a kid ran out to your car window, checking you out and asking what you wanted. You told him and he took your money and signaled to his boss. Then another kid ran up with your product and dashed off. You drove away happy. Meantime the runner was at the next car in line. It ran like this, 24/7, with a major rush before and after work, at lunchtime, and all night long on the weekends, except for when the cops came by. Every so often, they'd set up a checkpoint and start pulling over cars, especially those with Jersey plates. This scared the customers but they always flocked back soon enough—like pigeons that had been scattered from the roof. Other times, the cops tried to seal off the street, pulling up and blocking the corners, then sweeping up everyone in between. But the only ones holding drugs or money on the street were a few juveniles with a few bags each—the runners, who knew nothing useful anyway, except that if they just kept their mouths shut they'd be sprung in no time. The crew bosses, who sent them back and forth, were clean and the guards

who watched over everything would ditch their pieces in the sewer drain and bolt. The stash and the cash were held in one of the buildings and moved periodically—a basement, a hallway, an apartment where they paid the tenant for use of a window—but the cops never made it that far before all valuables were removed. The small amount Maria lost to the law was just a cost of business, like spillage.

That's what the lookouts were for. Stationed on key corners, stoops, and rooftops, they watched for cops, at which point they'd call out *"Llegada!"* (Coming!) and the whole operation would simply fold, disappearing into the woodwork. So, for anyone who wanted to do more than collect a few minor arrests and fill a quota, the first thing to do was take them down. The gray van pulled up, and two men got out. Both wore tracksuits, the camo of this neighborhood, and as they passed the lookout on the corner, one said, "Hey kid," and distracted him, while the other hit him with a taser. He fell and they dragged him between two parked cars to sleep it off. Then they broke into the basement door of the building and ran up the four flights. The lookout on the roof never saw a thing; he was too busy looking out, down the street, for police. The first man through the roof exit shot him, a silencer on his pistol, then took off his pack and set up in his spot. His partner got on his earpiece mic.

"Ready."

The van driver pulled out now and came down the block, stopping in the center, as though he were a customer looking to cop. The runner came up to his window. "What you need? C and D, man. Gran Diablo is on the money . . ."

"What I need, bro," the driver, a muscled-up white man with a blond ponytail, "is for you to tell your boss to close up shop. We're taking over this block. White Angel is moving in."

"Huh?" The white dude had an accent, sounded like a surfer or something, but that wasn't the problem; he was just talking nonsense. But he'd parked so that he blocked the whole street so, after a couple of tries, the runner ran back and told Miguel, who was overseeing the crew from the doorway of a nearby building. Miguel sighed, cursing in Spanish, and

grabbed his piece from where it was hidden in a disused planter, stuffing it into his jeans, then went down to see what this joker wanted.

"Sup?" he asked the white guy in the van.

"You the boss here?"

"Why?" Miguel asked. "You ask to see the manager or some shit?" He lifted his oversized Yankees jersey and showed the gun. "You want to talk to the complaint department?"

The white guy smiled. "No complaint, bro. Just letting you know, White Angel moves in here tomorrow. Giving you the chance to pack up and go in peace."

"Right," Miguel said. "Thanks for sharing. Now why don't you peace the fuck out man, before I lose my sense of humor." He half drew the pistol, finger on the trigger.

The white guy raised a hand. "No problem. Take care." He pulled away. Miguel spat in the gutter, shaking his head, totally unaware of the sniper's scope trained on his forehead. One shot took the top of his head right off.

Panic erupted, but there was no time to hide. In thirty seconds the key members of Maria's top crew lay dead or wounded on the ground. And the shooters were on their way out. They got back in the van and headed for another building nearby. Maria's own.

Maria's apartment, on the top floor of a building with a river view, was almost impregnable. She had another, fancier house in the Bronx, but this was home, where she had lived her whole life, and everyone in this building knew her. The kids sitting on the stoop worked for her and kept an eye on the whole block. The super's wife, who kept her ground-floor apartment door ajar, noted whoever got on the elevator. Even the guy who sold flavored ices on the corner would have alerted someone if a van full of armed men had pulled up. So they went in the one way she didn't think to worry about: from above.

First the van stopped one street over, on the other side of the block from her building. Four men slipped out, and unobtrusively broke into a basement door of a building. They took the elevator from the basement to the top floor and left via the roof exit. No one bothered to notice. They crossed over to the roof of Maria's building and, with a crowbar, busted open the door to her roof. Then they came down the stairs. Using a battering ram like the cops did, they rushed down the hall, broke her door open, and entered.

Their attack was flawless, and should have succeeded without a hitch, except for two things: First, Maria happened to be in her bedroom with her boyfriend, Paco. If she had been in the living room, watching TV with her Tia, she would have been killed instantly. As it was, they shot Tia, an old woman and the one truly harmless person on the premises. Her eyesight was too poor to shoot anyone, and the strongest substance she handled was hot sauce. But the commotion drew the attention of Maria, Paco, and Duque, who was the second problem.

Duque was Maria's dog, a ferocious pit bull. As soon as the action started in the living room, before Maria and Paco could even get out of bed, Duque was up and running. He tore into the living room, leapt onto the man who had just shot Tia, and sank his fangs into his groin. The man howled in pain, dropping his gun and struggling with the dog, who locked his jaw and ground in deep, chewing his way through fabric and skin. The gunman beside him was distracted, trying to get a clear shot at the damn dog, and the other two had gone to check the kitchen and the office. This gave Maria and Paco a chance. Paco was twenty-two and pretty, with a neat goatee, dark, deep eyes, a lean muscled chest and gold cross, wearing only his boxers. He was a good lover and a fine companion for Maria, who was at least twenty years his senior, but he was not the smartest guy in town. He grabbed his Tech 9 from under the bed and rushed out. Seeing the dog ripping into the man's groin, and distracted by the screaming, he yelled "Duque!" and shot the guy Duque was attacking, just as the second gunman shot him and the dog both.

This, however, gave Maria time to think. Dressed in her red bra and panties, she pulled her Uzi from where it was always strapped

under her bed, peeked carefully through the doorway, and opened fire, killing the man who'd killed her dog and boyfriend. By now the two other gunmen were coming back into the room and she shot the one pushing through the kitchen door first, blowing him back into the kitchen and sending the door swinging after him. But the one coming from the office got her.

He had dropped to the carpet when he saw Maria shooting, so when she swung back to pick him off, she missed, riddling the wall with bullets. From his prone position, he fired back at Maria under the dining table, shattering her shinbone. She stumbled back, firing wildly just to keep him pinned down, then threw her door shut and hit the button on the wall. By the time the gunman got up and across the apartment, he was too late. She was in her panic room and the metal door had bolted, essentially sealing her in a vault. The gunman tried to gain entry with the crowbar, but by now the whole building was in an uproar, so he fled the way he came. The last thing Maria had the presence of mind to do before she went into shock was text the super's wife the code to her panic room door. That way the EMTs were able to gain entry.

❖

Joe was watching *Jeopardy* with Gladys when Yelena came home. She knew the routine—no talking during Alex Trebek—so she went to the kitchen and got her vodka from the freezer, then sat on the couch and waited for a break, while Gladys called out the answers, getting an impressive number right. "What is phosphorous? Who was Bertolt Brecht? Where is the Suez Canal?"

At the commercial, Yelena followed Joe into the kitchen while he got himself a seltzer from the fridge.

"So," he asked quietly. "Who'd you see?"

"Someone I hoped never to see again. Unless my gun was in his mouth. Nikolai Kozlov, the SVR agent who threatened me with life in prison if I didn't work for them."

"Your Russian handler? What was he doing at the Wildwater building? Watching the show?"

She shrugged. "I saw him getting off the elevator. So I followed but he got in a car and left."

"It's a big building," Joe pointed out. "He could have been visiting some other office."

"Yes, if you believe in coincidence," Yelena said.

"I don't," Joe admitted. "So with Wildwater involved and now this Russian, this is starting to smell like spooks."

Yelena wrinkled her nose and poured herself another drink. "Smells like bad shit to me."

Joe nodded. "That's the CIA scent I remember, all right. As soon as the spies get involved, everything turns to shit."

"A lot of our oligarchs come out of the old KGB. Your Richards, the Wildwater CEO. He is like one of these too." She sneered. "They're just greedy pigs who don't have the courage to be real outlaws."

Joe grinned. "I didn't realize you were so politically engaged. You're an anarchist."

She laughed. "No. I met some of those anarchists. They talk too much. I'm just an honest thief, like you."

Joe clicked his soda bottle against her vodka bottle as Gladys called in from the living room. "Bring me a Fresca, will you? It's Final Jeopardy." So they went in and joined her, and then ordered Indian food, and Joe was pleasantly surprised to see how well his grandmother played host, matching Yelena drink for drink, regaling her with tales from her grifting days, and swapping shoplifting tricks. Then his phone rang. It was Gio. Someone had just tried to kill him.

❖

Gio had been busy all evening, taking care of one of his most boring chores, counting money. Like many businessmen with varied and far-flung enterprises, he spent a fair bit of his time simply making the rounds.

The difference was that while more conventional business owners hoped to be picking up earnings at these stops, Gio was dropping them off. He was laundering money, with Nero driving beside him and Big Eddie in back with a duffel bag full of cash, tribute that had been passed up the line from the many rackets Gio owned or allowed to proceed with his blessing.

His first stop was Laundry Town, and he braced himself for the same stale jokes. Like clockwork, Big Eddie held up the duffle.

"Hey boss I got your laundry right here. Drop if off dirty, pick it up clean. Fluff and fold, am I right?"

Nero chuckled obligingly, but Gio couldn't take it anymore.

"Let me ask you Eddie, how many years we been coming here?"

"I don't know boss, five, ten?"

"And every week you make the same fucking joke. I just can't stand it anymore."

"Sorry boss."

He turned to Nero. "And you laugh. How can you still think it's funny?"

"Sorry, Gio."

"Okay new rule. From now on, no jokes about laundry or dirty money or anything unless you just thought of it brand new and you are absolutely fucking sure it's funny. Got it?"

"Yes, boss."

"Sure, Gio."

"Great, thank you." Gio sighed. Still, as a way to clean illegal proceeds, he had to admit it was one of his brightest schemes. They showed up during a weekday night, a slow time, and immediately headed through the door marked employees only. Neither the senior citizen behind the counter nor the two West African women folding drop-off customers' clothes, nor the few bored civilians watching their underwear spin, took any notice at all. In the back office, Gio sat at the desk, opened the old fashioned safe, and began to fill it with money while Nero did the paperwork.

Laundry Town, which was now a small chain of six laundries that Gio had built up using the old Italian couple who owned the first one as fronts, was a cash-only business. People dropped off clothes or dry cleaning at the counter, or they slid bills into a machine that put credits on a card to use the machines. Either way it was easy to simply add more receipts and more income to the books. The only real supplies were detergent, cleaning fluid, and water, so there was little to worry about in the way of inventory. The managers, that is to say Gio's fronts, got to run the business and pocket the legit proceeds. Gio ran his own cash through, had the business show it as corporate profits, and then took it back as earnings from his stake in Laundry Town, Inc.

Next stop was Paradise Nail Salon. Same deal here. A Korean mother of three had been left to run the place alone when her husband died. Gio had stepped in to offer support and protection, and one of his corporate shells had bought the storefront where she worked. Now she managed three shops—two of them former video stores, another great cash business for Gio, and one of the few he enjoyed visiting, until the bottom dropped out of it—and Gio had the same arrangement with her.

The biggest hassle was Jocko's, a bar and music venue out on the island, simply because it was the loudest and most crowded and because of the added attention that anyplace with a liquor license got. Gio made it work for him though: he had the manager order more booze to offset the extra cash he pumped in, then took it as a write-off and used it to supply drinks for the illegal gambling parlors he controlled. That was Gio, smart, careful, and on top of every angle. So the last thing he expected, when he finally arrived, tired and bored, at his last stop, was to be stepping into a trap.

Especially not at Café Primo. This place had been in the family forever. It was in Carroll Gardens, which had been a deeply Italian neighborhood in south Brooklyn for decades, with the scent of semolina bread baking on the corners, bathtub Madonnas on the front lawns, and even a mural in salute to John Gotti. The space had once been a social club, one of those storefronts with painted-over windows where wiseguys

used to hang out, scattered all over New York. This one had become a Caprisi joint when Gio's father won the building shooting craps. It sat there, a neighborhood fixture, hosting card games and the occasional load of stolen merchandise, until the area began to change. Rents rose, new, wealthier people moved in, the bakeries became *boulangeries*. Pretty soon the little storefront was simply too valuable for three old guys to sit out front on folding chairs in shorts and black dress socks all summer. It already had a marble counter and a fine, old-fashioned espresso/cappuccino machine, the kind with the eagle on top, and all the character, tin roof and tiled floor, that a chic designer would charge you a fortune to copy. Gio got a new sign painted—Café Primo—and put his cousin's kid, who had "trained" as a barista, whatever that meant, in charge. The place did great business, though it was always a little sad to come by here. You know times have really changed when not even the Mafia can afford the rent. Still, he saved it for his last stop, so that along with dropping off the money, he could relax a little with a well-deserved espresso and a single pignoli cookie—his pants were getting tight.

So when Big Eddie came out with three coffees on a tray and set them down at the outside table that Gio's cousin had reserved for them, Gio had asked, "What about the cookies?"

"Sorry boss, I forgot," Eddie had said, turning back. Gio sighed and was blowing on his coffee when Eddie came rushing over, without any cookies, yelling "Boss!"

"What?" Gio had barked, impatiently, but before he could register anything else, Eddie had flung himself through the air, knocking Gio to the ground, toppling the chairs and tables and taking two bullets in his broad back.

Gio heard the shots and felt glass raining down, but from under Eddie's bulk he couldn't see what had happened. It was a drive-by. A car had pulled up, and a man had hung out the passenger window, raising a machine pistol. He'd opened fire at Gio, hitting Eddie instead and shattering the shop window behind them. Nero had dropped to the ground behind the upended table and drew his pistol, returning fire. Gio

was unarmed, but as he rolled Eddie off, he drew the gun from Eddie's shoulder holster and likewise shot at the car, which was now speeding away.

"Eddie!" Gio said, using all his strength to roll him over. "Eddie!" He was dead, with both rounds still inside him. It was only then that Gio realized some of the blood on him was his own. Splinters of falling window glass had sprayed his back like buckshot, shredding his white dress shirt, and now blood was soaking through.

The first call Gio made from the ambulance was to his family, to check on them and let Carol know he was okay while Nero dispatched soldiers to his house and his mother's house and raised the general alarm. The second was to Eddie's family. And the third call was to Joe.

PART III

20

W HEN J OE CAME DOWNSTAIRS the next day, Nero was waiting, standing at the curb with his car double-parked. They hugged and Joe told him, "Sorry about Eddie."

"Thanks." Nero nodded. "He was a stand-up guy to the end."

"No doubt."

Nero opened the rear door for Joe, and he slid in next to Gio, who shook his hand.

"Sorry," Gio said. "I can't hug with this fucking back."

"Right," Joe told him. "Sorry to hear about Eddie."

Joe could see his friend was distraught, so he waited while Nero got in and they started moving. Then Gio spoke, looking out the window at the tumult of Jackson Heights, silenced now behind glass.

"You know he took those bullets for me," Gio said.

Joe nodded, even though Gio couldn't see him, and waited for him to continue. "And the last thing I ever said to him was yell at him for forgetting my cookie."

He turned back with a bitter look on his face. Joe squeezed his hand. "I'm sure it rolled right off him. He was like that. Big shoulders."

"Yeah. You're right. He was all heart." Gio smiled. "And no brains."

"Better than the opposite."

"Ain't that the truth," Gio said, then yelled: "Fuck!" He punched the seat in front of him and Nero flinched. "I'm going to miss his dumb fucking jokes about the laundry."

❖

Nero took the Brooklyn–Queens Expressway into Brooklyn, then the streets. As they moved deeper into South Williamsburg, they seemed to be traveling not just through space but time. Soon they saw only men in black—black coats, black hats, black beards—and women in headscarves or caps and long skirts, pushing strollers or leading flocks of kids dressed like miniature versions of themselves. More and more of the writing on the storefronts was in Hebrew or Yiddish and Joe was struck, as he always was, by how many of the windows, whole sides of tall apartment buildings, were barred, elaborately so, with rectangular, cage-like structures. Were they to keep people from getting in, he wondered, or getting out?

This was the land of the Hasidim, the ultra-Orthodox Jews who formed a highly insular community of their own, an Old World town within the secular modern city, with their own institutions, schools, businesses, even their own neighborhood security patrols, and rabbis who ruled by their own religious laws. Of course, they also had their own outlaws. That's where Rebbe came in, as the oldest and most respected Orthodox gangster, a king among his tribe. And now they were in his land.

As they stopped for a light, Joe saw a man who was loitering on the sunny corner nod at Nero, who nodded back. He was a tall guy in a wide brim black hat with a pointed black beard, and a long black coat over his black pants, like wearing a solar energy panel, Joe imagined. His eyes prowled the street watchfully, and he had his right hand in his coat. He was armed.

Now Joe noticed other men stationed around, on corners and on stairs, watching from windows, even on the rooftops, black forms silhouetted

against the sky like scarecrows. They turned into a small, dead-end street and found it blocked by what looked like a bakery delivery van—Hebrew writing and a painting of matzoh. Nero stopped. A young guy approached the car. At first glance he looked more modern, in jeans and with a hipster vibe to his beard—but he wore a knit skullcap and had the telltale knotted strings, the tzitzit, dangling from under his Kurt Cobain shirt. Nero lowered the window.

"Caprisi," he said, and the guy peeked in back at Joe and Gio. He nodded, signaling as he stepped away. The truck rolled back.

"Tight security," Joe said as Nero pulled forward.

"After last night, we decided only Rebbe could guarantee safety for this meeting. All of us targets in one place."

Most of the block was taken up by a huge old warehouse. Nero turned into the driveway and a large, metal gate was rolled back by a bearded guy with a skullcap and a rifle slung over his shoulder. Another, who could have been his brother, stood watch, rifle in hand. Joe clocked two more on the roof as they rolled into the warehouse. The walls were as thick as a castle and light filtered in from high, barred windows. There was probably still coal dust on the pebbled glass. Inside, a row of delivery trucks stood against one wall, by the other, a row of expensive, late-model luxury cars and SUVs. The guests. And by itself in a corner was a private ambulance, with two EMTs sitting on the back bumper. Nero parked and they got out. The other drivers were gathered in a group, chatting and smoking. Cash waved at Joe from where he was leaning on his hood—no doubt he was driving his boss, Uncle Chen. Liam Madigan, who was there with his eldest brother, ambled over.

"Gio, I'm terribly sorry to hear of your loss. I always liked Eddie." He shook both their hands. "Anything I can do," he said. "Just ask."

"I'll be in touch," Joe told him.

"And I'll be ready."

Beside the trucks were towering pallets, stacked twenty feet high, with plastic-wrapped blocks formed of boxes of matzoh, each one emblazoned with a bright yellow Moische's logo. It was like a fortress wall towering

above them, with no way through or around it. Beside it stood Josh, with a headset mic and an Uzi on a strap over his shoulder.

"Joe," he said, with a grin, "good to see you," and then to Gio: "Just a second, sir."

Gio nodded and Joe winked as Josh spoke into his mic. They heard an electric motor and suddenly a large chunk of the wall lifted up and began to ease back, opening a doorway wide enough for both men to walk through. A forklift, manned by an old graybeard, dressed in black of course, had pulled back with the load. He waited for them, then rotated the forklift and backed out through the passage he'd made, sliding the brick back into the wall behind them. They were sealed in with matzoh on all four sides now—the warehouse was stacked to the ceiling, leaving a large open space in the center.

Several folding tables had been placed end to end, then covered with a long white tablecloth to form a single surface. Another nearby table held tea and coffee urns, pitchers of ice water, rows of cups and glasses, sugar, and milk. On folding chairs around the table were Uncle Chen, true to his name, a bald, round, avuncular-looking old man who was the ruthless boss of Flushing; Anton, from Brighton Beach, representing the Russian Mafia, furiously smoking acrid Russian cigarettes; Reggie, Alonzo's brother, younger and thinner than Alonzo, with a high fade where Alonzo had his head shaved, was dressed like a grad student in a button-down and jeans, and looked a bit out of his element; and in a navy blue suit and red tie, Jack Madigan. At one end of the table sat their host, Menachem "Rebbe" Stone. And at the other, still with red lipstick, polished nails, and diamond rings despite being in a wheelchair and with an IV dripping into her arm, was Little Maria.

"Gio," Rebbe called to them. "Yosef!"

He came around, arms open wide, and hugged Gio tightly. Gio flinched in pain, but took it, along with a ticklish kiss on the cheek. Rebbe had come up in the world with Gio's father and he'd known Gio his whole life. He shook hands warmly with Joe. "Thank you for coming. You want something? Tea? Coffee?" He shrugged at the stacks

around them. "Matzoh maybe? No? I don't blame you. Then sit, sit, please."

They took the empty chairs that were left and Rebbe stood at the end of the table. "Welcome friends and thank you all for coming. I'm flattered that you'd ask me to host this meeting, and I hope you can see that we are safe here, from our enemies and from listening ears. If you don't think matzoh can stop a bullet you haven't tried to use the can after Passover week at my house. Oy." He patted his belly as chuckles echoed in the cavernous space. "But no more jokes. I apologize. It's a sin in a time of mourning. And let me say, I know I speak for us all when I offer my deepest regrets to those of you who lost people last night—Gio, Maria. *Olav ha-shalom*, may they rest in peace." The others nodded. Anton and Jack crossed themselves. "And Reggie, your brother is in our prayers." Reggie nodded shyly and fidgeted in his chair. "Uncle Chen," Rebbe said, turning to the old friend and rival beside him, "I hear you were hit last night as well."

Chen nodded. "A Sunset Park operation. They took out one of my best dealers. A kid I've known since he was in the fifth grade."

"What a waste of a young life," Rebbe said. "So then, we know why we are here. Let's begin. First off, I know Maria wants to say something, and she can only stay a short time. Maria?" He nodded to her and took his seat.

"Thanks, Menachem." Her voice was raspy. "As you can see, I am still not good. All night I was in the hospital and they didn't want to let me out. But I told them I had to be here, even if I crawled, so here I am. So forgive me if I sound a little loopy, they gave me something for the pain." She shrugged. "Is pretty good shit, I should find out their supplier." This got a laugh. She grinned, then grew serious and raised a painted claw. "But this is what I came to say." She spat her words out. "*Rapa tu mai*, these *mama guevos*, who violated my home. I put my curse on them. They killed the ones I love most. My aunt, who never done nothing to nobody, except cook and pray for us all. And they took my precious boy, the love of my life, Duque."

"Was that her boyfriend?" Gio whispered to Joe.

"Not quite," Joe answered under his breath.

"And also," Maria went on, "while he was defending me, those bastards, *hijo de la gran puta*, they kill my boyfriend Paco too." She winced in pain, then took a breath, and continued. "So you know how me and my associates, in the import business, we offered five hundred thousand for this Zahir. I'm here to say that we talked today and now we are going to double this. One million dollars, for the head of the piece of shit who did this to me, and to us."

A murmur went around the room. Reggie raised a hand, like in a classroom. "I want to say I'm kicking in another hundred grand, on behalf of my family, for what they did to my brother."

Gio nodded. "Me too. In the name of Big Eddie."

Rebbe looked at Chen, who nodded at him, and then at Jack and Anton. They all nodded back. He spoke: "I know we all want to help with this. So let's make it two million. The price for justice against the enemies who attacked us here in our own hometown." He turned to Joe. "So. That's what we asked you here for. What do you say, sheriff?" He showed his crooked teeth through his snow-white beard. "Two million dead or alive."

While the others waited, Gio leaned in to Joe's ear. "Let's just make that dead."

Joe nodded at him, then smiled at the waiting bosses. "Let me see what I can do."

21

DONNA STOPPED AT THE coffee cart where Sameer, a cheerful young Yemeni man, stood in a plexiglass box steaming milk and buttering bagels.

"Make it a double today, Sameer," she told him.

"Coming right up." He poured her a latte with an extra shot of espresso. "Here you go. Now go catch those bad guys," he said, as he did every day.

"I'll try," Donna said, clipping her ID to her jacket as she headed toward the entrance to the Federal Building. She too said that every morning, though she rarely thought she'd have the chance to actually chase one. But that morning, before she even got to her office door, a passing colleague told her Tom was looking for her, so she knocked on his door instead.

"Yeah!" he yelled, turning from the window as she entered. Once again the endless parade of civilians was passing across the square, constantly threatening to ruin his day by getting killed. "Sit," he said. Donna felt like he was talking to a dog but she sat, swallowing her annoyance with a long sip of coffee.

"Well you're in luck," he told her.

"Really?" She asked, skeptically hopeful. He didn't sound happy about it.

"Yeah. As of last night we have a citywide drug war."

"Oh . . . great?"

"Anyway enough noise got made that the police department is assigning their Major Case Unit. And since our lab made the connection with that last case, they've asked us for help. But I've already got every agent on full alert for 9/11 with all days off cancelled and overtime coming out my ass, so all the help they're getting from me is you. Have fun," he added, and turned back to the window.

❖

Thanks to all his pushing, Fusco was now running the White Angel investigation, but the truth was, he wasn't even sure what he was investigating. He'd begun nosing around White Angel because Gio told him to. Then his own cop instincts, which were much more reliable than his terrible gambler's hunches, told him something was up, except no one but maybe his partner believed him. Now, with the FBI lab results and the half dozen bodies that had dropped all over town in one night, all of sudden everyone was sure there was a case, and that it was major as hell, but still no one, not even Fusco himself, knew what the fuck kind of case it was.

The FBI chick, Zamora her name was, came by just as he was pondering these heavy thoughts over a breakfast burrito with extra cheese. Parks was sipping some kind of tea that smelled like medicine.

"Detective Fusco?" she asked. A looker. The classy type, in one of those black power suits the feds favored.

"Yes, you found me, come on in." He moved his burrito to his left hand, wiped his right on his pants and shook. She held her smile. "This is Parks," he added.

"Nice to meet you," she said and shook Parks's hand too, transferring some of Fusco's burrito grease.

"Welcome," Parks said, grabbing a couple of deli napkins and handing her one. "Please sit down."

"Yeah, have a seat," Fusco said, taking another big bite. "We were just discussing the, uh, nature of this case. Maybe you'd like to give us the FBI's read on it."

"Well . . ." Donna looked down at the one empty seat and saw the greasy burrito wrapper. She leaned against a table. "We," and by *we* she meant herself, "think that Zahir, up till now, has been smuggling dope into New York and using it to fund terror overseas. Now it looks like maybe he's moved in. He's distributing here directly, and we received a threat about a possible terror strike as well."

"A threat?" Fusco asked. That was news to him.

"That's classified."

"Credible?"

She hesitated. "Semi."

"And you do terror or drugs for the FBI?" he asked.

"A little of everything," she said. "I handle information that comes in."

"Comes in how? You mean CIs? Do you have one on this case?"

"Mostly via phone or email actually. Some tweets."

"So like a receptionist?" Fusco asked, and Parks, like someone who sees another, metaphorical bottle of piss about to spill across the room, leapt in.

"Agent Zamora," he said. "Do you have any evidence to link the drug activity, or last night's violence, to Zahir? Or to terror at all? We've been watching this White Angel crew for a bit, and they just look like regular homegrown gangbangers to me."

Fusco waved his burrito at Parks and a spray of juice dotted the files on his desk. "He's got a point. No reports of guys in turbans and bathrobes slinging dope in the projects, yet."

"So what do you make it as?" Donna asked.

Parks shrugged. "Turf war. White Angel has the best package in town, maybe because of your Persian connection, sure. They use that leverage to poach more territory until, last night, war finally breaks out. Bound to happen sooner or later." He sat back and crossed his legs, revealing argyle socks and lovely brown wing tips. "And that's if these incidents are even all connected. New York City is known to have more than one shooting in a night."

"As you can see, Zamora," Fusco said, "Parks has a brain, rare in the NYPD, which makes up, somewhat, for the hassle of trying to eat lunch with a vegan. You're not vegan are you?"

"No, I'm not."

"Of course not. What was I thinking? Your people love pork way too much, like mine. Sorry."

Donna frowned, unsure of whether to be offended, or accept this apology, or what. Fusco marched on, running a thick, greasy finger over the pages spread on his desk. "But he is missing one curious aspect of last night's parties. Crime scene reports suggest that the shootings by the bridge last night were done with a high-powered rifle from a rooftop. That means a sniper, with some skills rarely seen among uptown corner boys. The device in the Brooklyn stash-house, as well as what I've got on the car bomb in Jersey—they're being very cooperative because it's a small town department hoping like hell this is our mess—both are high-tech gear of the sort used by commandos and shit."

"You're thinking what, military?" Donna asked, as Parks leaned over the desk to read the reports.

Finished with his breakfast, Fusco belched into his fist, then reached for his coffee. He dumped in a sugar and stirred with a finger. "I'm thinking, whatever kind of war this is, for dope or for Allah, it's being fought by soldiers." He took a sip and sat back, resting the cup on his burrito-filled belly. "I just hope we don't need an army to take them down."

❖

Joe called in the troops. But before he could take out the target, he needed to locate it, and the one spot where he knew they'd be was at work, selling dope. Or more precisely supplying it, since there was little chance the kids peddling bags of White Angel knew any more about their bosses than the kids who sold for Alonzo or Maria. It was like asking a gas station attendant the address of the CEO of Exxon's house. So what he really wanted to catch was the re-up, the moment when the invisible power had to show its hand, even if it was just dropping off a package.

From what he'd learned at the meeting, White Angel's busiest spot was in East New York, a largely ungentrified piece of Brooklyn where,

in parts, a certain degree of lawlessness still prevailed: hookers walked streets, boozers huddled on corners, and junkies lined up for junk, especially when word was out that the quality was this high. Reggie and his driver, who knew the area well and drove with a Glock on the console, picked up Juno and Joe. Juno got in back with Reggie. Joe rode up front with the driver, and asked him to cruise past the spot, rolling slow so that Juno could take pictures from behind the tinted glass.

The block was derelict and abandoned at night: the back side of lots where bus and delivery companies parked their vehicles, a vacant space full of monster weeds reaching over the toppled fence, a boarded-up auto repair shop and an abandoned, crumbling tenement. At the corners there were bustling tenements, where regular people tried to live their lives, a bodega, and a bus stop, but the middle of the block was a no-man's-land and that's where White Angel was sold.

Joe clocked the lookouts on the corner, teenagers slouching against a wall or a car, who'd send up a signal if the cops rolled by, then the touts, who steered you toward the product while singing its praises. Then a ragged row of junkies, lined up against a fence, trying to look casual while shuffling impatiently, like passengers on a really crap airline waiting for a flight to oblivion. One by one, they'd be sent in the vestibule of the abandoned building, then emerge a second later, now hurrying away as the lookouts admonished them to walk not run. The setup was secure, if simple. If anybody suspicious came along, they just closed up shop and locked the front door. No one standing outside would have anything more incriminating than a bad attitude—except for a few unlucky dope fiends with their hands in their pockets. Even if the cops charged in, Joe knew from circling the block that this building had a rear entrance that led to the vacant lot behind, then to the neighboring yards or the street. Any stash would be tossed along the way. Whether in the deserts or at the borders or on the corners, trying to stop the flow of drugs was like grabbing a fistful of water from a rushing river: it ran right through your hand. Maybe you caught a minnow.

Reggie waved at the scene, dismissively. "I've been telling my brother for a couple years now, all this is the past, man. I got us a chain of vape shops and joints selling CBD. That shit moves like crazy and it's legal. Sell it right out in the open, and no fear of drive-bys neither. I wanted to name it for Alonzo, like ALZ CBD or something, cash in on his profile but you know him, all secretive and shit, so I went with Doctor Vape and like a hip-hop vibe with graffiti for the packaging. And now, for the hipsters, we got the Brooklyn Sweet Oil Society." Excited, he leaned up between the seats and tapped Joe's shoulder. "Check it out, Joe, I got a factory making custom Doctor Vape Pens and I'm even designing my own vape juices. You should try some, like Mellow Fellow or Royal Crown Cream. Or I bet you'd dig my Professor Smooth Berry. I'll send you some sample cartridges."

"I don't smoke," Joe said, trying to be polite. He didn't want to say that those things looked ridiculous to him and they stunk. Every time he saw someone hit one, he had an urge to slap it out of his mouth.

"It ain't smoke," Reggie explained. "It's flavored steam with nicotine in it. And now CBD. And soon THC. All legal. That CBD stuff? We sell it in chocolate, oil, body lotion. White folks buy it for their fucking dogs! Soon it will be in their kids' milk. And when they legalize weed, like any minute now, we are poised to dominate that shit. That's what I told Alonzo, let them have the dope, dude. Let somebody else get shot up or blown up over this raggedy ass strip of dirt."

"You've got a point," Joe conceded. "Times change. There will probably be a Starbucks in that building soon. But addiction is addiction. There will always be dope."

"King Heroin. You sound like my brother." Reggie lowered his voice in imitation of Alonzo: "Change the names but the game remains . . ." He shook his head. "Yeah, he's old school like you. But now he's in a coma." He lapsed into silence as they turned a corner. They passed another bodega, a flat tire repair place, and a corner restaurant whose sign read Chinese-Burger-Chicken-Donuts. Reggie went on. "I say be more like your man, Gio. Now that's a cat I'd like to just study for a minute."

"I'll recommend you for an internship," Joe said.

"I worked for the man," Juno piped in, taking his face from the camera.

"Word?" Reggie regarded his skinny young seatmate with new interest.

"Yeah." He chose his words carefully, glancing at Joe up front. "I mean he's cool and he pays right but, all due respect, he ain't exactly some softy running a start-up, like riding a scooter around the conference room and shit. New suit and an MBA but you can't hide those cold-as-fuck shark eyes. Give me the willies."

Reggie sighed. "Guess that's why him and my bro are friends. Even stone killers get lonesome sometimes, need someone to talk to."

Juno cleared his throat, and when Reggie glanced over, he nodded his head toward the back of Joe's head. Reggie hastily added: "Not that being a stone killer is automatically a bad thing." But Joe's mind was elsewhere.

"You get what you need Juno?" he asked.

"Yes sir."

He pulled out his phone. "Okay, then let's get going. I need you, Cash, Liam, and Josh all together to explain what we're going to do. I'll call Yelena. And stop if you see a Salvation Army on the way. I need some clothes."

❖

They met in the back room at Club Rendezvous. It was convenient, safe, and—crowded and loud as it was—a random assortment of criminals wandering in one at a time drew no special notice. They just walked by past Sunny, the enormous African bouncer who was on duty when Joe was off, and who got that name because of the wide, gold-capped grin he gave the world—and also past the discreet extra muscle Gio had added since the attacks, a silent white guy in a suit, with a gun under the table—then crossed the busy room full of patrons, around the stage where the dancers played, and down the rear hall toward the restrooms, the dressing rooms, and the manager's office door. The manager, a pot-bellied, white-bearded dude they called Santa politely pointed them all to the couch and chairs,

then got up from his desk and left, shutting the door behind him. Liam and Josh were next to each other on the couch, self-consciously keeping a few inches apart, which no one else noticed. Juno was at the end of the couch, arranging the street photos he'd printed on the coffee table. Cash sat backward on a kitchen chair, leaning it forward on two legs to see the pictures. Yelena curled in the armchair. Joe rolled the manager's desk chair out and sat.

"Thanks for getting here so quick," Joe told them. "I don't have to explain why."

"Take out these bastards before they get us," Liam said.

"That's the goal, yeah," Joe said. "But the first step is identifying them. So tonight we follow the dope, see where it takes us, and learn as much as we can."

"Recon," Josh said, "like the army."

"Or like cops," Cash added.

"Funny you should mention that," Joe said. "We're going to need two cars. One I don't care, as long as it's clean enough not to get you pulled over. The other one, we need a Chevy Impala, like an unmarked cop car."

"Done," Cash said, nodding.

"And you two clean-cut, handsome young fellows," Joe said to Josh and Liam, "try to look like cops look when they're trying not to look like cops."

Liam laughed. "You're just saying that because I'm Irish."

"Well white anyway," Juno pointed out.

"You mean I have to shave?" Josh asked. Since leaving the military he had made a point to grow out his hair and beard.

Joe shrugged. "Well the mustache is good. Just trim it and tuck your hair up under a cap or something. Think Serpico."

Josh frowned. "You mean the sign?"

"That's Scorpio," Cash told him. "*Serpico* is an old movie with Al Pacino playing a cop. Pretty good though."

"Don't worry, Joe. We get it," Liam told him.

"Juno, you know what I need from you. The cars will be parked here and here." He pointed to the spots on the photos, then stood and went to the manager's desk. "And does this printer do color copies?"

"Shitty ones," Juno told him.

"Good," he said, pulling out a twenty-dollar bill. "Make me four shitty copies of this, both sides."

"And what about me?" Yelena asked, after listening to all this in silence.

"You are going to be my guardian angel, perched right here." He leaned over and tapped a photo. "But first I need your help with makeup and costume. And I need a clean syringe."

❖

A couple hours later, Juno and Cash were sitting in the Chinese-Burger-Chicken-Donut place, with a selection of those items on the table between them.

"The problem with this kind of place," Juno was saying as he fiddled with his phone. "The donuts taste like chicken. The chicken tastes like an old burger. The burgers taste like stale donuts."

"And the Chinese food just tastes like shit," Cash agreed. "It's cause they use the same oil for everything."

"That's what comes from trying to give people everything they want. You end up not wanting any of it."

Cash sat up, his head tilting slightly toward the window. "Check the Benz."

Juno turned casually, still holding his phone. Sure enough, a black Benz had stopped up the block, in front of the vacant lot that backed onto the White Angel cop spot. A kid slipped like a rat from a crack in the corrugated metal fence. He ran to the car and a hand came out, passing him a black plastic bag. He scurried back and disappeared. The car rolled.

"Get it?" Cash asked.

"Got it," Juno said. The high-quality lens he'd used to replace the one on his phone's camera had captured the car and its license. "Let's dip." They stood, leaving their plates untouched. "All this talk about food is making me hungry."

❖

Meanwhile, Yelena was in Joe's room, doing his makeup. First she skillfully used blush, powder, and pencil to do the opposite of what they were sold to do: make him look worse—paler and with dark circles under his eyes. She even used some of the stage makeup she'd bought to add a sore to the corner of his mouth.

"Perfect," she said, showing him in her hand mirror. "Now I won't worry about the other girls kissing you."

He laughed, trying to get used to the odd feeling of it. "Now what other girl would do my makeup and then hit me when I asked her?"

"Hit you?" Yelena gave him a searching look. "For real?"

"Yeah, here . . ." He held out his arm and pointed to the crook of his elbow.

"How hard?"

"Hard enough to bruise."

She shrugged. "If you say so . . ." and gave him a walloping slap.

"Good," he said. "Again. A bit harder."

She laughed and gave him a couple more.

"Ow, good, that stung . . ." he said, wrapping a belt around his bicep as he watched the redness swell on his skin. "Though you could pretend to enjoy it less. Now hand me the needle."

At that she frowned, watching as Joe broke the seal on the fresh syringe (Cash had obtained it from a diabetic neighbor). He found a vein and expertly eased it in, then pulled back, drawing a little blood, then booting it back in. He pulled it out, then repeated the process a couple times.

"You're very good at that. Too good," Yelena told him.

"Some things you don't forget," he said with a grin, but she was no longer in the mood to laugh. In fact, he was pretty creeped out himself. He had butterflies in his stomach, an edgy, empty feeling that had nothing to do with missing lunch. A little blood remained around the punctures and he let it dry.

22

JUNO AND CASH WERE in a car Cash had provided, stolen but with legit plates, feasting on jerk chicken from a takeout place Juno knew. They were parked around the block from the cop spot, with a receiver on the dash. Liam and Josh were in a black Impala, likewise borrowed, parked over a block the other way. Yelena was on the roof of the warehouse, overlooking the dope operation, with a sniper's rifle. It was dusk.

"Clear here," she said into the little mic attached to her earpiece.

"All quiet," Juno said. "Last time the re-up took a few hours, but they've been hopping since it started to get dark. Expect we'll see them soon now."

Liam checked in too. "Couple of hookers gave us the stink eye," he said. "So I guess we look like real cops. Otherwise quiet here too." His stomach grumbled. "Quiet and hungry. Wish we had some of that chicken."

"I know you do," Juno answered. "That's where all the cops in the neighborhood go."

❖

Forty minutes later, the black Benz pulled up at a traffic light down the street. Juno got on the line: "Showtime."

"Standing by," Liam said as Josh started the engine.

"I'm ready," Yelena said, pressing her eye to the scope.

Joe came shuffling into view. He was wearing clothes he'd bought at the Salvation Army, then had Cash drive over a few times: a polyester print shirt from the '80s with missing buttons and a tear at the elbow, worn pants from an ancient suit, his oldest pair of Converse. He had a ball cap pulled down low, one of Gladys's cigarettes behind his ear and dirty nails. He joined the line, standing behind a bent, bald man who looked seventy-five but might have been forty in dope years. The touts moved up and down, calling to the other passersby.

"Yo White Angel here! On the money!"

"Boy and girl! Boy and girl!"

A dark-skinned guy in his late teens, with a sleeveless undershirt, baggy jeans, and a heavy gold chain was working the door. The bent man went inside and then came back out, shuffling quickly off the other way. The door guy looked Joe over.

"You new around here?"

Joe nodded, avoiding eye contact, and shuffled his feet. "I heard your stuff was on the money."

The guy looked him over suspiciously. "Got tracks?" he asked.

Joe nodded again and, darting a glance up and down, rolled his left sleeve up then quickly down. The guy saw his marks, and also noted with distaste the blood-stained syringe poking out from his trouser pocket.

"Okay, make it quick," he said, tapping the door three times. "Cop and go."

"Thanks," Joe muttered, stepping by him as the door unlocked and opened from within. Another even younger guy stood in the vestibule, wearing a Nets jersey and jeans cut so low you could see the red briefs encasing most of his ass.

"What you need?"

"Dope. A bundle."

"Where's your money?"

Joe held out his folded bills and flipped the corners quickly. Five twenties. With a nod, the dealer opened one of the apartment mailboxes set in

the wall behind him and pulled out a small bundle of ten sealed baggies, bound with a rubber band. He handed them to Joe and took the money. Then, just as Joe was turning to leave, he put out a hand to hold him.

"Hey, this money's no good!"

Joe grabbed the dealer's hand and bent it behind his back until he howled, banging on the door. "Help! This dope fiend's ripping us off." As the door opened, Joe pushed him toward it while grabbing the waist of the dealer's low-riding jeans. With a quick jerk he pulled them down around the ankles.

"What the fuck?" the dealer yelped, and as the door guy came in, he shouted "His money's fake," stumbling over his pants and falling on the floor. The door guy reached over him and grabbed Joe's wrist. Joe pulled out his syringe and jabbed it deep into the meat of the door guy's arm.

"Ah! Shit! My God!" the door guy yelled in horror as he realized what it was. Joe left it poking out and ran, sprinting down the hall toward the rear of the building.

"Re-up's there," Juno said now, over the earpieces. "One guard by the back door and the runner."

Joe came tearing out the back door, surprising the guard, another teen, who was standing there, gun out, watching the other way, as the runner, a twelve-year-old kid, darted through weeds that were taller than him, toward the hole in the fence. Joe grabbed the guard's gun by the barrel, twisting it away while he tripped the teenager and dumped him on the ground. Pointing the gun, he ran toward the runner, who stared at him in shock.

"Out of the way," he yelled.

The kid promptly stepped aside, still watching in amazement as the guard and both of the door guys came out after Joe. As he ran, Joe popped the clip from the gun and then tossed the separate pieces into the deep weeds.

"Get that junkie! Get him!"

Joe felt them gaining as he reached the hole in the fence and slipped through, tearing the ass of his pants.

❖

At first, Donna had been thrilled to be invited on the stakeout. Detailed to the NYPD Major Case Unit as FBI liaison, she felt like she was on a field trip, or away at camp. After their preliminary peek into the heroin operation known as White Angel, they'd decided that the East New York location was the busiest, most-longstanding, and most likely to yield usable information, so they'd rigged up a realistically-crappy-looking delivery van with their high-tech equipment and parked it on the corner while the dope dealers grinded up the block. But the excitement wore off after the first six hours of total boredom, and when Fusco, who'd promised to bring food, surprised her and Parks with a load of inedible junk from the Chinese-Burger-Chicken-Donut place, which immediately stunk up the van, she began to wish she were back in her nice, clean, air-conditioned office.

She supposed that was why, lulled into a stupor, she took a minute to recognize Joe. She was actually in the middle of a yawn, or trying to yawn without breathing in too deep, as yet another scuzzy junkie crept up to the tenement door where they sold the dope. But something about his profile caught her eye, and she looked closer. And there he was: Joe Brody, always popping up in her life at the worst moments, like fate. Her first thought was that he was using, strung out, and to her surprise she felt . . . compassion. A desire to help rushed up in her, to save him from himself. He was a veteran after all, and even as a criminal, he had done more to serve and protect his fellow citizens than most of the cops and Federal agents Donna knew. Not to mention saving her career as well. But there was more to it, she knew. She had feelings about Joe, though she wasn't entirely sure what those feelings were; fear and distrust were as present as fascination or admiration, and moral horror mingled with physical attraction as she watched him on the screen. But then she took in his odd clothing; even his walk was different. Was he in costume or something? Was he a junkie or was he *playing* a junkie?

"Hey try to zoom in on that guy. The white customer."

"Why?" Parks asked. "You know him?"

"Maybe. He looks familiar." In fact, Donna, knew very well she couldn't say how she knew him, since he'd disposed of the body of terrorist Heather Kaan after Donna put a bullet in her. Fusco leaned in and took a look too.

"Just another junkie. Probably seen his mug shot or something." He finished a donut that smelled like a cheeseburger and wiped his hands on his pants. "He ain't going to lead us to the kingpin. That's for sure."

Donna couldn't argue with that, so she sat tight and just watched as Joe went in the door to cop. Then something weird happened—they heard yelling and banging from inside. The outside man, the door guy, ran into the building, and a beat later, the lookouts came rushing over too.

"Shit," Donna said. "Something's happening. We've got to move in."

"Move in on what with what?" Fusco asked. "This is just a low-key stakeout. It's not like we've got a SWAT team standing by."

"We don't even know what's happening," Parks added. "Or if it pertains to our case."

Donna nodded. She knew they were right—or rather they would have been right, if it were anybody but Joe. She had no idea what he was up to, but her complex feelings were suddenly a lot simpler: fury. He was up to something and she was pissed. Seconds passed by. "What's behind this building?" she asked.

Fusco shrugged. "A vacant lot full of dog shit, cat shit, and probably human shit too, if you're lucky."

"I'm going to check it out," she said as she made for the door. "Keep rolling!"

But as soon as he had recognized Joe, right after Donna had, Fusco had surreptitiously kicked the cable out of its socket and disconnected the camera's live feed from the recorder.

❖

When Joe came through the hole in the fence, the black Benz was there. As he emerged, a broad, white guy in a tracksuit was getting out of the back seat, holding a black plastic bag. He stared at Joe in wonder. Alarmed, he yelled, "Sergey!" Another guy, shorter, heavily-tatted in jeans, white sneakers, and a white V-neck T-shirt, opened the front passenger side. Joe went into a slide, and as his other pursuers came through the fence, he rolled under the car.

Breathing hard, but safe for the moment, Joe pulled the device Juno had made for him from his pants. It was a small tracker, coated on one side with a powerful epoxy. Joe switched it on and peeled off the backing, then stuck it to the underside of the car. It held. Meanwhile he saw feet surrounding him and heard the voices they belonged to.

"Grab that dumbass!"

"How? He's hiding under there like a bug."

Joe identified the white sneakers, who he figured to be in charge, and grabbed his ankles, pulling hard. As the guy fell, Joe rolled out, boxing his ear, leaving him dizzy and ringing. Joe scrambled to his feet, and the bagman and the guard both jumped him. He elbowed one in the nose, breaking it, and kicked the other in the shin, trying to disable them without seeming too professional about it, keeping his arms tucked close and taking some hits on the back and shoulders without exposing anything too vital. Then he broke free and ran with the whole crew pounding after him. That's when the cops showed up.

As Joe neared the corner, with the two door guys right behind him, the guard limping slightly after, and the rest trailing curiously, a black Impala came swerving across his path, with a red light spinning on the dash.

"Hold it," a loud voice that Joe knew was Liam's fake New York accent boomed over a speaker. "Police!"

Everyone scattered. But as Joe turned to run, Josh leapt from the car and grabbed him, throwing him onto the hood of the car. Liam jumped out too and held him.

"Where do you think you're going?" he asked. "What's the big rush?" He quickly frisked Joe and pulled the stolen bundle of dope from his pocket. "What's this?"

"Nothing," Joe muttered. "It isn't mine."

"Yeah, yeah . . ." Liam said as he pushed him into the backseat. Meanwhile up the block, the others had vanished, back through the fence or around the corner. The two men from the Benz had climbed back in, and after watching this unfold in the rearview, had decided to slowly pull away, holding their breath the whole time. As they turned the corner and drove off, free, they began to laugh at the whole crazy incident and lit cigarettes, feeling safe as they put more blocks behind them, and oblivious to Cash, who had smoothly pulled out, following from a distance while Juno tracked them on his iPad.

❖

When Donna came around the corner, she saw Joe getting arrested. She was breathless from dashing around the block, and didn't want to blow the stakeout unless she had to, so she paused when she saw the black Impala parked on the sidewalk, the dashboard flasher throwing red over the dim street, and the other suspects scampering back through the fence or into other buildings. Two white plainclothes cops were rousting Joe and pushing him into the car. Serves him right, whatever he was or wasn't doing. She watched them bounce over the curb and head off the other way. Then, as she turned to go, a black Mercedes that had been parked quietly in the middle of the block suddenly pulled out, turning its lights on as it cruised by. Automatically, she noted the plates as she headed back to the van.

❖

"You okay?" Josh asked Joe, handing him a bottle of water from the front seat while Liam drove them away. Both men were grinning wide.

"Yeah, I'm fine," he answered. "The hardest part was letting those mooks hit me and not breaking their arms."

Yelena's voice came over their earpieces. "You away clean?"

"Yes, ma'am," Liam said into his mic. "We are circling back to get you now."

Joe guzzled water, then peeled off his clothes and put on the clean black T-shirt and jeans he'd stashed in the car.

"What about this?" Josh asked, holding up the bundle of dope. He showed it to Liam too, who caught the symbol stamped on each bag, an angel with lifted wings. Liam's eyes flickered darkly.

"I don't care," Joe told him. "Just get rid of it quick. Otherwise Yelena's liable to do a cavity search."

When they stopped for Yelena around the corner, Josh leaned out and tossed the dope in the sewer. No more about it was said. Nor did Joe tell them how, for a second, he'd thought he'd caught a glimpse of FBI Special Agent Donna Zamora, running down the block after them, and then fading into the distance as they sped away from the scene.

❖

As Donna climbed back into the van, Fusco and Parks both turned from the screen.

"Anything?" Fusco asked.

"Maybe so," Donna said, taking her seat. "An unmarked department car just snatched someone up fleeing the scene. Two plainclothes. Can you call in?"

"Sure," Fusco said and got on the radio.

To Parks, she added. "Let's check the footage again. See what we got at least."

Parks nodded and began to rewind the recording, then cursed under his breath as he hit static.

"What's wrong?" Donna asked.

"I don't know." He sped the video back and forth and then with a sigh bent down to examine the equipment. "Goddamn it!" he called out.

"What?" Donna asked, getting frustrated. "Goddamn what?"

"This," Parks said, waving a cable, which he then plugged in. Sheepishly he sat back down. "The cable was loose. Sorry. It was my fault. I forgot to check."

"You mean we weren't recording? For how long?"

"I don't know, five minutes."

"Really?" Donna asked, thinking, *How could anyone be that lucky*, when Fusco also spun back on his stool.

"Nothing," he said with a shrug.

"What do you mean? Nothing at all? Total peace declared in Brooklyn?"

"As close as it gets. Uniforms responding to a domestic. A D&D at a bar. Car thefts. Vandalism. One assault on a bus. But no undercover activity or plainclothes busts anywhere in this sector. At least nothing's been called in. Sorry."

Sorry was the word, all right, Donna thought, her anger cooling and hardening into something more steely.

Fusco sipped from his Diet Coke and belched, loudly, like a roar. "Let's check again in the morning. See what came in." He offered her the bottle.

"No that's okay," Donna told him, calm now. "I have another idea for the morning."

23

"WATCHING YOU GET CHASED around by those kids was feckin' classic," Liam called over his shoulder.

"When you crawled under the car," Josh added. "They had no idea what to do."

As the Impala sped through Brooklyn, Liam and Josh were laughing uproariously, and even Yelena smiled slyly in amusement and relief at how well the trick had worked.

Joe grinned. "My biggest worry was that Yelena would get impatient and start blowing their heads off."

She laughed. "But no, I was very entertained. I can watch you get beat up by children all night."

Juno called in, "Looks like they've gone to ground," and sent an address.

"It's in Brighton Beach," Josh said as he drove. "I can pick up some borscht for Rebbe while we're there."

Joe and Yelena exchanged a look in the backseat.

"Okay guys," Joe said. "Let's not break the champagne out yet. That was amateur hour. Next stop we might be dealing with pros."

❖

Juno and Cash had tracked the black Benz to Zena II, a Russian nightclub in Brighton Beach, where the two men had valet parked and gone

inside. Josh pulled in behind Cash's car, up the block from the club, so that they could all observe the crowd outside. Shining cars came and went. Couples stood waiting at a velvet rope, men in expensive jeans or suits with women in miniskirts and heels, while a row of double-wide bouncers in black suits stood behind it, like trolls guarding a castle.

"You think that's the main stash?" Liam asked.

"A lot of extra muscle just for a club. Even a Russian one," Cash said.

"I don't know," Joe said. "It kind of makes sense. Thugs can come and go all hours without drawing suspicion."

"And they can keep close control of the entrance," Josh added.

Juno eyed a parade of young women, all hair and curves, who bounced and giggled as the door guy waved them in. He elbowed Cash.

"Yo Joe, you want me and Cash to check it out?" Joe frowned. Juno continued: "I know last time we got grabbed up, but that was because Cash here had to go ordering appetizers and shit."

Cash shoved him. "You the one had to piss so bad. You got snatched up in the bathroom."

"No thanks," Joe said. "That was fun but not tonight. Something's bugging me." To Yelena he said, "Let's take a walk."

Arm in arm, like a couple headed out for the night, they crossed the street to where the crowd was most dense. Multiple languages were shouted through a cloud of smoke and perfume. An old, white-haired man in a custom-made suit shook hands with the door guy who nodded at a bouncer big as the door he blocked. The crowd parted as the entourage came through—three girls whose ages just barely added up to his, plus two bodyguards of his own—the door opened, releasing a blast of ice-cold air-conditioning and throbbing bass, then resealed. The bouncers closed ranks like cyborgs in their wrap-around shades.

Joe muttered, "This could work as a pickup point for re-ups, and for bringing back cash. But where are they bagging the stuff, stepping on it? For an operation this size that must be a team of people. I can't see it all going down in here."

"The basement?" Yelena asked.

"Maybe." He considered the building, a cinder-block box painted black. "If this even has a basement. Looks like a converted warehouse on a concrete slab. Plus you'd need ventilation. Someone to watch the workers. And even then you'd still have your whole crew working right under the nose of the legit employees, with a few hundred people, some of them thieves, dancing right above you. Word would get out." He shook his head as they continued strolling, down the block and around the corner, where the darkness and quiet grew. "It's not safe. I wouldn't do it like that." He turned to her. "What would you do? If you were trying to protect your stash from someone like you?"

"Very difficult," she said with a smile. Then she nodded at a gated-up shop. "I'd hide it someplace like that."

Joe took the place in as they walked by. Grosskoff Caviar & Sturgeon, the sign read. Although the shop was closed, with a gate pulled over the front, the AC was humming. There were no other windows, but he could see dim light glowing in a skylight. There were security cameras at the building's corners. It fit. The shop was essentially a giant climate-controlled vault and no nosy passersby would question the security or the air-conditioner and power going night and day. There was a narrow alley behind it, where a small, refrigerated truck with the shop's logo was parked. Joe called loudly to Yelena in a drunken voice.

"One minute baby!" He veered into the alley, unzipping his fly, and saw that it also ran behind the club, which had a back door, for loading and unloading. Another hulk in a black suit stood guard, and he shouted as he saw Joe coming.

"Hey!"

Joe ignored him, drunkenly leaning against the truck.

"Hey," the guard yelled, coming closer. "This ain't the toilet. Get out of here."

"Sorry, sorry, no trouble . . ." Joe mumbled, waving an arm, and swayed back down the alley. As he passed the truck, the guard turned away to open the club door for someone coming out and Joe dropped, lying on the ground behind it. At first he just saw white sneakers. Then jeans.

Then he saw the tattooed Russian from the Benz, a black satchel over his shoulder, approaching the rear door of the caviar shop. He unlocked it and went in. Joe crept back to Yelena.

"Bingo," he said. "I knew there was a reason I liked you."

She laughed. "I can think of a few." She took his hand as they walked back. "One is that I know how to sneak in and get those fish eggs."

Joe laughed as they passed back by the club, another happy couple. "Just like a good alley cat."

❖

Yelena stepped back into the alley, in a spot where she knew the streetlight hit her hair and traced her silhouette. She lit a cigarette, pretending to be hiding from the wind. Immediately, the guard by the door took the bait. One thing about big, dumb, rude men: they were predictable.

"Pssst, pssst," he hissed, and made a kissing sound.

She regarded him, blowing smoke.

"You think you are talking to cat?" she asked, letting her Russian accent thicken.

He began to saunter over. "I know I am talking to good pussy."

She smiled. "Be careful trying to pet. You might get scratched."

He came closer, grinning dumbly. "Don't worry. I can handle this little kitten." And indeed he was twice her size, maybe three times her total mass. He put a big hand out, as if to stroke her hair. In a flash, her left hand was reaching between his legs, grabbing his balls and twisting as hard as she could. As he gasped, her right came up, wielding the cigarette, which she stubbed out into his ear. He howled in pain, lifting his hands to brush the burning coals away, giving her a clear shot, and she punched him, hard, with an uppercut to the nose, which broke with a crunch under her fist. He grunted, as the blood gushed, and reached for her in blind rage, but by then Joe had stepped from the shadows and knocked him out with the crowbar from the pack he wore on his back. The man dropped, and Joe caught him as he fell.

"Pig," Yelena said, and spit on him.

"A heavy pig," Joe grunted, handing her the crowbar and trying to balance. "Let's load him up."

With the crowbar, she popped the rear doors of the truck open and Joe dumped the unconscious guard inside. They rolled him in, removed his gun and phone, then bound his hands behind him with his own shoelaces. As they shut the doors, Joe spoke into his mouthpiece.

"Okay Juno, give us two minutes then knock out the cameras. Liam, get ready."

They strolled past the caviar and sturgeon shop to the building next door, a closed spice shop with a couple of apartments above it. This lock was so flimsy, it was beneath Yelena; Joe simply loided it open with a card himself. They moved quietly to the roof access, which was unlocked, then climbed down onto the roof of the caviar shop. Now they could see the skylight, the alley where the truck was parked, and the busier street out front. The cameras, pointed downward, could not pick them up, but they tread softly so as not to be heard inside.

Meanwhile, Juno and Cash were parked around the corner, and Juno had been hacking into the shop's Wi-Fi, which was on the same network as Zena II, allowing those inside the club to see the security cameras. When Joe said, "Ready," Juno hit a button and crashed the network. To anyone watching, it would appear that their internet service had dropped and needed to be rebooted.

"Cameras out, folks," Juno said.

"Think I'll stretch me legs then," Liam said over his mic.

He had been loitering on the corner, with a brown paper grocery bag in his hand. Josh had parked further up the block as lookout, in a spot that gave him a view of the shop and the cross streets. Now Liam sauntered across the street and along the side of the shop, pausing about six feet from the vent to the AC unit, which was humming away. He pulled a sealed plastic bag from the paper bag: it contained a liquid chemical with another, smaller, sealed bag floating inside it. He threw it hard against

the vent, bursting both bags and mixing the fluids, which drenched the vent. Then he ran like hell.

The bag had contained military-grade "Malodor," heavy doses of chemical compounds that when mixed released a noxious, repellent, and intolerable but essentially harmless gas; in other words a stink bomb so foul that the US and Israeli armies considered them weapons. In this case, the fumes were sucked into the vent and pumped into the sealed interior of the shop. Inside, four people were busy bagging dope: One mixed the raw heroin with cornstarch and powdered caffeine on a large tray. Another used a small scoop to weigh doses out on a digital scale. Two more packed these little scoopfuls into the small glassine envelopes, taped them shut, and stamped them with the angel logo. Another guy, the only one armed, watched over them: he was guarding the workers from anyone looking to rip them off and guarding the stash from greedy workers. He also had a rather delicate nose and was the first to react when a powerful scent of human feces began to fill the air.

"Jesus what's that smell?" he called out to the workers gathered around the table. "Was that you Louie?"

Louie, who was in his undershirt and surgical gloves, mixing, looked up. "Not me!" He sniffed and made a face of disgust. "Smells like a sewer pipe burst."

Sonya, who was bagging, stood up, covering her nose. "It's coming from the vent. I think a rat died in there."

Louie stood too. "Or a bum who's been eating rats took a shit in our air-conditioner."

Ronnie, the other bagger, was gagging. "I can't stand it. I have to get some air." She moved toward the back door but the guard waved her back.

"That door's locked from outside for security. Come on." He led them through the inner door, to the front of the shop, which was decorated with displays of caviar tins and vodka bottles. A long refrigeration unit held smoked fish and other treasure, worth slightly less than the heroin in back. Hurrying around the counter, he threw the deadbolt and opened the front door, then unlocked the gate and pushed it open.

"Hurry!" Sonya yelled. "I have to get out of here."

❖

On the roof, Joe and Yelena were waiting. Then they heard Josh laughing over their earpieces. "Here they come," he said. "They look traumatized."

"Thank God none of that shite got on me," Liam said. He was making his way back around to join Josh in the car.

"Yeah, you'd be walking home," Josh answered.

Yelena pulled two gas masks from the pack and handed one to Joe, who fitted it over his face. "Okay," he said. "We're going in."

With the crowbar, he chipped at the paint layered where the window-panes joined, then forced it in the crevice, and using his foot, levered the skylight open. They both stood back, instinctively, to avoid the invisible rush of poisoned air from within. Then, while Joe aimed his gun into the now-empty store, Yelena clamped a winch over the opening. Sitting on the edge of the skylight, she put a foot into the loop at the end of the cord and lowered herself in.

She checked quickly to be sure it was indeed empty, then slid the loop over the leg of the table and signaled to Joe. He slid down.

They were in the back room of the shop. Around them refrigerated cases held tins of caviar and sealed sturgeon as well as cartons of blinis, vodka, and other trimmings. The equipment for the legit front business was on a work bench, while the central table was covered with the bagging supplies. A door led to the front of the shop, where, in the daytime, customers were served from behind a counter.

Joe shut that door, keeping it open a crack to watch, while Yelena quickly checked around. One of the fridges held a large black plastic trash bag, which she untied.

"Here's the stash," she said, handing it to Joe, who hefted it.

"Must be at least a dozen keys here." He took hold of the cord and put a foot in the loop. "Let's go," he said, and then, over the mic: "We're coming back out."

Yelena joined him, sliding her foot in on top of his and wrapping her arms around him. Then she yanked the cord to start the winch,

and they rose. As they moved past the table, she flipped it over, spilling the rest of the dope onto the floor. Now the plan was simply to go out as they'd come, exit through the neighboring building, and hop into the car with Cash and Juno. When the dope crew summoned the courage to venture back in, they'd find their stash mysteriously vanished. But as soon as Joe and Yelena's heads cleared the window, someone took a shot at them. The bullet ricocheted off of the skylight's metal frame.

They ducked, heads down, and hung there.

"Josh?" Joe asked over the mic. "Any news?"

"Shit, sorry, Joe," he said. "I missed it. They must have a sniper in the building across the street." He was out of his car now and scanning the street. "I'm going to have to move to get a shot."

But now gunfire raked the roof above them, shattering the open skylight. Glass rained down and they swung together on the cord.

"Going down," Joe said, as they yanked it to restart, and it lowered. Yelena jumped off first and ran to the back door, while Joe knelt behind the toppled table.

"It's locked," she yelled. "Give me a minute."

Now the guard came back, hanky around his face, and opened the door, gun drawn. Joe sent a bullet whizzing past his ear and he fled.

"Whenever you're ready," he called back to Yelena.

"Done," she yelled, pushing it open, and he joined her as they went out the back into the alley. This time the door saved them. It was reinforced steel, designed to protect the stash house, and so even fired at close range from a high-powered rifle, the bullet got stuck halfway through its thickness. Joe and Yelena dropped to the ground.

"The truck," he shouted as they crawled around the far side and then climbed in the driver's door, ditching their gas masks. The guard he'd knocked out was just coming around, mumbling and shifting on the floor. In the side-view, Joe saw two men in body armor, heavily armed and set up behind a portable shield, blocking the mouth of the alley.

"Now what?" Yelena asked.

"Let's drive," Joe suggested. He took a folding camp knife from his pocket, busted open the ignition housing with the screwdriver and used the pliers to strip the wires. "This truck is refrigerated. All that metal should stop a bullet."

The engine sputtered to life. Meanwhile, the guard on the floor, stirred by the commotion, was climbing to his feet. But before Yelena could do anything about it, like shoot him, someone else beat her to it. An armor-piercing projectile came through the back of the van, burning through the layers of metal like they were paper and punching a hole right through the guard before exiting out the other side of the truck.

"Next idea?" Yelena asked as she threw herself to the floor, firing back as best as she could through the hole that shot had made.

Joe called over the mic. "We're taking fire back here."

"Damn it," Cash said. "We're on the wrong side of you." He was parked with Juno on the street, waiting to pick them up when they came out next door. Liam and Josh were pinned down by the sniper. "We can try to drive around and ram them," he suggested.

Now the two men in body armor were moving and, to close the trap, the club's alley door opened too, and another armored man stepped out. "Thanks but we got a ride," Joe said, and stomped the accelerator. He ducked his head as the man in the door fired, just one shot, before Joe ran him over, sending him flying and taking the door off its hinges. Joe braked hard, banging into the wall.

"This way," he told Yelena. Crouching low, they abandoned their equipment pack and darted out the driver's side door, into the open, or rather missing, door of the club. They were now in a dim loading area. A dumpster full of trash bags sat to one side, ready to be picked up. Music thumped through the walls. Joe dropped the bag with the stash into the dumpster. Then they tucked away their guns as they pushed through another door into a bustling kitchen and a young busboy, apron around his shirt, stared at them in surprise.

"Excuse me, but where is the dance floor?" Joe asked.

Confused, the busboy pointed toward the kitchen doors, from which the music came roaring every time a waiter hurried through.

"Thanks," Joe said, grabbling Yelena's hand. "Come on, honey, let's dance."

❖

Toomey was getting annoyed. Till now, all his plans had gone off like clockwork. As predicted, these street gangs had been nothing compared to his highly-trained, disciplined, and battle-hardened team. It was thugs versus soldiers and the soldiers had wiped the streets with them, giving them a taste of real urban warfare. Then word had come down that this Brody might be making a move against them. And perhaps, Toomey admitted, he'd been a touch too confident, after the string of easy victories. He'd posted his own man as a sniper in addition to the usual guards, local talent from Brighton Beach. Then, as soon as his point man had spotted Brody's people moving in, he'd sent in the hitters, armed, and armored, to the teeth, while he directed it all on camera. But then the cameras went down. And now he was told that, despite his overwhelming firepower and tactical surprise, Joe and Yelena had fled into the club. He couldn't exactly send storm troopers in to sweep the place with bullets, as much as he'd like to. Like a fly that you missed with the first swat of a magazine, and that zips out of reach, this minor annoyance had become a major hassle.

"Does anyone have eyes on them?" he asked Sergey, the beefy, tattooed Russian who ran this place as well as this end of the operation. That was the division of labor: Sergey peddled the product, handled the stash house and the street crews. Toomey handled security and ran the pipeline, bringing the product in. Victoria was the head case. Every covert network needed one, and Toomey was cool with it: let her chop people's fingers off and electrocute balls, she enjoyed it. Jensen kept Richards's ass well-licked. And Richards and Nikolai played the big shots, overseeing finance, connections, and long-term geopolitical strategy. Or so they

thought. Toomey had ideas of his own that would make them look like the spoiled brats they were, playing kiddie games. But for that he needed time, and that was what the large supply of heroin he'd brought in and stockpiled in the caviar shop meant to him: time. Now this Brody had snatched it.

Sergey was on the walkie with his people, the Russian knuckle-heads who threw drunks out of the club and guarded the dope on runs to resupply the dealers. "They are downstairs," he told Toomey. He shrugged. "I think they are dancing."

"Just make sure you seal all the exits. As long we have them trapped, we take our time cornering them. And get back our goddamn dope."

"Right," Sergey said, rushing out to deal with it, which mollified him a little. They'd boxed themselves in, and even if Toomey couldn't kill them right here, they would surely run them down and retrieve the product, maybe even take them prisoner. Endless seconds crawled by while he stared at blank monitors, fists clenched. Then he heard more squawking over the radios and Russian cursing, which he didn't understand, except for one word: *musar,* which in the dictionary means garbage but which everyone on the street, and in this club, knew meant police.

❖

Joe and Yelena were in the cavernous main room of the club. Colored lights streamed and strobed as a mass of bodies gyrated on the large dance floor. The columns that held the warehouse roof up had been lined in mirrors that multiplied the chaos, and tables, chairs, couches, and ban-quets covered in red plush filled in the sides, with a long bar along one wall and more mirrors above, old fashioned ones edged in gilt. A DJ ran the deafening techno and waiters rushed champagne and vodka back and forth. The air was thick with sweat, alcohol, cologne, and perfume. As Joe pulled Yelena into the center of the dance floor, he picked out the guards: more big men in black suits or tight T-shirts, looking grim.

"Two by the front door," he spoke into Yelena's ear. "And one by the kitchen."

"And more by the restrooms," she said, nodding toward the two men who stood glaring at them by the other hallway. A roped-off staircase led to a balcony above, and there was Sneakers, the Russian from the Benz, leaning over the railing, eyes on them, jabbering into a walkie, no doubt directing his troops.

Yelena looked Joe in the eye. "Well Joe, looks like you have no choice. It's a matter of life and death." She put her arm on his waist and began to sway her hips to the music. "You will have to dance with me."

"That sounds like an emergency all right." He pulled out the phone he took off the guard and dialed 911, switching to a frantic voice. "Help! Please!" he shouted into the phone. "I'm at Zena II, the club on Brighton Beach Avenue. The bouncer just pulled out a gun and threatened to kill a customer. He's a big guy in a black suit. Out front! Hurry!" He hung up and then dialed again. "Help! Fire!" he said this time. "I'm at the club Zena II, there's smoke and flames in the kitchen. Oh my God it's spreading please help. The sprinklers don't work." He disconnected the call. "Help's on the way," he told Yelena.

"So is trouble," she said, nodding as she swayed to the rhythm. The guards, having decided not to wait any longer, were converging, making their way through the dense crowd.

"Let's get a drink while we wait," Joe said and took her hand. As the guards drew closer, they pushed toward the edge of the crowd, where the most luxurious banquettes lined the dance floor. The old man they'd seen outside sat in the center of one, with his young female companions on either side, and two personal bodyguards on the ends. Joe reached over and dropped the Russian's phone into one of the girl's cocktails. "Excuse me, I'm so sorry. I slipped."

She stared at him blankly, batting her fake eyelashes. The old man yelled and waved him off. His bodyguards stood up and stepped toward Joe. By now the club guards had made it across the floor and were getting closer.

"You don't mind, do you?" Joe asked the old man, reaching for his expensive bottle of champagne. He pulled it from the ice bucket. "My girlfriend is thirsty." He handed the bottle to Yelena.

"*Za zdorovie*," she said, and took a gulp, just as one of the bodyguards, barking in Russian, pushed Joe. Joe sidestepped him, quickly pivoting like a bullfighter and tripped him, sending him reeling into the club guard, who got knocked to the ground. Angry and embarrassed, the club guard jumped up and punched the bodyguard in the gut.

Meanwhile, another club guard was reaching for Yelena and she spun, stomping his instep and grabbing his arm, then twisted it behind him, kicking his other tendon from behind. He stumbled into the table, dumping champagne and vodka onto the girls' dresses, and then falling into their laps. They screamed in anger and the other bodyguard leaned in to yank him off. He came up swinging blindly, hitting the guard.

The old man bellowed in Russian and the fight grew, as bystanders stepped in to defend him or the women and were confronted by club security, who had rushed over to pacify the bodyguards. Then Yelena noticed two firemen coming in the door, in full gear.

"Our bodyguards are here."

"About time," Joe said as they began to push through the crowd milling like angry bees around the growing brawl. "Fire!" Joe yelled now. "Fire!"

The firemen looked their way.

"I think there's smoke coming from the kitchen," he told them, as more people noticed and began to move toward the exit. Joe pulled his own phone out now and called Juno.

"Hey we're coming out the front now," he said. "How about that lift?"

"Um . . ." Juno said. He and Cash were observing the mayhem from the car. A fire engine was parked out front and cops were scrambling from their cars. "You do realize that there's a whole bunch of city employees out here?"

"Don't worry," Joe told him. "That's our free pass tonight."

They flowed with the evacuating crowd, out the doors and into the street, where firemen ran by three cops who were wrestling the largest bouncer to the ground, his wraparound shades getting crushed underfoot. The door guy was up against the car, getting frisked by other cops. Joe nodded as they walked by. Cash picked them up at the corner.

"Man," Juno said, as they got in. "Are we happy to see you. Uncuffed and bullet-free."

"I feel bad, dudes," Cash said, as he steered them away from the club and into ordinary, backed-up traffic. "I wish there was something I could do to make it up."

"There is, actually," Joe said, sitting back and finally breathing easy as they pulled onto Coney Island Boulevard. "You can pick us up a garbage truck."

24

AFTER DROPPING JUNO AT home, and Joe and Yelena at Gladys's, Cash, Liam, and Josh ditched one car and drove the other into the city, to a depot on the Hudson River where mountains of salt and sand sat, awaiting the roads of winter. It was controlled by a union official who was also a distant relative of Gio's. A call was made and a garbage truck borrowed. Then in the early hours, Cash drove it by the now peacefully closed Club Zena II, which had put out its trash for the night. Liam and Josh rolled the dumpster down the alley and tipped it into the truck, then retrieved the one bag with the dope, and ditched the rest in a construction bin before returning the truck and hiding away the stash. As dawn broke, the three shared breakfast in a Westside diner, then went home to shower and sleep. By then, of course, Joe and Yelena were already tucked in bed, and even Joe was resting peacefully for once, too far under to be stirred by nightmares and wake Yelena, so that, after jetlagged days and dream-scarred nights, they were both finally catching up on their sleep when at 7 A.M. there came a pounding on the door.

Joe stumbled into the living room, towel wrapped around his waist, while Gladys, in her bathrobe, peeked through the peephole. The pounding got louder.

"Open up! Police!" a voice came booming.

Gladys turned to Joe. "It's the cops. And your friend Donna's with them."

"Better open up then, before they bust it down," Joe said.

Gladys put the chain on and opened the door a few inches. "Hi Donna," she said.

"Good morning, Mrs. Brody," she said, strictly business. She was in a suit and she had Janet and Andy with her, as well as Fusco and Parks representing the NYPD. She held up her warrant. "We've got a warrant to search these premises ma'am."

Gladys opened up, stepping back to watch them troop in. "It's kind of early," Gladys told her. "Why don't you come back in a couple of hours for breakfast? I was up late playing cards with your mom."

This got an eyebrow raise from Andy. Fusco wondered if it was some kind of obscure insult. To him, this whole thing was an embarrassment and he was afraid of repercussions from Gio, but he himself had been woken only an hour before and told to mount up. Donna had wanted to let him sleep, considering the suspiciously convenient dropped cable. But Tom had made it clear: this was still an NYPD operation and no way would she be allowed to execute a warrant without them. So here they were, the whole gang, facing Joe, who gave them a shy wave, holding his towel up with his other hand.

"Good morning Agent Zamora," he said. "I hope you'll forgive me for not raising my hands."

"Mr. Brody," she said, with a curt nod. He looked tired, obviously, but otherwise fit, without the pallor and without any signs of drug use, no longer the shambling, wrecked junkie of the night before. Clearly that had just been a ruse. She was both relieved and infuriated, to see him smiling and apparently without rancor now. "You can go get dressed," she told him, "while Agent Newton accompanies you."

"After you, sir," Joe told Andy, and gestured toward the hall. Meanwhile, Gladys settled in to watch the search.

"Any change you find you can keep," she told Fusco as he dug in the cushions of her recliner. Sliding on her glasses, she read aloud from the warrant: ". . . conduct a search of said premises for evidence to wit . . . to wit! What's that mean? To wit heroin and paraphernalia related to the sale and use of heroin. What?" She laughed. "Good luck," she told Donna,

who was leading Janet into the kitchen. And to Parks, as he bent to peer under the couch: "You ain't going to find any heroin down there, but see if you can find my missing slipper, Detective. Now that's a real mystery."

"I'll try ma'am," he told her. He wasn't sure what he was even doing here, how this Brody character tied into the investigation. He pulled a remote control out from under the couch and brushed the dust off it. "Have you been looking for this?" he asked Gladys.

"What is that?" she asked. "I have my channel clicker right here." She held up her cable remote. "Then there's this one for the TV, I have to press that red button first."

"This is for the DVD player. See?" He pointed to the logo on the remote, which matched the player.

"Well I'll be," Gladys said, adding it to the pile. "You're gonna be chief one day, young man. That's fine police work."

Parks grinned. "Thank you, ma'am."

"Donna!" Andy's voice rang out from the back bedroom. "I mean, Agent Zamora. You might want to get in here."

Hearing the excitement in Andy's voice, Donna left Janet to check the sugar, flour, and other powdered products in the kitchen and hurried into Joe's room, eager to see what he'd discovered. Dope? A gun? Instead she found a girl, naked, or so it seemed, under a sheet. She was sitting up and smoking a cigarette.

"I asked you not to smoke in here," Joe was saying. He had jeans on now and was pulling on a T-shirt.

The girl shrugged and ashed in a cup on the nightstand. "I am doing by the air conditioner."

"So what?" Joe said. "That blows air in, it doesn't suck smoke out." He turned to Donna. "Maybe you can explain this to her?"

"Miss," Donna said, keeping her voice level. "We are sorry to disturb you. Can I see some ID?"

Yelena leaned over and pulled a passport from her purse, letting the sheet slip off. Donna looked away. Andy stared and smiled. "Here." She held it out.

"Irina Malecovich," Donna read.

"I am dancer at Club Rendezvous," she said, exaggerating her accent.

Joe smiled and shrugged. "Last night was so busy, she was exhausted, poor girl. So I let her sleep here."

"I'm sorry to hear that your job is so tiring, miss," Donna said. "But I'm going to have to ask you to get up and get dressed so that we can search this room. We will avert our eyes of course," she added, glaring at Andy.

Yelena shrugged, dousing her smoke in the cup with a hiss. "You don't have to avert," she said, and stood up.

At this Andy giggled, and Donna, to her horror, felt herself blush. Yelena pulled on her panties and then wriggled into jeans.

"You know how dancers are," Joe told them. "Very in touch with their bodies. I actually think it's a healthy attitude. We have so much shame in our culture."

"Mr. Brody," Donna said. "Please come into the living room while we execute this search."

"Right," Joe said and followed. Now Janet, having finished a fruitless search, was helping Gladys make coffee. Parks, after putting fresh batteries in the remote, was rooting in the hall closet, while Fusco checked Gladys's room.

"Put an extra scoop of coffee and a pinch of cinnamon in the pot, hun," Gladys told Janet. "That's my secret." She elbowed her. "A little sambuca in it doesn't hurt either." Janet laughed

Joe sat on the couch next to Yelena and watched as Fusco reentered. "Bedroom's clean," he said, although he had actually ignored a snub-nosed .38 revolver under the mattress. Parks came back with a paper grocery bag from Key Food.

"I found this in the closet," he said, holding it out for Donna to see. "Looks to be about twenty grand."

"That is mine," Yelena said. "My tips from club."

"Twenty thousand dollars? In tips? And you carry it around in a shopping bag?"

"In Russia we don't trust bank."

"Actually Irina needs to get going," Joe said. "She's due at the club."

"In the morning?" Donna asked.

"Staff meeting," Joe said. "Unless your warrant allows you to take her money."

Donna nodded angrily at Parks, who gave the bag to Yelena. She kissed Gladys on both cheeks. "Bye Joe," she said, then nodded at Donna, "Officer." To Andy, who was entering, empty-handed, from Joe's room, she gave a happy wave. "Goodbye Agent Andy!" And she went.

"Aren't you due at this staff meeting?" Donna asked Joe, in a resigned tone, now that she could see this search was going nowhere fast.

"No," Joe said. "I took the day off. For a funeral."

❖

Carol drove Gio to Big Eddie's funeral. His back was still stiff from where they'd dug the glass out, and too much driving, at least the way Gio drove in morning traffic, might pull out the stitches. She'd convinced him to let the kids stay at home. True, they'd known Eddie all their lives, but the manner of his death, shot dead protecting their father, was more than they should have to be exposed to. As it was, visiting Gio in the ER after "the accident" in Brooklyn was supposedly traumatic.

He'd relented, but he wasn't so sure he agreed. God knows, he understood the urge to shield one's kids from the world. What else was his life but a gigantic force field designed to keep them in a different reality than the one he knew so well, the same reality his own father and grandfather had exposed him to deliberately, making sure he knew exactly where the food on the table came from, how the house he slept in was paid for and protected? It was sick, twisted, a form of abuse, Carol said. It was trauma. And he saw her point, he wasn't asking his own son to defrost any severed limbs any time soon, but there was a lot of love there too, even if it was expressed in an odd way. The night his Dad made him watch him kill a man, an informer, was also the night he took him to a high-end brothel to pop his cherry, and then for steak at Peter Luger's. Rebbe was there for

the dinner; the hit had been to protect him too. He shook young Gio's hand and said, "Happy Bar Mitzvah, you're a man now," and everyone laughed. Later on, in college, when other guys would freak out about their parents visiting, about grades or asking them for money, he was amused. He knew his family would do anything for him, anything, and so would he for them. That was blood. And when it came time for him to go out into the world on his own, he was ready in a way that those punks never were, even with their degrees. Would his kids be? Wasn't it exactly the "trauma" he'd been subject to that made him strong? Then again, it also got him shot at. So maybe the safest thing for his own kids was to be sure they were nothing at all like their Dad.

The chapel was packed, with heaps of flowers and wreaths from all over the tristate area, even from Philly, Chicago, Boston, and Miami. And along with all the family and friends, and "family" and "friends," the nature of Eddie's death, in that wave of attacks, meant that all the other bosses sent people to show their respect and solidarity. This made Gio a kind of de facto host at the event, and he would need to shake hands with almost every single person there, but he went to the widow first, and hugged her, along with Eddie's kids. Of course he'd been to the house already. He'd explained how Eddie died saving him, a hero, left a fat envelope of cash on the coffee table, and told her not to worry, that he'd make sure her three kids' college got paid for. Still, that depended on them getting into college, and he couldn't make any promises about their elder son, Eddie Jr., known, of course, as Little Eddie, despite standing over six feet tall, and weighing two-fifty, all muscle. He'd barely made it out of high school and already had a criminal record far more impressive than his transcripts. He had inherited his dad's brains. But some of his heart too. What he wanted, he'd made clear, was to come in with Gio, and it might suit him. But could Gio say yes to that while shielding his own kids? Would Little Eddie, like his father, be the shield?

And speaking of shields, as he took his seat next to Carol, who'd found them a spot in the front row, he saw Joe, in a black suit, white shirt, and black tie, standing by the door. Always the bouncer. Though,

if he were going to carry the metaphor further, he'd have to describe Joe not as a shield, but a sword. He was the angel of Gio's justice, or vengeance, if there was a difference, slaying those who'd tried to slay Gio, who threatened his life, his family, his town. He nodded his head at Joe in greeting, and Joe returned a quick nod. They'd talk later, after the praying was done.

As it began, with the priest's arrival at the pulpit, Carol squeezed his hand and Gio held it. Their own relationship had shifted since the attack, when she'd rushed into the Emergency Room to find him lying on his stomach, with a doctor tweezing glass shards from his back. She'd said later that even though she knew he was okay—he'd been the one to call her after all—she still had this sudden image of him lying there dead, if not for a few inches and a few seconds, and she'd burst into tears. From that moment on, he knew his marriage would survive. He wasn't saying the problems were over, but rather that their connection, their family bond, would prove stronger than anything else. Her killing Paul—as a realist, Gio knew some of it was sexual jealousy, or possessiveness, or just rage, and that she might just as easily have shot him also, but the real reason, her most primal motive, was to eliminate a threat to their family. Her family. And so, in that way, despite all of her judgment, she was not as different from him and his own clan as she imagined.

As for the "issue," it was on hold, at least until they were ready to discuss it further, and that was fine with Gio. Again, he was a realist, and he knew sometimes, with some problems, just tabling them indefinitely was the best you could hope for. When he got home from the hospital, they had sex, great sex, for the first time since it all happened. It had been awkward, physically—he had to be on the bottom, to avoid pulling a stitch, but also sitting up straight, so as not to rub against his back—but emotionally it had been natural and real, the deep connection between two people who loved each other and who knew nothing, not one night or one kiss more, could be taken for granted in this world. So Gio decided fuck everything else, for now.

❖

Joe watched the service from the back, observing, like an anthropologist, the different social structures interacting as part of this solemn rite. It was, before everything else, a family tragedy, and the tears and moans of Eddie's wife and mother-in-law, the quieter sobs of his children, were the realest, rawest truth. They made him feel ashamed, or perhaps humbled was the better word. Even the bosses in the room, and there were some very powerful and dangerous men here, were humbled by the grief of a wife, or a mother, or a child.

But it was also the funeral of a soldier. Bullshit, of course, in a way: an enterprise like Gio's was about money first and last, money they bled illegally from society and protected with blood if need be. But by choosing to live outside society's laws (if choosing was the right word for someone like Big Eddie, who'd flunked out of junior high and been educated in the streets and juvenile detention centers), they had in effect chosen one another, and over time, developed their own social network, with its own bonds of support or affection, its own code of conduct—to which each one adhered or not, just as straight citizens chose which rules they obeyed: taxes, traffic, adultery—and its own rituals and rites of passage. This was one. Dumb and lazy, Eddie, for all of his faults, had lived closer to the code than most, and had died for it. He was one of them, he'd fallen, and so they came, these unsmiling men in black suits, standing along the walls or sitting in back, with faces that represented every ethnicity, every religion and culture in the city, but all of them marked with a certain hardness, a truth that set them apart from the regular people, the ones sitting in the front pews: they knew it could just as easily be them lying in the coffin, and might very well be, next time. RIP Big Eddie.

That was the thing about Donna. That's how Joe thought of her, still, as someone he knew, Donna, not as Agent Zamora who'd just tossed his crib. His grandmother's bedroom for fuck's sake. He knew that she had violated his privacy, deliberately, that she was making it clear she was onto him, that she was after him, that she was coming for him, and

yet he had been strangely elated to see her, to be, even in some sick way, the center of her attention. Like a lovestruck little boy who acts out in class just so his beautiful, brilliant teacher will look at him, yell at him. Angry, yes . . . but at him! He knew, too, that part of what drew her to him, made her come over and nearly kick his door down, was her own feelings for him, the bond that had grown between them, the times they'd saved and spared and covered for each other. Like it or not, they were joined. Their attraction was all the more potent for being unspoken, their complicity all the more binding for being unacknowledged. But it also drove her nearly crazy to know he'd broken the law. She couldn't stand it. Everything in her nature told her to chase him down and catch him, just as he was born and bred to run. She was a cop, a Fed, and when she put on black and stood in a row at a funeral, shoulder to shoulder with her people, it would be for her fallen comrade, not for his. She was law. And he was against the law. So how could they be for each other?

25

THEY BURIED BIG EDDIE in Calvary, the vast cemetery in Queens, a city of the dead within the city, with over three million souls, from Civil War veterans on down to Eddie, fallen on a Brooklyn sidewalk in the line of duty. The endless rows of gravestones created their own landscape, a necropolis mirroring, or perhaps mocking, the Manhattan skyline that blared triumphantly, and vainly, in the background: from ornate mausoleums proclaiming the persistence of ego beyond death, to the family crypts, layered generation over generation, to the crumbling forgotten stones of the poor, their names erased by weather as by history, to the lost traces of the past, sleeping under our feet. Everyone striving, fighting, buying, selling, loving, hating, and feverishly living in those towers across the river that reached for the sun would soon end up here, if there was still room for them. If some even worse fate hadn't already taken us.

After the interment, Carol took the car and went to help Annette get food and drinks ready for the mourners who'd be filling the family house with their sympathy. Gio lingered, to walk and talk with Joe, safe with those secret-keepers, who truly understood the code of silence. Nero waited by the car, finally enjoying a smoke, among those beyond caring about their health, or his.

"How's the back?" Joe asked, as the last mourners got into cars and left.

Gio waved it off. "Fine. Hurts. But I'll live. Unlike some." He looked at Joe. "So it's Anton? That Russian motherfucker double-crossed us."

"Looks that way. Hard to see how anyone could be running that operation in his territory, with Russian talent, without him knowing. And they were ready for us. They had a sniper on point and an ambush waiting. Someone told them we'd be coming sooner or later. Someone from that meeting at Rebbe's. Who else could it be?"

"I knew it. I never liked that prick. First of all, those cigarettes he smokes stink like burning dog shit. And who smokes inside, in a windowless room, with other people? And talk about milking a joke. You ever notice that? Every time I say something that gets a laugh he has to try and top it."

"Sounds like the death penalty to me."

"Petty bullshit I know. But my point is, I never liked him, but I held my tongue, and my temper. Now we have no choice. He hit first. We unite, all of us, and we take him out for good."

"Not yet," Joe said. "You've got to hold it a little longer."

"Why?"

"Even if we are sure Anton is running White Angel, he is not the one behind those attacks. Or the ambush last night. Those police reports Fusco gave you? Nero showed them to me and I read them in the car. The bomb in Alonzo's car was high-tech military stuff. The attack on Maria's crew used high-velocity sniper rounds fired from a distance by a sharpshooter. Last night they fired armor-piercing rounds at us."

"So?"

"That's the shit they shoot at tanks. It cut through the refrigerated truck like butter. I'm pretty sure they had infrared heat detectors on us too. Full body armor . . ."

"I get you," Gio said, nodding now, calmer.

"The guys at the service today? Sure they'd march into battle for you or for Eddie. But I don't care how tough they are. They're still street guys. These were trained soldiers."

"Army? Spies? Who?"

"Mercenaries. Just like the ones we ran across in Afghanistan. The way I figure it, Wildwater and their accomplices are behind the whole Zahir

thing, using it as a cover to steal dope, smuggle it, and make money to finance whatever shady shit they're up to, corporate, political . . ."

"CIA?"

Joe shrugged. "Why not? Wouldn't be the first time. And Yelena made a Russian spy at the Wildwater building. Let's say that's the connection to Anton. They bring him in to run their New York distribution, handle the street crews."

"And he's clever about it," Gio adds. "He knows the shit's so good he can expand fast, move in on new territory, but he hires neighborhood people to sling it on the corners, so it doesn't connect back to him."

"Right. These local crews don't even know who they're working for, just a smoking package and muscle if they need it. But the security, the deep security anyway, is Wildwater people. Has to be."

"And with all that money flowing in and all that firepower behind him, Anton figures it was time to step up and move against us."

"Or he knew that with us looking into Zahir, we'd get to him eventually. So he struck first."

"And you hit back hard last night. The street value of that stash once they cut it? You cost him millions. Not a knockout but you hurt him. Why back off now?"

"Not back off, stop to figure the next shot. Like you said, we hurt him, financially. And it is going to be hard to hold all that territory with no product. So what does he care about most right now? The next shipment. That's the key. How are they getting the stuff in? Until we figure that out, we can't cut the head off the monster." Joe shrugged. "Even if we wiped out Anton and his whole gang today, you'd still have that pipeline and that private army loose in the city, just looking for their next front man."

Gio nodded. "Yeah. You're right. It's not a local gang war anymore. It's an invasion. So . . . if we don't whack Anton, what do we do?"

"I wish I knew," Joe said. "I'm thinking about it."

"Think fast, brother. We are both walking on these graves instead of lying in one by luck and a couple of inches."

Joe smiled at him. "But hey no pressure, right?"

Gio laughed and clapped his old friend on the back. "That's right. Fuck it, we're alive today. Let's find Nero and go back to Eddie's house. Annette's aunt made eggplant parm. She can barely tell right from left, and her lips move when she reads, but I'm telling you, that woman is a genius."

26

Juno was in a fury; that is, a cold, controlled, brain fury. He still felt responsible, on some level, for the death of Hamid, and now these same people, these shadows, had outsmarted him and his friends last night. They'd made it out safe, by luck and by fast thinking, but he'd come this close to losing Joe and Yelena. For a loner who took a long time to build friendships, and who trusted only a handful of people outside his family, this made the matter very personal, especially since Joe had saved Juno's life at least twice, and come to trust him with his own. And for the whiz kid side of him, the brainiac gamer, hacker, and hustler, to be bested like this, first out of town and then in his home court? That he could not abide.

He went back to work, powered by Red Bull, cold pizza, and even colder fury. Cash came over too, just as pissed and just as loyal, but while he was an artist behind the wheel and an ace at video games, he wasn't much for crunching data and he quickly got bored and fell asleep. But it kind of soothed Juno to have his pal there, snoring lightly on the couch, while he ran the numbers like Cash ran the roads. And then, around two in the morning, he got it. The answer. Or at least a clue to the answer. He got something. And not by hacking or scamming. He got it by going full nerd, pulling some deep quant shit, running reports and combing through the heaps of mostly useless, boring, dust-dry data that Joe had dumped on him. But all once, staring through his glazed eyeballs, he

saw it: a pattern. And that pattern was an arrow, pointed right at Zahir. Or whoever the hell they were really chasing.

"Yo Cash, Cash," he shook his friend.

"What? What?"

"I got it man, I figured the shit out."

"Awesome," he jumped up, as though there were some place to go, then sat back down, rubbing his eyes. "Call Joe."

"Now? It's two."

"Dude call him. If you really have something, he needs to know."

Juno called, and it went to voice mail. He hung up.

"Voice mail," he told Cash.

"Why didn't you leave a message?"

"For Joe? Does he even check voice mail? I'll call back in the morning. He probably turned his phone off to go to sleep."

In fact, Joe was awake, also thinking about Zahir. He'd silenced his phone for the funeral service and forgotten to turn the ringer back on. Finally, he drifted off, only to be awakened around four by a nightmare. He sat up, breathing hard, bathed in sweat, heart pounding, trying not to wake Yelena, who slept beside him, naked on her back, a loaded handgun under her pillow. Startle her and she might blow his head off. Or if he made too much noise in the living room, his grandmother might think he was a prowler and kill him with that ancient revolver she kept under her bed. As the only unarmed one in the house, he grabbed his phone to see the time as he tiptoed to the kitchen for a glass of water. That's when he realized his phone was off. He flipped it on and saw the missed call from Juno. He called, but by then Juno and Cash had both fallen asleep, halfway through a video game that sat, paused, on the screen.

Donna had a hard time sleeping that night. When the search of Joe's place, of Gladys's place actually, turned up nothing, she was a bit embarrassed and a bit frustrated—okay a lot frustrated—but she took it in stride. She was a law enforcement officer, a federal investigator, and that's what they did, investigate and enforce the damned law. That meant follow

the trail of evidence wherever it led, and whatever it turned up. Even if that was nothing. Or a naked girl. Still, she told herself, it felt good to be on track, just doing her job, regardless of her feelings. And she believed that, she really did. At least until she laid down to go to sleep, and those other feelings came out to play, chasing each other around her head.

And what were these "feelings" she had about Joe Brody? She had to admit there was a spark, immediately. And the fact that it struck while she was handcuffing him outside the cheesy strip club where he worked was also the first glaring red flag. That was why, when she got on this case, potentially the biggest of her career, and Joe turned up in the middle of it, again, like a bad penny (or a bad omen or a bad conscience), she'd told herself, screw it, I'm just going to play it straight and do my job. Let the chips fall where they may.

And when the trail went cold in his bedroom, she did what a good investigator does, she went back to the last solid link: the dope operation. She dug out the plate number for that black Benz she saw leaving the scene and ran it. Turns out it was registered to Sergey Popov, who lived in Brighton Beach and worked as a manager at a nightclub, Zena II, that had been linked to the Bratva, the Russian mob. Not only that, when she checked the place out in the NYPD database, there'd been two 911 responses just last night, one a fire alert, which turned out to be false, and one a report of a bouncer with a gun. No arrests, but some of the very confused witnesses did say they heard gunfire nearby. And then there was the girl in Joe's bed: also Russian.

So there it was, a new Russian connection in her case. They decided to place this Sergey under surveillance. Parks and Andy were taking the night shift, and she was supposed to be resting up to take over tomorrow. It was all on track. Until she laid down and tried to shut her eyes. And the feelings came out to play.

❖

Anton was not the worrying type. He'd fought his way to the very top of a mountain made of broken bones and busted skulls largely because of what

he lacked: conscience, regret, shame, self-doubt. If he wanted something, he took it. If someone got in his way, he hit them. If they hit back, or if he thought they might, he killed them. That was his philosophy and his business strategy and, though it might be simple, it had worked extremely well so far. He was, in essence, a bully. A thug brutal enough to bully the other thugs and bullies. And in modern Russia, as the lines between businessman, politician, criminal, and spy had all dissolved, bullying was a growth industry. They'd elected one president, the thug-in-chief. And now, here too, in America, they'd chosen a bully to lead, a President Putin of their own. Anton had loved New York since the moment he'd set foot in Brooklyn, but it was only now that he really felt American.

That's why, when Nikolai Koslov had first come to him, the decision had seemed as simple as any other. Nikolai was SVR, a cop and a spy working for the Kremlin, so not to be trusted, but he'd offered a good-faith gift, the identity of his mole in the Russian New York underworld, Yelena Noylaskya. Good, they would skin her alive and stuff her as a trophy, an example to the others. Thank you, Nikolai. Then he'd proposed his real business: some friends from US intelligence and some mercenaries, disguised as jihadi, were stealing Afghani dope, and had a foolproof way of getting it into New York. All they needed was distribution. Through intermediaries, they'd reached out to Little Maria, and it didn't go well, especially not for the dead middlemen. But Anton had his own network, his own people. Maybe he could use an unlimited supply of pure Persian heroin?

Sure. He'd be happy to buy, for his own territory. But he couldn't move that kind of weight without expanding, and stepping on the toes of Little Maria, Alonzo, Uncle Chen . . . half the bosses in the city. Nikolai understood the problem. That's when he introduced Toomey. Ex–Special Forces and now a mercenary, Toomey was the one who stole the dope and shepherded it through. He'd brought a team of his fighters here to New York. They'd clear the territory, then Anton's people would move in. Anton liked this idea: as a bully he understood the difference between a real soldier and a fellow bully, and he knew that few street criminals

would be able to put up much of a fight against Toomey and his men. He talked to his top lieutenant, Sergey, who pointed out the problem: a bunch of white boys setting up shop on a Black or Spanish corner would be seen as cops or immediately attract the cops. It was Sergey's idea to recruit the local kids, young delinquents with just enough sense to run a cop spot without caring too much where the package came from, as long as it was on the money. And man was it ever. They called it White Angel because it took you straight up to heaven. The plan worked beautifully and they began to make a fortune overnight. Until Gio and the others began to connect this new dope, White Angel, with the Zahir business. That created new issues. It got Gio's friend Joe involved. Everyone knew he wouldn't do regular hits or enforcement, that was why he was given free reign as sheriff, but now he was on the track of Zahir and that meant he was getting closer to Anton. And if he did unmask him, then Anton would have all the other bosses, the whole town, lined up against him, at once. Not even the other Russians would stick by him, once they knew he was in bed with the SVR.

The one advantage Anton had left was surprise. So he talked to Toomey, and again, there was no hesitation. Like men of action, they acted. Coordinated strikes against their most likely adversaries—Maria, Alonzo, Gio, Chen—and a trap for Joe and Yelena as a bonus. But it hadn't gone the way Toomey promised. And now, suddenly, things were not so simple, and for the first time that he could remember, Anton was worried.

"What are you worrying about?" Toomey asked him. "We've got more firepower than any of them. More than the cops. And no one knows anything yet."

They were on the balcony of his party house, staring at the ocean, with a spread of caviar, coke, and cold vodka in front of him and warm hookers waiting inside, while his wife and kids waited in another, even bigger and better house nearby. The bully life was sweet, as long as you were top bully. But now he had no appetite for any of it, except the vodka and his cigarettes, which he lit end to end.

"It doesn't matter how big a gun you have, Toomey," he answered. "This isn't Chechnya. We can't hold that territory without product." He turned to Nikolai, who was lighting a fat Montecristo, playing the suave European, not concerned. "Do you realize what that bastard cost us, stealing the stash?"

"Of course," Nikolai said, with a shrug. "I can count." He nodded at Toomey. "When does the next shipment come in?"

"Day after tomorrow. We can hold out till then." Toomey smiled reassuringly, and Anton nodded, reassured. Toomey, however, was lying. Joe had thrown a major wrench into his own plans and he was as worried as Anton. But unlike Anton, he was a soldier, a warrior, not a bully or a dumb thug. He was still confident of bringing his mission off with a high likelihood of success, as long as he met that next shipment and kept control of it.

"Good, good," Anton was saying. "And I want Joe dead."

"He can't hurt us," Toomey said, not wanting to get distracted from his own primary objective. Anton slammed a fist onto the table and the caviar scattered, bouncing crushed ice onto the coke, probably a thousand dollars' worth of little fish eggs and white powder ruined. Nikolai cursed as some sour cream got on his pants. He dipped a napkin in water and began blotting.

"He has already," Anton thundered. "I want his head. And Yelena Noylaskya too."

"Fine," Toomey said, magnanimously. Sometimes bullies needed to be appeased. Toomey understood this: Richards, his theoretical boss, was just a smarter, better-connected bully. "We have an operative, a freelance hitter. The best there is. I will put her on Brody and Noylaskya."

"Her? You're sending a woman?" Anton leaned toward Nikolai. "You agree with this?"

"My friend," Nikolai said, tossing the napkin aside. "We are sending the devil."

Anton grinned. "Good." He turned to Sergey who'd been standing at a respectful distance, his stomach growling. He'd had no time to eat and had not been happy to see all the food hit the floor. "Sergey!"

"Yes sir?"

"I'm sending you with Toomey here, to make sure the next shipment comes home with no problems, understand?"

"Yes sir," Sergey said, and nodded at Toomey.

Fuck, Toomey thought, as he smiled and nodded back.

❖

But that wasn't the only new complication to come up that night. Toomey and Nikolai took their limo back to the Wildwater building, pulled into the parking garage, and rode the express elevator to the executive suite, where Richards, his sidekick Jensen, and their new CIA liaison, Powell, were waiting. Powell looked tired and a little freaked out—no wonder if Vicky had been sucking the life force out of him. Nikolai had called her a devil. Fair enough. He would have added succubus if that dumb peasant Anton had understood. Now, however, she'd have a new game to play, and Powell might be tossed aside, like a half-eaten fly.

"So . . . you settled things with our friend in Brooklyn?" Richards asked.

"Yes. No problem," Toomey said.

Nikolai draped himself over a chair. "We told him we'd send Victoria after that Brody."

Richards frowned, brow furrowing as he thought, which always caused him discomfort. He liked having Victoria around because she made him feel tough, like the guy with the vicious Rottweiler on a leash; on the other hand, actually unleashing her made him uneasy, like the guy with the vicious Rottweiler running loose. But, on the third hand, Brody had stolen his dope, not to mention shooting down his chopper and nearly killing him. His pride still stung. "Good idea," he declared, nodding, brow furrows vanishing as he finished thinking and made a command decision. "But now something else has come up. Jensen?"

"Sir." It was the nice, crisp way he said the word that had got him this job. He turned to the others. "Our sources in the FBI and local police

have told us that someone new is poking into our operation. They don't know much, but it could become a problem."

Richards pointed at Powell. "It's your ex-wife, Mike."

Powell blanched. "Donna?" he asked. "I mean, Agent Zamora?" Jensen pressed a button and her federal ID photo appeared on the screen. Powell hadn't spoken to her or even seen his daughter since he'd been back. He wanted to, he missed Larissa terribly, but somehow, even though he was home, he still felt too far away.

"What's your assessment?" Richards asked him. "Is she a serious threat?"

"No," Powell said immediately. "I mean, she knows her job, but I can control it, use the bureaucracy to throw them off or even shut it down. We can use national security. Say it's classified."

Richards nodded. "Good. That's smart," he said and gave Powell a firm, friendly slap on the thigh, like a good leader, to let him know he understood. "Thanks for being a team player on this." But still, after Powell left, he pulled Toomey aside, and asked him, "What do you think? Can Powell handle his ex?"

Toomey shrugged and looked at the photo of her. She looked smart. And sexy. Too much of both for Powell maybe. "Who knows?" he told Richards. "He obviously couldn't handle her when they were married. I better keep an eye on her myself."

❖

Yolanda put her reading glasses on and pulled her chair up so that her nose was just inches from the screen. She'd been told by her daughter that this was bad for her eyes, but she felt more comfortable this way, like when she was driving. She was on one of those sites, hunting and pecking among the keys, filling in a dating profile. It had been her friend Gladys Brody's idea; well actually, she had suggested it for Yolanda herself, urging her to get back out there and find herself a new man while she was still young enough. But Yolanda had another, better idea: she was making the profile for Donna.

She knew she'd be annoyed, and refuse if Yolanda asked her, so she didn't ask. She figured she'd just wait till the eligible bachelors started lining up, then show her the choices and let her decide, answer one or delete the whole thing. What was the harm? She added a nice photo she had of her and filled out the questions. Where it asked, *What type of guy are you looking for?*—she wrote: *Handsome. Brave. Honorable. Like law enforcement or fireman.* Actually Donna had never mentioned firefighters. That was Yolanda's idea. She'd seen one of those calendars at a friend's house. In some of the pictures they weren't wearing much more than boots and a helmet. Then, after thinking for a second she added: *Ex-military.*

❖

When Joe woke up on the couch the next morning, both Gladys and Yelena were standing over him. He sat up, rubbing his eyes.

"What?" he asked.

Gladys handed him a cup of coffee. Yelena handed him her phone.

"It's Juno. He's been trying to call you."

A couple of hours later, they had once again taken command of the manager's office at Club Rendezvous. As soon as everyone was settled with coffee or sodas and the door was shut, Joe spoke.

"First, before we get into it, Liam, is that stash safe?"

Liam smiled. "It's buried next to some bones that have been there since the seventies. So I expect they'll be all right a few days more."

"Good enough. Now Juno, why don't you tell everyone what you found? You'll explain it more clearly than I can."

"Right." Juno stood up, as though delivering a report to the class. "So basically what I did was set up an algorithm based on the dates we have for when the dope shipments came to town, more or less. I didn't know exact dates of course but within a one-week window. Then I searched the data and captured any events within that window or one week prior. This produced a mapping . . ."

"What difference do the dates make?" Josh asked. "We know they had to send it before it got here?"

"Jesus Christ," Liam added, "you say this is the clear explanation?"

Only Yelena nodded at him encouragingly. "Give him a chance. He'll get there."

Cash tugged Juno's arm and he sat back down onto the couch. "Bro I told you. You've got to translate it into like regular New York English for us. We don't speak brainiac."

"Right, right, sorry. Okay . . ." He took a deep breath. "Point is, I figured out how they're getting the shit in, all right? It's the returns."

"Returns?" Yelena asked.

"It's pretty clever actually," Joe said. "Almost foolproof. Wildwater supplies all kinds of junk to the military overseas. Random, boring shit . . ."

Juno nodded. "Exactly. Like shoelaces, cases for binoculars, tent poles, housings for flashlights . . ."

Joe went on: "It goes through the normal channels, purchase orders, delivery stateside, and then ships overseas. But if something is defective, or the wrong item shows up by mistake, then Wildwater's local office just issues a return authorization and ships it back."

"Get it?" Cash asked, proud of his friend. "Like when Nike sent me the wrong size sneaks, I popped them in the box, printed out the label and sent them back for free."

Juno stood up again, excited. "That's the brilliant part, see? It's coming in as US military property, not as an import, so now customs is nothing. And Wildwater has already accepted the return, so no need for a further military inspection here either. It just flows right through, via air freight, to the terminal for pickup and then back to Wildwater's warehouse."

Cash was grinning now, as the others began to get it. "Except now, those tent poles or flashlights or whatever . . ."

Yelena laughed. "They are full of heroin."

"That's pretty damned good," Liam said. "Just let the government deliver the gear for you."

Josh nodded. "Beautiful. The closest thing to an open pipeline you could have. No customs. No military police. No nothing. Ah, what we could do with that. I better not tell Rebbe. It will break his heart."

"When is the next shipment of returned goods?" Liam asked.

"Two days," Juno said. "Air freight to Newark."

Yelena hugged Juno. "Juno you are a genius."

"Thanks, Yelena," he said, blushing.

"Now how do we stop it?" she asked him.

"Oh . . . that . . ." Juno sat back down and reached for his Coke. "I haven't gotten to that part yet."

Silence descended, and everyone sat back, as though the elation were escaping from the balloon. After a couple of minutes, Joe realized all eyes were now on him.

"Anyone here know any dog trainers?" he asked.

❖

As it happened, the club manager, who'd been conducting business from a seat at the bar while Joe and the others commandeered his office, was a dog trainer himself. Johnny "Santa" Santangelo, who took advantage of his white beard and huge belly to play Santa at the club's Christmas party each year, took in rescued dogs, mainly German Shepherds, Dobermans, and Rottweilers, which he trained as guard dogs, and then sold, or failing that, gave away as housebroken pets. Many of the Caprisi family's warehouses, parking lots, and construction sites were patrolled by Santa's helpers. The dog Joe wanted was of a far more specialized and rare type, but Santa knew a guy who knew a guy and when Nero and Pete went to visit him on Gio's behalf, the trainer reluctantly agreed to fake some paperwork and lend out the talent for a day.

Meanwhile, Cash was busy. He had to obtain two vehicles. One, which he'd be driving, was the crash car. A crash car is what it sounds like, and it could be any make as long as it had some power. Cash chose a Camaro, which he modified with heavy-duty shocks, a reinforced steel

front bumper and some additional steel poles welded into the interior. The second vehicle was a specialty item for Joe, which he got from an Armenian guy who owned a salvage yard near Reliable Scrap, the huge auto junkyard Cash ran for Uncle Chen, and which was the center of his car theft business. Cars disappeared and dissolved into parts, then reappeared in new colors and shapes and under new names in that giant labyrinth, itself just a small corner of the junk kingdom that spread over that part of Queens.

Liam and Josh, who'd become familiar with the Newark Airport freight operations through their hijacking, stole a semi, switched the plates to make it pass as legit, and had it repainted. J&L Trucking—"In It For the Long Haul"—was what Liam stenciled on the door, which Josh thought was ridiculous, but sweet.

Yelena handled weapons and costumes.

And Joe tried to explain what he needed to Juno.

"I can get you in easy," Juno said. "But getting out the way you want is impossible."

"Sure, it's difficult maybe, but there must be . . ."

"No man, you don't understand. Am I generally given to hyperbole?"

"Somewhat."

"Okay. But right now I mean literally impossible." He sat forward and explained it slowly to Joe, as though to a large child. "Getting a truck in for a fake delivery is no problem, because it won't be fake. Anybody who wants to can ship some shit somewhere. It's America. I'll just go online with a made-up company name and manifest, say y'all are bringing in a load of whatever to be sent off to Lithuania or some place. You pull up in the truck, show the paperwork, and you're in. But for me to go into their system and find out exactly where they put the can from Wildwater, that's a whole different kettle of fish."

To save on money and logistical hassle, Wildwater, in its capacity as a legit corporation, would consolidate all the items from that general region going stateside and then send an entire truck-sized container, which would be loaded onto a gigantic plane and offloaded in Newark.

Any item in there could, conceivably, contain the dope. And the container could end up anywhere in the depot, since it would be slotted into an open space whenever it came in.

"But why can't you just hack in, even once it lands, and tell me its location? Don't tell me their security is too much for you. It's got to be in their system."

"Ah, but that's precisely what I keep saying, my dude. In *their* system. And their system is closed. It's basically just a local network for moving boxes around their yard. There's no internet access, nothing over phone wires or cell signals. Doesn't matter how good a hacker I am if there ain't shit to hack."

"So who does have access?"

"Folks working there. Shipping clerks at their terminals. And those dudes in the orange vests who drive around in carts, finding your can. They have handhelds, like UPS does, for checking it's the right package. Same idea, but the packages are the size of subway cars."

"So, if you had one of those handheld things?"

"The range isn't much. It wouldn't work outside the yard."

"But if you were in range . . . with one of those devices . . ."

"Then I can find you your Persian. Or at least the can it's in. How you're going to get me in there I don't know. Not to mention back out."

"Don't worry about that. I'll think of something."

Juno sighed. "Oh, I know you will. That's what I'm afraid of."

27

IT WAS BRIGHT AND early. The morning air was still cool and quiet, and you could even hear birds trilling in the wetlands (along with the roar of airplanes) and smell water on the breeze that shifted through the reeds (along with the burn of chemicals), as J&L Trucking's 18-wheeler pulled up to the gate of the high-security air freight depot adjacent to Newark Liberty International Airport, with Liam behind the wheel.

"Good morning," he told the head guard, a forty-something white guy with a flattop buzzed haircut and creases in his uniform pants. The credentials clipped to his ironed shirt read James Barker, Supervisor. Liam handed down the paperwork that Juno had provided. "We've got a drop off."

"Morning." Barker looked it over, while two junior guards circled the truck, checking underneath it with mirrors. "Says here you're hauling fertilizer? What does certified organic, single source mean?"

"Means this is the purest horseshit around, straight from Kentucky, home of the best horseshit in the world," Liam went on. "Now some folks will tell you Virginia, but for my money, the horseshit that you get from a diet of sweet bluegrass . . ."

"Well, we've got to open her up. Give them a hand, Myron."

"Yes, sir. No problem," Liam said, as Josh jumped down from his side. Barker led the way to the rear of the truck, followed by Myron, one of the other two who'd been checking the exterior, a young Black guy with

a smooth-shaven head and red eyes behind his glasses. Artie, a plump, fair-skinned redhead and the youngest of the lot, stood around trying to look useful.

"Does it stink bad?" Myron asked Josh.

"Not if you don't break the seals."

Liam, who was watching in the side view, pressed a button and the gate lowered, hitting the asphalt with a clink and making a handy ramp. Then he hopped out and joined them.

"Here it is," Josh said, walking Barker up the ramp. He unlocked the rear and he and Myron rolled the door up, revealing a solid wall of rich, brown fertilizer, sealed into large, plastic-sealed cubes, and marked "Kentucky's Finest—100% Pure Manure."

"How much you hauling?" Barker asked, peering at it.

"Twenty tons."

"Right . . ." He decided he'd seen enough. "All right, looks good." As he turned to descend, Josh slipped on the metal gate for a second and bumped him, then grabbed his arm to keep from knocking him off. Barker stumbled back and knocked into Myron, who dropped his clipboard while fighting for balance. The papers blew around. Artie and Myron chased them.

"Oops, sorry . . ." Josh said.

Liam too reached up to support Barker's back. "Careful!"

Barker regained his balance. "I'm fine," he said, defensively, then shouted at Myron: "Come on, quit fooling around," as he headed back to the front, Artie trotting behind him. Barker told him to lift the entry barrier while Myron reorganized the clipboard.

"Here's your authorization and delivery location," he said, handing Liam back the stack of papers and circling something with a pen. "I marked it on this map."

"Thanks very much." Liam hopped back in the cab while Josh locked up, then climbed back into his seat. Liam lifted the ramp. Meanwhile, the barrier rose and Barker, having regained his authority, stiffly waved them through. Josh pulled two small earpieces from the glove box and

handed one to Liam while fitting the other in his ear. He spoke into the tiny mic.

"We're in. You copy?"

"Loud and clear," Juno's voice replied.

While Liam followed the map, Josh removed a small panel that had been cut into the rear of the cab, then reached through and knocked on the wall of the trailer. Juno slid a panel open from the other side, inside the body of the truck.

"Here you go . . ." Josh said and he passed him back the handheld scanner that he'd lifted from the guard.

❖

Inside the trailer, Juno plugged the handheld into his laptop and began to search for the location of the Wildwater canister while Joe and Yelena moved the cubes of fertilizer. They had nowhere near twenty tons. There was just a single layer of large cubes, stacked like bricks, blocking off the rear doors, and now they shifted them aside.

"You find it?" Joe asked Juno.

"Looking, looking . . . Wildwater Corp, one canister, landed at four A.M., from Kabul via Frankfurt. Unloaded at five A.M. Here it is . . ." He spoke into his mic.

"Liam, I found it. I'm sending the location."

"Great," Liam answered. "I'll look for a quiet spot to unload."

The location of the container appeared on the truck's GPS and Josh told Liam to keep going straight, while he stuffed the paperwork from the guardhouse into the glove box. Even with the map they'd been given it was confusing: like a maze built of shipping containers, stacked several stories high and sprawling out for acres, with no one in sight but the occasional worker on a forklift shifting one in or out, or another truck looking to load or unload. Now they followed Juno's digital map, which led them like a red string through the labyrinth. Then Josh spotted a shed that looked like it housed unused forklifts.

"There," he told Liam. "Pull up alongside it."

"Right," Liam said, and backed in, so that the rear of his truck was hidden in the shade of the shed. Stacks of containers shielded the other sides.

"We found a spot," Josh said over his mic. "Get ready." Then he jumped down and came around the back while Liam lowered the gate, keeping an eye out the whole time. In the back, Josh took another quick look around too, then unlocked the door and pushed it up. The fertilizer wall had been cleared, revealing the interior, and Josh waved while backing down the ramp. Slowly, the Jeep rolled out of the truck and down the ramp. Joe was behind the wheel, clean-shaven and in an Army major's uniform, with a standard issue sidearm and his hair neat under the hat. Yelena, also in a uniform, sat beside him, cradling an army issue M-1. A German shepherd in a military harness and leash lay resting on the back seat.

Josh saluted as they drove past.

28

FOR CASH, WAKING UP so damn early was the hardest part of the day, or so he thought. Still he was there, at the salt depot on the West Side when Joe said to be, and at least Joe brought everyone coffee. That's the mark of a true leader. After they got the truck squared away, with the Jeep on board and a little desk set up for Juno, he helped Liam and Josh build the wall of—he was happy to know—hermetically sealed manure and then trailed them to Jersey. When they reached the outlet road for the depot, Liam and Josh got on line behind a row of trucks, pick-ups, and other vehicles waiting for entrance, including a number of ordinary passenger cars, couriers and such, as well as a few military vehicles, green trucks on giant tires, a Humvee. Another line slowly pulled out from the exit. There was a guardhouse with gates, and a chain-link fence enclosing the whole gigantic place, like a super-sized Lego-town built of brightly colored rectangles. Beyond that were the Jersey wetlands, miles of swamp and weeds, with chemical plants firing on the horizon, planes coming and going from the airport.

Cash pulled over. The whole road leading to the entrance was lined with parked trucks and cars, mostly long-haul truckers waiting for something to arrive or be cleared for pickup. Some had been there all night, with the drivers asleep in the cabs. Now a few stretched their legs and smoked. A couple of livery drivers were taking naps between airport runs. Cash slid into a spot that gave him a nice view of the entrance,

said "in position" over his mic, and settled in, watching as the truck got through, no problem, and not really expecting much of anything else to happen until it came back out. And for a while nothing did. He sat back and snoozed.

❖

Donna hadn't planned on going to Jersey that morning. She hadn't even planned on leaving Brooklyn. In fact, if Sergey Popov ran true to form, he wouldn't even stir till past noon. But there she was, parked down the block from his apartment building, fighting to stay awake in the car—she'd relieved Andy at six—when his black Benz came rolling out of the parking structure with Popov behind the wheel. She followed him onto the Belt and then through the Brooklyn Battery Tunnel into Manhattan, where he stopped at a corner in Tribeca to pick up a guy she hadn't seen before, an athletic-looking young white dude with a blond ponytail. Still it was nothing to get too worked up about. Maybe they were going to hit some golf balls. But the next thing she knew, they'd crossed the Hudson, if driving through a tunnel beneath it counted as crossing, and were heading to I-9 and the outskirts of Newark Airport. She reported in, as a matter of course, letting her office know she was in New Jersey, but when Popov arrived at the freight terminal and pulled over, as if waiting for someone or something, she decided that this might be more than a trip to see his grandma. So she called Blaze. The deputy federal marshal was just getting into her office in Newark and agreed to drive over and provide backup, if Donna would back her up later by being her wing-woman at a new lesbian bar she'd been meaning to check out that night. Donna agreed to one drink. Then she settled in, eyes on Popov, whose own eyes seemed to be dozing behind his mirror shades.

29

ARTIE WAS ON THE early shift today, pulling a double, covering for his buddy, who was hooking up with some girl he'd met. Artie didn't mind. He needed the money, plus Floyd had given him a little thank you gift for the favor: a fat juicy joint of primo bud that he went off in the reeds and smoked between shifts with his other pal, Myron, who was showing up for gate duty that A.M. The weed definitely made the shift go quicker, but it was stronger than he was used to, a special gift after all, and when this MP, Major Somebody, pulled up in a jeep and started talking about a suspected shipment of illegal substances, it was all Artie could do not to freak out.

"Officer," this MP said as he pulled right up and stopped Artie on his rounds, piloting the three-wheeled cart they gave him to drive. At first he didn't even know who he meant; Artie was just private security and nobody called him officer or anything fancy like that. His plan had been to do a quick tour of the depot then stop at the vending machines and pick up sodas and snacks for him and Myron.

"I'm Major Ardon," the MP said, pointing at a name on his uniform, H. Ardon. He looked serious and tough, like Artie's high school gym coach, and he had a girl, sorry woman, sorry female officer beside him, who was looking straight ahead through her shades, helmet low, and holding a German Shepherd by the leash. "And I need immediate emergency access to this container."

"Um . . . which . . ." Artie fumbled, flustered and already starting to sweat. He knew he was supposed to call this in, but the Major kept banging on the container. Artie checked: it was marked US MILITARY, described as "Returned and/or Defective Misc," and Wildwater Corp's agents were supposed to pick it up today.

"Open her up, pronto," the major ordered.

"Yes sir . . . I mean . . . don't you need some kind of warrant?"

"Warrant?" the major barked at him. "Is that what you said?" He closed in on him, poking him in the chest with a finger. "First of all, is this item under military authority or your private civilian authority?"

"Um . . . military?" Artie guessed. He had no idea.

"Good answer. Now . . . two . . ." He poked him harder, with two fingers. "We have reason to believe that illegal contraband, to wit heroin, is on that container, officer. But as you see, it is scheduled for pickup today. Is it your intention to deter us in seizing that heroin in time?"

"Um . . . no sir . . ."

"Right again." Now the major poked him with three fingers. "And three. It is for that reason of extreme urgency that I have the corporal here with me, and her highly trained K-9 investigator. This dog is able to sniff out any and all illegal substances, but the longer we spend talking and waiting for warrants the higher the likelihood of a false positive."

"False positive?" He glanced down at the dog with a new respect as it sniffed the wheels of his cart, then his own boots.

"Right. This dog's highly trained senses are so sensitive that if any person or vehicle or even clothing has been exposed to and/or ingested illegal drugs within the last month, the dog will know. Traces remain in the hair and skin cells. They store in fat and become detectable when the subject begins to secrete perspiration. Now, if while we are here chatting, the dog barks at anyone, then I am legally obligated to place said person under court-martial awaiting a full spectrum of blood, urine, and spinal fluid tests."

"Oh . . ." Artie said, sweat pumping from his pores. His armpits burned with fear, and the realization he was secreting panicked him even more.

But how could you hold in sweat? He wondered how red his eyes were and wished he'd worn shades too, like the MPs.

"Now then officer, it is oh nine hundred hours. Are you going to open that container or not?"

"Yes!" Artie shouted. "I mean yes, sir!" And with that he broke the seal and unlocked the can.

"Thank you officer. For doing your patriotic duty," the major said and saluted. "Now step back," he added. "And let the dog work."

"Right, right . . ." Artie said saluting as he gladly ran back to his cart.

The dog's qualifications at least were real, even if Joe and Yelena's were not. The trainer from whom Gio's people borrowed him supplied dogs to government agencies, and this one had just passed its tests with flying colors. The trainer had held up his delivery for a couple days, saying he needed shots from the vet before traveling. However, as far as Joe knew, the only substance he was trained to sniff out was heroin; certainly not people, and of course not for thirty days, but Joe knew a stoner when he saw one, and didn't need the dog's help to know this dude was baked, standing at attention by his cart and trying to hold his breath.

But now it was Joe who was sweating. They were inside the container, packed to the ceiling on both sides, with a narrow path down the center, and Yelena was leading the dog slowly along, while it sniffed at cartons and pallets that, according to their markings, contained all manner of stuff—from fluorescent bulbs and night vision goggles to smoke detectors and shoelaces, but none of it, according to the dog at least, contained a speck of dope.

Yelena looked at him and shrugged. Joe's mind raced. Was it possible to fool the dog? Theoretically yes, but he couldn't see any coffee or other items that might be used to throw off the scent, and it would take all day to search this can by hand. Was it possible there was no dope here after all? Sure. If they had cancelled the shipment for some reason. Then the

rest of this crap would just come in through the normal channels, with no one coming by to pull the dope from it.

But before Joe had time to think any further, he received confirmation that someone else did seem to think there was dope on the container. It was Juno, calling him over the earpiece.

"Hey Joe, FYI. I kept the tracking on that Russian's car live, and according to that, he's sitting right outside the gate. So you might want to get a move on . . ."

"Shit," Joe said. He'd hoped, by the time anyone showed, to have the dope and be back inside the truck. "Cash, you there?"

"At your service," Cash responded from his parked car.

"Can you take a look around, see if you can confirm that the Russian goon from last night is there?"

"Hang on . . ."

"Try again," Joe whispered under his breath to Yelena. She gave the commands that the trainer had provided, and the dog diligently sniffed his way up and down the container, then wagged his tail, licked Yelena's hand and lay down for a well-earned rest.

Cash came back on, "Well I've got bad news and totally fucked up news . . ."

"Let's have it," Joe told him. He could see that the guard was starting to get restless, and curious, as the fear faded.

"Bad news is the Russian is definitely here, about thirty yards back."

"And the totally fucked up?"

"That Fed, the female one. Starts with a Z?"

"Agent Zamora?" Joe asked.

"Yeah, that's the one. She's here too."

❖

Meanwhile, Josh and Liam were sitting tight, waiting for word from Joe, while Juno sat even tighter in the back. The plan was that once Joe and Yelena found the dope, they'd return to the truck, and drive back up into

the trailer to be escorted out like a backward Trojan Horse. Then the guard from the gate zoomed by in a little cart—the bald guy with the glasses. He paused, reversed, and got out.

"Shit," Josh said.

"What?" Juno answered, hearing him over the mic and squirming with frustration. He was certain he'd been correct in his calculations—the shipment had to be there. Yet they'd come up empty. But the very fact that the Russians and the FBI were both here only proved him right. Or almost right. They were missing something.

"Nothing. Just be cool and don't make any noise in there," Liam said, removing his own earpiece. He waved at the guard and leaned out, grinning big.

"Thank God, you found us," he called to the frowning guard.

"Found you?" he asked, looking up.

"Haven't you been looking for us? We're lost."

Actually, the guard, Myron, was heading to the vending machines behind the shed. He had terrible dry mouth, ever since he smoked that fat joint with his buddy Artie at the start of shift. Then Artie had gone off on his rounds, promising to pick him up a Mountain Dew, and never came back. Now Myron had no choice but to show these two foreigners the way back to the exit.

"Follow me," he said and, with a sigh—the vending machine and its load of cold soda was so close—he got back into his cart and headed off, reluctantly. Liam, also reluctantly, put the truck in gear and followed with Juno fuming in the back. The plan had gone off perfectly, but the results were nil, and now here they were, leaving empty-handed. Josh got back on his headset to call Joe and let him know that he'd need to find another way out.

30

WHEN TOOMEY ARRIVED AT the depot, everything seemed to be under control. He got on line at the entrance, waiting as the trucks and cars rolled up to the gate, showed their paperwork, got checked by security, and admitted. He was driving his own ride, a Jeep Wrangler Willys, the big, tricked-out Unlimited; it drove like the rugged military vehicles he was accustomed to, but with the leather seats, tinted windows, and top-notch sound system he preferred. He rolled slowly forward, sipping his coffee and adjusting the AC, classical music blasting. It was the same routine he had gone through each time since he began handling the shipments and there had never been a hitch. Nor did he expect one this time. He saw Sergey parked on the roadside along with the semis, pickups, and cars that were always there, and nodded as he passed. Toomey's number two, Trey, was beside him, riding along in an uneasy partnership with the Russian, and nodded back. He also noted two of his other men, Dirk and Baxter, sitting in a Hummer, ready to trail and observe from a distance. They were battle-hardened mercs who had accompanied him to New York on this mission. To Dirk this was just another deployment: he was Dutch and had spent a decade fighting wars around the world. To Baxter, an ex-Marine from Atlanta who decided to go into business for himself, operating stateside was a bit of a mind-blower. But he was furious when their ambush at the club went wrong: he was more than ready to prove himself again now.

Toomey reached the gate and showed his papers to the head guard, who remembered him. He was the kind of guy who got all warm and fuzzy around military, and the Special Forces sticker on Toomey's rear window might as well have been a free pass.

"Morning sir," the guard greeted him, standing a little straighter. Toomey gave him a warm smile and a commanding nod.

"Morning, Barker." His papers explained that he'd be loading up an assortment of random, very boring items from the Wildwater Corporation container. Barker gave the Jeep a cursory check then thanked him for his service again and waved him by.

❖

Joe came out of the container fast and called to Artie, who was getting sleepy leaning on his cart in the sun: working a double and getting stoned was catching up to him. He jumped as Joe barked.

"Officer!"

"Um, yes, sir . . ."

"This container has been cleared. Seal it up and then escort us to the exit pronto. We've just had another emergency call. National security."

"Right!"

That intense corporal who didn't talk came out, leading the dog, who sniffed suspiciously in his direction. Artie gave them a wide berth as they got in the Jeep and then shut the door to the container, slapping a sticker on it that said it had been opened and inspected. Then he got back in his cart and began to zoom through the stacks, leading the Jeep to the exit. He still didn't really grasp exactly what all this was about, but if it got these hard-ass MPs and their narc dog out of his life, so be it.

❖

Joe and Yelena sped toward the gate, cruising past the other vehicles waiting to exit as the security guard led them along the edge of the road.

They passed the truck, J & L painted on the door, with Josh and Liam in the cab and, Joe knew, Juno in back. Myron had escorted them this far before going back to his post at the gate, sadly without his soda. Joe shifted his cap casually as he passed, and Liam scratched the side of his nose, letting him know he saw him. Then they reached the front.

"Lift the gate," Artie called out as his cart pulled up, with the jeep idling behind. Myron stepped out of the guardhouse.

"Hey Artie," Myron said. "Where were you? I thought you were bringing me a Mountain Dew?"

"Sorry Myron," Artie said, trying to signal him by nodding subtly at Joe. "Got caught up with this. I'll tell you about it later."

Joe gave the horn a tap. Artie jumped.

"Shoot . . ." He turned back to Joe and saluted at him again, then turned back to Myron. "Listen these MPs got to get out of here. Lift her up."

"MPs?" Myron frowned down at his clipboard. "I didn't know there were any MPs here. Excuse me sir," he stepped up to Joe. "I'm sorry but I didn't see you come in. When did you arrive?"

Joe stared him down from under his hat. "Hours ago, officer," he said. "We were here bright and early. What time do you come on?"

"Nine."

"Then that explains it, doesn't it, officer?"

"Yes sir, but the guard on duty should have logged it here."

"Officer," Joe said, looming over him. "I have an emergency to deal with. A matter of national security. And you're going to hold me up because some incompetent forgot to log something, whoever it was?"

Myron nodded. "That's what's weird sir. The incompetent on duty? It was you, Artie."

Artie looked stunned. Was it possible he'd been so stoned he had forgotten about the MP? Or had he slipped by during one of his very brief naps? That's when Yelena, who'd been briefed on the commands for her highly trained dog, gave the defend command, "Take!" while also pulling back hard on the leash. As a result the dog began barking furiously at the two guards while straining with all his might.

"That's it!" Joe told them. "Hold it right there. I'm going to have to place you both under arrest."

"What?" Myron asked, backing away, looking from the dog to Yelena to Joe with equal fear. Artie groaned.

"You idiot. I told you to let them out."

"At least one of you," Joe said, "has been using illegal drugs or alcohol on duty, which is a violation of the Homeland Security Act, a federal court-martial offense."

"I wasn't on duty yet . . ." Myron said. "I mean . . ."

"Too late for excuses, son," Joe told him. "Now both of you are going to have to give us a bodily fluids sample while the corporal here observes. She's a trained expert interrogator." He turned to Yelena. "Get the specimen jars."

Yelena saluted sharply and directed the dog toward the guards, who backed away. "Let's go, you drugged-out losers. On the double!"

Barker, who'd been busy processing entries on the other side, saw the commotion and rushed over, saluting smartly when he saw Joe and Yelena.

"Good morning Major, what seems to be the trouble?"

"You the CO?" Joe asked, sternly.

"Yes sir . . . I mean I'm the supervisor, Jim Barker."

"Well I'm dealing with a high-threat-type national security crisis here and your men have seen fit to delay us. And now it seems we have a possible drug violation as well."

Barker glared at Myron and Artie, who looked back, wide-eyed with fear, and at least feeling stone-cold sober. The dog growled, and Yelena licked her chops, like they were both ready to rip them apart. Barker spoke in a lower tone to Joe.

"I apologize sir. We try to recruit good men, but it's not like in the Army. We don't have the same training."

"You served?" Joe asked him.

"Reserves. Mostly out of Fort Dix."

Joe nodded in appreciation. "Then you understand."

"Yes, sir, I do."

"Hold it," Joe said holding a hand up and listening to his silent ear-piece. "That alert has just gone code red." He told Myron and Artie: "I'm putting you two in each other's custody till we get back." Then he turned to Barker: "Now for the sake of America, lift that goddamn gate, soldier!"

"Yes, sir, right away. Lift her!" he yelled, and Myron jumped and ran to the guard house.

"Yes, sir!"

Yelena ordered the dog to fall back, and it happily hopped into the Jeep, tail wagging. Joe jumped behind the wheel and saluted as the arm of the gate lifted. Barker saluted and said, "Thanks for your service, Major!" Myron and Artie watched him leave with relief before starting to yell at each other. And as Joe and Yelena cleared the exit and pulled onto the access road, everything seemed to have worked out smoothly, until a bullet shattered the windshield.

31

TREY WAS THERE WITH Sergey to watch out for trouble, so after Toomey, his commander and employer, entered the depot, he put his binoculars on the exit gate and kept them there, waiting for him to return. When the Jeep with the military folks pulled up, he took note, and when he saw they had a dog and the dog barked at the guards, he got curious, but it was only when curiosity made him zoom in tight on their faces that he realized: it was them, the motherfucker who killed Tony back in the helicopter and the girl who rode the motorbike like a BMX champ. The same two who'd hit the stash and walked away untouched. This, he decided, qualified as trouble and he called Toomey, who told him to take them out. Immediately.

"Yes, sir. It's done," he said with satisfaction. He got on the phone to his back up, Dirk and Baxter, who had the sniper rifle. "Team Two come in."

"I'm here Team One."

"Dirk, we've got a target. The Jeep about to come out. Driver and passenger both. This one's for Tony."

"Negative," Dirk said. "We don't have a clear shot."

"Understood," Trey said, secretly pleased. "I will engage. Take the shot if you get it." He drew his machine pistol. "Pull out," he told Sergey, as he racked the slide, "we're taking these two down."

Sergey, however, did not take orders from Trey. Nor did he take orders from Toomey. He worked for Anton, a demanding and unforgiving boss, and Anton had ordered him to protect the shipment, nothing else.

"I'm not going without the dope," he said.

"We have to move."

"We're not moving."

"But Toomey's orders . . ."

"Fuck Toomey," Sergey said. "We wait."

Now the Jeep was moving, coming through the gate. "Fuck Toomey?" Trey asked. "Fuck you." And he leaned out and took a shot, shattering the Jeep's windshield. From that angle, with the target moving, he missed, but he left Sergey no choice: now they were going to move.

❖

Donna did not see that coming. She'd sunk into a torpor really, as the sun began to climb, toasting her face through the window, and the minutes clicked by, watching the slow traffic, like a lazy two-way river flowing in and out of the depot. Then, before she even registered what was happening, the guy in the car with Sergey, Unknown Subject with Ponytail, who'd been watching the same boring show through binoculars, swapped them for a gun and took a shot at a vehicle as it passed, shattering the windshield. A Jeep, with what looked like military personnel aboard. Actually, looking closer, as she drew her own weapon and pushed her door open to take a protected stance, it was a man, a woman and a dog, which was even weirder. And then, as if to twist her mind completely, she thought—or maybe she was just going crazy—that as the Jeep accelerated, swerving past her, that she saw Joe driving, no longer looking like a desperate shuffling junkie, but now in crisp fatigues with a cap and shades.

❖

"Get the dog down!"

When the windshield shattered, Joe hit the gas, and began to swerve deliberately, slaloming along the road to make it harder for the shooter to aim. Meanwhile, Yelena pushed the dog onto the floor, petting him swiftly and commanding him to lie down and stay, then raised her weapon and hunted for the shooter. But with two lanes of traffic, much of it big trucks, and two more rows of vehicles parked along the shoulder, it was hard to see exactly what was happening, and there wasn't anywhere to hide. So Joe floored it, and as the Jeep picked up speed, he saw Donna, out of her car, gun drawn, also searching for the source of the bullet.

That became clear when the black Benz, which Joe recognized, pulled out, drawing honks as it screeched through a U-turn and came after them, with a Hummer looming behind it. A few seconds later, Donna was back in her car and chasing them.

"You back there, Cash?" Joe asked over the mic.

"Yup. Right on your tail. Which keeps getting longer, by the way. What's with this Hummer?"

"I don't know but if you can help give us some breathing room, I'd appreciate it."

"Say no more."

Cash gunned his engine, which roared with power as he slipped onto the shoulder, passing the Fed in her Fedmobile—a black Impala, perfectly respectable but no match for what he had—then checking out the Hummer as he passed that—two guys, one white, one Black, clean-cut army types. Despite its power, neither the Hummer nor its driver were anywhere near as nimble as Cash, and he slid into the gap, nearly moving horizontally, like an expert parallel parker snatching somebody's spot. Then he braked. The Hummer driver hit his brake and his horn, both too hard, rocking forward and barely kissing Cash's bumper, and his ass, as Cash threw his car into higher gear and stomped the gas, slipping away. The big beast fishtailed as it tried to do the same, but the Fed, who Cash had to admit was not bad, swerved around it and took next place in the race, behind the Camaro. She hit her flashers and siren, trying to tell him to clear the way. He waved and hit his turn signal, as if he was going

to, but then kept swerving in front of her, slowing as did, like a dipshit driver who was panicking and had no idea what to do.

❖

Behind the wheel, Donna was on the radio now. "Calling all law enforcement. This is a federal agent, calling for assistance. In pursuit of . . . two or three suspect vehicles."

Newark police and the NJ State Troopers both responded and Donna identified herself and described the vehicles. Then Blaze came on.

"Zamora is that you?"

"Affirmative Deputy Logan."

"I was just on my way to meet you."

"Change of plans. Want to help me catch a couple suspects?"

"That's what I do. I'm joining up with the posse now at the highway junction. We'll cut them off at the pass."

"Thanks."

Now she had this black Camaro in her way though. It was a brand-new muscle car, jacked up and gleaming, but the dude inside it—and it was always a dude—had no idea how to drive. Typical. He had his blinkers on, first the left, then the right, then the hazards, and was slowing down, but couldn't seem to get out of the way. She got on the squawk box:

"Pull over to your right . . . Right!" she ordered as he swerved right, then started to skid on the gravel at the shoulder and swerved back left, cutting across her and dangerously close to the traffic coming the other way.

Jesus, she thought, how did this guy get a license? Then she heard automatic gunfire from up ahead. And a moment later, more gunfire, from her left, as the guy in the Hummer shot out her tires.

32

ONCE THE DOG WAS safely on the floor, and Joe was on the open road, Yelena crept into the rear seat and, aiming carefully out the back, opened fire on the Russian and his gunman in the Benz. She knocked out the windshield and both headlights before the driver took evasive action and peeled off, dropping to the rear of the pack, leaving Cash right behind them and then Donna in her car behind him. Cash smiled at Yelena, as he held Donna back, and the Jeep moved further away. Then Yelena saw the Hummer pulling up alongside Donna, roaring along the shoulder, full speed, with a gunner now upright through the opening in the roof, aiming an AR-15. He carefully took out Donna's tires, sending her skidding off the road. The Hummer's driver muscled in on Cash in the Camaro, threatening to push him into oncoming traffic, while the gunner took a shot at Cash through the roof.

"Shit, that was close," Cash called over the mic. "He's trying to get through me to you. I'll try to hold him back a little longer."

It didn't matter though. Riding high above the Camaro, the gunner was able to fire over Cash's car and into the Jeep. Yelena hit the floor, hugging the dog, as bullets tore into the back seat and the rear panel.

"You okay?" Joe asked, still speeding forward.

"So far," Yelena told him. "He hit the extra gas tank." The plastic container of extra fuel strapped to the rear of the Jeep was now leaking dangerously.

"Better ditch it then," Joe said, and reached under the passenger seat for the emergency kit. He pulled the flare gun out and handed it to her. "Give them this as well."

"Right."

The Hummer bucked against the Camaro, trying to brush Cash aside.

"Let them through, Cash," Joe said over the mic. "And watch out. Yelena's going to light them up."

"Cool. I'm out," Cash said, and swerved away, letting the Hummer pass. As it closed in on the Jeep, pulling in right behind them, Yelena rose up and threw the leaking gas canister. It thumped onto the windshield, gasoline spilling from the bullet holes. Immediately, she fired the flare, blasting it into the fuel can. It blew.

Like napalm, the gas caught, first the fumes from the ruptured container, then the liquid fuel splashing on the roof, and then, a split second later, the whole can. Instantly the hood of the Hummer was covered, as flames danced over the liquid, licking everywhere it spilled like tongues of blue and orange. The terrified gunner ducked back inside as the driver swerved, his windshield blind with flames. In a panic, he veered wildly, drove onto the shoulder, and banged into a tree, as they both bailed out of the truck.

Now it was just the Benz still trailing behind Yelena and Joe, and they had a decent lead. But there was trouble ahead. Juno had been monitoring the law's frequencies from the rear of the truck and he warned Joe about a roadblock a mile ahead, at the last exit before they joined the main highway.

"Are you clear back there?" Joe asked.

"Yeah we're like a quarter mile behind you," Liam put in. "Normal traffic now. No cops."

"Then we'll come to you," Joe said and made a hard left. Leaning on his horn, as on-coming cars honked and swayed around him, he cut the wheel, and skidded into a U turn, then straightened out, and rejoined the flow, going the opposite way. The Russian stayed with him, repeating the move, as terrified drivers veered away, honking frantically. Joe stayed in

the left lane, pushing as hard as he could, until he saw the truck on his left, coming toward them. Liam gave a quick wave. Then Joe did it again.

Cranking the wheel left, he cut across the double yellow, and swung into the traffic, which braked and honked and yelled, then gunned it and re-joined the flow, now a few dozen yards behind the truck. This time the Russian took a beat longer, but soon he was there again, behind them.

"Okay," Joe said over the mic. "Same getaway plan as before but with a slight change. We're going to have to keep moving."

Liam kept the truck rolling steady while Josh, watching in his side mirror, waited for Joe to work his way up, passing other cars, and finally falling into place right behind them. "Ready," Joe said, keeping about one car length back. Then Josh lowered the gate. The metal ramp came down on its hydraulics, and when the lip began to scrape along the asphalt, Juno flung the door up from inside. Joe slowly increased his speed, nosing the Jeep's front wheels onto the ramp. The Russian, seeing what was happening, sped up too, bumping them from behind. Yelena fired a couple shots, brushing him back, while Joe gave it some gas, racing the motor, and drove up into the truck.

"Lift it!" he yelled over the mic, and Josh hit the power, bullets ringing off the metal gate as it came up, shielding them inside. The Russian was right behind them now.

"Need a gun?" Juno asked, as Joe and Yelena jumped out of the Jeep.

"Nope," Joe said, "I got it," and pulled his folding camp knife from his pocket. He began to slash at the plastic-wrapped bales of manure stacked along one side of the truck. "Help me lift it," he said, and Juno and Yelena came to his aid. "Time to unload this shit."

Together they hoisted the bale over the gate and it dumped onto the hood of the Russian's Benz, where it burst open, spilling an avalanche of manure over the hood and through the blown-out windshield. The driver and passenger tried to brush it away, but another bale followed, burying them. Unable to see, and with fertilizer blowing around them like a small brown hurricane, the driver pulled onto the shoulder and stopped. His

passenger, the guy in the ponytail, leapt from the car and tried to take a shot, but the truck was gone in the flow of traffic.

Juno and Joe lowered the door. A few minutes later, the truck had slowed to a crawl, as they reached the roadblock, were waved on by bored state troopers, and made their way to the Lincoln Tunnel.

❖

Meanwhile Toomey, who had proceeded to the Wildwater container with no problems, selected the items on his pickup list, loaded them into his own Jeep, and left. By the time he reached the exit, the excitement was all over, and he proceeded on his way without impediment. He was a little annoyed at all the backed-up traffic; after all, he had a schedule to keep.

PART IV

33

JOE WAS TRYING TO think. They were in Old Shenanigan's Ale House, the sprawling, packed Irish pub in the West 30s, (or Irish-ish—it had green tablecloths and Guinness on tap but bore little resemblance to anything Liam remembered from home) that once belonged to Patty White and that Liam and his brothers now controlled. They were in a barren upstairs room, half-finished and in a permanent state of construction, off limits to employees and unknown to the tourists and local office workers who packed the street-level saloon. It was safe—swept regularly for bugs, windowless, and stripped to the beams. There was even a secret sub-basement where, decades ago, Pat had buried a rival, and where Liam had now hidden the stolen stash. All in all, Pat had been smart to use it for meetings; except, that is, for the night he came to meet Liam here and found Gio, who shot him.

Now the crew were on folding chairs with their drinks on a bridge table, mostly beers, with a Coke for Juno and a black coffee for Joe. But he hadn't touched it. He was pacing around, hearing the faint hum of the bass from the bar below, and trying to think while the others watched and waited. Finally Juno broke the silence.

"How come with this job I feel like we're always one step behind, you know?"

Yelena nodded. "Yes, right from the start in Afghanistan."

Cash put in: "A little more bad luck today and we would have been the ones eating shit instead of that Russian."

Juno grimaced in anger, waving his tablet: "That's what burns me most. I mean, at first I thought, okay, I got it all wrong about the delivery. But then why were all those cops and crooks there, if there was no damned dope?"

Joe, who had been standing outside the circle, staring into space, turned to Juno, as though he'd been woken from a nap. "You're right," he said, brightly. "Something went wrong."

Juno nodded. "I know, man, no need to rub it in."

Joe went on, as if talking to himself. "I mean with them. Look, you're right, all of you, we've been a step behind this whole time. Why? Because they knew more than us. But they must have thought there was going to be dope in that container also. And with no more product they're going to be feeling the pressure. So we keep turning the screw."

Liam nodded. "Now you're talking. How?"

"Maybe it's time for me to talk to the boss, directly."

Cash frowned. "You mean Anton?"

"I mean the little man in the glass tower who pulls the strings."

"Oz?" Juno asked.

Josh, who had been texting, turned to Joe. "Sorry to interrupt, Joe. But I have an urgent message."

"What is it?"

"It's not the kind of thing you text. It's waiting outside."

❖

Donna was trying to think. Andy, Blaze, Fusco, and Parks were all crammed into her little office, Fusco of course filling the armchair, Andy on a smaller straight-back chair, Blaze and Parks leaning on her desk, and Donna behind it. She was explaining what went down that day.

"Look, the way I see it, I had no choice. I played my hand. The suspect led me to Jersey. I called you, I called the office, and I called a friend who

was local for backup. Then it all went sideways before anyone got there. What could I do?"

"You could have caught somebody," Fusco offered. "Or found some dope. Or learned something. Or not lost track of our suspect. Any one of those would have worked."

Blaze gave him a dirty look, Andy and Parks groaned, but Donna laughed.

"I'm starting to like you, Fusco."

He grinned. "You too, Zamora."

"But you're only half right. Or three quarters. I did learn something. We know how the dope is getting in. What else were they all there for, armed to the teeth at a freight depot? Andy . . ." She turned to him. "Can you find out who had international pickups scheduled this morning? Let's see if anyone jumps out at us."

Andy nodded and opened his laptop.

"As for our lost Russian." She turned back to Fusco. "Who does he work for?"

"Anton Solonik," Fusco said. "I got it from OC Task Force."

"Right. Our files say the same thing. So now we know: the Russian mob is behind White Angel, they're using hired muscle to take more territory to sell it, and they're bringing it in via air freight from somebody in that depot."

"Well I can make a pretty good guess about that somebody," Andy said. With his FBI clearance he had logged into the listing of shipments. "There was a whole pile of pickups this morning, it's a busy place. But when I narrow the field, only one pops out."

He showed them the screen. Fusco squinted at it. "I can't read shit without my glasses."

Parks leaned in. "It says, defective merchandise. Shipped from West Germany."

"Amazing," Fusco said. "Thank God for the high-tech FBI."

"Even we have to scroll down," Andy said. "That's just where it was consolidated. The goods originate at offices in . . . Frankfurt, Rome,

Istanbul, Saudi Arabia, Tel Aviv, Iraq, and . . . hold your applause: Fucking A. F. Ghanistan."

"That's got to be it," Donna said, leaning in. "What's the company?"

Andy read: "Wildwater Corporation. Headquarters are right here in town."

"What do you say, detective?" Donna asked Fusco. "Is that a lead or what?"

He grinned. "Not bad for a f . . ." he began, but Blaze cut him off.

"You better not say for a female, or I will shoot you dead right now."

"I was going to say for a feeb," he said and winked at her.

Blaze laughed. "Sorry. I shouldn't presume you're an asshole. It's not fair."

"Oh, it's fair," Parks said. "He is for sure an asshole."

Andy added, "You just can't presume what kind."

Even Fusco cracked up at that, and Donna was leaning back in her chair laughing, when her computer screen flashed a flagged message alert at the same that her phone vibrated. She leaned in, still smiling and clicked to see what was so urgent. Zahir had sent her an email.

❖

Joe and Josh walked out of the pub. A black town car was idling in front. When he saw Joe, the driver, a young, bearded man in a black, wide brim hat, with a gun bulging the side of his black suit, hopped out and opened the rear door, then waited, bumming a cigarette from Josh, while Joe got inside.

"Good afternoon, Rebbe, how are you? We going to the deli again?"

Rebbe laughed and squeezed Joe's hand in both of his, kissing him on the cheek. His beard tickled. "I wish! Better than the dry corned beef Patty used to serve here, *olav ha-shalom*. But I'm going to the cardiologist after this. Never eat pastrami before you get your cholesterol checked," He sat back. "I'm afraid this is a business call. Unpleasant business."

"Tell me."

"I wanted to warn you, personally, since I know you're friends, that there's a contract out on the *rushish meydl*. The shiksa."

"Yelena?"

He nodded.

"Who put it out?"

"Anton . . . a curse on his name, he should crap blood and piss pus. Black sorrow is all that his mother should see of him . . . but . . ." He held up a finger. "The situation right now is complicated. We know he attacked us, but we can't prove it enough to get all the other New York bosses on our side yet, or convince the Russians to give him up. And he hurt our friends too bad for us fight him on our own, with his mercenaries." Rebbe shrugged. "On the other hand, he can't admit that the stash you took was his and that he is behind White Angel either. And he can't come after you, because you are with Gio and this . . ." He tapped Joe's chest, high on the right side, where the brand was. ". . . marks you as untouchable."

"You say that," Joe pointed out, "but the number of people who want to kill me keeps going up overall."

Rebbe shrugged. "What are you gonna do? But with Yelena it's different. No offense, but the word is out she was a snitch, informing for SVR in Moscow."

"She had no choice but to agree," Joe said. "But she told them nothing once she was here."

"I know, I know, boychick, but this way Anton has a legitimate reason no one will dispute, and she has no powerful friends to back her up."

"She has me," Joe said.

Rebbe smiled like a grandpa and patted Joe's knee. "Then we understand each other perfectly."

❖

When Joe got back upstairs, the others were waiting.

"We checked," Liam said. "And if you really want to see Richards, he will be hosting an event at his office tomorrow."

"What kind of event?"

"You know, a big 9/11 thing, full of important patriots."

"Can you get me in?" he asked Juno.

"Of course. But Joe, there will be a hundred witnesses."

"Don't worry, I'm just going to have a quiet word with the man. And what about the tracker on the Russian's Benz, is it still active?"

Juno shrugged. "Yeah but it's at a repair shop, no doubt getting the shit scrubbed off it."

Joe turned to Cash. "Keep on it, will you? I want you to see if he takes you to Anton." He glanced over at Yelena. "Looks like we are going to have to pay him a visit too."

❖

"Americans claim they remember 9/11 but they remember nothing of the terror they cause. This year we will remind them. I am bringing a gift to Ground Zero. The mountains of dead and the smoking wreckage I leave will be the true memorial."

Immediately after reading Zahir's message, Donna ended the meeting in her office and went to her boss, Tom's. She was told he was busy but when she explained she had just received a serious threat, she was called in anyway, where she found him in an important, classified meeting . . . with her ex-husband.

"Shut the door," Tom said, as she froze on the threshold. She shut it and stepped in. "Donna, you know Agent Powell here of course."

"Mike," she said, managing a polite smile. "When did you get back into the country?"

"Just now," he said. "I wanted to brief Tom on 9/11-related intel we gathered overseas."

"And when he mentioned Zahir, I figured we better bring you into the conversation," Tom said.

"You've been investigating Zahir?" Donna asked him, sitting down now.

"We pick up chatter, though it sounds like you might know more than us at this point," Mike said.

"You say there's a new threat?" Tom asked.

"Yes, sir." Donna opened her folder. "This message came in addressed to me." She read the whole thing out, facing Tom, but when she glanced over at Mike, his eyes were wide and his mouth hung slightly ajar. "Are you okay?" she asked.

"What?" He sat up and regained his composure. "Of course. I mean . . . it's an alarming development."

"Yes, it's bad news," Tom said, leaning back in his chair. "But we get a lot of threats. What makes this one credible?"

"It's from Zahir," Donna said. "We have reason to believe he is here, sir. Or his agents are."

Again, Mike seemed to jerk in his chair, like someone had yanked his chain. Then he turned back into the condescending, whining Mike she knew so well. "Are you sure of this Donna? I mean, where's your evidence? As far as we know, Zahir operates overseas."

"Then I guess there's a lot you don't know," she answered calmly. "What a surprise."

Tom stood. "That's exactly why I brought you in, Donna, since you and your team have been working this. Now look . . ." He pointed at both of them. "I know there's some personal feeling here, some anger and past resentment . . ."

Mike and Donna both looked at the floor in embarrassment as Tom went on: "But it's time to put that behind us. To drain the bad blood and bury the hatchet. And that's why I'm asking. Do you, Agent Zamora, think you can work with this man . . . even though he's CIA?"

"Sir?" Donna cleared her throat. "I mean, yes, of course, sir."

Tom waved a hand. "I know, it's tough on me too. But there's a bigger picture here. Don't you agree Agent Powell?"

"Ah, yes, sir," Mike said, sitting up straight. "I agree completely."

"There's one thing we all want: this Zahir's balls on a hook. Let's keep our eye on those balls. What difference does it make who does the actual chopping and who holds him down? And who wears them on a necklace?"

"Absolutely sir," Donna said. "That's why I came to work this morning."

"Exactly. Good. Excellent. So in that spirit, why don't you update us now on where your investigation is at present."

"Well . . ." Donna hesitated. She glanced at Mike, who was listening attentively. She still didn't trust him for shit, whatever the boss said. "Actually sir, I was just about to meet with my team when this threat came through. Perhaps I should prepare a report and submit it to you later . . ."

"Just give us the gist, Donna." Tom sat down and leaned back, ready to hear a tale. "Do you have a lead in this case or not?"

"Yes, sir, we do." Donna sighed. "We have reason to suspect that a corporation, or some of its employees, is involved, possibly cooperating with Zahir in the heroin smuggling or else being used by them."

"What corporation?"

Now Donna glanced sideways at Mike, while still addressing Tom. "It's called Wildwater, sir. They have an office here in Manhattan."

"Wildwater," Tom repeated. "Never heard of it. Ring any bells Powell?"

Mike shrugged. "Nope. But I will check it out and get back to you."

"Okay, then," Tom said and leaned over to shake his hand, signaling the meeting was done. "Back to work."

"I will keep you posted, sir," Donna said.

"Right," Tom said. "Do that. After tomorrow."

"Sir?"

"In case you forgot to look at the calendar today, or the paper, or the goddamn internet, it's September 10th. Tomorrow you will be on the ground with everyone else, working security."

"But you just said yourself we've got to hunt this Zahir down and chop his nuts off. Don't you think . . ."

"I think the place to be sniffing around for those nuts tomorrow will be down among the sweaty crowds of tourists at Ground Zero, Zamora. And that's where you'll be."

"Yes, sir."

As they walked into the hall, Mike touched Donna's arm, but she instinctively drew back.

"Sorry if that was weird," he said. "I had no idea you were working the case . . ."

"It's fine," Donna said. "But when were you going to tell your daughter you're back? Or were you?"

Mike looked genuinely stricken, and she felt a twinge of regret. "I was, I just . . . you know what it's like in the field for me. Just please, tell her Daddy will see her soon. I promise."

"Okay," Donna said. "I will." And for the first time that day, she believed him.

❖

Mike Powell was trying to think. As soon as he heard that message, purportedly from Zahir, he knew he had to get ahold of Richards and Toomey. What the hell were they thinking? Any hope he had of burying the FBI investigation and stonewalling Donna went out the window when they issued a domestic threat, in New York, the day before 9/11. Unless it wasn't them. Was it possible someone else was now posing as Zahir? And how to get in touch, now that he knew they might be under surveillance? He couldn't walk into the building. He couldn't use his cell. Even going to his own office and calling from a secure line suddenly made him paranoid. So he did it the old fashioned way: after much searching, he found an actual working payphone near the men's room in a hotel, called Richards, and told him to call the payphone from a safe line. But Richards was no help at all: Toomey had left early that morning to pickup the latest delivery, and somewhere along the way, he had shaken off the Russians and never returned. They knew nothing

about the Zahir message or who had sent it. Richards started going on about Donna, and how much of a threat did she pose, and could Powell still handle it? Powell lied and said yes; to his own surprise, he found himself worried about her now, about what it might mean if Richards decided to "handle" it another way. He was also worried by the edge of panic he now heard in Richards's voice. The shadow they had created had come to life.

34

AFTER WORK THAT NIGHT, Donna met Blaze at the bar as promised, though she hadn't promised to be a fun date, brooding in the beer Blaze bought her about work and the sudden return of her ex-husband.

"What a shit show," Donna muttered. "The most epic shit show in a long-running hit series."

Blaze shrugged. "You got to learn to let it go. Shit goes sideways sometimes. So be it."

"Yeah but the thing of it is, this was my first time really running with the ball, you know? My idea to begin with, my lead to Jersey, practically my team. Then it all blew up in my face."

Blaze shrugged again. "Not really. I mean, yeah, it kind of did, but you learned something, right? Wildwater. That's the next step. You keep going. And sooner or later you catch up. Like on a manhunt." While she talked her eyes wandered. A pale young woman with long red hair was alone at the bar, sipping a mixed drink and sneaking looks at their table.

"Or a womanhunt," Donna said.

"What?" Blaze asked, returning her own gaze to Donna.

"Nothing. Anyway, you're right. Got to persevere."

"Exactly."

"As long as we survive tomorrow's foreign invasion. And I mean tourists, not terrorists." Donna talked on, though now Blaze was back to smiling at the redhead. "Am I boring you?"

"A little," Blaze said, with a grin, then laughed. "No, sorry, of course not. Just tired."

"Yeah, me too," Donna said, and stood. "I'm going to go home and practice smiling for tomorrow. I'll let you stay here and . . . rest." She laughed and bent over to kiss Blaze on the cheek. "Thanks for the beer, buddy," she added and went.

"See you, special agent," Blaze called after her, then returned her gaze to the redhead. She stood and sauntered over, like marshals in saloons have been doing for over a century.

"Good evening," she said to the redhead. "Sorry if this is too forward, but my friend left, and there's an empty seat at my table, and I thought you might be tired of standing."

The redhead beamed. "How thoughtful," she said in an English accent, which was an added attraction for Blaze. "Not too forward at all. I'd love to join you."

"Great," Blaze smiled back and held out a hand. "My name's Blaze."

"Lovely to meet you, Blaze," she said, placing her soft, childish hand in Blaze's, the black nail polish chipped. "My name is Victoria. But my friends call me Vick."

❖

"So . . . I have a confession to make. Don't be mad."

"Um . . . okay." Donna had just walked into the house and found her mom there waiting, with her laptop in her lap. She put her bag down and stowed away her gun, then kissed her on the cheek. "Do I need to read you your rights?"

"No, but you have to promise not to be mad and not to just say I'm crazy."

"How can I?"

"Promise."

"Okay I'll do my best."

"Honey . . ." She opened the laptop. "I made you a profile."

"A what?"

"A profile."

"Like for a serial killer?"

"For dating!" She showed her the screen, which showed a dating website profile, complete with a photo of Donna.

"Oh, my God, you're crazy."

"I'm sorry but I had too."

"What do you mean had to? Of course you didn't have to."

"I felt so sad. Seeing you still so young and beautiful and so lonely. So I made a nice profile for you, and yes, most of the messages are from serial killers . . ."

"Great. I will forward them to the bureau."

"But tonight one came that I think you will really like. Mija, he's perfect! Just your type."

"My type? I don't even have a type."

"Look, he's a veteran. Special Forces. Got a whole bunch of medals. Purple heart. Now he does consulting. He's handsome. Strong jaw. Blue eyes. He's in town for 9/11."

Reluctantly, Donna glanced down at the profile her mom clicked on. She was right, he was handsome. And his service was impressive.

"He walks with a cane," Yolanda added. "Bad leg from a gunshot. But I think that's kind of sexy, you know, wounded warrior. Manly. I mean as long as what's between his legs wasn't shot off."

"Mom, please. You're going to give me nightmares."

"Anyway, I didn't want to lose him," Yolanda rattled on. "So I wrote back for you!"

"What? How could you? Jesus."

"And he wants to meet tomorrow! At the ceremony."

"Well I hope you two have a nice time," Donna said. "Because I will be busy working."

"Mija, please, you have to answer him at least. He's a war hero. You can't ghost him."

"Ghost? How do you even know about all this?" Donna sighed as she looked through the email exchange. He was literate at least, with correct

spelling and punctuation. And polite. And patriotic. A squared-away soldier boy. And she had to admit, to herself if never to her mother, he was her type. "God, I'm so sorry I ever taught you to use the internet."

She wrote back to him, just apologizing for her Mom's meddling and explaining that she'd actually be working tomorrow.

I understand completely, he answered. *My niece talked me into making my profile. Well, I will be down at Ground Zero anyway, paying my respects—I've lost a lot of friends since 9/11 and I've never seen the memorial. But it's hard to get around on this leg. Maybe you'll have time for a drink after?*

Donna smiled. He was a good guy at least. Her mom had decent instincts, after all, and she meant well. *I can't promise about the drink, but why don't you call me in the morning when you get downtown? I think the least I can do is arrange VIP access.* She sent her work number. *Ask for Agent Zamora. Donna.*

Really? He wrote back. *That would be outstanding. My full name is Rick Toomey. And thank you!*

Thank you, Rick. For your service.

❖

Blaze didn't realize her badge was gone till she woke up. She had a few drinks with that English chick (or British? She got them mixed up), then they started making out, then dancing, then dancing and making out, and then, just as she was about to suggest taking the party elsewhere, the damn girl went to the bathroom and vanished. Gone, just like that, a fugitive in the night. Cold feet, Blaze figured, and a wicked case of blue balls for her. Probably a pillow princess anyway, a soft pale redhead like that, with that stuck-up accent. But by then a couple of Blaze's pals had turned up and they bought her tequila shots to commiserate. By the time she made it back out to Jersey City, the room was spinning and she barely got her shoes off before hitting the bed.

The way Blaze figured it, there were a lot of places her badge could be: on her own floor somewhere, under the couch or table, on the floor

of her friend's car from when they drove her home, or on the floor of the bar, which she'd call as soon as they opened. And if she did think about the redhead, Vick (cute name), holding her close when they danced, grinding against her, she didn't think about how her nimble hand might have slid into her pocket. And as she washed her Advil down with Diet Coke followed by black coffee, she definitely didn't feel lucky to be alive. But she was.

❖

Vicky felt a bit sad leaving the bar. It would have been fun to go home with that tough, sexy marshal and play with her some more, in private. But, business before pleasure: she couldn't kill everyone cute she met, unfortunately. A dead federal agent, the night before 9/11, would kick up a lot more fuss than a drunk one who got her ID stolen. So Vicky, who still had a hard time finding her way around New York the second she left the Manhattan grid, got in a cab on Bleecker Street and took it all the way out to Brighton Beach. She suspected the cabbie took the scenic route, but who cared, it wasn't her money. She was on expense. She just relaxed and enjoyed the ride out to the address that Nikolai had gotten from his Russian connections. It looked nothing like the real Brighton of course. But it was a bit cooler than downtown had been. And she did smell the ocean on the breeze.

❖

The old man was suspicious at first—some girl he'd never seen before, and English too—but when she dropped Anton's name he could hardly refuse. So he let her in, offered her tea, which she accepted, took her picture, and then left her sipping on the couch while he altered the federal marshal's ID she gave him. He didn't ask any questions. He couldn't, since he barely spoke English and her Russian was rudimentary.

When he emerged with the finished product, she praised his work and then, reaching into her bag for the money, tasered him instead. He woke up chained to his balcony, dangling over the side, with the sound of the ocean in his ears and wind twisting all around him. Fear crashed in like the waves. His legs kicked helplessly like he was drowning.

"It's lovely out here," Vicky told him. She was smoking one of his Russian cigarettes. "Though you can feel autumn in the air, can't you? Makes me a bit sad. A poetic feeling really."

"Help . . ." he managed to croak in English. "Help. I give you money."

"Not money." She leaned closer. "Information."

He nodded. She leaned even closer, blowing smoke into his face. "Yelena Noylaskya. Where is she?"

He shook his head. "Don't know."

She took another drag and coughed. "Bit harsh this," she commented, and ground it out on his hand. He howled and yanked away, losing his grip on the railing and putting his full weight on the cuffs, which cut into his wrists. He grabbed the bar again.

"I'll stick to my own if you don't mind," Vicky said now and lit another, English cigarette. "Yelena?" she asked, holding it over him. "What name is she living under?"

He shook his head. "Don't understand English. Sorry."

She burned him again. He screamed again but held on. Then she asked him again in Russian. This time he looked her right in the eye and whispered something back that she couldn't translate but didn't need a dictionary to understand. It was a curse.

She tried a few more times, just to be thorough, but all he did was continue to mutter in Russian, curses and, she thought, prayers. She'd played him wrong, she realized: He'd made the connection between Anton and the SVR and Moscow powers, and probably hated them worse than death itself. He was a stubborn, tough old bastard and he wasn't going to budge. So instead of torturing him with it, she put the last smoke in his mouth and he sucked it eagerly, even gratefully, she thought, and then she unhooked him and let him go.

Joe and Yelena watched TV with Gladys, a *Parks & Recreation* marathon, the idea being to take their minds off of the day ahead, but Joe couldn't focus and went into the bedroom and read instead. Finally, when Gladys drained her last drink and went to bed, Yelena did the same.

"Still the poetry?" she asked, lying beside him. "You know, I didn't go to school, but in Russia we honor our great poets." She shrugged. "At least until we execute them." She shut her eyes. "Read me some?"

He read her the first of the *Duino Elegies*, and then told her the little he knew about their creation, how Rilke, in the midst of a severe psychological crisis, was invited by the Princess Marie von Thurn und Taxis to stay in Duino Castle, overlooking the Adriatic Sea, where walking on the cliffs, he heard the wind whisper the opening line in his ear: "Who, if I cried out, would hear me among the angel's hierarchies?" It was ten more years of struggle before he completed the poems.

Yelena liked that. She reached for the book: "Whom can we turn to in our need? Not angels, not humans," she read, approvingly. "And it says this, too, about lovers . . ." She ran a finger along the text: "They keep on using each other to hide their fate."

Joe smiled. "Oh yeah? That strikes a chord for you, does it?"

Yelena shrugged and tossed the book onto his stomach. "Anyway he reminds me of you." She laughed, as she stood and peeled off her T-shirt and jeans. "I bet you would go live in a castle alone and walk the cliffs." Leaving her clothes in a pile, she switched off the light and slipped into bed beside him. She pressed her mouth to his ear. "Then I'd be the angel that comes and whispers in your ear," she added, and stuck her tongue in his ear.

"Ha!" He squirmed and turned to face her, though his eyes could not yet make hers out in the dark. "You know what part reminds me of you?" he whispered back.

"Tell me."

He moved closer, his lips brushing her ear now. "Beauty is nothing but the beginning of terror."

35

DONNA'S DAY WAS GOING pretty well, if you didn't mind suffocating crowds, boring speeches, and a wide variety of New York smells, including hot dog, spilled beer, and overflowing toilets. Then her walkie squawked. It was NYPD.

"Agent Zamora, you on? Over?"

"Zamora here. What's up?"

"We've got a vehicle out here at the perimeter. Driver said you gave him clearance to enter. Name of Toomey. Rick. You know him?"

Donna scowled at her walkie. "I know him but I didn't clear him. Vehicle you say?"

"Yeah, he's a disabled vet. Trying to get into the memorial."

"Okay hold him there. I'm on my way."

"Roger that."

"Can you cover me?" Donna asked Andy. "My date's here."

"Date?" he asked, eyes automatically sweeping the crowd behind his shades while he spoke. "Are you joking?"

"I don't even know," she admitted. She moved through the crowd, forcing her way gently and showing her badge, until she finally got to the perimeter, where the cops had their barricades, the National Guard stood around in fatigues and rifles, and Homeland Security, slightly more discreet, moved around in Kevlar vests and sunglasses. Most discreet of all were her own kind, FBI and Secret Service, many of whom were dressed

as tourists, or vendors, or hidden in sniper positions around the area. She showed her badge and kept walking to the closest corner where a vehicle was allowed. She approached an NYPD sergeant, a dark-skinned woman with her braids up under her cap.

"Excuse me Sarge, I'm Zamora, FBI. Someone called for me?"

"Right." They shook hands. "I'm Cole. Hoping you can handle this for us. The guy's a vet, even got a Special Forces decal on his truck, but there's no way we can let him drive any closer. You understand. No disrespect."

"No, of course not. I've got it. And thanks."

The sergeant touched her brim and pointed, and Donna went around the corner, where she saw a Jeep Wagoneer, one of the big ones, double parked, with a big white guy leaning against it. He held a cane. He was handsome, she had to admit. And parked illegally.

"Mr. Toomey?" she called out as she drew closer. "I'm Agent Zamora."

"Hey . . ." he gave her a wide, craggy smile. Dimples even. "I thought we were Rick and Donna. Have I been downgraded?"

She laughed. "Not at all, just in work mode, sorry." She held out a hand and he shook, firmly but gently, and gave it just a second of extra pressure. "Now what seems to be the problem?"

"Didn't know there was one. Just another disabled vet trying to get in. I don't know where to park though. Thought you'd have some kind of VIP access for special needs parking."

"I'm afraid there's no way we could clear every car. Not to mention no place to park them. You'll have to use a lot or find the closest legal spot. But the upside is alternate side of the street rules are suspended. And if walking is a problem, I can get you a ride with the police." She smiled. "So don't worry, you'll still be getting the VIP treatment."

He laughed. "That kind of special attention I don't need. The walk will do me good."

Donna smiled. "Sounds like a plan," she said and got on her radio. "Sergeant Cole? This is Agent Zamora. You on? Over."

Her radio squawked. "I'm here. What can I do for you?"

"Mr. Rick Toomey is going to park his vehicle legally and return. Can you send him my way?"

"No problem."

"There you go," Donna told him with smile.

❖

Toomey kept his cool. As always. The parking problem had thrown a wrench into his plans but of course he had a backup. As always. So he reparked his truck and took a cab back down to the memorial, or as close as it would get him, fiddling with his cane in the back. Now that he'd ditched the vehicle, the whole disabled vet thing was a bit of a nuisance, and he considered "forgetting" his cane in the taxi, but no, he had to keep the limp. He was visiting a secular holy site, not Lourdes, and a little extra pity never hurt, he found, especially with women. Extra especially with women like Zamora—Donna—who clearly had a need to rescue and protect.

He paid his taxi, got out, leaning on the cane of course, then found that African-American sergeant, the one who had given him shit before, smiled, and called her ma'am and was waved on through, pushing his way through the crowd, his VFW hat and his cane helping, people more or less clearing a path, but still, a mongrel crowd, every kind of person mixed up together, like a garbage dump. Half the people selling food or drinks or goddamn 9/11 T-shirts and flags even looked like Islamics. Now what kind of mixed-up world was that?

He wouldn't be sorry when he had to leave New York.

❖

"Hey, Richards, I've got a question? How's your heroin import business going?"

Still with his gracious host's smile stuck to his face, Richards turned to Joe.

He was in his adventure gear: multi-pocket hunting vest over white dress shirt and khakis, though most of the men around him—and they were pretty much all men except for some of the caterers and a couple of sleek female PR operatives—wore suits and ties or formal military uniforms with rows of medals. Joe had noted the military vehicles in the parking lot when he'd come in—a few Humvees, limos with military plates, as well as expensive private cars with USMC or Army emblems on the windows and bumpers. Even a Jeep Wagoneer with De Oppresso Liber, the Special Forces motto, on a sticker on the back. He'd ditched yesterday's uniform himself, passing unnoticed now in a jacket and tie as he followed the crowd into the elevator and up to the mezzanine, pausing in front of the table where guests were checking in. Then his turn came:

"Good evening ma'am, I'm Yurami, first name Ken," he said with a slight country twang.

The woman smiled and searched the list.

"Here you are, Mister Kenneth Yurami," she said, writing his name on a tag.

"Mister Yurami? Only my mother calls me that," Joe said, with smile. "Just make it Ken please." He stuck the name to his chest and went through, getting a seltzer from the bar, then mingling with the crowd that circulated around Richards like a giant organism, or one of those huge trash islands that form in the ocean currents. Finally, he floated close enough to ask his question. That got Richards's attention.

"Excuse me? I'm afraid I don't know what you're talking about."

"Don't be modest. It doesn't suit you, Bob," Joe laughed. "I'm talking about your new product White Angel. You should be proud of it. It's killing more junkies than anything else on the street."

Now the men in suits and the men in medals were frowning and looking uncomfortable. Richards forced a smile, while his eyes searched for security. Jensen, seeing his master's discomfort, moved closer to Joe.

"I think our friend here has had too much to drink," Richards said. "I think he needs some air." He gestured toward a side door, which Jensen held open. "If you gentlemen will excuse us a moment?"

"Yeah why not?" Joe said. "Back in a moment, gentlemen. And waiter . . ." He handed his empty glass to a general. "Get me a refill meantime will you?"

He sauntered through the door after Richards and into the hall, where a security guard was waiting. Jensen shut the door and put a hand on Joe's left shoulder, while the guard grabbed his right. Richards turned to him with a snarl, hand clenched around his martini glass.

"I don't know who you are or what you think you know but look, Mister . . ." He narrowed his eyes at the name tag. "Ken Yurami?"

"Drop your pants and I'll consider it," Joe said.

The security guard snickered. Richards glared. Jensen pointed at the tag. "That's not a real name!"

"I'm Ken Yurami to you," Joe said. "Remember it. Because what I think I know is all about you and Zahir, about the dope coming in through the Wildwater returns, about your deal with the Russians . . ."

Richards laughed. "I have no idea what you're babbling about. Even if these things happened, they have nothing to do with me. There isn't a shred of evidence. Threaten me in front of witnesses, and you'll be the one to get arrested, Joe." He grinned. "That's right. I know just who you are. And those men in there? Generals, diplomats, millionaires. If I snap my fingers they will be happy to lock you up. If I don't have these boys right here snap your neck first. You think I broke the law? Son, as far as you're concerned, I am the law."

Joe smiled back at him. "You're right. But you've crossed into my world now, where the law can't protect you. Your money can't protect you. Not your powerful friends. Or your hired goons. I saw your speech the other day, about leaving war to the professionals. It's the same with crime. You should have taken your own advice. If you know my name, then you should know it would take less than ten seconds for me to cut your throat with that glass right now."

Richards laughed louder, and the two other men joined in, gripping Joe tighter. "Now that I'd like to see." He raised his glass to Joe in salute, then downed his martini.

"As you wish," Joe said, and dislocated Jensen's right arm. Jensen had made the mistake of grabbing Joe up on his shoulder, and though his grip was strong from working out, like a knuckle-buster handshake, his positioning had left him vulnerable. Joe was able to jump back and twist his left arm around Jensen's extended right, eluding the guard's looser grip. As Jensen stumbled forward, Joe forced the right arm up between the shoulder blades, till it left the socket with an audible pop. Jensen groaned. In a panic, the guard tried to grab at Joe while also reaching for his shoulder holster, but Jensen was stumbling between them and, with both hands busy, the guard had no defense when Joe hit him, hard and fast in the throat. He gasped for air, clutching his throat, and Joe quickly dipped into the holster and slid out his gun, then hammered him on the forehead with it. He dropped to his knees. Now Jensen was reaching for his own gun, awkwardly, with his left hand, and Joe grabbed that arm and bent it back the same way. "Sorry, but no guns. Someone could get hurt." Another pop. Jensen screamed.

Richards, who had been watching in shock, flinched as Joe moved toward him with the gun, swinging hard. He shut his eyes. The gun barrel cracked the glass in his hand, breaking it off at the stem, which Joe snatched in his left. Then he pushed Richards up against the elevators, with the edge of broken glass against his jugular.

"How did I do?" Joe asked. "Was that ten?" The guard was on his knees, still trying to breathe. Jensen seemed to be in shock, regarding his two arms, which dangled helplessly. Richards stared at him, frozen in stark terror. Joe could feel him tremble, like a rabbit in the jaws of the wolf. He pressed the elevator call button.

"I'm going to let you get back to your friends. But just remember. You're living in my world now. Not theirs. And there's no going back."

The elevator doors opened. Two uniformed waiters stood there with a serving cart. "Going down?" Joe asked.

They nodded. Joe dropped the broken glass and got on.

❖

Liam and Josh, who were dressed in waiters' uniforms they'd taken from Old Shenanigan's, waited for the elevator doors to shut before grinning at Joe.

"That seems to have gone well," Liam said.

Joe glanced up at the camera. Josh nodded. "We took care of it."

"It went just like we planned," Joe said, relaxing. "What about you and Yelena?"

"Ask her yourself," Josh said and tapped on the cart. The tablecloth parted and Yelena, who'd been curled beneath it, hopped out.

"How'd it go?" Joe asked, helping her to her feet.

"Fine," she said, brushing out her hair. "He'll never know I was there." She was wearing leggings and a sleeveless T-shirt. Now she pulled a clingy dress from her bag. Kicking off her sneakers, she stepped into the dress and pulled it up, then grabbed black heels from her bag and slid them on while Liam and Josh put her sneakers in the bag and stowed it back under the cart. As the doors opened on the lobby, she took Joe's arm and they walked out while Liam and Josh continued down to the basement.

Joe and Yelena smiled and laughed as they crossed the lobby, nodding at others who came and went. The PR woman was by the door, with a couple of guards.

"Goodbye," Joe said as he passed her.

"Goodbye, Mr. Yurami . . . I mean Ken . . ." she laughed. "And happy September 11th . . . I mean . . ." she looked disconcerted.

"I know what you mean," Joe told her. "God bless America."

Yelena waved happily and they went through the revolving door onto the street. Cash and Juno were waiting in a black limo with tinted windows. As soon as they shut the door, Cash pulled out, rolling half a block to where Liam and Josh had emerged from the parking garage. They'd abandoned the cart in the elevator, and now Josh had Yelena's bag over his shoulder. They hopped in and, as Cash drove away, Joe leaned to Juno. "Cameras?"

"I'm on it, Boss," he said, tapping away at his laptop. "I'm erasing the last hour to be on the safe side. Since before you all entered the building."

"Perfect," Joe said. "Now that Russian, Sergey. Tell me where his car is."

"Yeah," Juno said. "I've been checking like you asked. It was at the repair shop and detailing place all day. But now it's rolling again. Guess not even a Russian gangster can throw out a brand-new Benz just 'cause it gets a little shit on it."

"A lot of shit bro." Cash chuckled from behind the wheel.

"True that," Juno agreed. "Ol' Sergey had a real shit day."

Everyone laughed except for Joe, who glanced at Yelena.

"But not his worst," he said.

❖

Richards didn't move a muscle till the elevator doors closed. Then he rushed over to the others. The guard was curled in a ball, taking deep, measured breaths. Jensen was standing there stunned, arms hanging limp like a rag doll.

"Call for help," Richards ordered him, out of habit.

"I can't," Jensen said, staring down at his useless appendages. "My arms won't move. My walkie is in my pocket."

"Jesus Christ," Richards muttered, frowning in distaste as he reached into his underling's pants. He pressed a button. "This is Bob Richards. We need security in the South Hall on the mezzanine floor."

❖

Ten minutes later, he was back up in his penthouse office with Nikolai and the team of mercenaries. Trey, who'd had medic training, was seeing to Jensen. The other injured guard had been quietly taken to another room to recover.

"I'm going to have to pop his shoulders back in," Trey said to Richards. And to Jensen: "It's going to hurt. A lot."

Nikolai spoke: "Take him in the other room. All of you. We need to think."

"Yes, sir," Trey said, leading a reluctant-looking Jensen out, as Baxter and Dirk followed. As soon as the door shut, Nikolai asked, "Any news from Victoria?"

"She says she is on it," Richards told him. "And you know what that means."

"Good." Nikolai nodded. A blood-curdling scream came from beyond the wall.

"That's the first arm," he observed. He put a cigar in his lips and lit it. "And now," he said, "I take these soldiers of yours to Anton, and let them handle this Brody and his crew."

"And that girl, Noylaskya. She's your problem."

"In a sense, perhaps," Nikolai reflected. "After all, I created her." He waved his cigar. "And I will destroy her. She's just a tool after all. If she fails you, throw her out."

Another wrenching scream came from the other room.

"Speaking of which," he added. "Sounds like your tool is just about repaired."

Richards nodded, then glanced at his watch. "And I better get back to that party. Keep me posted." But he hesitated before leaving, suddenly feeling a wave of insecurity, remembering the pressure of the jagged glass against his throat, the totally dead, flat look in Brody's eyes. Until Brody was dead, was he safe anywhere, even here? As if to reassure himself, he looked around his office. Everything appeared to be in order.

36

Donna saw Toomey—Rick—making his way toward her in the crowd. She smiled. She wasn't sure what to make of him. In some ways of course her mom was right, he was her type of man—but seeing him here in his VFW hat, and the whole thing with the parking—it all reeked of a certain kind of arrogance and entitlement that she got more than enough of on the job, where dick-swinging was a major pastime, and the egos behind it were as fragile and volatile as an angry toddler's. Then again, at least he'd earned the right to swing his a little if he wanted.

"Hey, Rick," she said, smiling. "Glad you made it back. Sorry if walking in the crowd is a pain."

He shrugged and looked down at his cane as if he was surprised to see it. "You know, on a day like today, I carry this bullet fragment with more pride than any medal, because I got it defending America, and avenging 9/11."

"That's true," she said. "We all owe you a debt of gratitude."

"Not necessary," he said, with a shrug. "But a little respect would be nice." He sidled up closer. "You understand what I'm talking about, don't you? You've chosen a life of service too. You wear that badge. Live by a code. Whether or not others honor it."

"I like to think so."

"Donna, let me ask you, one warrior to another. Is there something in your life you love so much you'd do anything to save it, no matter the sacrifice?"

"Sure . . ." Donna said. "My daughter."

He smiled. "Of course. Your mother mentioned her." He took his hat off, looked around, and then put it back on. "Well that's exactly how I feel about America. Like a protective parent."

"Huh . . ." Donna said. "Well I guess everyone here feels that way."

"Do they? I don't think so. I think a lot of them need a reminder. A wake-up call. Before it's too late."

Too late for what? she was about to ask, definitely getting a bad vibe now, but also, as always, another part of her was working, eyes and ears scanning, and she heard a voice, a cop, saying, "Go right ahead, Deputy Marshal Logan," and she thought, *Oh, Blaze is here*, and turned and saw, coming through the crowd, a curvy blonde with a Yankees cap and dark glasses and a blue blazer, white shirt, and khakis who looked sort of familiar, and kind of like a Fed, but was certainly not Blaze Logan, despite holding up a Federal ID and walking with her other hand lightly on her side-holstered gun.

And just as it was clicking in Donna's head and she was remembering, *That's the redhead from last night*, she also saw her draw the gun, and extend her arm, like in slow motion, and point it right at, of all people, Rick Toomey.

"Gun!" she yelled as, instinctively, she threw herself on him and knocked him to the ground, and something seared across her back, like a burning ember, and the sound of a gunshot echoed in her ears. And then she didn't have time to think because total chaos broke out.

❖

Vicky was annoyed. With herself mostly but also with that Fed, Zamora, who she knew was Powell's ex and who was definitely on her to-do list now, though not yet at the top.

In the seconds after the shot went off, and she missed, her bullet nicking Zamora and then flattening into the ground, panic broke out around Vicky, with people yelling and pushing in every direction. She joined right in, pushing her way through the crowd, waving her badge, yelling "Federal Marshal!" and even holding the gun in the air, which scared the punters shitless. And witless. They turned and fled or ducked, as cops and Feds ran toward her and she waved them on, pointing toward the vortex of the disturbance. But the crowd was so big and so loud that within a few minutes she had crossed into another area where people had no idea anything was wrong, and she pocketed her weapon as she found a line of women waiting for a bathroom.

"Security check, step aside," she announced, brandishing the badge and brushing past the line. Quite useful really, these things, she thought, as she entered the first open stall, where she stuffed her hat and wig in the toilet, then removed her shirt and blazer, revealing a very tight T-shirt that said "Never Forget" on the front, with an image of the towers, and on the back, over a US flag, read "These colors don't run." Lastly she slid down her pants, stepping out of them to reveal a pair of cutoff shorts that barely covered her bum.

"That one's clogged," she said to the next woman in line as she opened the door to the stall, then stuffed her bundled clothing, along with the gun and badge, into the trash.

"I feel dizzy," she giggled in a high, Southern accent, weaving through the crowd, bumping off of men, who didn't mind, and then stumbling into a cop. "Oops! Sorry officer! I just feel so ditzy. I mean dizzy!"

He smiled and put a hand on her back. "No problem miss, let's get you some air," he said, and led her out to freedom.

37

"SURE YOU DON'T WANT us to come in with you?" Josh asked. He was turned around, talking to Joe and Yelena in back, while Liam drove. They were downtown, near Wall Street, but the quiet, dark block, a narrow gorge cut into the towering buildings of old stone that seemed to almost touch above them, was a world away from the noise and crowds that were fading as things wound down at the 9/11 memorial, right across the narrow island. They pulled up behind Cash and Juno, who had been tracking Sergey's black Benz, which was parked down the block.

"That's okay," Joe said. "It looks less suspicious if we just go in together. You wait out here and catch any rats who try to flee." To Yelena he said, "Ready?"

"Of course." She held up a bikini.

"Brilliant," Liam said, and to Joe. "Where's yours?"

He frowned at Yelena who was stuffing hers back into her tote bag. "I thought they gave you something. You didn't tell me . . ."

She shrugged and opened the door. "You better hope. Otherwise you will be fighting one handed."

He got out after her and shut the door, and they walked down the street, pausing by Cash and Juno as they passed.

"Sergey went in about an hour ago. And it's been a cast reunion since then."

"Anton?" Joe asked.

"Yup and the soldier boys we met in Jersey. I'm sure they'll be happy to see y'all." He frowned. "Though I know I'd feel safer if you two had guns."

"No place to hide it," Joe said. "Everybody has to strip in the locker rooms. We'd never get through to the baths." Both had also left their phones, wallets, and keys in the car.

Cash leaned across from behind the wheel. "This *banya* place. Is it like the massage joints Uncle Chen runs? A rub and tug?"

"Only if your idea of a happy ending is a big Russian dude beating you with birch branches and cracking your neck."

Cash shrugged. "To each his own."

"It's a *shvitz*," Yelena told him. "More like the Korean spa in Queens."

"Gotcha," Cash said. "Well maybe I will try it sometime. If it's still standing after tonight."

❖

"You do the talking," Joe whispered to Yelena as they walked down the steps. A young woman, blondly plump and rosy-cheeked, looked up from her phone. Yelena greeted her in Russian, and Joe paid cash for two. After a bit more back and forth, she handed over a brand-new pair of men's swim trunks, large, baggy, and decorated with a beach scene in tropical colors—sand, sea, palm, birds. Joe paid another twenty for it and she cut off the tags. Then they were given keys and sent to separate locker rooms. They changed quickly and met in the hall, Yelena emerging in her stylish black bikini and holding two rolled white towels, one of which she handed to Joe. He was in his new trunks.

"You look great," he told her.

"Beauty and terror?" She smiled and gave a little spin, then gestured for him to turn as well. He raised his hands as if under arrest and turned.

"Straight to terror?" he asked.

She laughed. "No, I like these for you. The parrot makes your ass look good."

"Thanks," Joe said, and opened the inner door for her.

They were in the banya, the Russian bathhouse, one of the oldest in the city. The signs on the wall were in Russian, Hebrew, Yiddish, and misspelled English. An underground warren, its hallways connected a series of chambers, including a restaurant, saunas, a steam room, a cold plunge, massage rooms, and, down a floor below, a large swimming pool and Jacuzzi. The overall decor was fake Roman grotto—white painted columns, patterned tiles, plaster statues of naked cherubs and demure maidens, and murals depicting pastoral antiquity—hills, sea, ruins—not a bad job on the landscapes, but the people looked like they'd been done by kids. Everything was warm, wet, dank—moisture clung to every surface and water dripped like you were in a cave. You *were* in a cave—deep in the bowels of the city, the old saunas built into the foundation of the building.

Yelena led Joe through the restaurant where wet customers wrapped in towels ate blintzes and drank borscht. A few ogled her as they passed, but no one seemed concerned, and she turned down the hall toward the Russian-style sauna. Two big, hairy men sat on a bench outside, one in baggy trunks and a heavy gold cross, the other with a wet towel around his shoulders and another around his waist. Yelena set their rolled towels on the bench and Joe reached for the door.

"*Sozhaleyu. Zakryto,*" the one with the gold chain said, standing to block Joe's way. "Broken," he added in English, though steam was visible through the small window in the door. Meanwhile the sitting man winked appreciatively at Yelena, who smiled back.

Joe nodded, humbly, and turned to go, then, spinning back for momentum, slammed his right fist into gold-chain's solar plexus, knocking the wind out of him. He gasped, leaning forward, and Joe stepped aside, grabbing his arm and tripping him in one motion. The big man slid smoothly on the wet tile and went down, knocking his head hard on the bench. Yelena, meanwhile, had moved fast, yanking the wet towel from around the sitting, leering man's neck and whipping it across his eyes. He cursed and reached for her blindly. She eluded him easily, kicking his ankle out from under him and, as he stumbled to his knees, she looped the wet towel around his throat, pulling it tight. Grunting,

he struggled, but she had her foot on his back now and gripped hard. After a few seconds, he passed out, and she let him drop. She grabbed her rolled towel and handed Joe his. He opened the door to the sauna.

The room was like the inside of a brick pizza oven, or a deep inner VIP chamber of Hades. Raw bedrock, granite blackened with age formed one whole wall, the others were stone and brick. Staggered rows of wooden benches ran along three sides, and, in the corner, an iron furnace wheezed and growled, radiating waves of stunning heat, a red heart flaming behind the window in the furnace door. A wooden bucket with a ladle sat under a dripping faucet. Anton was laid out like a lox in a smokehouse, face-down on the top bench, close to the ceiling, while a minion scrubbed him down with soapy water. Sergey sprawled on the other top bench, and man-spread across the lower shelves, legs wide, arms out, were the three mercs, Trey, Dirk, and Baxter, slicked in sweat.

The intense heat seemed to slow everything down, vision blurred, time melted, and it took a second for the men to react to the two new bodies in the room. First they all looked at Yelena, grinning like wolves. Then Trey looked at Joe.

"Hey." He opened his eyes wider. "You killed Tony!"

Joe frowned, trying to remember. He looked to Yelena. "Who's Tony?"

She shrugged, then, before anyone else could move, she kicked Dirk in the chin, as Joe snatched up the wooden bucket and whacked it across Baxter's head. Now everyone moved. Trey leapt up in a rage and came at Joe, swinging, while Sergey, thinking a bit further ahead, reached into a robe that was hanging on the wall and drew a switchblade, which he clicked open. Dirk bounced back up and dove for Yelena's legs while the big boy who'd been sluicing down Anton turned and swung his bucket at her head.

As Joe turned to block Sergey's knife with his towel, Trey landed a hard right to his head, knocking him off center, then came up with a roundhouse that caught his jaw. As he spun, Joe kicked back, catching Trey behind the ankle, and elbowing him hard in the chest so that he slid on the wet floor, landing with a hard thud. He stopped Sergey's blade

with his towel, which was slashed and, stepping back, drew a combat knife, a long, evil blade that had been rolled inside the towel. He faced both men, winding the towel around his arm for defense.

Yelena, meanwhile, having deflected the bucket, was twisting free of Dirk's grip while striking him hard across the ear with a cupped palm, rupturing his eardrum. By now, however, the big masseur was on her, leaping down from the upper bench. She pivoted into his body as he landed on her and both went flying back against the stone wall. Then, abruptly, he stopped, his broad body pressed against hers, gasping as his eyes went wide in surprise and pain. She stared right back into them, now holding him tight, as though in a dance she was leading. She let go and he slid away, torso covered in blood. Blood dripped from the combat knife she'd had sheathed in her own towel. He dropped to the floor and the red ran into the wooden slats and away.

By then, however, Dirk was back on his feet and Anton was in motion. Cursing in Russian, Anton lifted the squeeze bottle of soap and squirted it in Yelena's eyes. Blinded, she tried to slash out at Dirk but he slammed her hard and she skidded back, hissing like a scalded cat when her shoulder fell against the furnace door.

Joe saw this, but was too penned in to help, fending off Sergey's blade with his towel-wrapped arm and slashing and kicking at Trey, who was closing in. Then Baxter, who'd been stunned on the floor, reached under a bench and drew a .32, a flat automatic that he aimed up at Joe. Joe jumped. The bullet went under him and ricocheted off the stone wall, echoing in the small chamber. As he leapt over Baxter, who was crouching, Joe's left foot connected with Trey's chin, knocking him off balance on the soapy floor. He fell back. Sergey was lifting his arm high for a downward stab with his blade, and as Joe passed, he slashed deep across Sergey's wrist, severing the arteries and tendon. The switchblade clattered to the floor.

Gritting her teeth, Yelena caught the handle of the furnace and kept from falling as the door swung back, then shoved her towel into the open mouth. It caught immediately. As Dirk came at her, she flung the burning

towel onto his face and he stumbled back, panicked by the flames. Anton, seizing the moment, ran from the sauna, leaving the door open, yelling in Russian for help.

Now Joe, landing on the upper bench, spun around, kicking Baxter in the back of head, sending him sprawling, and stuffed the bucket down on Trey's head just as he regained his feet. He hurled his blade, which arced through the humid air and struck deep into Sergey's chest. Launching himself, Joe jumped onto Trey and knocked him forward, into the open door of the sauna. Sergey lay fallen against the furnace now, his eyes blank, his body steaming against the hot iron, but he felt nothing. He would never feel anything again. Joe pulled his knife free and grabbed Yelena, giving Baxter another hard kick in the kidneys.

"Come on." They pushed into the hall as Trey rolled under their feet. The two goons were gone, fleeing or maybe fetching weapons. There was no sign of Anton. "How's the burn?" Joe asked as they hurried down the hall. Now he heard yelling from upstairs.

"Hot," Yelena admitted.

"Maybe this will help," Joe said, and they jumped into the cold plunge. A small, chest-high pool full of frigid water, it was meant to shock the system after the hot rooms and it worked, dulling Yelena's burn slightly. Then, as the two goons returned and Trey came down the hall, they ducked low in the water, up against the wall of the pool where they hoped the extended concrete rim would hide them from view.

"You see where they went?" Trey asked the goons. Baxter and Dirk were following behind him from the sauna. The goons shook their heads. One now had a gun, the other a bat.

"Okay," Trey said. "Let's check everything. Spread out."

Joe and Yelena remained motionless, careful not to splash, heads still under the rim of the pool, breathing slow with their bodies still submerged in the water. It was very cold. Joe could feel his fingers and toes going numb. Finally, the men moved.

"Now," Yelena whispered, and they crawled up onto the floor. They ducked into the closest door, the steam room. Joe's towel was shredded

from Sergey's blade and soaked from the cold water. He tore it into strips and tied them around Yelena's arm while she kept an eye on the glass door. They were in a tiled box with benches and vents on the floor for steam. Joe climbed to the thermostat and stuffed the remains of his wet, ragged towel around it. The cold water triggered the mechanism and the room began to fill with thick clouds of hissing steam. Soon he could barely see his own hand in front of his face. Yelena was invisible beside him. Then the door opened.

❖

When Anton made it out onto the street, he couldn't believe his luck. He'd fled crazily through the banya, sending his men back to fight, and huffing up the stairs. He even had time to grab his robe, which contained his wallet and keys. He pulled it on now as he hit the sidewalk, tasting the fresh (or at least city-scented) air, seeing the night sky (or at least the city's lamplit ceiling), feeling the flow of normal life around him, and he realized, putting a hand in a pocket, even his cigarettes were there. He was alive and dying for a smoke. That's when a car door opened, blocking his path.

"Hey there, Anton, you need a ride?" It was Liam, one of the Madigan brothers, the pretty one with the smart mouth. "You'll get in trouble walking the streets in your dressing gown."

Now the other door was opening, and it was Josh, the Israeli, a tough-looking Sephardic who worked for Rebbe Stone. He was holding a gun. "You look tired," he said. "Puffing like you're going to have a heart attack. Better ride with us."

Anton stopped. Liam came up beside him. "It's the smoking," he told Josh. "I'm telling you. It's a killer, right Anton?"

Anton held his arms up. "Money," he said. "Lots of it. And the dope business too. I can tell you all about it."

"Excellent," Liam said. "We can't wait to hear. But we have to talk on the way. We're late."

"Late?" Anton asked, feeling the hope drain from his body.

"It's a surprise party," Josh told him. "And you're the guest of honor. All your friends are waiting."

❖

Joe and Yelena remained completely still, holding their breath. The fogged-over glass door to the steam room opened and enough light streamed in from behind for them to see it was the two goons from the hall, armed with a pistol and a bat. Then the door swung shut and the steam swallowed them. The men looked around, peering into the thick fog, failing to see the ghosts just in front of them.

"Let's go," one said. "I'm dying in here." They turned to go. Simultaneously, Joe and Yelena moved. They crept silently forward, emerging from the clouds. As the thug with the bat glanced right, he saw Yelena's blade, appearing as if from nowhere, slice across his friend's throat, releasing a ribbon of blood. He started, but it was too late. Joe's arm was snaking out around his own neck and Joe's blade found his throat too, cutting the jugular. He staggered forward, blood spraying, and fell. Then a bullet shattered the glass door.

Joe jumped back as the bullet cut through the clouds of steam and cracked the tile wall. Yelena dropped to the floor and felt for the goon's fallen gun. As the gunman approached, stepping into the doorframe, Joe saw it was Baxter and tossed the bat. That distracted him long enough for Yelena to raise the gun and fire, chasing him back. Yelena went into the hall after him, firing again as he took cover around a corner. A statue of Cupid had been shattered; now headless, it looked more like a real ruin than the cheap plaster copy it was.

"This way," she called back at Joe, who came after her, crossing the glass that now covered the steam room floor from the broken door. He felt it cutting into his feet, but there was no time for that now. Crouching low, he followed Yelena, who fired another shot to keep Baxter back and led Joe down the hall into the next room.

These were the massage booths. A long, low-ceilinged room, dimly lit and divided by curtains hung on crisscrossing cords, with a massage table in each nook. Yelena and Joe moved through quickly and quietly, brushing the curtains aside, she with the gun poised in one hand and the knife in the other, he with his knife hand cocked back and ready. Then, in a corner, there he was: Nikolai, laid out on a table, his back red and scored, while a big bald Russian in a tiny speedo worked over him with a leafy birch branch. He paused when he saw them, holding the branch aloft.

"You—back," Yelena said. He raised his hands and stepped back. Nikolai rolled over, squinting his eyes. "And you, pig," she told him, "wake up. I want you to see the bullet coming."

Nikolai blinked at her. "Ah," he said. "Yelena. I was hoping we'd meet."

Just then, from the corner of his eye, Joe saw the shape of Baxter's gun pushing against the curtain to his left. He grabbed the muzzle, forcing it aside as it fired, the bullet tearing through the curtain, whizzing past, and tearing the curtain beyond, leaving two smoking burn holes in the fabric. During that moment's distraction, the big Russian tossed the branch at Yelena and snatched up a knife. As he raised his arm to throw it, Yelena fired: the first bullet went through his knife hand, and the next two went through his heart. Then her gun clicked. Empty. She turned to the empty table and the rustling curtains. Nikolai was gone.

"Go," Joe said as he wrestled Baxter through the curtain, keeping him wrapped tight. His pistol went off twice more, burning more holes in the curtain. Then he heard Baxter's gun also hit an empty chamber. Holding Baxter in a hug, Joe reached high and brought his knife down in a sweeping arc, stabbing through the curtain. He felt him slump, as blood began to seep through the fabric, and let him drop.

Joe went after Yelena, out through the back of the room to the hallway, but stopped when he saw Dirk and Trey go by, calling to each other, "She went down here." He waited for them to pass and then followed, down the stone steps. He could see that he was leaving bloody footprints, but it didn't matter: he was the pursuer now, not the pursued. He didn't need to hide.

❖

Yelena entered the pool room. This was a large space, farther underground, and it felt cool and quiet, as if further from the city. A swimming pool filled its center like a blue window, sending reflected ripples across the ceiling, also painted blue. Beside it was a big Jacuzzi, a tiled circle in which the water churned and foamed. There was a bar, a mural along the long wall depicting a waterfall tumbling from forested cliffs into an ocean where a ship sailed to an island with a castle, where a poorly painted king and queen stood on a tower waving, their faces and hands pink smudges. There were tables and chairs and lounges, all empty.

From behind the bar came Nikolai, hefting a machete. He was wearing trunks and a gold cross but had no tattoos; he was not a criminal. He smiled as she came around the pool to face him, holding her blade.

"Do your American friends know what your tattoos mean, Lenochka? Or do these dumb hipsters just think it's cool? A fashion trend like theirs? You don't have to even hide them here in New York."

"I never hide them," she answered, moving closer.

"And what about your boy, Joe? Does he know that they mark you as trash? A whore and a thief? Scum born to scum in a sewer? The child of a junkie whore and God knows who? Some drunk who couldn't afford better."

Yelena smiled. "He knows. That's why he likes me." She waved the blade point at him. "But you don't need any tattoos do you? The mark of the pig is right there on your face for all to see. Now I'm going to carve it into your hide."

Nikolai laughed. "I'm sure you'd love to try." He shrugged. "But are you good enough? Remember, I taught you everything you know."

Now Yelena laughed. "You taught me to dress and fix my hair. To be polite. To eat caviar and to lie in five languages. But to fight? I was born into that, like you said. I inherit it from my whore mother. And now I'm going to kill you in her name. Whatever it was."

And she charged toward him.

When Joe came into the pool room, he saw Trey and Dirk, backs turned, in silence. Dirk's skull was buzzed close; Trey's long ponytail hung down. They were watching Yelena and Nikolai, across the pool, dueling. Well matched, they thrust and parried, dodged and darted, as tightly-focused and oblivious to their audience as any pair of champion dancers. Joe came up fast and kicked Trey, sending him into the Jacuzzi. Then, before Dirk could react, he drove his knife between his shoulder blades. Trey was fast, though, and strong, and he came up quick, grabbing Joe by the ankle. Joe lost his balance and fell into the whirlpool with Trey, his knife still in Dirk's back as he too plunged into the churning water, dyeing it red as he bled out.

When Joe felt his chin hit the bottom of the shallow pool, banging it hard, he pushed out with his arms, trying to propel himself back up. But he was too far under, and as Trey locked his grip on his legs, standing over him and forcing his head beneath the water, he had no choice but to struggle like a snake, arching his back, fighting to get his head up and breathe. He broke the surface just long enough to glimpse Yelena and Nikolai, clutched together now, each holding the other's knife arm, each raising a blade, topple together into the pool. Then he was under again, with the whirlpool swirling around him and the massage jet pummeling his face. Trey had the leverage, his own legs planted so that he was standing in the water, clenching Joe's legs with all his considerable upper body strength. Joe struggled and kicked, his head remained below the surface, and he knew it was only a matter of time. A couple minutes. The length of a breath.

Instead of fighting to rise up, toward the air, Joe went down, thrusting himself deeper into the water. Trey kept his grip, his clench was tight around Joe's ankles, but Joe managed to reach Dirk's body, to grasp his dead hand and pull it closer. As his vision clouded and he felt himself about to pass out, or just as bad, breathe in a lungful of water, Joe drew the knife from Dirk's back and then curled lower,

swimming between Trey's legs. He sawed across both his ankles, severing the tendons.

Trey let go. As his legs gave out, he dropped Joe and Joe somersaulted away. His feet touched bottom and he stood, gasping for air. Trey collapsed, sitting in the water as his useless legs folded, and Joe grabbed his right hand and cut the cord in his wrist too, squirting more blood into the already crimson whirlpool, which now seemed to boil like a cauldron. Limping on his bloody feet and still catching his breath, Joe hobbled up the steps and felt Trey grab him. His one good hand, his left, still with some strength in it, was holding Joe's ankle. Joe looked down to see Trey, grunting with effort, trying to come after him. A look of confusion came over him as he realized his body would no longer obey. Joe had cut his strings, severing the tendons in both feet and one hand. He sprawled back onto the lip of the Jacuzzi like a broken marionette, staring up at Joe. He nodded. Joe nodded back. Then he shut his eyes, in surrender, as Joe leaned over and sank the blade into his heart.

That was when Joe realized: Yelena was nowhere in sight. She and Nikolai were both gone. He stood and saw that the pool was rippling, stirred from below, and that a cloud of red was blooming across the blue skin. He held his breath. Then the surface broke and a body floated up. It was Nikolai with a knife in his back. A second later, Yelena emerged, rising from the water like a siren, or a nightmare, one of those avenging furies who haunt men's dreams. She came up the steps, back straight, head up, eyes forward, a newborn goddess, blood spreading in her wake.

PART V

38

"Holy shit," Juno said, when he saw Yelena and Joe come limping out of the bathhouse. Cash put the car in gear, honking once lightly to let them know he was there. Joe was in ridiculous clown-like bath trunks, like something a retired Jimmy Buffet fan would wear, and had what looked like bloody rags tied around his feet. Yelena was wrapped in a robe, and so seemed slightly less conspicuous, until she was close enough for Juno to realize she was more or less covered in blood.

Cash braked in front of them and Juno rushed to open the back door. "Damn, Yelena . . ." he said.

"Don't worry, Juno. It's not my blood."

"Hospital," Joe said. "Make a left on the next street."

Cash looked in the rearview as he hit the gas. "What's wrong? Who's hurt?"

"She is," Joe said. "A burn. She needs first aid fast."

"So do you," she said. "Your feet."

"She's got a point," Juno said. "You look like you been in Valley Forge with George Washington. I mean from the knees down. Knees up you look cool."

"I've got glass in my feet. It hurts like hell, but it can wait. And I can pick it out myself. That burn is for real and needs professional attention. Quickly."

Yelena sighed and rolled her eyes. "Okay Dr. Joe. If you say so."

"Thank you," Joe said, and smiled. Yelena smiled too. In the rearview, Cash noticed that she laid her hand over his.

"ER's coming up on the right," he said he drove down the narrow street. "You planning to escort her in or what?"

Joe looked down at his outfit. Juno was right, he looked like a mess. They'd throw a net on him. "Hey what size shoes do you guys wear?"

❖

It was tough but Joe managed not to limp. He was in his shorts, Cash's clean white T-shirt, and Juno's very expensive new sneakers, with his hair smoothed back. He didn't look much worse than a lot of the tourists who'd wandered into the ER. With one arm around Yelena, he went up to the counter and called to a woman in scrubs.

"Excuse me, please, you've got to help her."

Distracted, the woman regarded them over her glasses as she looked up from her desk. "Now calm down sir, I . . . oh my God." She goggled at Yelena, then reached and pressed a button. "Assistance! Now," she called into an intercom. Her eyes ranged over Yelena. "Miss, where is the bleeding coming from?"

"I think that stopped," Joe said. "But she's been burned." He pulled down the robe and revealed the raw and suppurating burn on her shoulder. He squeezed Yelena, who responded by beginning to wail loudly. "She's hysterical," he added. "It's the pain."

Two medics rushed over and took gentle hold of Yelena. The nurse turned to Joe, hand on keyboard. "What's her name sir? Is she your wife? Girlfriend?"

"No. I don't know her. I don't even think she speaks English. There was an accident at the spa. So I just brought her in."

"At the spa?"

Meanwhile the medics eased Yelena into a wheelchair, talking to her the whole time. She cried and yelled at them in Russian.

"Calm down, we're here to help you. What's your name?"

"Do you have ID? Do you have insurance?"

The nurse who was talking to Joe persisted, as Yelena was wheeled away. "I'm still going to need some info from you sir, for the file."

"Sure," Joe said, rubbing his forehead. "But can I get some water first? I feel a little faint myself. This was really scary."

"Right away," the nurse said, anxious not to have another intake. "Why don't you have a seat?"

She fetched a paper cup of water and came back, searching the seating area, but he was gone.

❖

When Victoria got to the banya and saw a young woman fleeing, followed by some other customers, a few still in their bathing suits, she realized she was late to the dance. And when she spotted first one and then two cars, each with two men in it, sitting and watching, she decided to stay and watch herself, moving to a discreet spot at the corner. And when Anton, the Russian mob boss, came running out, looking like he'd just seen a ghost, and the two men in the front car grabbed him up, she grinned. It looked like someone else besides her was on cleanup duty for a change. She was not surprised to see that it was Joe and Yelena who came out shortly after and got in the other car, looking ragged and bloody. And when no one else chased after them, she knew what that meant too: everyone else was dead.

Impressed, she watched as the car passed by, then followed after it. It was a tight space down here, at the bottom of the island, and the crowded ER was just a few short blocks away. So she waited for Joe and Yelena to enter, and the others to drive off, and then wandered in, picked up a discarded newspaper, and sat down with everyone else to wait. She wanted to see what happened next.

❖

By the time Donna could ask where Toomey was, he was gone. In the first minutes after the gunshot, while chaos reigned, they had tried to lock down the area, but the crowd was too big and the perimeter too wide, to search everything and everyone for one suspect. Plus, the description of the suspect—white, blonde, twenties—and the fact that she had fired just one shot at a tourist visiting the site, made it feel like some personal drama or random insanity, not a serious, organized terror attack. They put out an APB and had all the cops at all the checkpoints watching, but the rest of the event was allowed to go on. While a medic bandaged her wound—it was a mere grazing—Donna called Blaze, who was mortified and pissed but alive and well except for a brutal hangover. She went on the hunt for the shooter herself, walking the perimeter, searching the crowd, squatting in the van with the facial recognition boys. Nothing. Then Tom found her and made her sit still while she was extensively debriefed, and re-debriefed, and filled out a report. She said she wanted to question Toomey, and Tom told her that he'd given a statement and gone home.

Well, all she had to do was get on the laptop and dig a little for that statement of his to start melting away: Yes, Toomey was a vet, like he said, and he was in the Special Forces. But he was never wounded, as far as she could see. And his last known employment was indeed as a "consultant." For Wildwater. She bolted down a dinner of takeout beans and rice and plantains and café con leche from the Cuban place that was about to close—she hadn't eaten all day—and then she called Fusco.

"Hey," he said. "Where the hell you been? You're missing everything."

"I've been getting shot at and saving America, asshole," she said, realizing that she was actually happy to hear his voice. "What about you?"

"Shot at?" Fusco asked, sounding genuinely concerned. "By who?"

"By a Wildwater employee as it happens. What do you think of that?"

"I think you better get your ass down here to the bathhouse. The one by the Stock Exchange."

"Why?"

"Because almost everybody else who works for Wildwater is floating around here dead. We're still fishing them out."

❖

So she walked over. Tom had ordered her to get her wound looked at. It was nothing, but he wanted everything covered, so she said she'd go to the ER, then put an FBI windbreaker on over her torn shirt and walked to the bathhouse address, which was practically on the way. It wasn't hard to find: NYPD was out in force, with the block taped off and the whole circus set up. She waved her badge and a tech handed her booties and a zip up suit. Then on the way downstairs, she saw Parks, who was wearing a suit too, plus a hairnet and rubber boots.

"What is there—kryptonite down there?" Donna asked him.

"You're gonna need it, believe me," he said. "One stiff's ponytail got caught in a drain and the whole place backed up with bloody water. It's like a horror movie."

Donna put on the gear and followed him, then whistled when she saw the bodies laid out on tarps. The steam and heat were turned off and everything was lit, but there was still blood everywhere, on the floors and walls. "Yeah, we're up to seven dead."

"Eight," Fusco said as he came up from the pool room. He looked like a cartoon character, big and round in his baby blue hazmat suit, with his red, round face in the hairnet. It was hard not to smile. "We drained the pool and, guess what, found a Russian spy."

"A spy?"

"An intelligence officer. Nikolai something. Attaché for business affairs or whatever. But apparently he's with their CIA."

"I see," she said, thinking about Mike's impromptu visit yesterday.

"But most of the Russians are more familiar. Remember Sergey, who you lost at the airport?"

"Rings a bell," Donna said, through gritted teeth.

"Well the good news is you can stop looking. Someone stabbed him to death in the sauna."

"Mostly all knife wounds," Parks said. "I guess this is a tough place to sneak in a gun."

"And extra clips," Donna added. "I mean if you're taking on an army."

"And speaking of army, here's the other good news. The three dead guys who aren't Russian? They're all mercenaries."

"Mercenaries? Why is that good news?"

Parks grinned at her. "Because all three were contractors, supposedly overseas, working for the Wildwater Corporation."

"Really?" Donna couldn't help but smile big now too. "So I was right."

"It makes sense," Fusco said. "They landed here and tried to take over the dope trade."

"And now they got hit back," Donna said. "Hard."

Fusco nodded. "They should have learned their lesson in Afghanistan."

"But hit by who?" Parks wondered aloud. "And how many? I mean it had to be like an assault team right? And with knives. I mean who the hell knows how to cause all this mayhem with just a knife?"

He looked from Fusco to Donna, but now they both just looked at the floor, and shrugged.

❖

Donna called Tom to check in and let him know about the new developments, ask about getting some more FBI down there, maybe Janet to help with forensics.

"What bathhouse? I thought you were at the hospital."

"I was on my way, sir, but this is an important piece of the case . . ."

"I understand, but if you get an infection and they amputate your arms or something, it's going to fuck up my whole week, so get your ass to the ER and then report on this tomorrow."

"Yes, sir," she said, and told Fusco.

He shrugged. "Take your time. This party is going to go all night."

She walked down to the ER, which was madness like always, a hundred other dramas playing out, less bizarre than hers maybe but just as important to those caught up in them. She showed her badge to the woman behind the counter, hoping to get bumped ahead in line.

"You here for the Russian girl?" she asked.

"Russian girl?" Donna asked, feeling a tingle go up her spine. "What Russian girl?"

"I don't know her name, she doesn't speak English so I hope you speak Russian. I mean I guess it's Russian. But she came in with a bad burn and all covered in somebody else's blood. So we called the police, but they never came so I figured you're them. Except, like I said when I called it in, you got to speak Russian."

"What room is she in?"

The nurse gave her the number and pointed and Donna went down the hall, but when she pushed the door open and entered there was no Russian girl and no patient in the bed at all. The only person there, sitting in a chair in a nice gray suit, was Gio Caprisi.

When Victoria saw Donna her first impulse was to kill her. After all, she'd ruined her play, so beautifully planned and staged, and caused her a fair bit of trouble. It was extremely annoying, and as with anything annoying, a bug let's say, your first impulse is to crush it. But then again, she reasoned, this Donna was only doing her job, and doing it bloody well actually, better than most of these clods, and she felt she should really be more supportive of a fellow woman excelling in such a male-dominated field. It really was a boy's club still, and what with the Russian, Noylaskya, this was turning into a real female empowerment kind of moment. So, good for her. Besides, Victoria knew that impulse control was one of her issues, and that part of what made her a professional was focus—in this case, focus on her primary targets. Who were still out there. So when Agent Donna spoke to the nurse and then rushed off down the hall, no doubt looking for Yelena, whom she was not going to find, Victoria silently wished them both well. And she left.

39

"GOOD EVENING AGENT ZAMORA," Gio said, with a big smile, standing politely. "Lovely to see you again."

"Mr. Caprisi," Donna said, taken aback. "What brings you here? Visiting a sick Russian friend maybe? Or business associate?"

Gio shook his head, still smiling. "I don't think I have any Russian associates."

"Not anymore maybe. There's a bunch of dead ones floating around in the bathhouse."

Gio shrugged it off. "My family business is ices and gelato, as you know. Actually, we had three trucks out here today. All spotless. Not even a dead fly floating in a melted sundae, I promise."

"I'm impressed you didn't get a spot on your suit either," Donna noted.

"Well I mostly supervise these days."

"Then why are you here? Trouble in the ice cream world? A tummy ache? Brain freeze?"

"What do you think? I'm looking for you. It's urgent. I called my office line and they referred me to another agent, Newton I believe. And he sent me here. I have a tip."

"About?"

"A guy named Robert Richards. Maybe you've heard of him. He's the CEO of a company called Wildwater."

Donna breathed in sharply, but she kept her poker face. "I've heard of him. What's he got to do with you?"

"Me?" Gio shrugged lightly. "Nothing. As far I know, they don't sell ice cream. But I've been told, by reliable sources, that if you search his office, particularly the safe, you will find the evidence you need to prove he's been selling heroin and using it to fund a terror cell. I believe that's your business, Agent Zamora?"

She stood and leaned over him. "Who told you this?"

"Sorry. I don't remember."

She raised her hand and was about to put a finger in his face, something that even an FBI agent would be wise to think twice about, then thought twice and lowered her hand. "Enough games," she said, calmly. "I can take you in as a material witness."

He shook his head, sighing heavily. "Agent Zamora, don't you even read your own website? I did, when I checked for your phone number. You know what it said? Anonymous tip line. No questions asked." Noticing the mirror on the wall, he shot his cuffs and buttoned his jacket. "I'm going to go now. I had a long day. And I suggest you get some rest too. You have a big worm to catch. Get there early."

Then, with a smile and nod, he left. Donna kept the frown on her face until he was out of sight, then pumped her fist once and broke into a grin as she called Andy. "Get started on a warrant. We're going into Wildwater tomorrow. Early. Bob Richards's office. Right. I'll see you back at the office. And I'll bring the coffee. Thanks, bro." Then she called Fusco and Parks. Then she called her mom and told her she was pulling an all-nighter.

"But what about the date, mija?" her mom wanted to know. "Did Toomey come? Was he nice? How did it go?"

"It went so-so," Donna told her.

❖

Gio kept his face blank until he left the hospital, but as he got into Nero's car, he was grinning. He was riding shotgun. Pete and Little Eddie were in the back.

"Liam called, Boss," Nero told him as he pulled out. "They're all ready for us."

Gio looked in the rearview at Little Eddie, who looked like he was sitting in a dentist's waiting room or the principal's office. "You ready for this?" he asked. "It's Okay if you're not."

Eddie nodded, a little too quickly. "I'm ready Uncle Gio . . ." Then he blushed. "I mean Boss."

Gio laughed. "Uncle Gio is fine. I held you when you were a baby. Now you could put me on your lap." He turned around, making a serious face. "But you better not fucking try it."

"I would never . . ." Eddie blurted and everyone laughed. Pete patted his arm.

"Relax, kid. You're among friends. And I know your Dad is looking down now too, and he's proud."

❖

Old Shenanigan's Public House was packed with a raucous, roaring crowd, but they entered through a rear alley, where one of the Madigan crew was waiting to lead them directly into the basement storeroom and then to a long-forgotten sub-basement, the stairs to which were normally hidden behind a painted-over metal door concealed by storage cabinets. They filed down the narrow stairs—Little Eddie had to go sideways—and found Liam and Josh waiting by the light of a battery-powered lamp. It was a low, damp, dusty space with a dirt floor. Now a couple of yards of that floor had been dug up, and Anton was sitting in the hole among the soil, broken concrete, and rock, still in his bathrobe. On closer inspection, you could see that some of the debris in the hole with him were actually fragments of old skull and bone.

"Gio!" Anton said when he saw him, and started to get up. "Thank God you're here . . ."

"Relax, Anton," Gio said. "Have a seat." Josh kicked him in the chest and he sat back down. "You must be tired. But it's over now. Your crew are dead. Your dope operation is shut down."

"That wasn't me. It was Sergey." Anton put a cigarette in his lips with shaky fingers and searched for his lighter.

"Sergey didn't take a leak without your order, we all know that," Josh said.

"You were White Angel," Liam said. "That crap almost killed me brother."

"Now I'm responsible for addiction?" Anton asked. "It's a disease. They'll find some other poison."

"Never too late to quit though," Liam said and snatched his cigarette.

"Hey!"

"Sorry, New York State law. Smoke free environment."

"Gio, these kids are crazy," Anton went on. "They can't just kill a boss. You have to listen to me. We're friends for fuck's sake."

"You're right." Gio nodded. "Old friends."

"Yes!" Anton agreed.

"I saw another old pal of yours today," Gio added. "Alonzo."

"How is he?" Anton asked.

"Better. Talking, eating, you know. It's a slow recovery but boy did he smile when I told him I'd be seeing you tonight. Really cheered him up."

"Oh . . ." Anton wasn't sure how to respond.

"And another friend of yours, Maria, she sent a message too. What was it again? You know her funny way of putting things, right?" He chuckled and the others grinned.

"She's a pisser," Nero said.

"She sure is," Gio said. "Oh, now I remember. She said, when you chop him up, save his balls and I'll feed them to my new puppy."

Everyone laughed except Anton.

"Funny, right?" Gio said. "I guess she thinks they'll help the puppy grow up stronger. Me, I'm not so sure." He looked at Anton critically. "I think we'll just feed you to the rats and worms."

Anton snarled. "You'd know all about licking balls and sucking dick, wouldn't you? Faggot."

"Hey!" Liam kicked him in the head. "Show some respect. Me and Josh are the faggots here."

Still smiling, Gio raised his gun. "Suck on this," he said, and fired. The first bullet entered his gut and he sat back, grunting and holding the wound. Gio handed his gun to Nero, who aimed carefully as Anton shook his head.

"This is for Eddie," Nero said and fired. He passed the gun to Pete.

"For Eddie," he said, and shot him again.

Now Anton was on his back, bleeding into the dirt, eyes rolling, and gasping like a fish on dry land. Pete put the gun into Little Eddie's hand and Nero whispered to him, "Just aim right in the center of his chest. Take a breath. And then squeeze the trigger, don't pull."

Little Eddie nodded. "This is for my father," he said, and then carefully squeezed.

❖

Afterward, Gio took Nero, Pete, and Little Eddie for a steak at Peter Luger's, then they drove out to the island and Nero dropped Gio at home. The kids were in their rooms for the night and Carol was in bed reading, wearing his old Mets T-shirt. When Gio walked in, she looked up from her book and took off her glasses.

"There you are, I was getting worried."

He made a face. "Why? I called. Only danger I was in was from a massive red-meat coronary."

"I know. It's just. You know. Ever since what happened."

He sat on the bed and took his shoes off. He was supposed to take them off downstairs but forgot about half the time. Then you still had to

remember to carry them up and put them in the closet, or you got scolded for leaving them in the hall. It wasn't really a good system.

"Listen," he said, squeezing her foot under the blanket. "I don't want you to worry anymore. As of tonight, that problem is taken care of."

She sat up and put a hand on his shoulder. "You worked it all out? You found a solution?"

"Yeah. A permanent one."

"Oh . . ." A chill went through her as she realized people had died tonight. But she didn't remove her hand. She squeezed his shoulder.

"Wow your shoulders are tight," she said. "You need to relax."

"What's that mean?" he asked, lying down with his head across her legs. "I forgot."

She kept kneading his shoulders. "Maybe we should have a barbeque, you know, before the weather turns. Invite your sister and Jimmy and your mom. My family. The kids can ask their friends to use the pool. And you can invite Joe, and some of your friends, like . . ." She hesitated, wondering who that might be. "Nero. And Pete."

"Sounds great," he said into the blanket. He knew he had to get up and brush his teeth, but he was already half asleep.

Joe entered quietly, because that was his habit and training. His grandmother was so used to his coming and going at odd hours that she rarely woke up. He moved through the dark apartment and into the bathroom, silently shutting the door before he hit the light. Sitting on the toilet cover, he ran the cold water in the tub, unwrapped his feet, and washed away the dried blood. Then, with a tweezers and a bottle of hydrogen peroxide, he began to pull the little slivers of glass from his feet and drop them into the wastebasket one by one.

40

THEY SERVED THE WARRANT at six. Donna was first through the door, Fusco stepping aside and gesturing for her to precede him, which she acknowledged with a nod. It was her tip, but it was also a tip of the hat, and she took it as such. Then came Parks, Andy, and a swarm of others, plenty of work for everybody sorting through this large, sprawling office, collecting the evidence—papers, computers, files, phones—that would take many hours to process. Donna, however, led her party straight to Richards's office, while he was being woken up and fetched from his private apartment. It was like some duke's den—polished wood and burnished brass, old carpets and oil paintings, even a fireplace—all transported, through the magic of money, to a glass lookout floating in space, far above Manhattan. Andy went by, leading the executive assistant, Jensen, with one hand and carrying a laptop in a plastic evidence bag with the other. Then came Fusco, half-guiding half-dragging Richards by the elbow, while Parks had his camera out, taping everything. He grinned at Donna, who kept a straight face for the camera. Richards was dressed in rumpled khakis and an untucked dress shirt, but his feet were bare and his sparse hair floated around his head. Minus his toupee, he already looked defeated, like he'd been scalped. As luck would have it, Donna was sitting in his luxurious desk chair, behind his grand mahogany showpiece when he came in, going through his drawers.

"What the hell are you doing?" he roared.

"Executing a search warrant sir," Donna said and stood up, holding his day-planner in her gloved hand. "Can you direct us to the location of your safe please?"

"Safe? What safe?"

"Janet," Donna called to the forensics specialist who was busy directing two men as they loaded a filing cabinet onto a dolly. "Can you get some guys with tools in here to start tearing out the walls?"

"Gladly."

"Wait," Richards said, looking at his gorgeously polished and grained woodwork. "It's behind that painting."

"The one of the hunting dogs, sir?" Donna asked.

"Hounds, yes."

"Grab the hounds, will you?" she asked Janet, who carefully removed the painting. There it was, a built-in safe with a digital keypad. Parks moved in closer for a shot. Fusco dragged Richards over.

"Now then sir," Donna continued, speaking loud for the camera. "Will you confirm that this is your safe?"

"Yes, obviously, but it has nothing to do with the business. It just has purely personal items in there and I haven't even opened it in weeks. I almost forgot about it."

"Does anyone besides you have the combination?"

"No. No one."

"Then, for the record, will you state that no one but you has access to this safe or has used it, to the best of your knowledge? And all items within are your personal property?"

"That's what I said," he barked, losing his temper. "You're wasting your time. There's nothing but my personal private property in there."

"Did you get that?" Donna asked Parks.

He gave her a thumbs-up.

"Sir, please open the safe." She stepped back and Richards, after a push from Fusco, stepped forward, grumbling. He punched in a code and reached for the handle.

DAVID GORDON

"Sir, step back now please," Donna said, and Fusco pulled him back. Parks stepped up, focusing in, as Donna pulled open the door. Along with some files and manila envelopes, she found a large black plastic garbage bag. "Can you tell me what this is, sir?"

Richards stared. His mouth was open.

"Sir?"

He shook his head. "I don't understand. I've never seen that before."

She lifted it out, it had some heft to it, and put it on the desk, Parks panning along with her. Carefully she opened the bag and revealed the nice neat bricks of Persian heroin, vacuum sealed and taped. She spoke to the camera. "This bag contains what seems to be fifteen kilos of a powdered substance. Mr. Richards, for the record, do you know what this substance is sir?"

She kept her face totally blank, like a pro, but she could see, behind the camera, Parks, Fusco, Janet, and, from the doorway, Andy, too, all smiling at her. But it was the look on Richards's face that really struck her. Stark terror, which makes sense for someone about to go down for heroin smuggling and murder conspiracy, but also total confusion. He looked like he was having a nightmare.

❖

Looking as though he had aged ten years in ten seconds, Richards sat silently on the couch while the evidence against him was exhaustively photographed, measured, packed, and transported. It wasn't until Donna and Fusco headed over to get him on his feet and out to the car that he spoke.

He addressed her. "Agent, I have some important information I want to share."

"You'll have a chance to make a statement when we get to the office, sir."

"There's no time," he said. "I want to inform you right now that I have firsthand information about a possible terrorist attack. Here in New York."

Donna looked at him. Then she looked at Fusco, who was also staring in surprise. "When?" she asked him.

Richards shrugged. "Any second."

Richards went dumb again after that. Donna demanded to know the details, when, where, who, and Fusco was this close to turning the camera off and beating it out of him, but when he refused absolutely to talk any further without a deal, Donna decided not to waste time arguing and got on the phone to Tom, who was already on the way, having heard about the big dope score. He told her he'd call for a US Assistant District Attorney to meet them there. So when the elevator doors opened, she expected a few extra suits, but she didn't expect Mike, though she supposed she should have. This was, no doubt, why he'd been nosing around all along.

"What do you know about this?" she muttered as they all trooped into the Wildwater conference room, which had been searched and cleared.

"Right now probably less than you," he said, and while she had given up trying to guess when he was lying—the answer, she'd found, was pretty much always—he did look genuinely freaked out. So did they all, except for Richards, who had recovered a little of his cockiness, now that he was back in the driver's seat.

They all took seats as the ADA put out a recorder and turned it on. "I am here with the full authority of my office to offer you consideration on the charges of drug possession with intent to sell and smuggling of a prohibited substance in exchange for all information regarding terrorist activities."

"I want full immunity," Richards said. "From all charges, including murder and conspiracy to commit murder, stemming from all federal and local investigations into Zahir and Wildwater."

"Bullshit . . ." Fusco muttered under his breath.

The ADA shot him a look. "Agreed," he said.

"And . . ." Richards began.

Fusco erupted. "There's more, you scumbag?"

"Sit down and shut up!" Tom yelled at him and Fusco snarled. Parks put a hand on his arm and he sat.

Richards waited for quiet. "And," he went on, "I want a new identity and permission to leave the country freely. No offense . . ." he looked around, eyes lingering on Powell, "but with what I know, US agencies are the last people I'm going to trust."

The ADA huddled with Tom and Powell for a moment, then faced Richards. "My colleagues from the FBI and CIA assure me this can be done. You'll be placed under my supervision with Secret Service protection."

Richards nodded. "Deal," he said.

Now Tom, who'd barely moved, leaned over and spoke. "Start talking."

Richards sat back. "The name of the man you are hunting is Rick Toomey."

"Shit . . ." Now it was Donna who muttered under her breath.

"Where is he?" Tom asked.

"I have no goddamn idea."

"What is your relationship to this man?"

"He is, or was, my employee. He led my security forces overseas . . ."

"Mercenaries," the ADA put in.

"Whatever. Soldiers. All perfectly legal."

"And illegally? What else did he do for you?"

"He seized heroin shipments from suppliers. Smugglers and warlords. He also handled transporting it to the US and delivering it to our partners here."

"He was the one who attacked the other dope operations?" Fusco asked. "Here in the city?"

"Yes. He and his men."

"Where are his men now?" Fusco asked.

"You'd know that better than me, detective," Richards said. "I assume they are dead."

Tom interrupted: "Tell us about the terrorist connection."

Richards cleared his throat. "Part of our strategy, politically, was to use this money to seed small terror strikes overseas . . ." He held a hand up and raised his voice. "Only overseas! In order to keep elected officials and the American people focused on what we thought was the real threat to our way of life."

"And what threat is that?" Tom asked.

"Islam, of course."

Parks, who'd been the calmest one there, finally leaned in. His voice was bitter. "And that also kept government funds flowing into your bank accounts, and paid for all this, did it not?"

Richards nodded.

"What happened?" Fusco asked. "What could have possibly gone wrong with this brilliant plan?"

Richards clenched his jaw. "It was Toomey. He's a fanatic. He went off on his own."

"When did you become aware of this?" the ADA prompted.

"When the last shipment never arrived. You were there," he nodded at Donna, "at first we thought you grabbed it and him. But then he disappeared, and we realized you hadn't gotten anything either. So the product was never there, even though Toomey told everyone he'd sent it like always and was going to pick it up. That's when I checked with our people in Afghanistan and found out that Toomey had been making secret purchases on his own with our dope money. And that he sent his own shipment through instead."

"What was in his shipment, Mr. Richards?"

"Uranium. We estimate about sixty kilos."

"Jesus . . ." That was Mike, saying the first thing he'd said. Audible sighs went around the room.

"How could that just come through in a normal container?" The ADA asked.

Richards shrugged. "It's benign until it's weaponized. More or less. The same radiation as kitty litter."

The ADA spoke carefully, controlling his rage. "And what did you do when you realized that your colleague had perhaps smuggled material

into the area suitable for building a nuclear weapon?" Everyone stared at Richards, like a jury about to order execution. But now Richards stood up, defiantly.

"What did I do? I tried to stop him. I sent our best operative to take him out, and she would have too, she was this goddamn close." He pointed at Donna who stared back, stunned. "And then you saved him." He sat back down, waving an arm, dismissively. "And the rest of you let him go. Congratulations."

❖

By the time they got Richards cuffed and shod and downstairs, there was quite a crowd. The caravan of law enforcement vehicles stretched down the block and someone had tipped off the media, so reporters were buzzing, and that drew an outer ring of onlookers, many of whom had no idea what they were waiting to see. They probably would have been disappointed when it turned out to be a disheveled old man being escorted into a black Tahoe by a bunch of exhausted government workers in suits. But that's not how it turned out. As they were leaving the building and crossing the courtyard to the waiting cars, with Parks leading the way, parting the crowd, and Fusco and Donna holding Richards by the arms, with Tom, Mike, and the ADA bringing up the rear, suddenly Parks clutched his chest as if he were having a heart attack and fell. Donna knew it was not a heart attack though, because she saw the exit wound erupt, like a red blossom opening in his coat. The bullet flattened itself on the sidewalk.

"Shooter," she yelled, drawing her own gun, but with no idea where to even look. Then the top of Richards's head came off, and she knew, as he collapsed into a heap, that there was a sniper somewhere in one of the gigantic buildings across the street. But before she could even think about taking cover, she was knocked off her feet by someone grabbing her by the shoulders and yelling, "Lookout!" As she fell, she realized it was Mike on top of her. By then the pileup had begun, with bodies covering

each other everywhere and people pushing to get away and everyone yelling, so it wasn't until a few seconds later, when she tried to move that she felt the wet spot on his back and realized that he too had been shot. "Agent down!" she yelled as she rose up on one knee. Across the street, in a window, she saw a muzzle flash, and another shot entered Mike's chest. She fired at the window, glimpsing a female silhouette with long hair and, she could have sworn, a quick wave. Then she was gone.

Donna leaned over Mike now as she heard the ambulance sirens coming. He smiled up at her and whispered something. She leaned in.

"Tell Larissa I love her," he said.

"Tell her yourself," she answered and he smiled. And then he was dead.

Vicky hadn't planned to kill the cop. But then again, until the night before, she hadn't planned on killing Richards. But once the hit on Toomey had—she hated the word but it was unavoidable—failed, she was told that it was time to cut their losses, to tie up loose ends and go. The call came from a familiar voice, one of those who had sent her to work for Richards in the first place. Now he'd become a liability and she had a new primary target. The cop was just in the way. As she watched through the scope, from the window of an office that wouldn't open till 9:30, she saw that the only way to get a clear shot at Richards before they reached the car was to clear the path. So she shot the cop. Then she took out Richards, who'd always rubbed her the wrong way. She was going to put one more in him, just to be safe—no more unfortunate accidents—when that cute CIA boy Mike Powell stepped in front of it. Heroic or suicidal? No one would ever know. But it was just as well; he was a sweet playmate but one more loose end who needed to be tied off. As for the FBI agent, his ex, Donna Zamora—good luck to her. Vicky bore her no ill will and rather hoped she caught Toomey, since he was part of the mess Vicky had been sent to clean up. And those other two, Joe and Yelena: she was sorry not to be playing with them any further, after seeing what they

were capable of. They were her kind of fun, especially the girl. But for now, she was walking away. In five minutes she was back on the street, mixing with office workers who had no idea something awful had happened a block away. In an hour she'd be on a train to Boston. And then on a plane back to London, for a well-deserved rest. But before leaving, she did bend over the rifle and press her mouth to the stock, leaving a lipstick print, just as a kind of farewell kiss.

41

JOE WAS STILL IN bed. He'd slept deeply, physically exhausted, but also with the clear mind of someone whose labors were at an end. He had no nightmares and woke up feeling good. Even his feet were okay, now that he'd cleaned and bandaged them; the cuts were minor and staying off them for a day or two sounded fine to him. By the time he got up, Gladys had the coffee brewed. She brought him a cup and was suggesting scrambled eggs and toast for breakfast when the door buzzed.

Gladys went to the hall and opened the door but kept it on the chain. It was Donna. "Sorry, hun, but if you're going to keep doing this I'm going to have to call Mrs. Padera in 3B. Her son's a lawyer."

"I'm sorry about last time Gladys. I was wrong. I apologize. But this is serious, really serious. People will die. And I need Joe's help."

Gladys didn't ask any questions. She undid the chain and stepped back. "Have a seat. Coffee's fresh if you want some," she said. "I'm about to make scrambled eggs."

"Nothing for me, thank you." Donna said, walking into the living room. Joe, who'd heard them, was dressed now, in jeans and a clean black T-shirt. He held a cup of coffee.

"Don't worry about Mrs. Padera's son," he said. "I think he just does housing law."

❖

Joe took Donna into his room and offered her the chair.

"Thanks for seeing me," she said. "But first I owe you something."

"An apology for tossing the place? I heard it."

"No, that was for your grandmother," she said, "this is for you," and slapped him hard across the face.

"Ow," he said and then sat on the edge of the bed. She took the chair.

"Do you want to know what that's for?"

Joe rubbed his cheek. "I'm not sure it matters now."

"It does to me," Donna said. "It's for violating my professional integrity. For using me to further your goals, and in so doing, leading me to compromise my core values of honesty, fairness, and justice. I don't care if you're a criminal. But making me one." She shook her head. "I can't forgive that."

"Remind me. When did I do this?"

"The tip? About the safe in Richards's office?"

Joe shrugged.

"I know, I know, you sent your buddy Gio Caprisi, another patriot, and he fed me the info about the safe."

"And?"

"It was full of heroin, as you well know, heroin that I'm sure will connect to the dope being brought in by Zahir and to White Angel. Case closed."

"So? What's the problem? Congratulations."

"The problem is that I could tell from the expression on Richards's face when we popped the safe, he had no fucking idea how that dope got there. And why would he? Hide dope in his own safe? Confirm the contents were all his? He was set up by someone very clever."

"Is that what he said?" Joe shrugged again. "I'm not Mrs. Padera's son or anything, but that sounds like a pretty weak defense. He won't make that work in court."

She shook her head. "It doesn't matter now. He's dead."

"What?" Now she could see Joe was genuinely surprised. Thrown.

"And that's why I'm here," she went on. "Ready to grovel and ask for help, even from you. Because lots of people are going to die, innocent people. Some already have. And it's all my fault."

Then she told him the whole story as best she knew. Joe listened in silence, except for when she got to the part about there being uranium in the container, when he said "Of course . . ."

"What?"

He shook his head. "Nothing, go on," but he was thinking of the strange assortment of items on the shipping manifest Juno had dug up, all objects that emitted a small, harmless amount of radiation, nothing that would throw up a red flag with anyone. Certainly nothing that would alarm a dog trained only to sniff for drugs.

"So," he said, "when he tried to get you to arrange disabled parking . . ."

"His truck was wired the whole time. He wanted to set it off at Ground Zero. A goddamn truck bomb, right there, and I let him drive it away."

"At least you didn't let him in. You followed protocol. That saved hundreds, maybe thousands. You did your job."

"And then I saved his fucking life."

"That's also part of your job," Joe said. "Just like trying to save Richards." He started to put on his sneakers. "But fortunately it's not part of mine. I'll call you."

"Where are you going?" she asked, as he tied the laces, wincing just a little and leaving them a bit loose. "What are you going to do?"

"Something that violates your core values. But don't worry." He put his phone and keys in his pocket and then headed for the door. "You won't be involved. I'm used to government officials needing my help, but not wanting to know anything about it."

"Joe, wait . . ."

He turned back. She stood and came closer. "I'm thinking about, just in case it goes bad, having my mom take Larissa out of town, just to the beach or something. Your grandmother can go too. They can go to AC. They won't need to know the truth."

Joe smiled. "Thanks, Donna, but if anyone can spot a bluff, it's Gladys. That's why I just don't say anything." On the way out he grabbed a piece of toast. "Sorry, I've got to run. But Donna is staying for breakfast."

42

WHEN JOE TOLD DONNA that she didn't want to know where
he was going, it was partly because his feelings were hurt, but it was
also because he actually didn't know himself. He called Gio, keeping
the details vague, just to be sure he and his family were all out on Long
Island, then began walking aimlessly. He just needed to move, to feel
like he was doing something, if only wandering through the streets of
his own neighborhood. As always, in Jackson Heights, the world was
on display. Women in saris shopped at the Mexican-run fruit stand.
Dominican and Ecuadorian kids rode their bikes to the Yemeni candy
shop. Taiwanese businessmen from Elmhurst walked into the bank,
crossing paths with the delivery guy from the Thai place. The colors,
sounds, voices, tastes, and smells of the whole globe mingled and
merged around him. He'd been told, back in PS 69, that over a hundred
languages were spoken just in his school. No doubt that figure had only
grown. But to him this was normal. It was only when he grew up and
ventured into the big world that he realized how special his little corner
was, a unique and wondrous ecosystem. But to someone like Toomey,
it was more like a petri dish, which he'd be happy to wipe out with a
nuclear blast, to cleanse with radiation.

His feet started to hurt; he needed to sit, but felt like he had to keep
moving, so he climbed to the train and rode into the city, descending into
the darkness under the river. He surfaced finally in Columbus Circle,

walking uptown now, lost in thought, drifting up Broadway, until, thinking he should be heading somewhere at least, and that it might be good to try talking to someone other than himself, he called Frank. He didn't sound happy to hear from him.

"Oh hey kid what's up?"

"I'm in your neighborhood, well almost, and I wanted to see what you thought about something. Can I come by?"

"I'm kind of in the middle of something. Is it urgent?"

"You could definitely say that."

"Okay. Give me like half an hour to finish this up and I'll make coffee. Do me a favor and pick up some milk?"

So Joe walked the rest of the way to 125th Street, the main drag in Harlem, where Frank had kept his studio for more than thirty years. It was a large space, half a high floor of a building that had once been offices, then illegal dwellings, and now luxury apartments above and cool offices below with trendy retail—an organic market, a silly clothing shop, a fusion restaurant, a chain café—on the ground floor. Joe got on the elevator with a blond family, a bearded dad and slim mom both in expensive jeans, with one kid in a stroller and the other holding mom's hand and gazing up at Joe.

"You're sweaty," the little girl said.

"Shhh . . . that's rude," the mom said, and smiled at Joe. "Sorry."

"Not at all," he said and smiled at the kid. "You're right. I am. Stinky too I bet."

She giggled.

The dad noticed that he'd pressed ten and said, "You're going to see Frank Jones?"

Joe nodded.

"I want to see Frank!" the little girl yelled. "Let's visit Frank!" The baby seemed to agree, gurgling and shaking his rattle.

"Frank's busy honey," the mom said. "He's uh . . . got a friend visiting." The elevator stopped at their floor and she smiled apologetically as they got out, the husband still looking back curiously.

"Yeah the kids like me, because I'm always covered in paint," Frank said when Joe told him this, "but the parents hate me. They paid millions for their lofts and I still pay less than it costs them to park their cars. Plus I'm always covered in paint." He was wearing house slippers, worn cotton pants that had frayed at the cuffs, and a T-shirt so old it was disintegrating, revealing gray chest hair through the holes, with a blue Cuban-style guayabera shirt over that, leaning on his cane. Everything was indeed covered in paint.

"Fuck them. You were here first," Joe said, following Frank down the hall to the big open raw space, which commanded a view of 125th Street and the city beyond. There was an easel with a half-finished nude, larger than life–size, an iron-framed daybed—pictured in the painting—an armchair with the stuffing falling out of the cracked leather, a straight-back chair, and a bunch of tables, shelves, and stools, all covered in heaps of brushes, tubes, rags, books, papers, magazines, cans, cups, art supplies, and other random debris.

"It's not just money though," Frank went on. "It's guilt. Harlem is like an Indian reservation. First the white folks said, you better stay up here. Now, a century later, they're saying, actually we need that space. Deep down they know it and feel bad. Which they resent me for. I'm hanging around, haunting them like the ghost of Harlem past."

"Coffee's ready." A woman came out from the curtain that separated the living quarters from the larger work space. She was a voluptuous white woman in her early thirties, with red hair loose to her waist, barefoot and wrapped in a kimono that slid from one bare shoulder as she carried out a tray that held a French press full of steaming coffee and three mismatched, chipped cups.

"Eva," Frank said, "meet Joe."

"Nice to meet you Joe." She set the tray down on top of some old newspapers.

"Hello Eva," Joe said. He set a quart of milk on the tray. "Thanks for the coffee. Here's some milk." He realized that Eva was the nude in the painting. "Sorry if I'm interrupting."

"You're not," Eva said, pouring the coffee and adding milk to hers. "I'm about to take a shower. Then Frank is taking me to an opening at a museum."

Frank groaned. Eva laughed and waved as she wandered back behind the curtain with her cup. Frank shook his head. "Goddamn openings. Too crowded to see anything. Too noisy to hear anything. And a bunch of people you don't want to see or hear anyway." He lifted both cups and handed Joe his. Neither took milk.

"Sounds like she still wants to go," Joe said.

"She has to. She's the director of the museum." He sipped his coffee. "Makes better coffee than I do too. Have a seat."

As always, Joe took the straight-back chair and Frank sprawled in his armchair.

"So . . ." Joe cleared his throat. "Well . . . when I told you that I worked as a bouncer at a strip club for a living, that was only party true."

"I suspected as much."

"I mean I really do work there."

"I believe you."

"But sometimes I get asked to . . . help out in other ways."

"Right. A man of your talents."

"Yeah. So to speak. But right now I'm afraid those talents aren't cutting it . . . I need help . . . it's kind of a bad situation . . ."

Frank waved his cane. "For fuck's sake kid, spit it out already." So he did. More or less. He told him about Toomey, the uranium, the truck bomb, and the 9/11 memorial.

"Jesus fuck," Frank said when he was done. "You weren't kidding. That really is a bad situation. You better catch this guy. What the hell are you doing wasting time here?"

"I need your help."

"Mine? True, I've seen some shitbag officers like him. And back in the day I would have fragged this bastard no problem. But I'm an old man with a bum knee. I can't do shit about shit."

"I need your brain. I've got no leads, nowhere to look. The FBI accidentally let him go, the asshole who he worked for got taken out, and everyone else who worked for him or knew him . . ." Joe shrugged guiltily. "I might have already killed."

"Damn Joe. No wonder you get bad dreams."

"No shit. But what I need now is someone who can help me think like he thinks. Figure his next move."

"How the hell do I know? I just hope he doesn't decide to blow up a museum opening. Okay, okay . . ." Frank leaned back and rubbed his eyes. "No chance he's just gonna say fuck it and go home? Retire and coach Little League?"

"No way. He's a fanatic."

"You know him?"

"I know the type. So do you. Gung-ho and juiced up on all that warrior code bullshit. He's just full of rage and looking for a reason to destroy. Thinks he's serving a cause, but really it's just an excuse."

Frank cocked an eyebrow. "That does remind me of someone a little."

Joe looked at him in confusion. Frank leaned forward on the cane. "Look. He's hard core, right? Special Forces badass, right?"

"Yeah."

"So. You're the only other Special Forces badass sitting here. What would you do? Let's say you're dropped behind lines, on a mission, search and destroy, and it goes to shit. You can't reach the primary target. Would *you* just pack it in and go home?"

Joe narrowed his eyes. "I'd proceed to the secondary."

"Right."

"So when Donna—I mean the FBI agent—chased him away from Ground Zero and he was driving that truck bomb . . ."

"That was his primary, sure."

"He told her he'd park it and come back."

"He fell back and got in position for his secondary target. So where did he go?"

"Someplace he could park and not get towed or messed with. A parking lot? A vacant? No, he needs another high-value target. Someplace busy, with people." Joe stood and pulled out his phone. "A building with underground parking." He dialed. "I'm going to call the FBI. Tell them to start checking."

"You do that." Frank stood, too. "I'm going to get changed and go to an opening. And pray you take this motherfucker out." He clapped Joe on the shoulder as he limped by. "De Oppresso Liber, brother."

43

DONNA HAD THE SAME idea, more or less. After trying and failing to convince Gladys to take a trip out of town—"I live here so might as well die here too, hon"—and insuring that her mom was taking Larissa to an amusement park in New Jersey (she said it was because of a measles outbreak that had been kept out of the news), she had headed back toward her office. Thinking about the time interval from when Toomey tried to get what she now knew was a truck bomb into the memorial, and when he returned on foot—was it an hour? A bit more?—she called and suggested to Tom that they begin searching soft targets where a truck could be parked without suspicion, like indoor parking structures or busy streets that had legal parking that day. Tom assured her that they were on it, then ordered her to go home. She'd been wounded yesterday and had her ex-husband killed in her arms today; officially she was off-duty until she could be de-briefed and cleared by a shrink. She'd even had to turn in her gun after it was fired.

"You've done good work, Donna," Tom said, using her first name for the first time she could recall. "Excellent work. But we'll take it from here. And who knows? If Toomey's got half a brain he is long gone by now. He knows we're onto him."

Fusco, who never agreed with the bosses about anything, sort of agreed: "We're on it. The whole force is out, for Parks. Working with the

FBI and even the goddamn CIA with no bullshit for once. We've got hundreds of people to go door to door if we have to."

Finally, she headed home and was on the subway when Joe called her, but she was in a tunnel and the signal was too weak. So she got off, and checked her voice mail in the station. He'd left a message, more or less suggesting the same plan. She thought about getting back on another A uptown, but what would she do then? Sit in her now-empty apartment and wait by the window for a mushroom cloud? Watch CNN? Go to the local church and pray? Not her style. She needed to be doing something, to work—though she might throw a few prayers in there too along the way.

So, okay, back to basics: when you lose the trail, what do you do? Go back to the last clear spot, the last solid link in the chain and find a fresh clue. It worked before in this case, when she checked a license plate and it led to Sergey. What the hell, she was just a short walk from the Wildwater building, anyway, so she left the station and walked over.

❖

Joe was on the train heading downtown. He was not sure why. He'd already called Donna to suggest she look into large buildings with underground parking, and he doubted the cops were going to let him help with the search, but his instincts drove him to move toward the center of the crisis. Standing still was unbearable and walking away felt like . . . walking away. He knew it was in large part his conditioning, his training, and he knew that in some ways it was a dubious, even bedeviling, impulse: a strength that became a weakness in the wrong hands. That's how you ended up like Toomey, perhaps. Because the people who sent people like Joe and Frank and yes, even Toomey, into the shit, turned out to be people like Richards. That's why Joe knew that, despite the scars on his body and the still-unhealed wounds in his mind, he was one of the lucky ones; he had kept his soul. De Oppresso Liber indeed. Free the oppressed. And start with yourself.

That's when Joe froze, right in front of the train doors as they opened, so that the person behind him bumped right into him, and had to divert, muttering, "Damn tourist."

"Motherfucker," Joe said aloud, more in amazement than anger. The guy who'd bumped him looked back, insulted, but by then Joe had started running, pushing through the mass of people who were waiting to board the train.

"Fucking asshole!" the guy shouted as Joe sprinted up the stairs to the street. Joe pulled out his phone, dialing 911 as he began to run down the street. He knew where Toomey had parked the truck.

❖

Richards's office was still taped off and there was a young cop standing guard, but he respectfully lifted the tape when Donna showed her ID. The place seemed more than just physically empty. Even its opulence, its preening and power, seemed hollow now, a pointless charade. A bunch of big shots, trying to run the world as they saw fit, and taking it to the edge of ruin. What else was new? It would be a joke, this extra-toxic brand of vanity if it weren't so deadly to so many. Mike's face flashed in her mind. Why did he take a bullet? Was it for her? For Richards? How could he be that man and also the one who'd tormented her? How did love and hate, insecurity and honor, fear and rage get so hopelessly tangled? What the fuck was wrong with men?

Then, as if on cue, her phone rang again. Speaking of fucked-up men, it was Joe. She sighed and answered.

"Where are you?" he asked, out of breath.

"Back at Wildwater . . ."

"Meet me in the basement. I know where the truck is."

"Where?" she asked, but just then the uniform ran in.

"Ma'am!" he yelled.

"Hold on," she told Joe. "Yeah?"

"We've got to evacuate. A bomb threat."

She nodded and spoke into the phone. "Never mind. I'm on my way down."

"Good. I'm a block away," he huffed and she realized he was running. To the bomb not from it.

"Joe?" she asked, louder into the phone.

"Yeah?"

"Are you sure about this?"

"No," he said and hung up.

❖

The irony was not lost on Toomey, although his patience was wearing thin. For as long as the Wildwater building was a crime scene, swarming with cops and feds, surrounded by reporters and gawkers, he couldn't gain access and actually commit his intended crime. So for most of the day he wandered the surrounding streets, imagining what it would all look like destroyed, once the device he had in his truck turned the Wildwater tower into a flaming torch, a column of smoke rising into the sky, visible for miles and miles, like a beacon of destruction, sending out shock waves that would flatten all these blocks, shattering the stores, apartments, restaurants around him, the schools and offices, blasting them into bricks and stones and girders, blowing them into dust, sending the trucks and buses and cars flying like toys, like specks of dirt through space, tossing them like a tornado, along with trees and streetlamps and benches. And the people, the people who walked around him now, talking, laughing, cursing, eating, drinking, minding their own business or butting into someone else's, each busy with his own thoughts, her own problems or desires or joys or fears, dressed in every kind of clothes, from suits and dresses to shorts and rags, every kind of person, every race, religion, class, gender, type, and taste, strangers gathered by chance in this one place on this one day—they would all die together. Most before they knew what happened, vaporized instantly or melting into air. The less lucky slowly

and painfully, from fire or wreckage. And then, last of all, the lingering deaths of the radiated.

That would wake them up. Perhaps there would be a statue of Toomey in this place one day. A monument to victory this time and not a remembrance of defeat, like down in Ground Zero. For this, his strike, would be the opening blow in a final battle for the soul of America and the future of the world. It would be a battle cry, leading the forces of civilization, white Christian civilization, to final victory, and to a glorious future. And the rabble who died today? Expendable. Ready to be flushed out and erased, plowed into the earth from which the new world would rise.

Feeling good, Toomey ate a couple of hot dogs and a soda from a stand and then felt not so good—the goddamn foreigner who sold him this crap probably hadn't washed his brown hands—and then he had to pay for a coffee at a diner just so the bitchy tattooed waitress would let him use the john—probably a freak with those piercings, or a lesbian. Then, finally, feeling better, he walked back over and found the building open again. Thank God, he could finish up his mission and go. He'd had a bellyful of New York.

So he went through the revolving door and took an elevator down to the parking levels in the basement. The bomb in his truck was remote-activated, and he had the control, but no cell or radio signal would reach it underground unless he was close—another inconvenience caused by the loss of his primary target, and his own relatively basic bomb-making skills. He was a fighter, not an engineer. His plan now was to set the timer and then walk away, leaving plenty of time for him to get on a subway and be out of the blast area and deep underground by the time it went off. If he rode the train under the river, he could even pop out in safety and watch the smoke rise from the other side.

44

DONNA WAS ON THE elevator going down to the basement, while the cop went floor to floor on the stairs, herding people out. But too many people were now trying to desperately jam onto the elevator, which was completely full but still stopping on every floor, like a local train at rush hour. So she got off and ran down the stairs to the underground garage instead, then began searching among the cars, looking for Toomey's Jeep, working her way down the levels, trying to call Joe, though there was no signal on her phone. Then, on the bottom floor, she saw him, standing in front of the truck. He'd broken a side window, the one with the Special Forces sticker on it, and opened up the back. And now he was just standing there, staring, holding an unfolded camping knife in one hand. Then she got close and saw why.

"Hey," she said, softly now, catching her breath.

"Hey," he answered.

They were both looking at a very large explosive device—cakes of uranium, stacked in metal canisters, wired to dynamite that was taped in bands around it, with a detonator on top.

"Do you know how to disarm one of these things?" Donna asked.

"Not really," Joe said. "Do you?"

"Sort of. I mean, I took a class. Twice. But I failed it both times."

Joe handed her his pocket-knife. "Better luck this time."

"Thanks."

"Is it activated?" he asked, as she leaned in closer, looking at the mechanism, still not touching anything.

"Not yet," a voice behind them said. It was Toomey. He stepped out from where he'd been watching, between two parked cars, holding a remote in one hand, and a Glock in the other. "Easy now." He pointed the gun as them as they spun around.

"Toomey," Donna said.

"Nice to see you again Donna," he said. "Sorry our date didn't work out."

"Date?" Joe asked.

She shook her head. "Wasn't a real date."

"And you are Joe Brody. I feel like our date has been coming a long time."

Now Donna glanced quizzically at Joe, who shrugged.

Toomey went on. "I guess I should thank you too, Donna, for saving my life."

"Why not return the favor then?" she asked.

He smiled. "Actually, I mean to. You see, once again you two have fucked up my plan. I was going to set this timer and go. Be long gone before it blew. But now, with the alarm out, it's all a big rush. Even if I kill you both, the techs will be here to defuse it in what, ten minutes? So here's my proposal. I set the timer for half an hour, you cancel the emergency call, say it was a false alarm, and we all walk away alive together. Or I set it for three minutes, and we just see what happens." He looked at Donna. "What do you think?"

"I think this is definitely our last date."

He laughed. "Full disclosure," he said, "there is a trip wire on the bomb," and then he pressed the button on the timer. "Go."

Donna turned to the device, silently praying under her breath.

"You got this," Joe said softly.

"Joe . . ." she said, grabbing his arm as he turned. "I . . . what I said before . . ."

"It was all true," he said, squeezing her hand back, then: "See you in a few minutes." Hands raised, he walked across the garage toward Toomey.

❖

"I'm impressed with you both," Toomey said, when they were about twenty feet apart. "But not surprised. You're warriors. Too bad we can't all be on the same side, the right side, together. But the next best thing to dying with a brother-in-arms is at the hands of a worthy adversary. Don't you think?"

"I can think of a few I like better," Joe said. "Like getting really old and dying of boredom on a beach in Florida."

Toomey smiled and shook his head. "You're kidding yourself. That's not going to happen to you. Family? Marriage? Retirement? Not for our kind. The most we can hope for is an honorable death." He set the gun and the control down on the pavement in front of him and stepped back. "Red button stops the bomb," he said, and then, like he was running into the arms of a lover or a best friend, he ran at Joe.

❖

In the split seconds that he had, as he ran toward Toomey, Joe thought of the many ways he knew to kill a person. Most of course required weapons, however simple—a piece of glass, a pencil, a straw. But he had none of that here. Then he thought of the ways he could kill with bare hands—shattering the larynx, breaking the neck, choking the carotid—but these depended to some extent on surprise and an opponent who did not share the exact same knowledge. Toomey was right about one thing: they were evenly matched, and in an even match, even if he won, he'd lose, when the seconds of his life, of many lives, ran out.

So he did the one thing that would surprise Toomey, the thing a true warrior would never do—he retreated. As Toomey gained speed and momentum, crouching to lower his center of gravity and ducking his head for protection, hiding the vulnerable organs and swinging a fist at Joe, Joe, who was running full speed toward Toomey, jumped instead—he

jumped as high as he could, clear over Toomey, and landed on the hood of a parked car behind him.

Toomey stumbled forward, hitting his knees, then jumped up and whirled around to face Joe as Joe hopped up onto the car's roof. Joe saw Donna look up at him for a moment, her face a mask of fear and despair. Just for an instant, their eyes connected, as Toomey closed in.

"Fine," he said. "You want to play games. It's your last wish. Let's play." He jumped up onto the hood of the car, taking a karate stance, but Joe immediately leapt to another car. Toomey came after him, but Joe simply hopped back to the first one, bouncing off the roof, and jumped higher to the roof of a minivan that was parked next to the wall.

"Fuck this shit, Brody," Toomey said, leaping to the ground and trapping Joe by getting between him and the next vehicle. He was cornered. Toomey reached into the back of his waistband and drew a knife, short, curved, and vicious.

"I thought you were playing fair," Joe called to him.

"And I thought you were the real deal, Special Forces. Bullshit! You're just a coward." He moved in swiping the knife, as Joe backed into the wall. "You fight like a fool. And now you'll die like a fool, after I cut those strings."

He came at Joe, lashing out with the razor-sharp blade, and Joe jumped, like he was jumping rope, knowing that if the blade caught him, it would do what he'd done to Trey, sever his tendons and drop him like a ragdoll. He jumped high as Toomey sliced the air, closer and closer, knowing one false move, one slow jump, would end him. He could feel the cuts on his feet opening again. The knife flashed, catching his pants, slicing the skin. Toomey smiled at the blood. Joe jumped.

Then a shot rang out, shattering the side window of the van and echoing in the basement.

"No more fools are going to die today, Toomey. Except you maybe."

Toomey swung around and looked. Donna was holding his own gun on him with her right hand. In her left she held the control, which was

stopped at 0:09. She shrugged. "There's no way I was going to disarm that thing in time. I've got to retake that class."

Toomey roared. A howl of rage came up in him, clenching every muscle, every tendon, distorting his face, and his arm came up, to throw the blade. Donna shot and killed him.

45

THE TWO MILLION DOLLAR bounty was paid. After expenses, for everything from the flights to Afghanistan to the fake military uniforms and the weapons and vehicles, the payment, split seven ways, came to $264,285 each for Joe, Yelena, Cash, Juno, Liam, Josh, and the family of Hamid. They met in the basement of the building behind Club Rendezvous where once before they had come together and branded Joe with their mark. Once again, Joe stood before the gathered bosses with Gio at his side.

It was Little Maria who presented the cash. She'd lost the foot—infection set in and it had to be amputated. She was on crutches now, with one leg in a cast and the other still in a stocking and red high heel shoe; rumor was that her prosthetic would be shaped to fit into stiletto heels. Her new boyfriend, a beautiful young man with a goatee, black T-shirt, and heavy gold cross, carried the bag of money and led a pit bull pup on a leash. Everyone stood up when she entered. First she kissed Gio on the cheek. "*Hola guapo*," she said. Then, leaning on her crutches, she hugged Joe and kissed him on the lips.

"*Gracias amigo, con todo mi corazón.*"

Joe nodded in acknowledgment, a smear of bright red lipstick on his mouth. Alonzo was home but still not ready to travel; Reggie was there to represent him. He shook Gio's hand, earnestly thanking him, then

said to Joe, "My brother said to give you this," and gave him a big hug. Jack Madigan was there, in a navy suit, white shirt, and red tie, with Liam at his side.

Jack shook Gio's hand respectfully, then pumped Joe's hand hard. Liam clapped his back.

"How's your brother?" Gio asked them.

"Fine, Gio, thanks for asking," Jack said.

Liam shrugged. "Anyway he's better. The fucking eejit."

Rebbe, escorted by Josh, kissed both Joe's cheeks. "You did it, boychick. Just like I knew you would," he said, eyes twinkling, a sweet and kind old man with ice water in his veins. "Though I don't think I'll be going to that shvitz anytime soon."

Uncle Chen chuckled at this, and patted Joe on the back. Then he told Gio, "We know you made your father proud."

"Thank you Uncle," Gio said. "That means the most coming from you, who know."

Anton's name went unmentioned. In his place at the table, representing the Russian gangs, sat Yelena, regarding Joe with a sly, ironic smile. She looked different: she wore a tightly tailored black suit skirt and jacket, with a sleeveless silk blouse beneath it, and her hair was up. She barely spoke, but shook hands elegantly with the others, and gracefully accepted kisses from Rebbe and Little Maria.

No one questioned her presence or authority. In the days since Joe stopped Toomey, Gio's men, along with the other crews, had mopped up the last of the White Angel gang, brutally reasserting their domains. Bodies were still turning up in alleys and dumpsters all around town, but overall, things were returning to normal. A couple of Anton's men were rumored to have fled back to Russia; others turned up dead in Miami or LA. And one was hauled out of the water near Brighton Beach, at least whatever had been left by the fish.

Afterward, the group left separately, and Joe walked Yelena to her car, a sleek black Mercedes. She had taken her jacket off in the stuffy basement, and now, as she leaned back against the hood and lit a cigarette,

Joe could see the scabbed over scar from her burn—like an arrow—where the corner edge of the furnace had seared her.

"It's healing well," he said. "But you'll have a mark."

She shrugged. "We all have marks. That's life." She laughed. "But this one doesn't suit you." She wet a finger and scrubbed away Maria's lipstick.

"Speaking of new marks," Joe said. "You've been busy." Yelena had several new tattoos to join the ones that had already decorated her body: Now an eagle soared above the church cupola on her back, beneath which, Joe knew, a Madonna and child indicated that she was born in prison. A dollar sign and a skull rode on each hip, indicating a safe-cracker and a killer, and a dagger ran down her left thigh, entwined with roses and a snake, whose raised head signaled "I began in stealing and robbing." Another dagger, piercing a heart, ran down her right, and Joe could guess what the several newly added drops of blood meant. A new devil's face had been inked on her arm, next to her burn mark.

"What's that?"

"Enemy of the authorities. For taking out the SVR man."

"Right," Joe said. "And these?" he asked, brushing the row of stars on the top of each shoulder. He squeezed her right ring finger, which now bore a small crown. "And this?" He touched her chest, where between her breasts and under her clavicle, an eight-pointed star now shone.

"As you think," she said, looking him back in the eye.

Joe smiled. "Congratulations. You're a boss now. Is that what you want?"

Yelena laughed. "Want? It's like your grandma taught you. We play the cards we are dealt. And we win."

"Do we?" Joe asked her.

She leaned up and kissed him, very gently, on the lips. Then she knocked on the roof of the limo. Immediately, a huge man in a black suit jumped out of the passenger side and opened the back door, waiting with a respectful nod. The driver started the engine.

"I have to go to Moscow," Yelena said. "To settle a few matters."

Joe nodded. "Fly safely."

"You too Joe," she said, smiling, and got in the car. The bodyguard shut the door and nodded to Joe as he got in front. Joe stepped back and watched them drive away. He looked down at Yelena's cigarette, still smoldering on the ground, and stamped it out.

"Hey," Gio called to him. He was leaning from the window of his car. Joe wasn't sure how long he'd been there, listening. "Need a ride?"

46

"So you'll come to the cookout?" Gio asked. They had been driving several minutes in silence. "Next Sunday?"

"Sure," Joe said.

"Bring Gladys."

"Right."

"I'd say bring Yelena too, but I get the feeling she is going to be busy for a while."

Joe smiled and nodded. "Off to Moscow. On business."

"They won't know what hit them," Gio said. Then he shrugged. "Just as well maybe. The sight of her in a bikini might blow my kids' minds. But then you'd know."

"Well, when I saw her, there was a lot more blood than I expect will be in your pool."

"Right." He snuck a look at Joe then put his eyes back on the road. "Might be just as well for you too."

"Probably so."

Gio had been thinking; they had gathered today to reward Joe and his crew for saving their city, as well as delivering justice for themselves. That's what Joe had been recruited for and what he'd agreed to do. Nevertheless, this whole thing had ended up working out pretty well for Gio. His enemies had been vanquished and replaced with friends who owed their own positions partly to him and to Joe. His allies were grateful, and

his own strength was reinforced. He had never been so rich, so powerful, and, now that accounts had been settled, so secure. Much of this was due to his own cunning. Gio was very smart and very careful. But there was more: he had a gift for playing the game of power, a Machiavellian prince's instinct for turning crisis to profit, even when he didn't realize he was doing it. It was in his guts, the legacy he'd inherited from his father and grandfather. But he also had Joe. And that was why he turned to his friend now, as they cruised through the old neighborhood, and said, "I was thinking."

"Yeah?" Joe turned back from staring out the window, catching the tone in his voice.

"Now that you've got this fat nest egg, maybe you want to do something more with it than hide it under Gladys's bed."

"I do. I hide most of it in your safe."

"That's what I wanted to ask about. What if I helped you do something else with it?"

"Like what? You going to open me up an IRA?"

Gio shrugged. "It's not a bad idea. But I was thinking more along the lines of a house, for starters."

"A house? Where?"

"Out on the island. Near me. We could hang out, take the boat out or whatever. Don't worry, I won't let Carol bug you too much. This cookout is just a special thing. You won't be expected to come over every weekend unless you want to. Really it would be for Gladys. She might like a little bit of luxury, you know, some space, a yard, a pool even."

"I didn't realize houses on the shore in Long Island were going for two fifty these days. With a pool."

Gio laughed, then looked shyly out the windshield as they turned down Joe's block. "I could help out. You know, with the deposit. And with the paperwork to get you a mortgage or whatever. We can run it through the club. Or make you head of security for one of the other companies." He stopped in front of Joe's building and put the car in park, then turned to Joe. "I'd be happy to do it, brother."

Joe nodded. "Thank you, brother. That means a lot." Then he grinned at him. "But you know Gladys, she'd never move anywhere in a million years. She'll never change."

"Right," Gio said, smiling. "Gladys will never change."

Joe tucked a large chunk of cash into his own pocket and left the rest in the shopping bag on the seat. "Pop that in the safe for now, will you?" he asked, and opened the door. "And thanks for the ride."

Gio called after him: "You back to work at the club tomorrow? Or you too rich now?"

"I'll be there," Joe said and shut the door. Gio drove away.

❖

Liam and Josh went to see Sean at detox. They decided on the way not to mention the money Liam had just received, since it would just tempt his brother to hit him up for a loan. Nor, it went without saying, did they bring booze. They brought a deck of cards and a box of brownies instead.

"Hey!" Sean shouted when he saw Liam. He still looked a bit shaky, but his eyes were clear and wide open, the pupils a normal size. "What's in the box? A file I hope? I'm ready to bust out of here."

"Brownies," Liam said. "They got any coffee in this joint or is that off limits too?"

"They've got it. But you're a harder man than me if you can drink it."

"You remember Josh," Liam said. Josh nodded to him. Sean peered back.

"You the Jew poofter?" he asked.

Liam spoke: "He's the poof who saved your worthless fecking life. You'd be in a box right now if it had just been me there that night. Serve you right too."

Sean stared at Josh thoughtfully. "Then I've just one question."

"Go ahead," Josh said.

"Isn't it a sin for you to suck my brother's cock? Tain't kosher!"

Josh smiled. "I say a special Hebrew prayer."

"And I sprinkle some holy water on his prick before it goes up me bum," Liam added.

"Well all right then," Sean said. "That's all I wanted to check. Now hand over those fucking brownies, and let's play some cards."

❖

The medals were presented at 4 P.M., so Yolanda was able to pick Larissa up from school before coming to the ceremony. Donna had mixed feelings. Of course she was very proud to have her daughter see the mayor, the chief of police, and her local city council member present her with a plaque expressing the city's gratitude, and the assistant director of the FBI hang a medal on her. On the other hand, she had hidden the fact that she had been wounded and shot at, not to mention the bomb. And then there was Mike. But in the end it was decided that his name would go unmentioned in the public ceremony, and Donna alone would represent the family at Langley, CIA headquarters, when they added another star to the wall that represented those who died in the field, secret and nameless. As for the gory details, the PR people assured Donna that none of the politicians would say anything that a child couldn't easily digest. No one wanted to needlessly upset the public.

So she stood on the stage, beside Fusco, who was there to accept on Parks's behalf. It was the sight of Parks's two young boys, sitting as if stunned in their suits and ties, on either side of their weeping mother, that broke Donna's heart. The tears that ran down her face when the medal was placed around her neck, and the assembled officers saluted, were for them.

Fusco's eyes were dry. When he looked down at the plaque and the little velvet box that contained the medal in his hands, he was only thinking of Victoria. "I'll feel better when I bring them that bitch's head. They can mount it next to these on the wall."

"She's long gone," Donna answered. "And all we've got is a description and a lip print."

Fusco nodded. "Well, we ain't the only ones hunting." He knew that for Gio and the other bosses, she was unfinished business.

"And you're okay with that?" Donna asked him. "With them?"

"Okay?" Fusco laughed. "They scare me shitless. But I will say one thing, for better or worse. No matter how long it takes, they never let a debt go unpaid."

47

DONNA'S MOTHER THREW A party on the roof. The view was fantastic, the river and the bridge and the city. They strung up lights and set out heaps of food—Yolanda and her friends cooked for days. (Gary sent lovely flowers, which were displayed on the table, and asked about another dinner date, but when she texted thanks, Donna didn't mention it; God only knew what kind of fantasy he'd want to act out now.) Andy and Janet and an assortment of other cops and Feds came and mingled with her relatives and neighbors. Fusco and Blaze huddled in a corner, laughing darkly and sharing a flask that either of them might have produced. And Gladys came. Tom stopped by too and, at one point, Donna's heart skipped a beat when she saw him talking to Joe's grandma, but the old grifter charmed him, going on and on about what a wonderful girl Donna was. He assumed she was an old family friend, and maybe, at this point, that's what she was, though Donna sighed when she saw a card game shaping up. But then they cranked up the music and the dancing started and she didn't think about it anymore until after midnight, when Gladys came over and kissed her goodnight.

"How are you getting home?" Donna asked. "Let me call you a car."

"I'll call Joe. He said he'd pick me up."

"Really?" Donna hadn't heard or said his name since they last saw each other in the basement. Moments after Toomey fell, he was gone, blending into the crowd that was still fleeing the building. Seconds later a tac team

and bomb squad showed up, Donna still standing over Toomey, gun in her hand. She smiled now at Gladys, keeping her tone light. Casual. "Tell him to come say hi," she said. "Have a beer. Or a soda."

"Joe up here?" Gladys rolled her eyes at the law enforcement officers dancing and drinking. "Like inviting a cat to the dog pound."

"Or a fox to the hen house," Donna said.

Gladys laughed. "Tell you what. I'll ask him to meet me at your apartment. I'll tell him I need to use the john. But don't rat me out."

Donna smiled. "I promise."

❖

Joe knocked. Donna answered the door.

"Hey," she said. "Caught you."

"Hey! It's the national hero."

She laughed. "I wouldn't say national. New York City and Puerto Rico for sure."

Joe shrugged. "Where else matters? You're the princess of the city."

"Exactly. I'm getting free Yankees tickets, if you want to come."

"I'm a Mets fan," Joe said. "Queens boy. Another tragic history keeping us apart."

"Of course," she said. "You'd pick the losing the side."

He laughed. "Someone has to."

"Really though, Joe," she said, lifting off the medal that she'd been wearing all night, suddenly embarrassed by it. "You should have one of these too. Shit you should have a collection. Wear them all like a rapper. Here." She tried, playfully, to put it on him, but he pressed it back into her hands.

"Not my style," he told her. They were close now, and he was still holding her hands, with neither one letting go. "It looks much better on you."

"That's right, I forgot," she said, looking up at him, their faces close now. "You already have a star, don't you? Right here." She touched the spot on his chest. "Can I see?"

"It's nothing. It's just a burn."

"Please?" she asked. Her hand was on his heart now, her eyes on his. "Show me? Share that with me at least?"

He took a breath, about to say something, then changed his mind. He pulled off his T-shirt and raised his arm. He put her hand on his star.

"Here it is. You see. Just a scar. I've got plenty of others. It's nothing. Yours is better."

"No," she said, shaking her head, and tracing lightly with her fingertips. "Yours means much more. The people who gave it to you—they don't make speeches and they don't do PR." She looked him in the eye now, both of her hands on his chest, his hands on her shoulders. "And you can't ever take it off, can you? Not even for one night?"

He shook his head, as he slid her medal back over her head, and then wrapped her in his arms, holding her close, his mouth just a whisper from hers. "No. But we can both shut our eyes and pretend. For a minute," he said, shutting his. She shut hers too, and clung to him tightly, as she felt his mouth on hers.

❖

Neither of them spoke after that. Not when they clung to each other, arms and legs entwined, swaying together as their devouring mouths joined. Not when they found themselves, blindly, in her room, leaving their clothes in a trail. He spoke her name once in the dark, *Donna*, as she lay naked on top of him, pressing her skin against his. She laughed, feeling the medal knock against him, and tossed it on the floor. She gasped his name once, as he slid inside her, and moaned it once later, as he looked into her eyes, holding her face, and then whispered *Donna* again into her ear. After, they rested in silence, and slept for a little, and then made love again. Finally they lay still, her head on his chest, and she saw that the moon had set. It was very late. She glanced down at her phone: The party was over, Larissa was asleep at her mom's, Gladys had been driven home by Fusco. But still she said nothing, just curled back

up, and he held her close in silence, as if they both understood that the moment they spoke, it would break the spell and reality would come crashing back in. Time passed. Then, as the first flush of dawn began to glow outside her window, she saw a cat, her neighbor's, a black tuxedo with a white shirtfront on his chest and socks like spats on his paws. He meowed and they both laughed which scared him and he darted away up the fire escape, but that was enough. Their night was over. She turned to Joe then, looked at him frankly, pale and rumpled in the dawn.

"Now what happens?" she asked.

"Now?" Joe repeated, returning her gaze. "Now our troubles really begin."

ACKNOWLEDGMENTS

As always, I want to thank Doug Stewart, the world's greatest agent, for his invaluable foresight and friendship, without which I'd be lost, as well as everyone at Sterling Lord Literistic, especially Szilvia Molnar, who has helped my books find their way around the world. Thank you also to Danielle Bukowski and Maria Bell for all their help. I am immensely grateful to Otto Penzler, my editor, whose idea it was to embark on this serial adventure, and who has guided me every step of the way. I am also thankful to everyone at The Mysterious Press and at the Mysterious Bookshop. Thank you to Matilde Huseby and William Fitch for reading the early drafts, and a very special thanks to Nesa Azimi, Antonio Chinea, Nivia Hernandez and Anastasia Lobanova for their generous assistance with the various languages spoken in this book. Lastly, I want, once again, to thank my family for their infinite love and support. I could never have done it without them.

Read on for a preview of *The Wild Life*,
David Gordon's next Joe the Bouncer novel
coming soon from Mysterious Press...

1

JOE WAS AFRAID TO MOVE. He stood, holding his breath, listening intently for the creak of a floorboard, a telltale rustle or sigh. Every muscle tensed as he eyed the small bathroom window, doing the math—or, he supposed, physics—in his head: even if he managed to edge out sideways, onto the narrow ledge, could he make the reach to the fire escape without falling the eight floors to the sidewalk? Unlikely. But he would almost rather risk it than face what awaited him on the other side of the bathroom door. Why hadn't he thought to lock it? He stared at the flimsy handle now, waiting to see it turn from the outside, wondering if he could simply reach out and twist the locking mechanism, if he dared. Then he heard a voice. It was the law: Special Agent Donna Zamora of the FBI.

"What's the matter, honey? Why are you up? Do you have to make pee?"

Ears straining, Joe awaited the answer that could seal his fate. Why did the shower curtain have to be translucent? He heard the tiny voice of Donna's six-year-old daughter warbling in the living room.

"Don't worry, it was just a dream," Donna said. "Let's get you some water and tuck you in Mommy's bed."

As their steps faded, Joe breathed a sigh of relief, then smiled sardonically in the mirror. He'd hidden in sewers from cops and in bomb craters from jihadists without getting quite this tense. Then again, he'd sooner

go up against a trained killer in mortal combat than have a small child discover him naked at two in the morning. Finally, there came a soft knock, at the height of an adult hand.

"It's me," Donna whispered.

He opened the door. Donna was in her robe, dark hair glistening in the shadows. She handed him his clothes, his Converse Chuck Taylors on top of his folded shirt and jeans. From her robe pocket, she pulled his crumpled boxers and one sock, with a hole in the heel.

"I couldn't find the other sock," she whispered, while he quickly dressed. "It must be under the bed."

He sat on the toilet lid to tie his laces. She ran her fingers through his hair. "Sorry if she startled you."

"She nearly gave me a heart attack."

He could see her smiling in the dim light that slipped in from the window. Joe Brody, veteran of ops so black his military record had been deleted, an ace criminal who commanded respect throughout the five boroughs, afraid of a little girl.

"Come on." She took his hand. "I'll grab your coat. You can get out through her window."

Joe followed her to Larissa's room, a magical, candy-colored cave where teddy bears and stuffed unicorns snuggled with lambs and frogs, Disney figures populated the walls, and shimmering stars hung from the ceiling. Glitter was everywhere. He drew on his jacket, pulling gloves from the pockets, winding a scarf around his neck, while Donna opened the window. That iron fire escape was going to be cold.

"It's your own fault, you know," she told him. "Ever since she spotted you that time she has dreams about a man creeping past her window."

"My fault?" He pulled his hat on. "In that case, I will just stroll out the door like a gentleman."

She shook her head. "You can't. You know Mrs. Ruiz will see you leave."

"Doesn't she ever sleep?"

"Not since 1975, according to her."

"That's what my grandmother says, too. Then you hear her snoring." He sat on the windowsill; already he could feel the chill from the river. She perched beside him.

"Point is, you're supposed to be a master at this stuff. Professional criminal."

He smiled. "I'm out of practice, thanks to you."

"Well, we are going to have to have a serious talk. Figure this out."

He sighed. It seemed like they spent half their time rolling deliriously in each other's arms, and the other half seriously discussing the problems with it. "I'm sorry if I traumatized your daughter. I will pay for her therapy out of my ill-gotten gains."

Donna smiled. "She's a city kid. She's seen worse. Luckily, she decided you were Spider-Man. God knows why. His outfit is way cooler."

"Because she's smart. She can tell we're both from Queens." Joe kissed her. "Speaking of which, come over tomorrow."

"Larissa has a playdate."

"Your mom can take her. We need a playdate ourselves. Gladys will be out all day."

"Sneaking a girl in when your grandma's out? Definitely not the solution to our problems."

Joe swung his legs out onto the fire escape and braced himself for the climb. "At least you get to come in the front door."

2

Swift and silent past the darkened windows, slow and careful past the few with lamp-yellow or screen-blue leaking through their curtains, Joe felt the cold leach up from the iron into his hands and feet, the wind from the river already stinging his cheeks and neck. The reason he was crawling up the fire escape now was not only because of Donna's impressionable young daughter, or her nosy neighbors, or even her mother who lived across the hall. It was not because of his grandmother, whom he had not told, or any family problems at all. It was not religion or politics or culture or any of those traditional issues. It was not even a romantic dilemma—they were both free and single. Donna and Joe were a twenty-first-century Romeo and Juliet, with the most modern of personal problems, a career conflict: Donna was a federal law enforcement agent, finally on the rise after thwarting a terrorist plot and saving much of New York. And Joe was a professional criminal, lifelong pals with a Mafia boss and deeply entangled with the city's top organized crime leaders, who had empowered him to hunt down a terror cell lurking in their midst. When that terrorist ended up with a bullet in the head, they declared him their "sheriff," giving him free reign throughout their territories, and making him the fixer they called on when they, too, needed 911 to protect them from the nightmares that kept even Mafia dons up at night: Al-Qaeda cells, white-supremacist plots, terror-financed

heroin pipelines, homemade nuclear bombs. While the citizens slept, relying on Donna to keep them safe from dangerous criminals, the most dangerous criminals in the city relied on Joe.

For Donna, to have their relationship go public would mean the death of her career. For Joe, it would just mean death.

To Be Continued in The Wild Life...